Advance praise for
Unlocking Africa's Business Potential

"*Unlocking Africa's Business Potential* insightfully guides entrepreneurs, investors, and policy leaders to new realities of profitable businesses in African economies, which are also a powerful force for good. Landry Signé's evidence-based and powerful insights showcase and confirm that he is simply the best, brightest, and most passionate of his generation when it comes to enlightening the world with the fascinating transformation and potential of African economies."

—H. E. Prof. Ameenah Gurib-Fakim,
6th president of the Republic of Mauritius

"*Unlocking Africa's Business Potential* is an outstanding and well-researched book that all business and policy leaders interested in Africa must read. Landry Signé presents winning business and investment opportunities and strategies in Africa's most promising sectors during an era of shifting global policies and rapidly changing markets. Signé does an exceptional job of highlighting the key political, demographic, and economic trends that make it an imperative for companies to look to Africa to grow and expand their businesses."

—Florizelle Liser, president and CEO, Corporate Council on Africa

"Africa is home to many of the world's fastest growing and most profitable markets. In *Unlocking Africa's Business Potential,* Landry Signé offers a thought-provoking, powerful, and compelling guide for any global business leader interested in understanding the incredible transformation taking place and turning the enormous opportunities into high impact returns to all stakeholders."

—Paul Polman, co-founder and chair of IMAGINE, former
CEO of Unilever, and co-founder of the Global Commission
on Business and Sustainable Development

Unlocking Africa's Business Potential

Unlocking Africa's Business Potential

TRENDS, OPPORTUNITIES, RISKS, AND STRATEGIES

Landry Signé

BROOKINGS INSTITUTION PRESS
Washington, D.C.

Library of Congress Cataloging-in-Publication Data.
Names: Signé, Landry, author.
Title: Unlocking Africa's business potential : trends, opportunities, risks, and strategies / Landry Signé.
Description: Washington, D.C. : Brookings Institution Press, 2020. | Includes bibliographical references and index.
Identifiers: LCCN 2019048079 (print) | LCCN 2019048080 (ebook) | ISBN 9780815737384 (paperback) | ISBN 9780815737391 (epub)
Subjects: LCSH: Economic development—Africa. | New business enterprises—Africa. | Africa—Economic conditions—21st century.
Classification: LCC HC800 .S539 2020 (print) | LCC HC800 (ebook) | DDC 338.96—dc23
LC record available at https://lccn.loc.gov/2019048079
LC ebook record available at https://lccn.loc.gov/2019048080
ISBN 978-0-815737-38-4 (paperback : alk. paper)
ISBN 978-0-815737-39-1 (ebook)

9 8 7 6 5 4 3 2 1

Typeset in Adobe Caslon Pro

Composition by Elliott Beard

Contents

Illustrations

Figures

Acknowledgments

This book would not have been possible without the support of incredible people and institutions, for whom and for which I am extremely grateful: John R. Allen, president of the Brookings Institution; Vartan Gregorian, president of the Carnegie Corporation of New York; Brookings Trustee David M. Rubenstein, co-founder and co-chief executive officer of the Carlyle Group; Homi Kharas, interim vice president of the Brookings Institution's Global Economy and Development program; Brahima S. Coulibaly, director of the Brookings Africa Growth Initiative; Sanjeev Khagram, dean and director-general of the Thunderbird School of Global Management; and Bill Finan, director of the Brookings Institution Press.

I am also very grateful to the following people for having graciously written an endorsement for the book: H. E. Prof. Ameenah Gurib-Fakim, 6th president of the Republic of Mauritius; Dr. Mo Ibrahim, founder and chair, Mo Ibrahim Foundation; Paul Polman, co-founder and chair of IMAGINE, former CEO of Unilever, and co-founder of the Global Commission on Business and Sustainable Development; Florizelle (Florie) Liser, president and CEO, Corporate Council on Africa.

Writing a book requires the collaboration and unique contributions of many individuals. I would like to express my deepest gratitude to Chelsea

Johnson, my postdoctoral scholar during my tenure as an Andrew Carnegie fellow, who closely collaborated with me on this project and provided incredible support at each phase of the research, including the drafting phase. I am also grateful to Wilfried Youmbi, Zezhou Cai, Dhruv Gandhi, Amy Copley, Genevieve Jesse, and Nirav Patel for contributing to research and illustrations, and to Merrell Tuck-Primdahl, David Batcheck, Christina Golubski, Jeannine Ajello, and Joshua Miller for editorial and design work on some of the chapters. I am also grateful to my former students from Stanford University's Continuing Studies program, who enrolled in my course "Emerging African Markets: Strategies, Investment, and Government Affairs" and who have contributed to the evolution of this content. At Stanford University, Larry Diamond, Francis Fukuyama, Richard Roberts, Jeremy Weinstein, and Laura Hubbard have been incredible hosts and mentors.

I am very grateful to the Brookings Institution Press team, including Cecilia González, Kristen Spina Harrison, Fred Dews, Robert Wicks, and Yelba Quinn. I am also thankful to anonymous reviewers as well as scholars who have provided valuable feedback, including Witney Schenedman and Eyerusalem Siba.

I would like to thank my fantastic parents and siblings, whose unconditional support has been a constant source of motivation: Joséphine, Michel, Nadège, Carine, Gaël, Marcelle, and Ange. Last, but not least, I am grateful to my dearest love, Nadine, who not only provided invaluable moral support, but also was so kind as to read the manuscript, and to my son, Landry Signé Jr., for spreading joy and happiness in our life every single day. I dedicate this book to my son, Landry Signé Jr., and to the "Cheetah Generation."

This book was made possible in part by a grant from the Carnegie Corporation of New York and the Rubenstein Fellowship program at the Brookings Institution. The statements made and views expressed are solely the responsibility of the author.

ONE

The Evolution of African Economies and Their Tremendous Business Potential

In May 2000, a cover of the periodical *The Economist* featured an image of the African continent, in which was depicted a man holding a firearm. The title read, in large golden letters, "The Hopeless Continent." In an article titled "Hopeless Africa," the periodical proceeded to highlight a range of challenges that plagued the continent and explained both its past poor economic performance and prospects. It mentioned diseases such as AIDS and malaria, and natural disasters such as floods. It underlined governance issues, such as corruption and "government-sponsored thuggery." When covering the security state of the continent, the article went as far as to state that conflict—though not exclusive to Africa—persisted on the continent due to "reasons buried in their culture." The continent was not just considered as the home of failure and despair by *The Economist* (2000) but also by scholars, who described it as being in permanent crisis (1979–1999, Van de Walle 2001), with slow economic growth (Collier and Gunning 1999a, 1999b; Easterly 2001a; Guillaumont et al. 1999; Sachs and Warner 1997) and overall poor economic performance despite various experiences (Acemoglu and Robinson 2010a; Bates 1981; Fosu 2010; Monga and Lin 2015a, 2015b; Ndulu et al. 2007).

More than 11 years after the publication of the "Hopeless Africa" article, *The Economist* published an article with a slightly different tone. In

1

December 2011, the cover of *The Economist* featured a young child flying a kite shaped in the form of Africa. The cover reads "Africa Rising." In the featured article, the periodical praised the economic growth Africa had experienced over the past decade and partly attributed the high growth to the commodity boom. It also stated that the overall health of Africans had improved, due to antimalarial measures and other health precautions. Since the December 2011 publication, the periodical has published a number of reports praising the opportunities on the continent (*The Economist* 2013, 2016), which aligned with numerous optimistic studies (Fick 2007; Grosskurth 2010; Mahajan 2009; Roxburgh et al. 2010; Radelet 2010).

The two contrasted publications of *The Economist*, though a little more than one decade apart, paint two starkly different pictures. One might argue that the continent was not as hopeless as *The Economist* painted it out to be in 2000, and that in 2011, Africa may not have been as prosperous as *The Economist* claimed it was. The statistics show that the truth lies somewhere in the middle. While the African continent has made significant progress in recent years, there are challenges that have yet to be overcome. Moreover, Africa is not a monolith, and there are key differences among the fifty-five countries present on the continent. The reality is quite nuanced, and even within countries, certain sectors are performing well, whereas others are not.

Numerous scholars have tried to demystify Africa's economic performance over the past six decades, exploring a broad variety of drivers. For example, some scholars have focused on institutions and political regimes (Acemoglu and Robinson 2010b; Azam et al. 2009; Bates 2006; Bates and Block 2011; Herbst 2000; North 1990; Radelet 2010; Przeworski 2004) in explaining economic trends on the continent, whereas others have used policies (Collier and Gunning 1999a, 1999b; Ndulu and O'Connell 1999), political instability (Brun et al. 1999; Fosu 2001), geography and the environment (Bloom and Sachs 1998; Collier 2006; McCord et al. 2005), ethnic fragmentation (Collier 2000; Easterly and Levine 1997), and historical legacy (Nunn 2008), among others, to explain Africa's mixed economic performance since independence.

Contrary to publications that are either excessively pessimistic or overly optimistic, often without sufficient evidence, this book continues the tradition of axiological neutrality, avoiding bias and oversimplifications in the study of African economies (Signé 2017, 2018). The study therefore provides a cutting-edge but accessible perspective on the transformation of African economies and their tremendous business potential, with a particular focus on eight major sectors throughout the African continent, to which each chapter is devoted: consumer markets and distribution, agriculture and food industries, information and communication technology, manufacturing and industrialization, oil and gas, tourism, banking, and infrastructure and construction. The book adopts an accessible data and evidence-driven framework to analyze Africa's tremendous business potential, and it assesses for each of the eight selected sectors the trends, drivers, key players, business and investment opportunities, and challenges and risks, as well as the business strategies to mitigate risks, transform opportunities into high return, and achieve inclusive growth. The book is a pivotal contribution to understanding the transformation of African economies and business opportunities.

The next sections discuss the evolution of African economies, from the perspective of many growth narratives, competitiveness, governance and business environment, demographics and youth, continental trade and integration, emerging partners, and the Fourth Industrial Revolution.

One Continent, Many Growth Narratives

Over the past decade, Africa was one of the fastest growing regions in the world. Moreover, the continent was largely able to dodge the negative effects brought about by the 2008 financial crisis. The skeptics will state that this is because Africa was not well integrated into the global economy in the first place. Nevertheless, the shield provided by the lack of integration was beneficial in the long run. In 2017, four of the fastest growing economies in the world were located in sub-Saharan Africa—Ethiopia, Ghana, Côte d'Ivoire, and Senegal. This contrasts with the year 2000, when only one of the ten fastest growing countries in the world was in Africa (see table 1.1). In reality, in 2000, five of the ten countries with the slowest GDP growth rate were located in Africa—Democratic Republic of the Congo, Gabon, Côte d'Ivoire, Niger, and Zimbabwe—against four in 2017—South Sudan, the Republic of the Congo, Equatorial Guinea, and Chad (see table 1.2). The tables show the large difference in the growth performance of African countries. In 2017, there was a 20-percentage point range in the growth rate of African countries, with Ethiopia at the higher end and South Sudan on the lower end. No other world region had such large disparities in growth rate within their countries.

TABLE 1.1. Fastest-growing countries in the world (2000 versus 2017).

2000 Growth Rate		2017 Growth Rate	
Turkmenistan	18.587	Ethiopia	10.861
Myanmar	13.746	Macao SAR	9.258
Belize	13.020	Ghana	8.439
United Arab Emirates	12.329	Ireland	7.808
St. Kitts and Nevis	12.259	Côte d'Ivoire	7.771
Estonia	10.568	Nepal	7.499
Russia	10.046	Armenia	7.478
Ethiopia	9.838	Senegal	7.164
Kazakhstan	9.800	Tajikistan	7.140
Ireland	9.575	Bangladesh	7.137

Source: World Bank data.

TABLE 1.2. Slowest-growing countries in the world (2000 versus 2017).

2000 Growth Rate		2017 Growth Rate	
Solomon Islands	–14.277	Venezuela	–14.000
DR Congo	–8.136	Yemen	–13.839
Iraq	–4.341	South Sudan	–11.096
Zimbabwe	–4.231	Puerto Rico	–7.674
Niger	–2.584	Republic of the Congo	–4.608
Papua New Guinea	–2.455	Equatorial Guinea	–4.384
Paraguay	–2.314	Dominica	–4.172
Côte d'Ivoire	–2.068	Chad	–3.143
Gabon	–1.883	Trinidad and Tobago	–2.563
Uruguay	–1.776	Kuwait	–2.530

Source: World Bank data.

The tables not only showcase the large disparities in the growth performance of African countries, they also show the ways in which said growth performances fluctuate over time. Three groups of countries emerge. The first group comprises countries such as Senegal, Côte d'Ivoire, and Ghana, whose GDP growth rates have seen significant improvement over the past decade and a half. This is largely showcased by the case of Côte d'Ivoire, one of the largest success stories on the continent over the past decade. After emerging from the 2011 civil war, which left more than 3,000 people dead (Sturm 2013), the country has managed to go from one of the slowest growing economies in the world to one of the fastest. Since 2012, the year following the end of the Ivoirian civil war, Côte d'Ivoire has seen some of the largest growth in the net flows of foreign direct investment in sub-Saharan Africa; the net flows of foreign direct investment (FDI) into Côte d'Ivoire more than doubled over the past 5 years.

The second group comprises countries who have seen their economic performance remain steady since 2000. Said group includes countries such as Rwanda and Ethiopia. With the exception of a slight regression in 2002, since 2000, Ethiopia has grown at a steady rate of 7 percent or higher. The flow of FDI into the country has been multiplied by 25 since 2000. According to the World Economic Forum, Ethiopia's growth is largely driven by an increase in industrial activity, notably through investments in infrastructure and manufacturing. The growth in FDI is partly attributed to the creation of industrial parks and privatization, as Ethiopia continues to sell goods to China (Gray 2018). Some scholars have even referred to Ethiopia as the new China, given its potential to attract low-wage manufacturing (Gelb et al. 2017). The International Monetary Fund predicts that Ethiopia will continue to grow at a rate surpassing 8 percent yearly. Despite the strong growth in investment, last year, Ethiopia faced challenges brought about by droughts; the Ethiopian government increased the number of people requiring food aid by nearly 38 percent, thus averting a famine. This goes to prove that even when growth figures look promising, there can be other challenges a country faces that can create disasters if they go unchecked.

The third group of countries includes those whose economic performances have stagnated over the past few years. This group includes the Central African Republic, Chad, and Zimbabwe. Up until 2009, Zimbabwe's GDP was constantly on the decline. It slightly improved in the early 2010s and is now stabilizing at 3 percent, on par with the African growth rate of 3 percent. Over the years, investments into Zimbabwe have remained meager. While, in aggregate numbers, FDI into Zimbabwe has been multiplied by 12, the country attracts less than 1 percent of the total FDI into all of Africa. Zimbabwe's poor economic performance can be tied to a list of factors, ranging from poor macroeconomic governance to corruption and poor political governance. The country performs poorly according to business indicators and has not been successful in attracting the foreign investment necessary to kickstart its economy. Today, Zimbabwe is under new leadership. In January 2018, President Mnangagwa reassured the international community that "Zimbabwe is open for business" (Quest and McKenzie 2018), and that his administration will work hard to tackle corruption and create the infrastructure necessary to attract investment, but numerous challenges remain.

In its 2011 article, *The Economist* largely attributed the growth in African countries to the commodity boom; this nearsighted view hides the large disparities in the economic performance of African countries over the past years. As exemplified by the three different countries and the groups of countries that they represent, there are various narratives to describe the ways in which Africa operates, and they should be studied individually. Regardless of the stage of its economic growth, every African country presents a particular set of opportunities across various sectors, as will be highlighted throughout this text.

The Competitiveness of African Economies from Global and Comparative Perspectives

The Global Competitiveness Index 4.0, developed by Klaus Schwab at the World Economic Forum, is a new measure of productivity and performance. The majority of sub-Saharan African countries rank toward the bottom of the list, though a few are performing above countries typically categorized as high performing, such as India and Turkey. Mauritius, South Africa, Seychelles, Botswana, and Kenya all rank within the top 100 countries on the Global Competitiveness Index 4.0.[1] Another report on seventy-one emerging economies lists Ethiopia as the only outperforming African country, having achieved an annual GDP per capita growth of more than 5 percent for 20 years.[2] Ghana, Mozambique, and Rwanda are considered "recent accelerators" in the same analysis, having experienced significant growth at a 3.6 percent compound annual growth rate, which is higher than long-term outperformers but during a shorter period.[3] Recent outperformers, like Ethiopia, evidenced the highest percentage of capital accumulation as a factor of labor productivity, suggesting possible solutions to recent accelerating countries and consistently growing countries on the continent.

The majority of African countries find themselves among the "underperforming" or "volatile" emerging economies, which can be attributed to overall lower levels of investment, income, and domestic demand. Underperforming countries also often have limited domestic savings resources, which hinders industrialization and subsequent growth in employment and wages. As a continent, Africa will have the fastest and highest growth rate of GDP at 7.3 percent from 2016 to 2022, which is 1.1 percent higher than the next highest continent, Asia.[4] Thus, while high-performing countries will drive this continent-wide growth, low and underperforming economies have the potential to increase their GDP per capita through the growth of large firms and foreign investment. Competitive companies from emerging economies have proven to outperform their counterparts in advanced economies, so large firms may begin to drive the growth of economies across the continent by growing domestic income, advancing innovation, and sustainably using resources. The projected growth of Africa will be a general incentive to foreign investors, and improving governance indicators and greater political stability will lead to more investment.

October 2018 saw nine African countries reporting annual GDP growth of 6 percent or higher, with Libya recording the highest annual change at 10.9 percent.[5] This high percentage of growth rivals the GDP growth of emerging economy powerhouses India and China, and a majority of other African countries are close behind in terms of rapid growth. Twenty-eight African countries reported annual GDP growth between 3 and 6 percent in 2018, including Burkina Faso, Cameroon, Chad, Madagascar, Niger, Tanzania, and Uganda.[6] The International Monetary Fund also monitors annual changes in inflation based on average consumer prices, which gives more insight into the real growth potential of African economies in terms of demand, income, and fiscal stability. Numerous countries showed moderate inflation rates between 0 and 3 percent in 2018, indicating the potential for higher returns for investors. These countries include Benin, Burundi, Cameroon, Chad, Côte d'Ivoire, Djibouti, Equatorial Guinea, Gabon, Guinea Bissau, Mali, Morocco, the Republic of the Congo, Senegal, and Togo.[7] The rest of the continent is projected to experience some moderate increases in inflation within the next 5 years. However, these fluctuations are all projected to occur slowly, likely reflecting growing wages, decreasing risk to foreign investment in African countries, and the development of the private sector.

Improved, Accountable, Effective Governance and the Business Environment

African populaces across the continent are supporting a trend toward improved, accountable governance through the use of democratic elections, term limits, and increased citizen responsibility. In 2014–2015, Afrobarometer surveys reported more than 77 percent of the continent supported democracy, almost 75 percent wanted leaders to be limited to two terms, and more than 53 percent said it is important for citizens to hold governments accountable—even if that translates to slower decisions. Recent leadership changes in Africa signal that accountability and citizens' demands for constitutional checks on leaders are growing stronger. Since 2016, meaningful elections have led to changes in numerous countries, including Benin, Comoros, Ghana, Lesotho, Liberia, São Tomé and Príncipe, and Sierra Leone. Elections are the first step toward improving government accountability and have the potential to directly impact African business environments.

During the period from 2008 to 2017, the Mo Ibrahim Foundation reported that thirty-four countries had improved their overall governance, affecting 71.6 percent of Africa's citizens.[8] Improvements in overall governance reflect higher levels of accountability: vertical accountability that citizens exercise through elections; horizontal accountability of government checks and balances; and diagonal accountability, or the effect of personal responsibility on institutions. Comparing countries' levels of accountability with the World Bank's data on the ease of doing business, Mauritius (25), Rwanda (41), Kenya (80), Botswana (81), and South Africa (82) were the five highest-ranked sub-Saharan African countries with the most business-friendly regulations. These countries have either maintained high levels of accountable, effective governance or have significantly improved their scores in recent decades. Rwanda, for example, has increased its levels of governmental effectiveness, regulatory quality, rule of law, and control of corruption each by at least 20 percentage points from 2008 to 2017.[9] The *Doing Business 2019* report projects Rwanda's ease of doing business rank will jump from 41 to 29 within the year, indicating further correlation between improving governance and maturing business environments.[10]

Table 1.3 indicates the challenges that the continent still faces in regard to improving the overall business environment and becoming a more attractive destination for investors. Focusing on trade and customs regulations in the past has led to improvement in customs procedures, but this intersection of governance and business may continue to decline in effectiveness as states focus on other deteriorating aspects of the business environment. The increasing improvement in government development of regional integration points to the implementation of the African Continental Free Trade Area (AfCFTA) and other regional economic agreements. These and other efforts to improve the business environment convey the promise of trading and investing on the continent. And this book's assessment of the opportunities and risks to doing business in each sector will provide additional insights for those seeking to mitigate risks and capitalize on the high returns that African countries offer elsewhere.

Africa's Demographics and the Opportunities It Presents

The demographics of the African continent paint an interesting and encouraging picture. Estimates show that by 2030, Africa's population will reach about 1.4 billion people; in 2050, about 2.1 billion; and in 2100, about 3.8 billion. In 2030, over 50 percent of the population will be concentrated in seven countries (Nigeria, Ethiopia, Democratic Republic of Congo, Egypt, Tanzania, Kenya, and South Africa). Four of those countries will have over 100 million people: Nigeria (264 million), Ethiopia (139.6 million), Democratic Republic of Congo (120.4 million), and Egypt (119.7 million). In addition, Africa's population is becoming increasingly urban. Today, Africa is the fastest urbanizing region in the world (figure 1.1). By 2035, more than half of Africa's population will live in cities, and by 2050, nearly 60 percent of Africa's population will be urban (figure 1.2). Cities present opportunities that investors should move toward capturing, such as a skilled workforce and a relatively wealthy consumer base.

Today, Africa has one of the highest dependency ratios in the world. However, a closer look at the figures indicates that Africa has a relatively low old-age dependency ratio. In other words, the high dependency ratio can be attributed to the large number of children below age 15. This represents a key asset as said children will be an important share of Africa's

FIGURE 1.1. Average annual rate of change of the urban population by world region.

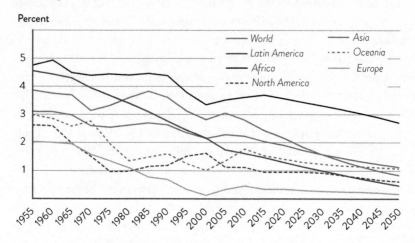

Source: World Economic Prospects, 2018.

FIGURE 1.2. Percentage of population at midcentury residing in urban areas by world region.

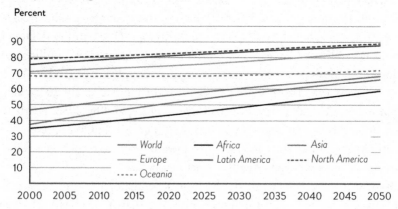

Source: World Economic Prospects, 2018.

TABLE 1.3. Business environment across Africa.

Business Environment	2017 African score/100.0	10-year AAT* (2008–2017)	5-year AAT* (2013–2017)	Trend Classification
Business Regulatory Environment	46.7	–0.04	–0.03	Slowing Deterioration
Absence of Excessive Bureaucracy & Red Tape	24.4	–0.47	–0.88	Increasing Deterioration
Absence of Restrictions on Foreign Investment	55.3	–1.68	–0.48	Slowing Deterioration
Efficiency of Customs Procedures	48.7	+0.78	+0.48	Slowing Improvement
Robustness of Banks	46.3	–2.34	–2.10	Slowing Deterioration
Satisfaction with Employment Creation	30.2	–0.34	–0.28	Slowing Deterioration
Government Development of Regional Integration	58.8	+0.18	+0.60	Increasing Improvement

*AAT = Annual Average Trend

Source: Mo Ibrahim Foundation (2018).

consumer base by 2030. In recent years, child mortality has declined as fertility rates remained unchanged, thus creating what demographers call the demographic dividend. If harnessed properly, the dividend can serve in furthering Africa's development. By 2030, today's African youth will be the workers and consumers of Africa, providing businesses with opportunities that are not to be overlooked. In order to benefit from Africa's large workforce and customer market in 2030, investments are to be made today.

In addition to offering an increasingly young and urban population, Africa is also presenting a growing class of consumers with discretionary income. This group is often referred to as the middle class, but there is significant debate over the methods by which to determine membership in a cross-national "global middle class," which spans diverse social, political, and cultural contexts. Many researchers have relied on a variety of income-based definitions due to the difficulty of operationalizing sociologically based definitions of class. These researchers may define the global middle class as a grouping that (1) falls in the middle of the global income or consumption distribution (see Easterly 2001b and Quah 1996); (2) enjoys a sufficiently high standard of living to be free from severe economic deprivation without rising above a threshold of affluence (see Banerjee and Duflo 2008; Birdsall 2012; Kharas 2017; Lopez-Calva and Ortiz-Juarez 2014; and Ravallion 2010, among others); or (3) constitutes a consumer market with defined features, such as sufficient contribution to global aggregate demand or to the demand of specific industries (see Barberena et al. 2006; Court and Narsimhan 2010; Dadush and Ali 2012; and Kamakura and Mazzon 2013).[11] Within each of these definitions, the size of the middle class may vary significantly based on the cutoff values used; Jayadev et al. (2015)[12] compared five definitions of the middle class and found that its estimated size for sub-Saharan Africa ranged from 32 million (Kharas 2010) (updated to 114 million in Kharas 2017) to 425 million (Roxburgh et al. 2010) people, with projections ranging from over half a billion by 2030 to 1.1 billion (out of 2.6 billion) people by 2060 (Deloitte 2014).

The foregoing approaches have strengths and weaknesses; however, the goal of this analysis is not to end the debate on the definition of the middle and upper classes but to provide practical analytical tools for a broad variety of global and local business leaders and policymakers so that they can make decisions based on their own goals and target market segments related to Africa's opportunities. It is important for businesses to embrace the conceptual diversity of Africa, and to understand that sub-Saharan Africa went, for example, from 45 percent of people living above the poverty line in 1990 to 59 percent in 2015, marking a considerable improvement (while acknowledging the broad variety behind such a number, including the unique needs of people above the poverty line but at risk of falling back below; low-, middle-, and upper-middle classes; and the upper class). Both the percentage of people above the poverty line and the evolution of this number are important, as the percentage includes both people with discretionary income—even if limited—and the middle and upper classes, and the evolution helps to understand the growth of Africa's consumer markets. The substantial improvement of such statistics represents a tremendous opportunity, both because it shows an improvement of living standards and because consumers with incomes above the poverty line have at least some access to discretionary income, depending on the sector, country, and type of service or product. Furthermore, even people living below the poverty line still have needs that require innovative and sustainable business solutions from creative entrepreneurs to leave no one behind. The tremendous potential of African countries is therefore correlated not only to population growth but to income growth as well.

Emerging International Partners for Africa

Much of the innovative and productive potential in Africa has already attracted substantial foreign investment. In the agricultural sector, European, Chinese, Saudi Arabian, North Korean, and Indian companies are presently investing funds, ranging from several million to billions of dollars to buy or lease mass hectares of land in order to promote various agricultural projects. Currently, countries such as Cameroon, Democratic Republic of Congo, Ethiopia, Kenya, Madagascar, Mozambique, and Senegal are growing a variety of marketable produce, including flowers, lentils, palm oil, rice, sugar cane, bananas, and corn.[13] Chinese lending to sub-Saharan African countries is particularly noteworthy because bilateral loans account for an estimated 14 percent of total debt contracts. These loans are only a small portion of the economic relationship between Africa and China. African countries also trade a significant amount with China.

African countries are increasingly building ties with other emerging economies. Trade with Brazil, India, Indonesia, Russia, and Turkey increased by over 100 percent between 2006 and 2016. African countries, as shown in table 1.4, have imported an estimated USD 156,632 million worth of imports from India and exported USD 310,787 million worth of goods.[14] Trade with China, the United States, and the European Union still represents more than 30 percent of the continent's total imports and exports, but these emerging trade relationships are taking increasingly larger shares of African imports and exports.

The African Continental Free Trade Area

When the AfCFTA went into force on July 8, 2019, fifty-four of the fifty-five African countries were party to the agreement. Only Eritrea had neither signed nor ratified the document. The AfCFTA, which establishes a single continental market for goods and services as well as a customs union with free movement of capital and travelers, will also contribute to unlocking business potential, generating opportunities for industrialization, and creating desperately needed jobs. This free trade area is expected to dramatically expand intra-African trade: some studies have shown that the creation of the AfCFTA could increase intra-African trade by about 52 percent by just 2022. In the long term, the United Nations Economic Commission for Africa estimates that the AfCFTA will increase the value of intra-African trade by between USD 50 billion and USD 70 billion by 2040, compared to a situation without the AfCFTA. As noted by Signé (2018b), the market size will include 1.7 billion people with over USD 6.7 trillion of combined consumer and business spending in 2030.

The AfCFTA will have cascading effects. Policymakers anticipate that the trade deal will drive the structural transformation of economies—the transition from low productivity and labor-intensive activities to higher productivity and skills-intensive industrial and service activities—which in turn will produce better paid jobs and make a positive impact on poverty. Indeed, by promoting intra-African trade, the agreement will foster a more competitive manufacturing sector and promote economic diversification. The removal of tariffs will also create a continental market that encourages companies to benefit from economies of scale—enabling countries to accelerate their development.

TABLE 1.4. Trade with Africa.

Countries	Change in imports (2006–2016) (%)	Total value of imports (in US$ millions)	Share of total imports (%)	Change in exports (2006–2016) (%)	Total value of exports (in US$ millions)	Share of total exports (%)
Brazil	12	51,849	1.5	66	95,516	2.7
India	181	156,632	4.6	186	310,787	8.7
Indonesia	107	30,825	0.9	147	32,847	0.9
Russia	142	19,675	0.6	168	5,241	0.1
Turkey	192	26,139	0.8	61	10,023	0.3
China	233	435,737	12.7	53	459,206	12.9
European Union	22	874,981	25.5	−5	827,417	23.2
United States	7	219,091	6.4	−66	482,189	13.5
World	56	3,432,539	100	18	3,573,221	100

Source: IMF, Direction of Trade Statistics, 2017.

The Fourth Industrial Revolution in Africa

The Fourth Industrial Revolution (4IR) describes a range of innovations and disruptions that aim to reshape the global economy, using the Internet of Things, artificial intelligence, biotechnology, 3D printing, among other technologies. Academics and investors alike are dedicated to capitalizing on the potential of the 4IR around the world, and the African continent stands to benefit exponentially from the 4IR.

African firms have limited drawbacks to integrating 4IR technology into current operations by leapfrogging legacy infrastructure, revitalizing public sector support, and establishing mutually beneficial public-private partnerships. Africa also benefits from the rapid expansion of mobile broadband networks across the continent, which can attract investors to the information and communications technology sector in particular and to other enterprise opportunities facilitated by increasing interest in the adaptation of local infrastructure to new technologies. States like Kenya and Rwanda are proactively adopting national strategies for technological adoption and fostering innovation with policies that enable heightened technical capacity. Other countries, like South Africa, Nigeria, and Egypt, each host more than thirty tech hubs. And creative entrepreneurs are launching a broad distribution of services to meet the needs of Africa's markets with technology, from mobile applications for agricultural finance to 3D printing of titanium metal parts.

This book provides guidance to people interested in doing or understanding business in Africa, and those looking for a clear and straightforward analysis of the new transformations and economic opportunities on the continent. This book offers explanations for what is at play in Africa, how to identify business and investment opportunities and transform them into results, thus creating value that contributes to economic growth, poverty alleviation, and a brighter future for the cradle of humanity. The book is also intended for leaders involved in the formulation and implementation of development strategies in Africa. These include policymakers and experts in government, international, and nongovernmental organizations geographically located in developed and developing countries interested in creating conducive environments for doing business or generating inclusive growth and development. The book's chapters cover the following sectors: consumer markets, agriculture and food industries, information and communication technologies, manufacturing, oil and gas, tourism, banking, and infrastructure and construction. Each chapter presents the key facts and trends, the relevance of the sector for the economy and development, key players and spending trends, specific opportunities with country cases, the challenges, risks, and strategies to transform the opportunities into results, and the perspectives for the future.

TWO

Africa's Consumer Markets and Distribution Transformation and Potential

Africa is one of the fastest-growing consumer markets in the world. Household consumption has increased even faster than its GDP in recent years—and that average annual GDP growth has consistently outpaced the global GDP.[1] In light of the increasing affluence, population growth, urbanization rates, and rapid spread of the internet and mobile phone access on the continent, Africa's emerging economies present exciting opportunities for expansion in retail and distribution.

Studies have shown that African consumers are savvy and brand loyal. Local vendors are entrepreneurial and present key assets for distribution chains.[2] At the same time, the vast majority of consumer spending on the continent currently takes place in informal, roadside markets, even in countries with well-developed retail and distribution markets. This disconnect signals enormous potential for growth as African consumers shift from the informal to more formal consumption—including shopping malls, supermarkets, and, eventually, even e-commerce—a process that is already underway in most countries.

Throughout Africa, consumer expenditure has grown at a compound annual rate of 3.9 percent since 2010 and reached $1.4 trillion in 2015. This figure is expected to reach $2.1 trillion by 2025,[3] and $2.5 trillion by 2030. By 2030, with the full implementation of the African Continental Free Trade Area (AfCFTA) and its single continental market for goods and services, international corporations will have multiple points of entry to the continent's increasingly integrated markets.

Even relatively frontier markets are receiving increasing attention from foreign investors, who consider factors such as the favorability of the tax and regulatory environment, the stability of the political system, access to human and financial capital, and proximity to key markets.[4] For example, in light of the political and security risks associated with investment in Nigeria, the common West African target of foreign investors hoping to capitalize on its large population over the past few decades, many companies are now looking to Ghana as their regional hub of operations. Ghana's healthy business climate is bolstered by a stable, civilian-led democratic regime, a population of over 28 million, and comprehensive security policies.[5]

Meanwhile, analysts have targeted Ethiopia as the future for growth in African consumerism. It was one of the fastest-growing economies in the world between 2005 and 2015, with an average annual GDP growth rate of 10.5 percent from 2005–06 to 2015–16.[6] In addition, with one of the highest savings rates on the continent, its economy reflects a more stable and secure consumer sentiment. Moreover, progressive government initiatives have reduced the burden on doing business—specifically, the time estimated to start a business dropped from 44 days in 2004 to 32 days in 2018, and the cost from over 400 percent of income per capita to around 50 percent of income per capita. The administration has also capitalized on the country's connectivity boom by setting up the Ethiopia Commodity Exchange (ECX) to help overcome market distortions, especially in the agricultural sector.[7] The ECX call-in service already receives over 1.5 million calls each month. Foreign companies, such as Coca-Cola and Heineken, have recognized Ethiopia's potential and are thus making substantial investments.[8]

This chapter offers business leaders an accessible overview of Africa's biggest opportunities in the consumer markets sector, discussing trends and perspectives in the period between now and 2030. It provides policymakers and leaders with an accessible perspective on the options likely to attract private investors, accelerate consumer market development, and contribute to growth and poverty alleviation, which will all facilitate the fulfillment of the Sustainable Development Goals and the African Union's Agenda 2063.

Background Facts and Trends

Africa is home to roughly 1.2 billion consumers today, a figure that is projected to increase to 1.7 billion by 2030. The potential for future growth in retail and consumer spending is, therefore, bright. On the other hand, despite recording some of the fastest economic growth rates in the world since 2005,[9] income levels in Africa have not kept pace, and household spending in the region has remained relatively stagnant.

GDP AND INCOME GROWTH

The McKinsey Global Institute notes that increases in income and labor productivity in Africa have been among the fastest in the world and have consistently exceeded projections. Since 2010, though, Africa has experienced a slowdown in real GDP growth, owing largely to declining commodity prices on the world market; economic growth fell from an average of 5.4 percent per year between 2000 and 2010 to 3.3 percent between 2010 and 2015. At present, Africa ranks third among world regions in real growth terms, behind East Asia and the Middle East, though it continues to outpace the global average.

HOUSEHOLD CONSUMPTION AND CONSUMER MARKETS

Household consumption in Africa exhibited a compound annual growth rate (CAGR) of 3.9 percent between 2010 and 2015, reaching an estimated value of $1.4 trillion in 2015. Despite the region's growth, though, changes in household spending in Africa have remained relatively stagnant, failing to keep pace even with the increase in average income levels.[10] At the same time, the formal consumer spending levels in sub-Saharan Africa have been rapidly outpaced by increases in developing East Asia, Central Asia, and Latin America. Notably, many of these trends reflect the fact that household consumption is generally measured in terms of revenues of formal retail markets, whereas the vast majority of spending in Africa takes place in informal markets that remain overlooked by traditional measures.

Africa's formal consumer markets are currently the least developed in the world, signaling enormous potential for future growth as the region's emerging markets undergo a process of economic modernization and demographic transformation. Already, Africa's total consumer expenditure accounts for roughly 8 percent of all spending in the world's emerging markets, roughly on par with that of Russia or Brazil.

Within Africa, the largest consumer market in terms of total volume is Nigeria, worth roughly $370 billion in 2013, followed by Egypt, South Africa, Algeria, Angola, Morocco, Sudan, and Kenya. At the same time, the fastest-growing market is Angola,[11] where expenditures increased at a CAGR of 34 percent between 2000 and 2013 alone.[12] Increased spending among households in Nigeria will likely amount to nearly $200 billion between 2015 and 2025, or 30 percent of Africa's overall consumption growth over this period.[13]

GROWTH IN THE FAST-MOVING CONSUMER GOODS AND DISTRIBUTION SERVICES SECTORS

As a share of Africa's total economy, consumer spending is now the fastest-growing source of demand, compared to government and business spending, and this trend is projected to continue through 2030.[14] By that time, the population of Africa will have surpassed that of either China or India. In light of these projections, even the most conservative estimates expect the value of consumer spending in Africa to surpass $2 trillion within the next few years—an increase of more than 30 percent from 2015 levels.[15] As a result, industries supplying Africa's consumer markets are expected to increase revenues, with household consumption projected to grow by $645 billion by 2015, with the largest benefits expected to accrue in food and beverages, housing, luxury goods, transportation, and hospitality and recreation.[16]

Given the relatively low purchasing power of African consumers, the greatest increase in household expenditure over the short term is likely to occur in the fast-moving consumer goods (FMCGs) sector, comprising low-cost products with a short shelf life that are constantly in high demand, such as consumables and cleaning products. According to the Economist Intelligence Unit, African retail spending surpassed $1.4 trillion in 2016, with the FMCG subsectors of food, beverages, and tobacco accounting for roughly two-thirds of the total consumption (figure 2.1).[17]

Substantial growth has also occurred in the distribution services sector, which notably includes services that take produce from farmers to the customer's table, particularly in East Africa. This has contributed to the marked growth rates exhibited in purchases of food, beverages, and clean-

FIGURE 2.1. African consumer expenditure in major retail subsectors, 2011 and 2016.

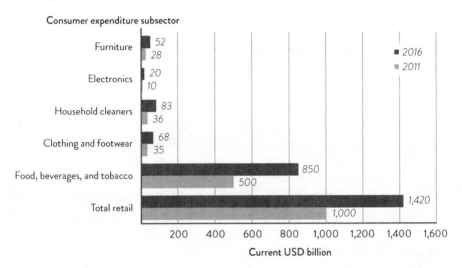

Source: The Economist Intelligence Unit.

ing products in 2011 and 2016 (see figure 2.1). Between 2001 and 2008, distribution services grew by a yearly average of 12 percent in Kenya and Tanzania and 20 percent in Uganda. This trend has contributed to the rapid increase in revenues among supermarkets in the region—CAGRs of supermarket retail sales had reached 13 percent in Uganda, 12 percent in Tanzania, and 7 percent in Kenya by 2010.[18] Still, only about 20 percent of sales go through retail outlets in East Africa, and this figure dips to less than 5 percent in other major markets, such as Nigeria, Ghana, and Cameroon.[19]

Importance of the Consumer Market Sector

There is a general consensus in the literature on economic transformations around the world that labor productivity gains are central in the shift toward a modern, developed society, a process that eventually culminates in what Rostow (1959) has famously coined "the age of mass consumption." Although the original focus was on agricultural revolutions in the early industrializers, especially the United Kingdom, the same logic of modernization has since been applied to the late developers, such as China and

India.[20] In general, the process through which this initial transformation occurs has two stages: first in agriculture, and second in manufacturing.

An agricultural revolution must first generate an increase in per capita output, allowing substantial portions of the population to shift away from engaging directly in farming and migrate toward urban areas, which are supplied by the nation's growing food surplus.[21, 22] While these productivity gains directly contribute to expanded employment in a formal, wage-based economy, they also increase the value of labor, thus laying the foundation for a population of consumers. Second, with larger segments of the population concentrated in productive sectors, productivity gains in industry are likely to be caused by technological innovations and advancements in human capital, such as improving education and health indicators. As the value of labor continues to increase, thus raising the average worker's level of income, manufactured consumer goods also become more affordable to a growing number of households, thereby expanding the range and quantity of goods consumed.[23]

Thus, in the stages-of-growth model of development, achieving both of these substantial transformations is thought to generate a period of self-sustaining growth in which productivity gains across economic sectors become mutually reinforcing. As income levels rise, a growing segment of the population is able to move beyond subsistence toward discretionary spending, increasing demand for a broader range of manufactured goods; for the construction of vital infrastructures to improve distribution and personal travel; for access to formal financial services for savings and credit; and for improvements in education and health services. The robustness of any country's consumer market is, therefore, a crucial reflection of the health of the underlying economy, as well as itself an important driver of growth in other vital sectors.

Key Drivers

Consumer demand and sales volumes have peaked in the developed world, and now developing economies are projected to account for the lion's share of growth in spending and consumption over the next few decades.[24] Although most investor attention has been focused on markets in Asia, Latin America, and eastern Europe, Africa currently contains nine of the twenty fastest-growing economies in the world, with income levels increasing among all socioeconomic groups.[25] Meanwhile, the continent's target markets and categories remain substantially underdeveloped and less competitive than those in other developing regions, since the vast majority of African consumers currently shop at informal outlets, such as roadside and tabletop stands.[26] Thus future growth in the retail sector will be driven largely by factors that increase discretionary household spending and contribute to the shift toward modern, formal consumption patterns.

URBANIZATION

Recent empirical data from Africa show that urbanization does, in fact, tend to produce greater gains in consumer spending, at least during stages of early development. Analysts estimate that, over the next few decades, the proportion of the population living in cities is projected to increase from 40 percent to more than 60 percent, with some of the most lucrative markets—such as Nigeria, Ghana, and Angola—likely to top 80 percent. An additional 187 million Africans will reside in cities within the next decade, and by 2050, roughly 800 million more people will be consolidated in Africa's urban megacenters. With productivity in cities three times as high as in rural areas, this signals vast potential for increased consumption by households and businesses.[27] According to The Economist Intelligence Unit, the largest eighteen cities in Africa could have a combined spending power of $1.3 trillion by 2030.[28]

POPULATION AND DEMOGRAPHICS

In 2030, 1.7 billion Africans will need critical products and services, such as food, beverages, access to pharmaceutical products and health care services, education, and security, in addition to other important products and services. Food and beverages alone will represent $740 billion in spending. Reaching billions of customers in Africa and abroad will require effective agriculture and food processing; well-organized distribution channels from transportation, wholesale, and retail sales; and well-educated professionals supporting an effective value chain. Corporations should prioritize the countries with the highest (optimal) population and spending relevant to their sectors.

The future growth potential for Africa's consumer market is bolstered by positive demographic forecasts. While the global population is aging, Africa's workforce is increasingly young, urban, and affluent—particularly in comparison to other developing regions, where productivity gains have largely stagnated in recent years. The continent's population is growing at an average rate of 2.2 percent, more than twice that of Asia, and nearly two-thirds of its inhabitants are under the age of 25.[29]

These young consumers are sophisticated, globalized, and cost-conscious, representing important drivers of consumer trends in emerging markets more generally, particularly as they become household decision-makers over the next 10 years.[30]

THE GROWTH OF THE POPULATION WITH DISCRETIONARY INCOME

Indeed, the tremendous potential of African countries is correlated not only with population growth but with income growth as well. One in five of the world's consumers will live in Africa by the end of the next decade, and more and more of these people will fall into the category of consumers with discretionary income.

In the next few years, more than half of all African households are expected to have discretionary income—that is, approximately 59 percent of Africans by 2020. In the five largest consumer markets alone—Nigeria, Egypt, South Africa, Morocco, and Algeria—the African Development Bank estimates that there will be 56 million households with disposable income of nearly $680 billion.[31] Consumers who are considered "better off than middle class" according to Organization for Economic Cooperation and Development standards are expected to spend an additional $174 billion per year over the same period, accounting for another 27 percent of the region's total consumption growth.[32] At present, the population with discretionary income is expanding so quickly that total consumer expenditure is expected to double by 2020.[33]

Special attention should be paid to the number of people with discretionary income and their purchasing power. Figure 2.2 shows the daily personal income distribution in Africa in 2030, compared to 2013. An approximate number of 582 million Africans will have estimated revenues of $2 to $20 a day, and an additional 116 million people will have revenues higher than $20 a day, for a total of 698 million people with discretionary income.

Second, while it remains relatively small compared to other world regions, an upper class is beginning to emerge in certain African countries, demanding high-quality, niche, and foreign-produced goods as a mark of

FIGURE 2.2. Personal income distribution in Africa by 2030 (per day).

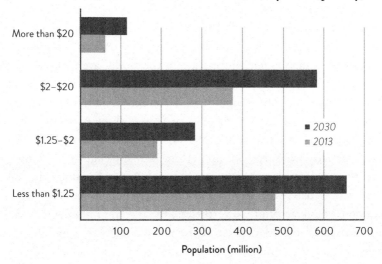

Source: The Deloitte Consumer Review, Africa: A 21st Century View, 2014

social status. Particularly if the price of oil rebounds to pre-2014 levels, oil-producing countries like Angola, Nigeria, Algeria, and Egypt are poised to see an increased market share for luxury goods. By 2030, the number of consumers in the top income bracket is projected to double in Algeria and potentially nearly triple in Morocco, while per capita income in Tunisia is expected to increase at more than twice the regional average, at 4 percent per year.[34]

INFORMATION AND COMMUNICATIONS TECHNOLOGIES AND FORMAL MARKETS

A robust consumer market requires sufficient maturity in sectors that support citizens' abilities to act as modern consumers. In particular, adequate financial development is necessary so that the workforce can efficiently save, spend, and borrow from financial markets. Relatedly, the spread of information and communications technologies (ICTs) provides new and innovative avenues for consumer spending—such as e-commerce—and marketing campaigns. There is also an increasingly recognized, complementary relationship between these two sectors, as the internet and mobile phones have increased the range of financial services available to previously underreached consumers.[35]

The rapid diffusion of ICTs in Africa over the past decade has facilitated access to consumers in new and varied ways. Africa is currently the fastest-growing mobile telecom market in the world, averaging a roughly 30 percent increase in mobile phone connections per year since 2000, and recently overtaking Latin America to become the world's second-largest mobile market behind Asia.[36] Roughly two out of three Africans now have internet access, 75 percent of whom report going online on a daily basis, and connectivity has surpassed 80 percent in many countries.[37] However, formal financial development in sub-Saharan Africa is among the lowest in the world to date, with less than one-in-three people claiming access to a traditional bank account. Nevertheless, the spread of mobile phones has rapidly increased the proportion of the population with a mobile money account, raising the number of people who have access to either a financial institution or a mobile-money service provider to 43 percent, according to World Bank data. Africans are especially likely to prioritize their ICTs over other needs—in recent surveys, many respondents even reported skipping meals in order to pay for mobile airtime and internet use.[38]

At present, informal markets overwhelmingly dominate the scene for private consumption in Africa. The modern trade sector is largest in South Africa and Angola, yet formal retail still accounted for just 39 percent and 34 percent of shopping visits in 2015, respectively.[39] In Nigeria, there were more than 200,000 roadside or tabletop vendors in 2015, which are the primary source of daily purchases for more than 80 percent of consumers.[40] In many of Africa's foremost emerging markets—such as Ghana, Cameroon, Ethiopia, and Egypt—these informal stalls and markets still accounted for more than 95 percent of consumer spending in 2015.[41]

Subsectors

In light of these trends, two consumer subsectors offer particular opportunities for growth across the African region: FMCGs and luxury goods. First, unlike other sectors, FMCGs tend to be household necessities with relatively constant, inelastic demand across all consumer classes. Demand for these types of products is likely to correlate with population growth rates, especially as single-person households are forecast to exhibit the fastest growth in consumption through 2030.[42] More significantly, as consumers become increasingly affluent and purchasing power increases in the region—particularly among the majority, low-income tier of buyers—the sector will exhibit a gradual trading up in prices along the value chain, ultimately boosting profit margins for both producers and retailers.[43]

In East Africa, a recent boom in the distribution services sector has contributed to a notable shift in consumer spending away from informal markets and toward formal retailers—a trend that is likely to be replicated across the continent in the coming years. The distribution sector now contributes to more than 10 percent of GDP in Kenya, Tanzania, and Uganda, and regional growth in distribution and retail has more than doubled the rate of GDP growth in the region over the past few years. At the same time, it continues to be outpaced by consumer demand, and research by Nakumatt Holdings—one of the region's largest formal retailers—indicates that the East African market has the potential to sustain significantly more retail stores.[44] Thus the potential for growth in Africa's formal retail sector is enormous, representing a key driver of future investment in the region.

Key Players and Spending Trends

As an indication of growing recognition of Africa's market potential, foreign direct investment to the region increased fivefold between 2000 and 2010, and it now exceeds that received by many of the world's largest emerging markets, including Brazil.[45] In terms of domestic firms, however, Africa currently possesses only 60 percent of the number of large corporations that one would expect when compared to peer regions, and their average revenue of $2 billion per year is half that of the large firms in India and Brazil. Given that consumer spending in Africa is largely concentrated in the informal sector, a small proportion of retail outlets account for a disproportionate amount of sales revenues. There is certainly room for growth.

In Nigeria, for example, there are approximately 700,000 informal stalls that sell soft drinks, yet there are relatively few of the most prominent supermarket chains: just seven Spars, sixteen Shoprites, six Massmarts, and two Game stores in the whole country. In contrast, South Africa has a much more developed formal retail sector, with nearly two thousand Spar and Shoprite supermarkets.[46] Yet the share of modern retail in countries like Nigeria is growing rapidly—as fueled by population trends and urbanization, among other factors—and growth rates are expected to increase in the coming years with the development of large-scale shopping centers.

African retailers like Shoprite (South Africa) are likely to continue benefiting from this trend, fueled by rapid improvements in regional distribution networks.

Brand recognition is highly important to African buyers, who often refer to products by an associated brand name, such as Tide for laundry detergent or Gillette for razors. As a result, multinationals providing recognizable international brands continue to report strong profitability in their African investments.[47] More than 70 percent of the fifty largest packaged goods producers in the world are already tapping into Africa's rapidly growing consumer market. Of these corporations, one in three generates more than 5 percent of its global sales in the region—as high as 14 percent for Diageo and 10 percent for Parmalat, for example. In contrast, consumer goods that are produced locally tend to be focused on a single, country-specific market, and they generally lack the funding and distribution needed to achieve recognition and loyalty among a critical mass of consumers.[48]

Opportunities

Although competition is increasing, as highlighted by the recent entry of significant multinational players like Walmart, Africa's consumer market is currently much less saturated and developed than that of other developing regions, such as Asia and Latin America.[49] Thus the opportunities for growth are high across the continent, and certain countries offer particularly lucrative investment opportunities due to their potential for rapid and sustained growth over the next decade. In the continent as a whole, already eleven countries account for roughly 80 percent of total wealth and consumer spending: Algeria, Angola, Egypt, Ethiopia, Ghana, Kenya, Morocco, Nigeria, South Africa, Sudan, and Tunisia. All of these countries have exhibited marked growth in household consumption since 2000, particularly in the post-2005 period, although growth in Nigeria, Egypt, and South Africa has significantly outpaced all other markets, as illustrated in figure 2.3.

Although these three countries now dominate the rest of the continent in terms of consumer spending by volume, a number of factors suggest that their future growth trajectories may be more restrained than some other emerging markets, where private consumption is just starting to take off. For example, although it is worth nearly $200 billion per year, South Africa's retail market is already considered overly saturated—as there exists a

FIGURE 2.3. Household spending in Africa's ten largest consumer markets, 2000–2017.

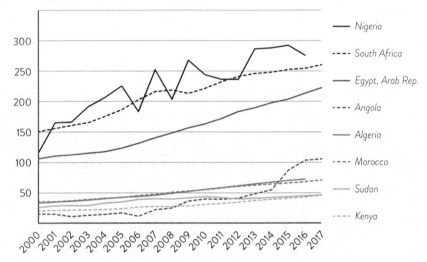

Source: World Development Indicators, 2018.

plethora of vendors—especially by regional standards.[50] In Egypt, growth in per capita income over the past 6 years has been one of the lowest among the top eleven consumer markets, suggesting a potential downturn in consumption in the near future. In November 2016, the International Monetary Fund even approved a $12 billion bailout for Egypt over the next 3 years, aiming to restore investor and consumer confidence in the economy.

In light of the drivers of growth in consumer markets identified earlier in this chapter, we provide a systematic comparison of Africa's top consumer markets based on their current market size and potential for future growth. We develop a multivariate index of market potential, ranging from zero (low potential) to 40 (high potential), which combines countries' rankings on recent indicators of GDP per capita growth rates, urbanization rates, mobile penetration rates, and compound annual growth in sales of FMCGs. This comparison is illustrated in figure 2.4, while table 2.1 provides a descriptive summary of relevant data.

TABLE 2.1. Descriptive data on factors related to potential future growth in Africa's top consumer markets.

Country	Household consumption (US$ billions)	GDP per capita growth (%)	Urban-ization rate (%)	FMCG sales growth (%)	Buyer sophistication (1–7)	Intensity of competition (1–7)
Nigeria	377.33	0.93	4.51	23	3.3	5.1
Egypt	275.74	0.77	2.23	8	3.1	4.8
South Africa	176.93	0.32	2.34	6	3.9	5.4
Sudan	74.37	4.60	2.80	14	—	—
Angola	74.47	0.28	5.35	34	2.33	2.6
Algeria	68.04	1.32	2.86	10	3.1	4.1
Morocco	60.02	2.03	2.26	9	3.2	5.2
Kenya	54.97	2.82	4.31	12	3.2	5.5
Ethiopia	50.80	6.97	4.92	15	3.2	3.7
Tunisia	29.94	0.52	1.43	7	2.9	5.0
Ghana	28.43	4.54	3.60	16	3.0	5.0

Source: World Development Indicators (December 2017). Household consumption are data for 2016; average income growth and urbanization rate are annual averages over the period 2011–2016; fast-moving consumer goods (FMCG) sales growth are the annual average over the period 2011–2015; "Buyer sophistication" and "Intensity of competition" are from World Economic Forum Global Competitiveness Report (2017–2018) and scored from 1 (worst) to 7 (best).

NIGERIA

With the largest population on the continent, Nigeria is also Africa's largest consumer market by volume, with roughly $380 billion in household consumption per year. Although its economic growth rate has been outpaced by many other African countries in recent years, including neighboring Ghana, recent compound annual growth in FMCGs is second on the continent behind Angola, at 23 percent. This is reflective of a number of positive conditions that suggest enormous market potential for Nigeria in the near future. With eight cities already reporting a population above one million people and with one of the highest urbanization rates on the continent (see table 2.1), Nigeria will be home to Africa's greatest number of urban megacenters in the coming decades.[51] This trend is already driving the shift from informal markets toward modern retail centers, although informal trade still accounts for the vast majority of consumer spending.

FIGURE 2.4. Comparison of market size and potential in Africa's top consumer markets.

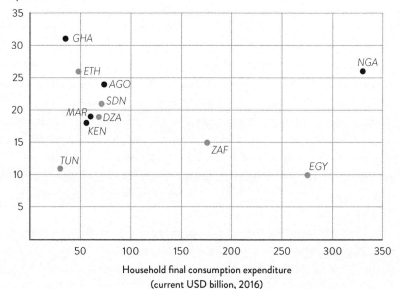

Market potential index

Household final consumption expenditure
(current USD billion, 2016)

Source: World Development Indicators, 2018.

Note: Market potential index is calculated by ranking each country in terms of the urbanization rate (average annual %, 2011–2016), GDP per capita growth rate (average annual %, 2011–2016), compound annual growth rate in fast-moving consumer goods (2011–2015), and mobile penetration rate (subscribers per 100 people, 2016). Each of the eleven countries is scored according to its ranking for each variable: highest score = 10, lowest score = 0. The four scores are then added together to achieve a composite index score ranging from 0 to 40 (true range is 11 to 31). Case study countries are indicated in red. Note that market potential score in Sudan has been positively impacted by the secession of South Sudan to unknown magnitude, so this country is excluded from case discussions.

Major international retailers are rapidly expanding their operations in Nigeria, such as Shoprite and Spar, and Nigeria now reports one of the highest levels of market competition in Africa.[52] E-commerce has even taken off with the launch of Jumia, a local version of Amazon, which allows for payment-on-delivery in order to overcome the deficiency of formal financial accounts and mobile money services.[53]

However, there are a few reasons to be wary of the current economic and regulatory climate. Nigeria ranked 145 out of 183 countries in the World Bank's Ease of Doing Business Index in 2018—a decline from a height of 133 11 years ago and the result of burdensome contract, licensing, and tax regulations and energy shortages. Moreover, due to the heavy reliance on oil rents as a share of total GDP, the recent decline in world oil prices has constrained markets and impacted local prices and demand, while also causing fuel and power supply shortages. At the end of 2016, consumer confidence scores were at their lowest point in the 3-year history of the Nielsen Global Survey of Consumer Confidence and Spending Intentions. Meanwhile, devaluation of the naira, constraints in access to foreign exchange, and a resurgence of security concerns led the IMF to revise the 5-year forecasted GDP growth rate from 3.2 percent to 2.3 percent. Concerns related to these factors have kept investment in Nigeria's consumer market below full potential in recent years.

In light of the sheer size of local demand for consumer goods, however, Nigeria presents an attractive investment option looking to the future, particularly for affordable basic products and FMCGs. Its retail market remains dominated by low-income consumers, and current GDP per capita growth rates and projections indicate that this is not likely to change in the near future. However, as consumers' purchasing power increases over the medium-term, investors' profit margins will improve through a gradual trading up along the value chain.[54]

GHANA

Although the annual volume of consumer spending in Ghana is presently much lower than that in neighboring Nigeria, it provides a relatively free and stable operating environment by comparison, leading many investors to view it as the new "gateway to the West African region."[55] Major multinationals have already started capitalizing on this by setting up manufacturing facilities in Ghana—Unilever, PZ Cussons, and Fan Milk Group—thus allowing retailers to purchase consumer goods locally and at lower cost. Yet only a small number of international retailers have set up shops in the country to date, and they are mainly restricted to the capital, Accra. Over the past decade, though, at least ten new, large retail centers—ranging in size from 8,000 to 27,000 m^2—have been completed or are near completion, and reports indicate that the total amount of retail space could increase by 180,000 m^2 in another 10 years.[56]

Ghana's middle class, though currently small, is growing at a rapid rate and increasingly demanding the convenience of modern supermarkets and retail outlets. The Nielsen Global Survey of Consumer Confidence and Spending Intentions (2016) reports that consumer confidence scores increased by 10 percent in 2016 alone and are now on par with those of Nigeria. This is reflective of the country's impressive economic performance in recent years, with population growth of roughly half a million people per year, average annual growth in GDP per capita being above 4.5 percent over the past 6 years, and CAGR in FMCGs of 16 percent (see table 2.1)—the third highest on the continent behind Angola and Nigeria.[57] Businesses working in Ghana report noticeable improvements in the ease of doing business in recent years, as well as in consumer spending and economic growth outlooks, in exchange and inflation rates, and in power supply.

ANGOLA

Angola is another attractive market for international retailers. Growth rates in FMCGs have been highest in all of Africa, at 34 percent compound annual growth over the past 5 years, and sales of packaged food alone are now worth $1.8 billion per year.[58] Angola's population growth rates and average income levels are especially high, with a rapidly expanding middle class—which presently stands around 16 percent of the country's total population—despite substantial inequality. According to Euromonitor International, the "Angolan middle class is increasingly able to afford a growing range of essential products, such as food and beverages, and demand for non-essential items is also expected to increase" (KPMG 2016).

Moreover, its consumer market has already started to show signs of rapid movement away from informal markets and toward formal retailers. South African–based Shoprite already has nineteen retail outlets in Angola, which have recorded higher sales of products like Red Bull and LC Le Roux sparkling wine than in all of its 382 domestic outlets combined. A number of large retail centers have opened in and around the capital Luanda over the past 10 years, including Luanda Shopping, with 208 shops, a six-screen cinema, and a gym.

Yet, at present, Angola's retail market remains significantly less saturated than that of Nigeria, South Africa, or Egypt. More international retailers and manufacturers have demonstrated their intention to invest more heavily in Angola in the immediate future, however, despite the macroeconomic imbalances and reductions in consumer spending caused by the recent decline in world oil prices, in order to avoid losing out on market share and the rapid growth in consumption that is likely to occur once the economic climate stabilizes.[59]

MOROCCO

Unlike in sub-Saharan Africa, growth in consumer markets in North Africa is largely being driven by expansion of the most affluent sector of society, or households earning more than $50,000 per year. Thus, although Morocco has not exhibited particularly impressive growth in sales of FMCGs in recent years, there is greater potential for growth in consumption of nonessential items, especially high-end products and services.[60]

Domestic retailers currently dominate the market in Morocco, the largest being Marjane Holding, Hyper SA, and Group Chaabi, but international brands and outlets have already started making inroads by focusing on the market for luxury goods.[61] Retailers have also capitalized on the boom in internet penetration, as the country's online shopping scene has taken off since 2013.[62] Morocco is thus poised to be at the forefront of Africa's broader shift from informal to modernized consumer markets.

To manage the changes and encourage investment, the Moroccan government has established a strategy known as Plan Rawaj, which aims to triple the value added in formal market trade and to create 450,000 new jobs in the commerce and distribution sectors—which already account for 13 percent of employment in 2013.[63] The plan includes development of 600 new large and medium-sized retail markets, including 50 "hypermarkets" and 30 malls and outlets, with the baseline goal of growing the consumer market by 8 percent per year through 2020.[64]

KENYA

The volume of consumer spending in Kenya is already the largest in the East African region, and several trends point to enormous potential for continued growth in the immediate future. First of all, the East African region, and Kenya in particular, has seen some of the most impressive improvements in transit infrastructure in all of Africa in recent years. Combined with process innovations related to the incorporation of ICTs in the industry, this has contributed to marked growth in the region's distribution sector, which supplies Kenya's exponentially increasing number of retail centers and supermarkets. Kenya's Vision 2030 lists distribution as a "strategic sector" to target and, recognizing the centrality of the distribution sector in driving regional growth, the governments of East Africa have worked to harmonize their customs and tax regulations and to encourage the movement of goods across borders.[65]

There is also a vibrant and growing domestic industry for the manufacturing of consumer goods and food products in the country, and a range of analyses consider Kenyan products to be among the top four countries in Africa that score above the global average in terms of the competitiveness of products on the international market.[66] While domestic production will continue to drive growth in domestic consumption, Kenya is also emerging as one of the continent's top exporters of manufactured consumer goods over the medium to long term.

Finally, Kenyan consumers indicate a positive outlook for the market. According to Nielsen (2016), consumer confidence scores increased over the last three consecutive quarters in 2016, with 53 percent of survey respondents feeling that "now is a good time to spend." Moreover, 72 percent of respondents reported favorable sentiments about personal finance and savings, with an increasingly large segment of the Kenyan population—the largest in Africa by a wide margin—using mobile money services to spend and save. The majority (54 percent) of growth in consumption in Kenya is being driven by middle-class households earning between $5,000 and $20,000 per year, and with the current trend of stable, positive growth in income levels and urbanization rates (see table 2.1), this segment of the population is likely to continue expanding over the coming years.

Challenges and Risks

The decline in global commodity prices is one of the foremost challenges facing the short-term development of the consumer market in Africa. The country with the largest population and the biggest consumer market in the region, Nigeria, is also the largest oil producer in sub-Saharan Africa. In Angola—which experienced the most rapid growth in consumer spending over the past decade while oil prices were high—oil rents account for more than 30 percent of annual GDP. Five of Africa's eight largest consumer markets are heavily reliant on oil exports—Angola, Algeria, Egypt, Nigeria, and Sudan—and, as such, the short-term prospects for growth in household income and spending in these countries will depend on whether commodity prices stagnate or rebound.[67]

Beyond the economic climate, investment in Africa's consumer market presents many similar challenges affecting all sectors in the region.

DISTRIBUTION COSTS

Weak infrastructure, especially the poor quality of road networks in rural areas and traffic congestion in cities, drives up the cost of transporting goods. Distribution networks can also be disrupted by hijacking and extortion from organized crime groups, such as in the "mungiki"-controlled areas on the outskirts of Nairobi, which generates hidden costs. Most companies working in the region therefore choose to invest in insurance and increased security.[68] Market entry is often obstructed by regulatory measures, which can be burdensome and prone to change without notice. Retailers importing consumer goods report cumbersome customs processes caused by bureaucratic hurdles and port congestion. This raises the cost of imports and makes it more difficult to maintain inventory at appropriate levels.

REGULATIONS

Companies interested in investment in the distribution sector in East Africa should know that despite efforts to simplify the process, all countries in the region have some form of regulation on market access.[69] Kenya, Tanzania, Uganda, and Rwanda require that new businesses formally register, get approval from authorities, and obtain the necessary commercial licenses and permits, which carry various fees depending on the type of business. There are typically multiple licenses required in distribution, such as approval from authorities in each of the local territories serviced and individual exporting documentation for each product. In one instance, a distributor reported needing export documentation for every individual flavor of yogurt transported.[70]

Complications also arise due to the fact that different countries have different regulations and requirements for doing business (table 2.2). Rwanda regulates tax registration even for microretailers, small franchises, and kiosks, whereas Uganda prohibits foreign retailers from establishing outlets outside the city limits. On the other hand, Burundi has relatively few regulations on distribution services beyond pharmaceutical providers, which has actually constrained the growth of retail and distribution businesses due to legal uncertainty and opportunities for corruption.

The foremost regulation-related restriction facing the retail and distribution sectors, however, is caused by price controls. Most East African countries have imposed pricing regulations as a measure of consumer protection, despite opposition from the private sector, which has a negative effect on competition. The most commonly controlled goods are fuels, but other price controls include sugar in Burundi, pharmaceuticals in Rwanda, and various food products in Kenya. Tanzania has implemented the most wide-reaching regulations, with controls on water, electricity, public transit fares, and telecommunications.

INFORMATION GAPS

For businesses trying to appeal directly to African consumers, on the other hand, a major impediment is the availability of market data. At present,

TABLE 2.2. Comparison across indicators of challenges of doing business in Africa's top consumer markets.

Country	Number of procedures to start a business	Number of days to start a business	Impact of policies on FDI (1–7)	Burden of customs procedures (1–7)	Transport infrastructure quality (1–7)
Nigeria	9	25.2	5.1	2.9	2.9
Egypt	4	6.5	3.4	3.9	5.1
South Africa	7	43	4.3	4.2	5.6
Angola	8	66	2.61	1.84	2.37
Algeria	12	20	3.1	3.4	3.7
Morocco	4	9.5	5.1	4.5	4.8
Kenya	7	22	4.5	4.1	4.9
Ethiopia	14	35	3.6	3.6	4.2
Tunisia	9	11	4.5	3.1	3.9
Ghana	8	14	4.6	3.9	3.9

Source: World Economic Forum Global Competitiveness Report (2017–2018). Note that the impact of policies on foreign direct investment (FDI), the burden of customs procedures, and transport infrastructure quality are scored from 1 (worst) to 7 (best). Scores for Angola are from the 2014 report. Sudan is excluded due to lack of data.

consumer research and data-mining companies have a minimal presence on the continent. Much of the data that is publicly available, both in terms of market supply and consumer demand, is unreliable and easily contradicted by field surveys. Multinational companies will have difficulty determining which socioeconomic groups demand which products, which products can command a premium, where consumers prefer to shop, how they respond to marketing techniques, and which markets have the highest growth potential.[71] This problem is particularly acute for distributors at the bottom end, where market fragmentation is high. In the absence of performance indicators and information about market share, it can be difficult for companies to effectively develop and market products and to plan strategically for the future.[72]

Strategies and Risk Management

When investing in Africa's retail and distribution sectors, most large companies have traditionally favored one of two models. In the first case, the organization is highly centralized and hierarchical, with most decisions and activities taking place at a central headquarters. This allows companies to capitalize on economies of scale, but it hampers adaptability and responsiveness to local specificities. In the second model, country-based operations dominate, and decisionmaking is largely decentralized, which can mitigate the disadvantages of the centralized model but can also result in duplications and undermine coordination.[73]

In light of these trade-offs, many companies have started to adopt a middle-ground model by restructuring operations around Africa's regional economic communities. This approach allows for effective local market coverage and subregional, country-level variation, while centralizing management in a strong, regional headquarters—a hub-and-spoke model. Another advantage is in the ability to coordinate shared services at the regional level, including supply chains and distribution, as well as in contributing to the development of a regional manufacturing presence. The most successful FMCG retailers working in Africa are increasingly following this strategy of focusing on country clusters in developing and marketing products.[74]

No matter which model of operational structure a company chooses to adopt, effectively entering Africa's consumer market requires attention to certain key strategies.

INVESTMENT IN MARKET RESEARCH

While the growth potential of Africa's consumer market offers enormous opportunities, purchasing power on the continent remains among the lowest in the world. In order to achieve short-term success, companies will need to target consumer segments with the greatest potential and to tailor their marketing and distribution. Doing so requires gathering a significant amount of data on the tastes, preferences, and behaviors of consumers across localities and demographic groups.[75]

For distributors, a census of local trade outlets will be necessary to develop a profitable strategy. It should attempt to measure the quantity, type, size, and accessibility of all existing outlets in target countries, as well as the products that they stock and the characteristics of their customer base.

For any company, determining the most lucrative markets to target will also require analysis of data on the following key factors: market fragmentation and saturation, allegiance to traditional trade channels, availability of third parties for joint ventures, tax and licensing regulations, quality of contract enforcement, potential for expropriation, corruption risks, strength of infrastructure, ease of movement and barriers to trade, and access to capital.[76]

LOCALIZATION

In addition to assisting in decisions at the regional level, market research will help retailers to localize product offerings and thus to ensure that they meet the needs and lifestyles of consumers in varied localities. As shown by some studies, companies that have successfully entered the consumer market in Africa have had two strategies in common: adapting products and services to the needs of local customers and building linkages and investing in the local community.[77] Establishing a local presence is vital to success in Africa, where community remains central to most people's daily lives.

Analysts have shown that collaborating with local partners and businesses and investing in education are key determinants of growth in emerging consumer markets, which not only increases returns to investment but ensures that companies remain relevant to their core consumer base over the long term.[78] Only one university in East Africa offers a formal course in retail management, so most companies working in the region currently rely on on-the-job training.[79] More effective businesses have invested in specialized training programs, which help to overcome these local talent shortages and to convey modern techniques, such as inventory management and merchandising.

Consequently, establishing a local presence is key to effectively penetrating Africa's consumer market, and it also significantly enhances the likelihood that companies will thrive over the long term. While there is no one-size-fits-all strategy for success, many analysts have pointed to a few other common tactics in attempting to explain why some firms have been able to expand and grow their business in Africa.

IMPORT SUBSTITUTION

Africa currently imports roughly one-third of the processed goods it consumes, compared to 20 percent in the Association of Southeast Asian Nations (ASEAN) trade bloc of Southeast Asia and 10 percent in South America's Mercosur trade bloc. Of manufactured products like cars and chemicals, 60 percent of Africa's supply is imported, which is twice that of Mercosur. And despite Africa's abundance of natural resources, 15 percent of its cement needs are imported, compared to 5 percent in ASEAN and Mercosur countries. There is, therefore, ample opportunity for African distributors to target more local suppliers and manufacturers in the future, which would ultimately cut costs and boost profit margins while contributing to job creation and rising incomes in targeted emerging markets.[80]

TRADITIONAL AND MODERN TRADE

Successful multinational companies working in African markets recognize the role of both traditional and modern retail outlets in reaching consumers. Penetrating informal markets means providing goods in small, manageable packages and educating informal vendors about product information.[81] The most effective companies have found innovative solutions to localized conditions and demands and have provided training courses for kiosk sellers on merchandising, sampling, and promotion techniques. Combined with locally targeted marketing campaigns, allowing customers to try new products has proved effective in overcoming their reluctance to switch away from preferred brands, a notable challenge in Africa given the relatively high brand loyalty of its consumers.

At the same time, the progressive shift from traditional to modern trade gives producers and distributors a chance to capitalize on the additional shelf space by creating product extensions and new varieties that are more likely to appeal to target demographics. As this shift is more broadly reflective of increasing purchasing power on the continent, companies should not limit their marketing efforts to affordable products with an existing consumer base, as aspirational brands tend to become the preferred option when incomes rise.[82]

INNOVATION

The varied challenges of doing business in Africa mean that successful companies will constantly need to adapt to reaching new markets. Companies choosing to pursue the regional operations structure are increasingly moving their research and development teams into regional hubs in order to better respond to local consumer preferences and behavior.[83] The result is likely to be more products designed to strike the optimal balance between durability and price and to address local conditions in emerging markets—existing examples include Renault's Dacia automobile and Samsung televisions with built-in power surge protectors.[84]

Rural and low-income consumers in Africa tend to be neglected due to the difficulty of access and economic constraints, signaling vast growth potential for companies that find workable solutions.[85] According to Herman Heunis, founder of the free mobile chat service MXit, his company has had marked success in reaching low-income Africans by targeting early adopters in communities and promoting education about new services offered.[86] Meanwhile, Nestlé has successfully penetrated traditional outlets in rural areas of South Africa by using informal distributors, who walk or use bicycles to deliver goods. Not only does this strategy minimize costs and increase market coverage, it has also enhanced brand awareness.[87]

Expanding access to Africans on the bottom tier of the consumer pyramid also demands innovative approaches to financial services. Due to the historically volatile nature of the economic climate, most of Africa's low-income consumers are accustomed to living without a social safety net, formal savings, or access to credit. Purchasing power will be significantly enhanced in these conditions where companies aim to facilitate customers' access to services like microcredit, mobile money transfers, savings accounts, and insurance policies.[88]

Growing a consumer-facing business in Africa means remaining flexible to changing conditions and seeking to leverage a first-mover advantage whenever possible. Emerging markets in Africa are characterized by market fragmentation, quickly evolving political and legal environments, and a shortage of strong local businesses. In order to take advantage, global companies must be prepared to jump on growth opportunities as they emerge, for example, when companies become available through privatization or market exit. According to analysts at Bain & Company, this is the strategy that helped Heineken to develop a coast-to-coast presence as one of the largest beer providers on the continent.[89]

Looking to the Future

From the perspective of international producers and retailers, therefore, the appeal of Africa's consumer market already exists, and several ongoing developments on the continent bolster the region's growth potential in the coming years.

According to the McKinsey Global Institute, the region offers "robust long-term economic fundamentals" driven by the advantages of a young and growing population, a rapidly growing workforce, the fastest urbanization rate in the world, and accelerating technological change.[90]

Production of consumer goods in Africa remains cost-competitive when compared to other regions. Meanwhile, studies of African consumers show that they tend to be entrepreneurial, ambitious, well informed, and disproportionately heavy users of the internet and mobile technology. African consumers are also more likely to prefer international products than consumers in markets such as China and India, where many local brands have already reached a broad scale. African consumers also appear to have more brand loyalty than their Asian counterparts, preferences that are commonly shared within families and social groups, and they are willing to make sacrifices for more durable, high-quality products, even when doing so requires saving and pooling resources.[91]

For creative and innovative businesses, rural consumers present a vast and untapped market, particularly in expanding services—like banking, food and beverages, and mobile phones and internet—outward from already established urban market centers.[92] Distribution services will be critical for increasing access to rural populations, as well as in the rapid expansion of business-to-business trade and the broader shift from informal to formal retail markets.[93] Therefore, governments should demonstrate a willingness to invest in the necessary infrastructure, such as roads, and to reduce regulatory restrictions on the movement of goods, as has already been the case in East Africa. This will allow investors in distribution to increase their gains.

The technology and connectivity boom also presents enormous potential for reaching new markets, as well as providing services that are profitable, while increasing the spending power of African consumers. In the next 5 years, at least 250 million Africans will have mobile phones and a monthly income of over $500. Since 75 percent of people on the continent do not have bank accounts, this signals vast potential for investment in financial services such as bill payments and money transfers. Some analysts project that the financial mobile services market will be worth $1.5 billion in revenues by 2020.[94] And while online shopping is currently rare—only 25 percent of Nigerians report having done so, the highest on the continent—improvements in small-scale distribution networks, power reliability, and internet penetration signal massive growth in e-commerce and online advertising in the coming decades. Meanwhile, social networks are also becoming an increasingly critical—and affordable—tool for marketing and consumer education in the region. These technological developments are helping the continent to overcome infrastructure gaps and improving consumers' access to information and products.

The current state of Africa's consumer market and the demographic changes that are already underway mean that certain markets are poised for investment over the next few decades. In just five countries—Algeria, Egypt, Morocco, Nigeria, and South Africa—an estimated 56 million households will reach the status of middle class by 2020, with disposable incomes of more than $680 billion.[95] In sub-Saharan Africa, nine countries will account for nearly 75 percent of all consumer spending by 2020—Nigeria, Senegal, and Ghana in West Africa; Kenya, Uganda, and Ethiopia in East Africa; and the southern states of Angola, Zambia, and South Africa.[96]

Future consumption in Africa is now characterized by stabilizing incomes, increasing purchasing power, and strong confidence in the future, while its consumer market remains relatively unsaturated and uncompetitive.[97] In this light, a recent report by Bain & Company concludes that "companies with no presence in Africa may want to seriously reconsider [since] skipping Africa means potentially missing significant growth opportunities."[98] Across the continent and across all sectors, the forecast for Africa's consumer market is bright—it is expected to be worth $1 trillion by 2020 and as much as $2 trillion by 2025.[99]

THREE

Africa's Agriculture and Food Industry Transformation and Potential

By 2030, agriculture and agriprocessing will remain the largest sector for business-to-business spending at $915.3 billion. Sixty percent of the world's unused arable land is located in Africa. It is paradoxical that the continent represents only about 3 percent of global agricultural exports and is home to millions of undernourished people. Since the mid-1990s, agriculture and agribusiness have been among Africa's fastest-growing sectors, despite the decline in the relative market share of agriculture. Nevertheless, since 1990, agricultural output has increased at an annual rate of 3.1 percent, compared to 2.3 percent in previous decades. The growth in the sector has been largely driven by improvements in political and social stability, macroeconomic policy reforms, reduced tax burdens on the sector, and increasing global commodity prices. Moreover, African governments have made agriculture a priority and increased the budgetary allocation to the sector. Sectoral challenges include the small-scale nature of agriculture, as it remains dominated by smallholder farmers. The growth of agroindustry has also revealed key investment opportunities, but it is still necessary to increase the competitiveness and productivity of small-scale farmers to enable them to compete at a global level.

Currently, Africa's agricultural intensification remains lower than predicted by the Boserup-Ruthenberg theory, which posits that population change and market access drive the intensity of agricultural production.[1] However, fertilizer and agrochemical use is becoming more widespread across the continent: In Ethiopia, Malawi, and Nigeria, for example, more than 40 percent of farming households use inorganic fertilizer.[2] Furthermore, recent research from McCollough (2017) suggests that the labor productivity gap between agriculture and other economic sectors is smaller than generally assumed in Africa and is mainly due to underemployment, suggesting that there are many potential economic gains to be made from investing in agricultural labor. Overall, improving agricultural productivity will be key to reducing poverty in Africa, especially for the extremely poor, for whom agriculture plays a particularly important role.[3]

This chapter discusses the key trends, drivers, opportunities, and challenges, and the strategies to transform challenges into superior returns in the agriculture and food industries.

Trends and Opportunities

Farming remains the main source of employment, income, and food for Africans—especially those living in rural areas—as well as a major source of revenue for African governments. There is substantial variation across the continent, however, with agriculture accounting for just 2.4 percent of GDP in Equatorial Guinea, compared to more than 70 percent in Liberia, for example.[4] Overall, the sector continues to generate the majority of GDP in many countries, such as Côte d'Ivoire, the Central African Republic, Ethiopia, and Sierra Leone.

However, although agriculture is still a major source of economic activity in Africa, its market share has been on the decline in recent decades. Volatile world commodity prices, policy-induced market failures, and debt crises in the late twentieth century have led to a marked shift away from the reliance on agriculture toward other economic sectors, especially services. Farming now accounts for between 40 and 65 percent of all primary employment in Africa, down from 70 to 80 percent at the turn of the century.[5] Furthermore, despite employing roughly half of all working-age adults, the sector accounts for just 25 percent of the region's GDP, signaling that agriculture has not kept pace with the growth in value added among other economic sectors. Moreover, the continent continues to import more agricultural products than it exports, generating a regional deficit of nearly $10 billion per year.[6]

But although the market share of agriculture has declined relative to other sectors, agriculture and agribusiness have been among Africa's fastest-growing sectors since the mid-1990s.[7] Despite variation across the continent, agricultural output has increased by an average annual rate of 3.1 percent since 1990, compared to 2.3 percent annually over the preceding decades.[8] Some subsectors have seen a particularly notable increase, such as fruits, vegetables, cereals, and flowers, while coffee exports have declined from 100,000 to 40,000 tons since 2000, evidencing the variation in agriculture exports.[9]

Much of the growth in agricultural output has been driven by improved political and social stability on the continent, macroeconomic policy reforms, reduced tax burden on the sector, and rising global commodity prices.[10] Most importantly, though, African governments have increased the proportion of their budgetary expenditures toward agricultural investment. The average level of annual public expenditures on agriculture increased from approximately $130 million between 1995 and 2002 to more than $185 million between 2003 and 2008, and in recent years it has averaged nearly $220 million, so the level is still growing.[11]

In terms of the private sector, agribusiness investment in Africa is low relative to other regions but has exhibited growth in recent years, especially in value-adding processes. Foreign direct investment has increasingly targeted subsectors related to food processing, distribution, and marketing. Commercial lending to the sector has also increased in absolute terms over the last decade, although it still accounts for less than 10 percent of total commercial bank credit in many sub-Saharan African countries, and less than 5 percent in Ghana, Sierra Leone, and Kenya, in particular.[12]

Despite these trends, smallholder and subsistence farming continues to dominate agriculture in Africa. Smallholder farmers cultivate low-yield crops with minimal use of mechanical inputs and irrigation, leading to relatively low levels of agricultural productivity and high incidences of undernourishment. As many as 60 percent of smallholder farmers have to purchase their staple food items and, despite informal trade networks, end up buying more food than they sell over the course of a year.[13] Moreover, poor processing and management practices mean that roughly 30 percent of total agricultural production is lost after the harvest, resulting in a loss of $4 billion each year.[14]

On the other hand, many African countries are starting to show signs that they are undergoing the same kind of agricultural transformation that has already been witnessed in the world's largest emerging markets. These processes include the commercialization of agriculture, a transition from self-sufficiency to specialization, the growth of upstream and downstream markets, the use of new technologies, the adoption of sustainable cultivation techniques, and integration into the global agricultural economy.[15] The rental market for farmland is becoming increasingly important in these countries too, and the distribution of farm size is changing rapidly with the rise of medium-scale farms (between 5 and 100 hectares). These medium-sized farms now represent approximately 20 percent of total farmland in Kenya, 32 percent in Ghana, 39 percent in Tanzania, and over 50 percent in Zambia.[16]

Another recent trend is the rise of an agroindustry sector, a component of manufacturing that adds value to agricultural raw materials through preparation, preservation, and processing. As a share of total manufacturing, the value of agroindustries is as high as 50 or 60 percent in countries like Ethiopia, Ghana, Madagascar, and Senegal.[17] There is still significant room for growth in this sector, however. Despite producing roughly two-thirds of the world's cocoa beans, none of Africa's cocoa producers make it into the top-ten chocolate-exporting countries.

Poverty and Agriculture

Current figures indicate more than 60 percent of the people in Africa live in rural areas and rely on agriculture for their livelihoods, and more than half of the rural agricultural labor force is made up of women.[18] The prevalence of poverty is highest among this rural population, with as many as 80 percent living on less than $2 per day in many countries. A 2014 Food and Agriculture Organization report found that the average African farmer is over 60 years old, signaling that the industry has failed to incorporate young people (aged between 15 and 24), who make up 60 percent of the continent's total population.[19] Sub-Saharan Africa's youth unemployment rate is already the highest in the world at 40 percent, and 250 million more young people will enter the labor force over the next 10 years. Despite a clear preference for urban and capital-intensive jobs, population pressures mean that roughly 40 percent of them will be primarily engaged in agriculture, the majority as smallholders.[20]

Demographic patterns indicate that Africa's share of the global population is likely to increase from 12 percent now—nearly one billion people—to more than 30 percent by 2050, and its urban population is projected to double in the next 15 years alone. In this light, the continent exhibits the fastest-growing demand for agricultural products of any region in the world, with its food and beverage consumer market projected to be worth more than $1 trillion by 2030. Even if part of this demand will be met by increasing imports—which the lowest figures estimate to top $110 billion per year in the next decade[21]—this will still require increasing domestic agricultural output by $630 billion per year.[22]

Worldwide investment in agriculture is expected to grow exponentially in the medium to long term. Due to its rapidly growing demand and its abundance of land, the geographic focus of this investment has shifted noticeably toward Africa. Consequently, many analysts predict that Africa is on the verge of a "green revolution," which will increase the value of its agricultural output from its current level of roughly $300 billion per year to more than $500 billion by 2020 and nearly $1 trillion by 2030. This increase has significant implications for the growth of upstream and downstream activities as well, such as in fertilizers and pesticides, machinery, transport, storage, food processing, and biofuels. The total market value for these activities is estimated to reach nearly $300 billion per year by 2030.[23]

Notably, there is variation across the continent, as coastal countries with large amounts of uncultivated, arable land are expected to account for about 70 percent of this growth potential. Indeed, a 2014 McKinsey Global report specifically identifies Angola, Cameroon, Côte d'Ivoire, Ethiopia, Ghana, Kenya, Madagascar, Mozambique, Nigeria, Sudan, and Tanzania as the most promising in terms of rapid productivity growth.[24] The forecasts claim that there will be an increase in cultivated land of up to 500,000 hectares per year in these countries. Other countries, such as Burkina Faso, Chad, Democratic Republic of the Congo, Mali, and South Sudan, have significant amounts of uncultivated cropland as well as an agriculture industry that comprises over 25 percent of GDP. Agricultural value per hectare also has the potential to increase due to the conversion of as much as 20 percent of cereal land to more high-value crops. In light of these targeted investments, growth in area cultivated and output has the potential to increase value added of the region's agricultural sector from $150 billion to $500 billion by 2030, when the entire agribusiness industry in the region is likely to be worth as much as $1 trillion.[25]

Overall Importance of the Agriculture Sector

In recognition of Africa's natural assets and comparative advantage, agriculture has been identified as key to regional efforts to spur growth and development. The African Union considers agricultural growth vital to improving food security and reducing poverty—as it has been more effective at improving human development than growth in other economic sectors.[26] Thus the AU is working to combat market inefficiencies that have created a reliance on subsistence farming and informal trade.[27] Indeed, in the late twentieth century, many African governments established agricultural marketing boards that held prices artificially below world market levels, which limited market competition and diversification and reduced the incentive for farmers to invest in expensive new methods and technologies.[28]

Over the last decade, agriculture has been placed at the top of the development agenda for many African governments, leading to increases in agricultural investment from both public and private sectors.[29] African leaders and development partners adopted the Comprehensive African Agricultural Development Program (CAADP) in 2003 in order to promote agriculturally based development, reduce poverty, and improve food security.

Investment in Africa's agricultural sector will therefore be vital to the achievement of the region's development goals, as well as its long-term sustainability, and it will also be necessary in order to meet the increasing worldwide demand for both food and biofuels over the long term. Due to its relatively low population density, arable land in Africa is still relatively affordable and abundant, although its value is increasing markedly due to a recent wave of interest in purchasing farmland.[30] Moreover, since average yields are currently lower than those in comparable geographic regions (figure 3.1), targeted improvements in knowledge, technology, and management practices have the potential to substantially increase the profitability of African agricultural products in the near future.[31]

The rise of agribusiness offers a vital opportunity for rapid and inclusive economic growth by creating new jobs, increasing productivity and income levels, and reducing food prices. Spillover benefits arise as well, since agribusiness contributes to the creation of a variety of subsectors, including input delivery, primary production, processing, and marketing and distribution.[32] It is, therefore, central to the goal of economic diversification, as well as improving employment and market linkages in rural areas, where roughly 70 percent of Africa's rapidly growing youth population lives.[33]

FIGURE 3.1. Average value of food production, three-year average.

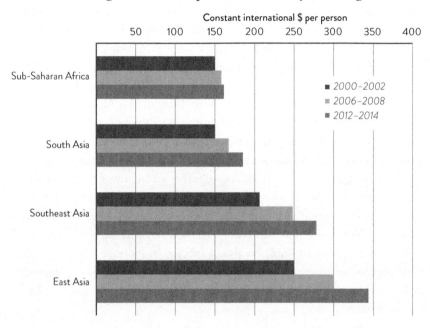

Source: FAO, 2017.

Key Drivers

While most other regions in the world have already maximized the use of their agricultural production resources, Africa is comparable only to South America in the abundance of its untapped agricultural assets.

DEMAND

The UN estimates that the global population will reach between 8 billion and 10 billion people by 2050, and between 2 billion and 3 billion of these people will live in Africa—an increase of roughly 200 percent in just a few decades.[34] In order to feed the world's growing population, global food production will need to increase by 70 percent from current levels.[35]

More specifically, cereal production will need to increase by 43 percent, from roughly 2.1 billion to 3 billion tons per year. Africa's market share for cereals will increase markedly over the same time period, as developing countries are expected to both produce and consume roughly two-thirds of the world's cereals by 2050. Currently, growing demand is driven by the consumption of cereals for biofuels, especially in the developed world. Sixty-one million tons of cereals were used as biofuels in the developed world in 2005, but this figure had already more than doubled to 135 million tons by 2010 and is projected to reach 180 million tons per year by 2020— 130 million of this total to be consumed in the United States alone.[36]

Although the demand for biofuels in Europe and North America is likely to peak in the next decade due to the shift toward clean and renewable energy sources like solar and wind power, cereal production in Africa is still expected to continue increasing over the medium to long term, especially to meet domestic demand. As a cheaper alternative to hydrocarbons, the use of biofuels is likely to continue expanding in the developing world, and the regional market for biofuels crops has the potential to reach $11 billion per year by 2030.[37] Moreover, Africa is the only region in the world where consumption of food cereals is expected to increase in the future— estimates are an increase in annual per capita consumption of 21 kg in sub-Saharan Africa, compared to a decrease of 27 kg in East Asia and 11 kg in Latin America.[38]

Domestic demand for cereals is also driven by the need to feed a growing livestock industry. Global meat production will need to increase by an estimated 74 percent by 2050, and Africa's consumption of meat is projected to triple over the same period.[39] The meat export industry on the continent is now almost nonexistent, despite Africa's rich history of nomadic cattle cultures and available land for grazing. However, developing countries are already starting to take over as the primary producers of the world's meat and milk due to land constraints in the developed world, and global trade in meat products is likely to increase from 16 million to 64 million tons per year by 2050.[40]

Beyond strict population growth rates, global consumption patterns are also changing as a result of development and urbanization patterns. The market for luxury items like cocoa and coffee is likely to increase by 25 percent in the next 5 years due to rising affluence among developed countries.[41] In the developing world, meanwhile, increasing income levels and the rise of an urban population with discretionary income are contributing to higher levels of caloric consumption and changing consumer preferences toward animal proteins and processed foods. In most of the world's emerging markets, daily per capita consumption will surpass 3,000 kcal in the next few decades.[42]

Although the projections in Africa are slightly lower—roughly 2,750 kcal per capita per day—many of the cities on the continent are among the fastest growing in the world. For example, Lagos, Nigeria, is already among the ten largest cities in the world, and it is on pace to grow by 75 percent over the next decade. Overall, Africa's urban food market, where per capita consumption value is already 25 percent higher than that in rural areas, is expected to increase fourfold by 2030.[43]

QUALITY OF LAND AND YIELDS

In light of the rapidly increasing demand for agricultural products in Africa, many analysts have concluded that food imports to the region will increase more rapidly than domestic production in order to meet these needs.[44] On the other hand, given Africa's comparative advantage, the unprecedented growth in its consumption markets, and the expected increase in agricultural area and yield, the World Bank suggests that Africa's $10 billion annual agricultural deficit could become a $20 billion surplus by 2030.[45] The difference will depend on whether Africa's agricultural sector receives the investments necessary to commercialize the market, since increasing agricultural output will require substantial improvements in productivity and yield rates.[46]

Key Players

Africa is already a major source of the world's agricultural supply. South Africa and Côte d'Ivoire are the region's largest exporters, with $6 billion per year in agricultural exports, followed by Kenya, Ghana, and Ethiopia. Since 1990, the latter, along with Mozambique and Zambia, are among the fastest growing in the world in terms of agricultural export market share.

In the past, private investment in agriculture was relatively limited in comparison to other world regions, largely due to risk perceptions and—as both a cause and a consequence—the low availability of commercial bank lending. However, private companies have started to invest heavily in Africa's agricultural value chains over the past decade, contributing to the development of new markets for seeds, fertilizers, technical resources, and marketing and distribution.[47] For example, in 2013, Standard Chartered invested $20 million in the horticultural market in Zimbabwe and $74 million in grain and fertilizer trade across the continent.[48] Major African and foreign companies are now involved in agricultural inputs, including BASF, Dow Chemical, Bayer, Sasol, and AECI; in food processing, including Nestlè, Unilever, Tiger Brands, and Tongaat Hulett; in beverages, including Coca Cola, InBev, Anheuser-Busch, and SAB Miller; and in food services, including Compass Group, McDonald's, Anglovaal, and Astral Foods, among others.

Beyond the upstream and downstream components of the market, large quantities of land in Africa have been purchased or leased over the last decade for agricultural production (table 3.1). Domestic investment, although relatively overlooked by media reports due to the relatively small size of individual purchases, has constituted the majority of agricultural projects to date. As of 2010, private domestic investment accounted for $54 million and 362,000 hectares of developed farmland, as compared to $24 million and 240,000 hectares for foreign investment.[49] This pattern is starting to change, however, with rapidly increasing interest from foreign sources of investment.

Much of the largest recent land acquisitions come from climate-constrained and capital-rich countries seeking to secure long-term supplies of food and biofuels sources, such as China, Korea, and the Gulf States.[50] The United Arab Emirates' Abu Dhabi Fund and Saudi Arabia's Hail Agricultural Investment Co. are developing a combined 50,000 hectares of farmland in Sudan. Recently, Qatar entered into negotiations to lease 40,000 hectares in Kenya in exchange for the construction of a new shipping port in Lamu, the terminus of Kenya's proposed oil pipeline.[51] European and American companies are also increasingly interested in African farmland. D1-BP Fuel Crops, a United Kingdom–based company, has acquired land to grow jatropha in Ethiopia, Madagascar, Swaziland, and Zambia, while Germany's Flora EcoPower cultivates castor seeds on 8,000 hectares of land in Ethiopia's Oromia Province.

These recent acquisitions and developments are evidence of the increasing rate of return in Africa's agricultural sector, resulting from the cost and availability of land and labor, rising global commodity prices, and philanthropic benefits to the company. Many of the investments have been directly facilitated by African governments themselves. For example, Zambia has set aside thousands of hectares of land to be demarcated into farm blocs and sold to foreign investors, while the Angolan government has discussed plans to revive its coastal banana industry with US companies Dole Foods and Chiquita Brands.[52]

TABLE 3.1. Examples of recent African farmland developments: country, investors, and crops.

Country	Investors and crops
Angola	140,000 ha mixed crops, AgriSA, South Africa; 25,000 ha rice, Lonrho, UK
Benin	350,000 ha crops and 300,000 ha oil palm, South Africa
Ethiopia	815 foreign-financed agricultural projects approved between 2007 and 2010; a 150,000 ha livestock farm; 300,000 ha farmland to an Indian company, Karuturi; 50,000 ha crops by a number of South African companies, including Richmond, New Dawn, Dinaledi, Batau
Congo	68,000 ha eucalyptus, Mag Industries, Canada; 200,000 ha mixed farming, AgriSA, South Africa
Cameroon	55,000 ha mixed crops, Gp Bollere, France
Ghana	13,000 ha under crops by Kimminic, Canada
Gabon	Olam (Singapore) acquired 300,000 ha to produce palm oil
Kenya	160,000 ha biofuels by Bedford, Canada
Liberia	A Malaysian conglomerate signed a 63-year lease for 230,000 ha to grow palm oil and rubber; an Indonesian producer signed an agreement to develop 220,000 ha to produce palm oil
Madagascar	Daewoo (Korea) attempted to lease 1.3 million ha for farm production; a 450,000 ha biofuel project; mixed crops on 100,000 ha by Osho of South Africa; 30,000 ha under Jathropa by Neo, France
Mozambique	35,000 ha teak and 140 000 ha pine, Gsff, Sweden; 15,500 ha Jatropha, Avia Spa, Italy; 20,000 ha livestock, Agriterra
Mali	540,000 ha rice project; 50,000 ha rice project by Saudi Arabia; 40,000 ha crops, Seed Rock, Canada
North Sudan	South Korea companies bought 700,000 ha for wheat farming
South Sudan	800,000 ha land lease near Darfur; United Arab Emirates acquired 750,000 ha farm lands; Saudi Arabia leased 376,000 ha to grow wheat and rice
Sierra Leone	45,000 ha mixed crops, Sierra Gold, Canada
Tanzania	45,000 ha sorghum, Cams Group, UK; 100,000 ha trees, Norway; 100,000 ha Jatropha, Diligent Energy, Netherlands; 100,000 ha crops, KRC, Rep of Korea
Zambia	200,000 ha crops, United Arab Emirates; 15,000 ha sugar, Agzam, South Africa; 27,000 ha crops, DWS Galof, Germany
Ethiopia, Kenya, Madagascar, Senegal, and Mozambique	80 Indian companies invested around US$2.4 billion in buying and leasing plantations

Sources: Connolly et al. 2012; The Land Matrix 2013. *Note:* Some of these "deals" only record intentions to invest, and others are projects in the implementation phase. The listings however show the degree of intent and interest in African agricultural investment.

Despite—or perhaps because of—the limited availability of commercial lending from African banks, private equity funds and investment banks have also joined the bandwagon in recent years. UK-based Emergent Asset Management has announced plans to raise between $450 million and $750 million to invest in farmland in sub-Saharan Africa, and Cru Investment Management has already launched a fund called Africa Invest and piloted a farming scheme in Malawi.[53] Others have focused their fundraising and investment on businesses along the agribusiness value chain, such as Actis Africa Agribusiness Fund, African Agricultural Capital, and the more recent Agri-Vie, a $100 million private equity fund formed by Strategy Partners and Sanlam. These groups allow investors to pool their capital in order to take advantage of larger investment opportunities, and they provide technical assistance to businesses along the value chain in order to improve the prospects for sustainable investment returns.[54]

Opportunities

Since the early 2000s, agriculture has reemerged as a top development priority for African governments. At the moment, and beyond the obvious structural constraints related to natural endowments, the most promising opportunities for private investment in agricultural production, agribusiness, and agroindustry are shaped by favorable public sector policies and programs. The past decade has seen promising and innovative efforts to stimulate investment at both regional and national levels.

The first regional initiatives were launched in 2003 during the Maputo Declaration on Agriculture and Food Security, when African Union member states adopted the Comprehensive Africa Agriculture Development Program (CAADP) and the Alliance for a Green Revolution in Africa (AGRA). As a signal of political commitment to revitalize agriculture as part of the regional development agenda, signatories committed themselves to allocate at least 10 percent of annual government expenditures toward developing the agricultural sector.[55] In addition to increasing public investment, specific policy goals for signatories include extending the area under sustainable land management, improving rural infrastructure and market access, eliminating trade restrictions to create a common food market, and improving agricultural research and knowledge dissemination.[56]

With the help of the New Partnership for Africa's Development (NEPAD), the CAADP Multi-Donor Trust Fund has been established in order to harmonize and channel financial support from the major donors toward facilitating these reforms, and the NEPAD Infrastructure Investment Facility (NIIF) involves the private sector in funding projects to build local capacity and develop necessary infrastructure. Meanwhile, AGRA works in partnership with private investors to promote credit access—especially to provide small, low-interest loans—for small-scale farms, input suppliers, and agroprocessors. So far, AGRA has supported over 100 programs in thirteen African countries. One partnership with Equity Bank established a \$50 million account that has supplied loans to roughly 2.5 million farmers and 15,000 businesses along the agricultural supply chain in Kenya alone.

Africa's regional economic communities (RECs) have also been active in stimulating foreign direct investment. For example, the Common Market for Eastern and Southern Africa (COMESA) has established a Common Investment Area in order to standardize the rules, regulations, and procedures for investing in agriculture. COMESA has also set up institutions like the Regional Investment Agency and the Africa Trade Insurance Agency, which promote investment and provide risk coverage against political and economic instability. In other regions, the Economic Community of West African States (ECOWAS) and the Southern African Development Community (SADC) are both working to implement investment and finance protocol that will promote regional integration, cross-border investment, and public-private partnerships.[57]

TANZANIA

Due to its history of stability and socialist policy orientation, the foundation for agricultural productivity is particularly strong in Tanzania, with the government now pushing to spur growth through liberalization and privatization. New land laws permit long-term leases up to 99 years for foreign investors, and private businesses are allowed to enter the market for processing and marketing cash crops with the goal of exporting. The government has also launched an Integrated Road Project to develop and maintain transport networks in rural areas with a specific focus on connecting agriculturally productive regions to markets. Other policy reforms have simplified the regulations regarding land registration and provided credit guarantees for export-oriented businesses. When these policies were in their early stages, between 2001 and 2005, an average of \$125 million flowed into the country per year in new agriculture investments.[58]

ETHIOPIA

Agricultural Development Led Industrialization is key to Ethiopia's long-term strategy for economic development. Since 2003, policy efforts have focused on creating an enabling macroeconomic environment for investment such that growth is ultimately driven and sustained by the private sector. The Ethiopian government's goal is commercialization of agriculture through both small- and large-scale businesses by taking a market-oriented approach with a specific focus on the agroprocessing and exports subsector of the agribusiness supply chain.

MOZAMBIQUE

Agriculture is also at the top of the development agenda in Mozambique, where the areas prioritized for policy intervention include rural infrastructure development, ease of regulation and certification processes, dissemination of information about markets and weather, rural financing, capacity building, supply chain development, and diversification. The country's income tax regulations are also highly favorable to agricultural enterprises, which pay just 10 percent compared to the 32 percent tax rate for standard businesses, and an extension of this benefit allows for a further 80 percent reduction in the tax rate for new investments in agriculture.

NIGERIA

A number of specific incentives have been implemented in Nigeria, including credit guarantees of up to 75 percent of all loans granted by commercial banks for agricultural production; 60 percent repayment of interest on loans to cassava producers and processors; zero restrictions on capital allowance for agribusinesses; a 100 percent tax exemption for 5 years for new agroprocessing businesses; duty exemption on machinery for agricultural production and processing; export incentives for agroprocessors; and import restrictions on certain food items.

GHANA

An ECOWAS member, Ghana already offers a relatively liberal business environment, and it has a comparative advantage in agriculture due to an abundance of uncultivated, fertile land, and low-cost labor. Moreover, foreign agricultural investors are offered long-term leases of up to 50 years, with the option of renewal, and excused from paying import duties on seeds, plants, machinery, and other input products needed to set up an agricultural enterprise.[59]

The Role of Policy

Many national-level policy efforts have been successful in standardizing entry and operating conditions within regions and reducing the risk of investing, which has effectively increased the amount of foreign direct investment in Africa's agriculture sector in recent years.[60] In terms of future opportunities, it will also be necessary to keep an eye on changes in international trade and financial systems over the coming decades. Much of the recent growth in agriculture since 2000 can be attributed to improvements in the terms of trade, especially rising global commodity prices, and not to productivity gains. Specifically, changes in global trade and financial regulations, US and EU bilateral trade agreements with Africa, and foreign aid policies are likely to have a major impact on the sector.

Governments that are serious about attracting investors are laying the foundation for long-run dynamism and sustainability at all levels of the agribusiness value chain. In many African countries, farmers already have more options in terms of the seeds and fertilizers they use and the markets available to distribute their products due to policy strategies launched more than a decade ago.[61] Although productivity remains relatively low, these early changes signal potential for exponential growth as market linkages grow and the supply chain becomes more efficient.[62]

Risks and Challenges

Between 2000 and 2010, Africa's combined GDP grew at a rate of more than 6 percent per year. Over the same period, however, agricultural GDP grew at just over half that rate, at 3.4 percent, signaling that agricultural development is lagging behind the region's economy as a whole.[63] Agricultural productivity in Africa remains the lowest of any world region, largely due to underinvestment, stemming from the following challenges.

FINANCIAL AND TECHNICAL REQUIREMENTS

Africa has not yet experienced the "green revolution" that has occurred in other world regions, whereby technical advances and development of high-yield crops generated a dramatic increase in agricultural productivity.[64] In order to improve efficiency and take advantage of economies of scale, this kind of economic transformation requires specialization, increased sophistication of techniques and instruments, and market diversification. Although we have described the signs that Africa's revolution is newly underway, the financial and capital requirements are massive, and previous initiatives failing to account for capital needs beyond start-up costs have proven unsustainable.[65]

So far, there has been relatively little extension of the "outside" technologies that helped to catalyze Asia's green revolution, such as irrigation techniques and chemical fertilizers.[66] Currently, only 4 percent of total farming land is irrigated in sub-Saharan Africa, which is less than one-quarter of the global average and one-tenth of South Asia.[67] Given its unique agroecological conditions and relatively diverse range of staple crops, the World Bank has stressed that a tailored and contextual approach will be necessary to improve productivity in Africa, with a particular focus on increasing yield and reducing labor requirements for root and tree crops.[68] Increasing irrigation will be a necessary component of this transformation—fortunately, Africa south of the Sahara has significant groundwater resources and river systems that remain largely underexploited.[69]

Beyond agricultural production, building an agroindustry sector requires well-developed market linkages, access to information, and high levels of technical capacity.[70] With the exception of Nigeria and South Africa, where the agroindustry sector is relatively well developed, these requirements will often need to be built up from scratch, relying heavily on imports of machinery and expertise, as well as investment in infrastructure. For export-oriented businesses, it will be necessary to develop ports, railroads, warehouses, and storage facilities, as well as the technical capacity for product testing and certification to meet world food trade standards.[71] In Africa, weak infrastructure has proven more of an impediment to agricultural investment and, hence, productivity than trade barriers.[72]

POLICY AND MARKET FAILURES

Poor policies have distorted the agricultural market in Africa, limiting the adoption of productivity-enhancing technologies and inputs like fertilizers, pesticides, and machinery. In the late twentieth century, many African governments established agricultural marketing boards that held prices artificially below world market levels, which limited market competition and diversification and reduced the incentive for farmers to invest in expensive new methods and technologies.[73] More recently, infrastructural gaps—especially in transportation—have resulted in high transport costs, which translate into high prices and low market volumes of such items.[74] Surveys of agricultural traders in Benin, Madagascar, and Malawi found that transport accounts for up to 50 to 60 percent of total marketing costs.[75]

Although most countries are actively reforming in order to reduce market inefficiencies, many policy-induced obstacles to investment remain. Foreign investors most frequently point to macroeconomic instability, especially inflation and exchange rates, and burdensome and multiplicative tax requirements as the main barriers to productivity.[76] Across Africa, there is a tension between the informal and formal sectors, resulting in unreliable contract enforcement, ambiguous land tenure (especially where customary law exists), and inefficiencies caused by corruption and bloated bureaucratic processes.[77] In light of the perishability of agricultural products, many private investors have reportedly allocated as much as 5 percent of annual revenues toward informal payments to expedite the movement of goods, as importing and exporting goods can take upwards of a month in many African countries. Moreover, inconsistencies in regulations and enforcement across countries, even within the regional economic communities and despite efforts to harmonize policies, often contribute to uncertainty.

To date, many governments have failed to meet the target set in the 2003 Maputo Declaration of allocating 10 percent of budgetary resources to agricultural investment. In fact, average government spending on agriculture declined from 4.5 percent of total expenditures in 2001 to 2.5 percent in 2012, although there is significant variation.[78] The low levels of public funding have been matched by underinvestment from the private sector, ultimately resulting in limited support for biotechnology and agricultural research specific to the African context, as well as in the weak development of upstream and downstream agribusiness markets.

ENVIRONMENTAL RISKS

Although there is much variation, Africa's soil tends to be less fertile than the alluvial valleys and volcanic soils of Asia, placing limits on the degree to which yield rates can be improved. Moreover, the amount of rainfall varies from region to region and from year to year, with frequent risk of drought—especially in the northern, landlocked parts of the continent—which is compounded by the limited use of irrigation and overwhelming reliance on rain-fed crops.

Environmental risks caused by weather shocks, pests, and disease are among the primary reasons that commercial bank lending to agricultural enterprises remains exceedingly low—less than 10 percent of all loans to major agricultural producers like Ghana, Kenya, Mozambique, and Uganda.[79] In addition, commercial banks tend to favor short-term investments, which are relatively low risk but not conducive to promoting long-term growth investment.[80]

The United Nations Food and Agriculture Organization considers Africa to be one of the regions most vulnerable to climate change, with projections that water will become increasingly scarce and drought more frequent across the continent.[81] The commercialization of agriculture is likely to put further strain on the already fragile environment, since commercial production often relies on the use of chemicals and heavy machinery, which can reduce soil fertility over time.[82] There is also growing evidence of soil degradation on the continent caused by unsustainable cultivation techniques among smallholders, especially in higher-density areas.[83] Already, 28 percent of African farmers are working on land considered to be degrading, and clearing land for farming has contributed to widespread deforestation and desertification, especially along the southern border of the Sahara desert.[84] Any new investments in agricultural pursuits in Africa will, therefore, need to consider strategies for sustainable productivity and adapting to climate change.[85]

Investment Strategies

Given that Africa's agricultural sector is at a relatively low stage of development, uncertainties about the growth potential for productivity and demand—as well as the policy and climate risks identified earlier—have hampered private investment. There is marked variation across Africa in terms of the external forces that are likely to affect investment potential, such as climate, soil, and market access conditions. Bearing this in mind, forward-looking business assessments can help identify areas for future commercial potential and opportunities that might prove to be "game-changers" in the industry, especially as Africa starts to undergo its green revolution.[86] The following are strategies for maximizing investment returns at various levels of the value chain.[87]

SUPPLY

Although agricultural input imports have increased rapidly over the past decade, Africa still accounts for less than 3 percent of total agricultural machinery imports in the world.[88] In addition, although 1 kg of fertilizer has been shown to increase crop yields by 7 to 10 kg, depending on conditions, fertilizer consumption in Africa is currently less than 5 percent of the developing world average.[89] At present, suppliers are hampered by the relatively high marketing costs for agricultural inputs in Africa, which represent at least 50 percent of the farm gate price.[90] In this context, targeted investments that are effective at reducing marketing and transport costs will lower the price faced by farmers, significantly increasing demand and, ultimately, profitability for suppliers. As much as possible, businesses should seek to reduce costs by coordinating the timing of port clearance with up-country distribution and by minimizing fuel expenditures.

Early and context-specific interventions have proven successful in both creating market demand for inputs and helping suppliers identify and access that demand. For example, in the 1990s, an experimental program in western Kenya relied on participatory testing and blending of fertilizers in order to create a product tailored to the acroecological conditions, which led an estimated 50,000 Kenyan farmers to start using fertilizer.[91] Another strategy that has proven effective is packaging fertilizer or related products in smaller quantities, or "mini-packs." This allows farmers to experiment with different varieties without substantial financial commitment, thereby increasing their willingness to buy while also improving their technical experience and knowledge. Of Kenya's smallholder farmers who use fertilizer, roughly half purchase it in packages smaller than 10 kg.[92]

In recent years, however, many African governments have shown a commitment to increasing the supply and uptake of agricultural inputs like fertilizer and machinery, making themselves prime targets for first movers to gain a market advantage. For instance, there are indications that many countries will return to subsidies in order to incentivize private suppliers to enter the market. Businesses seeking to take advantage of subsidy programs should work with governments to ensure that they are designed to be "market smart," meaning that farmers are encouraged to purchase a product that offers sufficient productivity gains so that subsidies can eventually be phased out while ensuring the long-run sustainability of demand for inputs.[93] Moreover, as many African countries seek to liberalize their agricultural sectors, effective public-private partnerships create incentives for private investment to build and diversify the market during the transition period. In several West African countries where the government still has a hand in steering the agricultural sector, the supply of fertilizer is provided through contracts with private importers.

In the immediate future, while African farmers' demand for inputs remains low at the national level, businesses should capitalize on regional markets in order to reduce marketing costs and capture economies of scale. The East and Southern African regional economic communities, for instance, have worked to harmonize policies for distributing seeds that are produced for specific agroclimatic regions that cross borders.[94] It will be necessary for businesses to invest in coordinating with and consulting these regional institutions in order to push forward the national-level reforms that will further facilitate the movement of inputs across borders. This entails lobbying for the removal of duplicative and overlapping protocols and contributing financially to the development of necessary infrastructure, especially roads, ports, and market research and information institutions.[95]

PRODUCTION

Biofuel crops, especially oils, are likely to be a major target for investment in the near future, especially in light of the farmland area expansion projects of many African governments. Oil crops are relatively land intensive and generally rain fed; as such, they have low technical and labor requirements compared to other types of crops, such as cereals.[96] On the other hand, there is substantial potential for more labor- and capital-intensive pursuit in certain areas of the continent, particularly for high-value-added exports in niche agricultural products, such as fruits and nuts, which have higher market values than traditional cereal grains and export crops. The Guinea savanna contains 400 million farmable hectares of land, much of which is currently uncultivated and home to low-cost and underemployed laborers, signaling vast potential for maize, soybean, and livestock production in countries like Ghana, for example.[97]

Given the current dominance of smallholders in Africa, who have difficulty capitalizing on economies of scale, agribusinesses are increasingly partnering with these small-scale farmers and landholders, for the benefit of both.[98] The primary impediments to improved productivity among small-scale agricultural enterprises are access to credit and information. As such, there is ample opportunity for private investments that improve the linkages between agriculture and finance and encourage the uptake of new skills and technology.

International banking and nonbanking financial institutions can help offset risk by pooling available investment capital in funds with highly diversified portfolios. Using these funds, as well as institutional expertise, to extend opportunities for microcredit loans and formal savings to the grassroots level has proved effective at increasing the profitability of small-scale enterprises and reducing the volatility of investment. Interested financial institutions should also work to coordinate resources in order to pressure governments to continue reforming their macroeconomic policy environments, especially in reducing vulnerability to commodity price fluctuations, stabilizing interest and inflation rates, and easing regulations on capital flows.[99]

In order to effectively shift toward high-value production, African farmers require access to machinery that will increase productivity rates, most of which needs to be imported. Wheeled tractors already make up more than 50 percent of all agricultural machinery imports on the continent.[100] Just as important will be training and education programs that improve farmers' technical knowledge about the use of machinery and other inputs, as well as the quality, safety, and regulatory standards of processors and wholesalers.[101] Targeted programs training African farmers how to comply with organic or fair trade requirements, for example, can substantially increase the value of agricultural output, often with minimal investment. Exploiting the technological boom that is currently sweeping across the continent is another cost-effective way to overcome the information and infrastructural gaps between rural farmers and markets, such as in the establishment of an online information clearinghouse or the use of mobile money transactions.

PROCESSING AND DISTRIBUTION

Significant investment will be necessary to develop the infrastructure to support agroprocessing and trade in Africa. Gaps in electrical supply are a particular impediment to the "cold chain" that is necessary to preserve meat, fruits, and vegetables for storage and long-haul transport. With a view to the future, effective private investments should contribute to building up much-needed roads, railways, ports, and storage and processing facilities in the short term. Strategic businesses are those that partner with governments to achieve these infrastructural development goals, while securing favorable policy outcomes in exchange for their investments, such as lucrative government contracts or tax breaks that allow them to gain an early market advantage.

Forward-looking strategies for downstream agribusinesses include lobbying to create markets for exports and partnering with African governments to implement safeguards against volatility. For example, the EU retains tariffs on processed products from Africa—a holdover from a colonial-era policy that artificially created markets for European manufactured goods—and the traditional donor countries in the EU should be particularly receptive to appeals to remove these barriers in support of the goal of economic diversification in Africa.[102] At the same time, given that the value-added and export-oriented components of the agribusiness chain are at the forefront of African governments' development strategies, businesses should aim to secure protection from import surges in low-cost competing goods and from severe fluctuations in global commodity prices.[103]

Returns on investment at this end of the value chain can be significantly enhanced by capitalizing on shifting consumer demands and international norms. First, by 2050, the largest growth in demand for food products will come from Europe, North America, and China, and these increasingly affluent consumers are shifting away from brand recognition toward an interest in localized, small-scale, handmade, and niche products.[104] Significant value added can be created by integrating agribusiness with the tourism industry, for example, as has already been done with luxury products like coffee and cocoa.[105] At the same time, investors can capitalize on the rise of corporate social responsibility norms by linking products with charitable feedback loops at relatively low cost, such as by linking purchases with funding for development projects at the source or by obtaining certification from activist organizations.[106]

At all levels of the value chain, achieving long-term returns on investment in Africa's agricultural sector requires forging both partnerships with the public sector and linkages with small-scale enterprises. There are significant gains to be made as the region's industry modernizes and commercializes and as the global demand for food multiplies. However, success in the coming decades will necessitate adjusting to issues of sustainability, environmental impact, and ethical practices, especially as international regulations continue to adapt.

Looking to the Future

Economic transformation driven by increased agricultural productivity has been extremely limited in Africa, where most farming remains subsistence oriented and market linkages are weak.[107] In order to produce sufficient surplus to keep up with urbanization rates, the agricultural sector will need to evolve rapidly, which requires specialization of crops, modernization and sustainability of techniques, adaptability to climate conditions, and development of the upstream and downstream components of the value chain.[108] According to the United Nations Food and Agriculture Organization, feeding the roughly 2 to 3 billion people who will inhabit the continent by 2050 requires net investment of at least $11 billion per year.[109] At the moment, however, and largely due to underinvestment, agricultural import dependence is on the rise.[110]

At present, the agricultural sector is the primary employer and source of livelihood for the vast majority of Africans—as many as 70 percent of the population in some countries.[111] Due to the availability of land in Africa, large agricultural enterprises are not likely to replace smallholders. Instead, their entry into the market will help develop the input supply and downstream distribution components of the value chain, which increases the profitability of agriculture for all scales of producers. However, in order to remain competitive, small-scale farmers will likely need to shift toward high-value, labor-intensive activities, particularly those with relatively low knowledge requirements.[112] The benefits to Africa are clear, though, as economists have shown that growth generated via agricultural productivity is several times more effective at reducing poverty than growth in any other economic sector, particularly among women, who make up the majority of smallholder farmers in the region.[113]

Recognizing the importance of a vibrant agriculture sector to development and prosperity, leaders from across the continent met in Dakar, Senegal, in October 2015 to recommit themselves to the goals of the CAADP and the Maputo Declaration and to map out a strategy for unlocking Africa's agricultural potential. Targets include exploiting regional comparative advantages, improving opportunities for trade, increasing resilience to environmental shocks and climate change, and making the continent a net exporter in the near future.[114] Their ability to achieve these goals is promising, as Africa has an abundance of natural resources that should make it appealing to private investors: relatively low-cost arable land, soils and climates suited to a diverse range of crops, low-cost labor from its majority rural population, and exponential gains to be made from incremental development of the value chain.[115]

In light of this, as well as the rapid increase in global trade of food products, the private sector has become increasingly interested in Africa's agriculture sector, laying the foundations for its sustainability and vitality from inputs and knowledge, to production, to processing and distribution.[116] By 2030, the market for African biofuel crops alone is likely to reach $11 billion per year. The forecast for the region's agribusiness industry, including all upstream and downstream components, is even more astounding—the World Bank predicts that the sector will be worth $1 trillion per year by the end of the next decade.[117]

FOUR

Africa's Information and Communications Technology Transformation and Potential

The concept of information and communications technology (ICT) encompasses a broad range of products and services that enable the storage, delivery, or exchange of information.[1] By its very nature, then, ICT is integral to processes of enhancing productivity and efficiency, which produces growth at all levels and in all sectors of the economy. There is no debate among development organizations and policymakers about the centrality of ICT uptake to Africa's prospects for economic development—promoting ICT is considered a key objective of the African Development Bank (AfDB), and the sector has been prioritized in the future economic "visions" of a number of African countries.

There are significant challenges to ICT development in the region, especially in the form of infrastructure gaps, weak legal and regulatory frameworks, and poor local capacity. Internet use is lower in Africa than anywhere else in the world, resulting in a deficiency of technological literacy, as the cost of ICT products and services tends to be too high for the majority low-income consumer base. However, even some of the most challenging environments on the continent have experienced positive trends in ICT development in recent years. In Somalia, for example, where the ICT infrastructure was destroyed by the period of anarchy and civil war, multiple internet and mobile service providers have since established a presence, and penetration rates are now higher than in neighboring countries like Ethiopia and Eritrea. Meanwhile, innovation in mobile money services has driven rapid growth in phone penetration across the continent, such as notable initiatives by Orange in Senegal and Safaricom in Kenya, while also contributing to increasing financial inclusion among previously unintegrated segments of the population.[2]

Kenya is now regarded as a leader in ICT development in Africa, with robust foundations for future growth.[3] Businesses working in Kenya have shown remarkable levels of uptake and integration of ICT into their daily operations, even since the 1990s, and even as the market has advanced and become saturated in recent years, a number of small enterprises have been successful in carving out niche markets in areas such as call centers (KenCall), data entry (DDD Kenya), and IT maintenance (Horizon). Meanwhile, the Kenyan government has set an example of proactive ICT policy by working to reduce tax, trade, and market entry barriers in the sector; facilitating public-private partnerships to develop infrastructure; implementing e-government services in education, health, business licensing, taxation, and corruption reporting; and even building a technology park in Konza in 2013 in order to attract investment and create jobs in the sector.[4] Yet, as in the other large ICT markets in Africa, there is still substantial room for growth in Kenya's ICT sector; in particular, increased affordability will help expand ICT services into rural areas and across borders.

This chapter explores the relationship between ICT and African development. It first examines some of the recent patterns and contributors to growth in the sector, before examining four of the prime opportunities for ICT investment on the continent: Tunisia, Botswana, Ghana, and Rwanda. The chapter also considers some of the remaining challenges to the industry in order to highlight specific strategies for investing effectively in ICT. Given the current trends and drivers in the sector, most businesses working in ICT are working to improve data connectivity to support increased traffic and to diversify their product and service offerings, with the key objective of reducing operating costs in order to increase ICT affordability for consumers and businesses.

Despite remaining market failures, Africans are hungry for access to personal devices for communication and entertainment, as well as to integrate innovative ICT solutions—such as cloud computing—into their small- and medium-sized enterprises (SMEs). While ICT penetration has increased exponentially over the past decade, latent demand remains much higher than the current supply. As the affordability of ICT goods and services improves due to infrastructure development and innovation, and as income levels continue to exhibit rapid growth, the potential for growth in Africa's ICT sector becomes enormous.

Background Facts and Trends

With the exception of a few outlier countries, ICTs were relatively slow to take off in Africa. As early as the 1980s, a range of initiatives started being introduced across the continent in order to address barriers to connectivity and capacity. In 1995, for example, the Capacity Building for Electronic Communications in Africa (CABECA) project, funded by the International Development Research Centre (IDRC) and the United Nations, aimed to promote sustainable, computer-assisted networking for a range of private- and public-sector uses.[5] Yet donors working in countries as diverse as Ethiopia, Senegal, and Zambia noted that significant barriers—especially those related to infrastructure, lack of skills, and cost to users—inhibited the uptake of new technologies.

Some of the more developed countries, such as South Africa and, to a lesser extent, Egypt, managed to keep up with technological advancements, maintaining internet and mobile phone usage rates on par with the world average, and even becoming relatively advanced in the development of fields like e-commerce. And even some of the most fragile states on the continent experienced some advancement, such as the establishment of an internet service provider (ISP) in Somalia's capital, Mogadishu, in 2000.[6] In general, though, and despite an influx of international funding, Africa lagged behind the rest of the world for the first decade of the ICT boom.

By 2005, however, ICT infrastructure on the continent had started to take hold, and the price of the internet and mobile phone subscriptions had reduced to sufficient levels to be accessible to broader segments of the population. The most rapid period of growth in mobile phone subscriptions occurred between 2006 and 2010, when compound annual growth rates surpassed 40 percent.[7] During the same period, total internet bandwidth usage on the continent grew even more rapidly, with 85 percent compound annual growth between 2007 and 2011.[8] Although the rapid uptake of the internet and mobile phones started between 5 and 10 years later in Africa than in the rest of the world, growth in penetration of both technologies has largely kept pace with the global trend over the past 10 years.

In fact, while penetration rates in the rest of the world have started to plateau in recent years—especially in mobile phone usage—Africa remains the fastest-growing region in the world for the uptake of ICTs. Although absolute usage levels remain lower than in other developing regions, the proportion of internet users in Africa has increased sixfold and mobile phone subscriptions threefold since 2006, faster than any other region except South Asia. Internet adoption still lags considerably behind, however, with just 20 percent of the population in sub-Saharan Africa reporting internet access, compared to roughly 73 percent mobile phone usage.

There is also substantial variation in the region, both across and within countries. In general, development of the ICT sector has occurred more rapidly in North and Southern Africa, while East and West Africa have lagged behind.[9] Although the mobile subscription rate in Nigeria is over 87 percent, the actual individual penetration is likely lower, as multi–subscriber identity module (SIM) ownership is widespread due to variable network quality.[10] On the other hand, Kenya has seen remarkable uptake of mobile technologies, with over four out of five individuals in urban areas using mobile money services to date. In terms of corporate ICT uptake, a 2016 survey found that 40 percent of manufacturing and 46 percent of agriculture service firms in Kenya rely on the internet to manage inventory, a rate roughly five times higher than that in Uganda, Tanzania, and the Democratic Republic of the Congo (DRC).[11]

Overall, however, ICT has now penetrated most African communities and transformed the economy and way of life.[12] As of 2015, there were more than half a billion subscribers to mobile services in Africa;[13] the mobile market contributed 6.7 percent to the region's total GDP, with more than $150 billion in revenues and 3.8 million jobs. More significantly, the positive trends in mobile adoption are projected to continue into the near future, with an estimated $210 billion in revenues and 7.6 percent of GDP attributed to mobile services and products by 2020.

Currently, smartphones represent a relatively small proportion of the market, apart from more developed countries like South Africa (51 percent).[14] However, smartphone adoption continues to see rapid growth in the region, now totaling 250 million and accounting for roughly 33 percent of all connections.[15] As a result, much of the current growth in the ICT sector is driven by data. Many of the least advanced ICT markets, such as the DRC, already have 3G networks, and 4G networks are becoming increasingly common in the more developed markets. As of 2016, there were seventy-two active Long-Term Evolution (LTE) networks in thirty-two African countries, compared to thirty-six just 2 years earlier. And while voice accounted for 80 percent of telecom companies' revenue 5 years ago, data revenue now accounts for an average of 15 percent of total revenue and is growing. Mobile data traffic has exhibited 77 percent compound annual growth since 2011—most operators in the region reported a 50 percent increase in data traffic in 2015 alone—and global telecom companies predict that Africa will continue to report the strongest growth in mobile data traffic of any region in the world, ahead of East Asia and Latin America.[16]

Significant gaps in ICT access remain. Most women and rural dwellers lack access to mobile and internet services, and even the most optimistic projections estimate that 60 percent of Africa's population will remain unconnected by 2020.[17] Yet the barriers to access are starting to decline with the emergence of second-hand and low-cost alternative markets, as mobile phones are quickly becoming the primary means of individual Africans' access to the internet.[18] This signals potential for an exponential increase in both mobile and internet penetration, and observers predict that the direct and indirect economic benefits of this transformation will generate $110 billion in GDP.[19]

Importance of the Sector

The range of technologies that fall within the umbrella definition of ICT are, by nature, revolutionizing the way that people and countries exchange knowledge and ideas. The potential benefits of this process are innumerable. For example, cross-fertilization and integration of cultures is thought to contribute to a more cohesive and peaceful global society, as well as the growth of cross-national social movements. Meanwhile, the autonomous nature of mobile and internet services improves accountability by improving citizens' ability to check oversteps of power in the public and private sectors. Perhaps most significantly, however, the ICT sector is increasingly thought of as a panacea for development due to its advantages to various economic sectors, to the competitiveness of individual firms, and to the livelihoods of individual consumers.[20]

At the micro level, ICT is argued to have important implications for organizations by helping to reduce costs and enhance efficiency and productivity.[21] These technological developments provide enormous strategic tools for firms that help to improve competitive advantage by creating opportunities for companies to access information in real time about their customers and competition (Lal 2004; Ongori and Migiro 2010; Ramsey et al. 2003), and by reducing distance-related barriers to sharing knowledge.[22] Particularly for small and medium-sized enterprises, ICT can enable the upgrading of processes and strategies that improve firms' ability to compete against large corporations in an increasingly globalized economy.[23] E-commerce, for example, helps local businesses to reach a larger, global consumer base.

The same logic applies to the improved competitiveness of developing countries, as ICT increases opportunities to tap into global markets (Grace, Kenny, and Qiang 2003), and it improves the functioning of markets by reducing transaction costs, increasing information flows, and enhancing arbitrage.[24] Thus, according to Khuong (2005) and Datta and Agarwal (2004), the economic benefits of the ICT sector are not only direct in terms of traditional investment and employment (Lewin and Sweet 2005), but also indirect by improving social standards and by boosting efficiency in growth across sectors.

As a tool of development, specifically, ICT is shown to increase flows of foreign direct investment—which improves resource-strapped governments' balance of payments—and to improve access to services and employment opportunities among previously unconnected populations, especially in nonagricultural economic activities and microbusinesses.[25] The public sector also stands to benefit by the reduced cost of information storage and exchange, and new technologies are at the foreground of innovative governance strategies in many areas, such as education.[26] Cloud computing, for example, which refers to low-cost solutions to managing and securing large-scale data, has been shown to facilitate distance learning and to overcome linguistic and cultural barriers to schooling.[27] In health, ICT can improve cost and functionality at the clinical, research, and administrative levels.[28] Electronic and telecommunications tools, such as video chat, increase access to traditionally underserved patients (Durrani et al. 2012; Lucas 2008; Shaqrah 2010), such as those in removed areas, while providing a low-cost tool for disseminating health-related information, such as vaccination campaigns.[29] A mobile-phone health campaign improved knowledge about HIV/AIDS in rural Botswana, for example.[30] The uptake of ICT in Africa's health system has been remarkable, and it has transformed the sector over the past decade.[31]

Beyond social indicators, the impressive economic growth rates observed in Africa over the past decade have also been attributed to the post-2005 ICT boom, especially the rapid spread of mobile phones.[32] One recent, notable analysis found that a 10 percent increase in mobile penetration rates improves overall economic productivity by 4.2 percent, while a number of studies have shown telecom growth to have a positive impact on household income levels.[33] May et al.'s (2014) survey of East African households, for example, finds that access to ICTs results in a net gain of $21 per month, and Diga (2013) argues that internet access in Tanzanian villages contributed to a reduction in poverty across seven different criteria.[34] The spread of mobile money services, an efficient and cost-effective facilitator of economic transactions, has been particularly impressive in East Africa, and has generated innovative solutions in banking, insurance, health, consumer markets, and many other vital economic sectors.[35]

Empirically, the data appear to lend strong support to the positive relationship between ICT uptake and economic and social development in Africa. Vu (2011) found that, in decreasing order of magnitude, internet penetration, mobile phone penetration, and personal computer access all have effects on economic growth.

On the other hand, a handful of critiques have arisen in recent years suggesting that the ICT literature has failed to establish the causal pathway connecting technology to economic growth and development,[36] and more significantly, that there might be some potentially harmful side effects, such as the opportunity cost of investment in ICT rather than directly into education or health services.[37] Low-income households in Africa spend a disproportionate amount of income on mobile services—as much as 27 percent in Kenya, for example[38]—which reduces the budget available for other essentials, like food and medicine.[39] However, the perceptions of individual Africans tend to indicate that ICT has improved the daily lives of people on the ground. Roughly two-thirds of survey respondents believe that mobile phones have made their household better off, and three-quarters note that phones have lowered their travel costs.[40] Thus many of the benefits of ICT in the developing world might be difficult to measure and analyze statistically—benefits like convenience, security, connectivity, and quality of life.

Among the policy and development community, there is a widespread consensus about the importance of ICTs to Africa's ability to compete in the global economy in the future. According to the World Bank and African Development Bank, "information and communication technologies have the potential to transform business and government in Africa, driving entrepreneurship, innovation and economic growth,"[41] while the African Union Development Agency (AUDA-NEPAD) views ICT as a vital "springboard" to the achievement of the Millennium Development Goals (MDGs).[42] As a result, there is now a wealth of well-funded initiatives to improve ICT infrastructure and capacity across the continent. For example, one of these organizations' primary objectives is to ensure that all of the major cities in Africa are connected by broadband infrastructure, both to each other and to the rest of the world. These initiatives promise to lay the foundations that will encourage private investment and innovation in the sector over the next decade.

Drivers of the Sector

In Africa, the latent demand for ICTs is already high—much higher than the existing supply. Individual consumers aspire to access innovative communication and data-based services, as well as rich-form online entertainment, while businesses and governments are eager to find new, affordable ways to store and access information that will make it easier and cheaper to meet the needs of their clients and citizens. At the same time, the increase in Africans with discretionary income means that more people on the continent can afford investing in ICTs, both for personal use and for their SMEs. In many places, multi-SIM ownership has become commonplace, especially for business owners and urbanites. Moreover, while a small minority of Africans to date have opened an account with a formal financial institution, this growing stratum of the population is increasingly seeking access to financial services that will facilitate economic exchange and savings, and such services are often provided more easily and affordably via innovative solutions linking banks with telecom providers. In fact, the World Bank views innovation in the financial services sector as a "primary driver" of growth in networking and communications technologies.[43]

In this light, the key determinants of future growth in the ICT sector are those factors that will enable producers and distributors to fill the gap between supply and existing—and increasing—levels of demand, specifically by reducing the cost of ICT products and services. For one thing, innovation in product manufacturing means that devices are becoming more accessible to individual consumers, such as mobile phones, computers, and smart televisions.[44] African manufacturers are increasingly targeting the domestic consumer market with ICT goods designed to be durable and affordable, such as the Huawei 4Afrika smartphone.[45]

In the literature, however, the primary determinant of the consumer-facing costs of ICTs is the level of development of network infrastructure, such as broadband internet and mobile data networks. Economies of scale are generated as the appropriate infrastructure is built and consolidated, both within countries and across borders.[46] While network coverage outside of major urban areas remains limited and data prices in Africa are still relatively higher than in other developing regions, the network infrastructure has increased rapidly over the past 10 years. A range of data technologies, such as mobile (3G/4G), satellite, DSL, and cable, have spread in more developed and urbanized areas, generating competition that has reduced the price of making calls and using data. In fact, the diversity and availability of connectivity offerings in Africa's urban centers have now reached a level comparable to that of more developed economies.

Market scale is also improved when innovative solutions to infrastructure gaps are realized, such as the advent of submarine cables for international data connectivity, which has the potential to reduce the price of internet access by half. Since 2009, a wave of submarine cables launched off of Africa's western and eastern coastlines has resulted in a huge increase in data availability on the coasts and a rapid decline in the price of data services, which also led to a concomitant decline in the price of satellite connectivity. Meanwhile, more satellites have been launched over the last 5 years, and a new generation of network cables serves to connect Africa directly to the Americas and Asia (WASACE, SACS, Sa-ex, BRICS, SES Astra). All of these developments are reducing the cost of data access for the average African consumer, nearing the $15 per month level identified as a tipping point for mass penetration.[47]

The ICT boom coincided with a period of increasing market liberalization in Africa, and while this allowed private investment and competition to drive growth in the sector,[48] it also meant that the private sector was responsible for much of the development of the infrastructure needed to meet demand. In this light, the relatively high cost of building fixed broadband and cable networks means that wireless broadband has developed more rapidly and, as a result, mobile phones are now becoming the primary source of internet access for the average African. Thus, while broadband connections accounted for roughly 25 percent of all mobile subscriptions in 2016, this proportion is projected to increase to two-thirds in just the next few years.[49]

In recent years, however, African governments are increasingly recognizing the need for cloud computing services and storage centers to host public data, which will necessitate further investment in broadband net-works.[50] Mobile and online initiatives in health, education, and other gov-ernment services are driving demand for further development of network and storage infrastructure in order to improve service provision. In Uganda, for example, the government has launched e-government projects in voter registration, biometric registration and National Identity cards, technology-enhanced learning, the development and dissemination of a national cur-riculum, and medical education for rural health workers.[51]

Therefore, in all facets of the market—government, business, and con-sumer services—the most important factor driving future growth in ICTs will be declining costs, which is primarily determined by infrastructural development and innovation. These factors will help to reduce the price of SMS services and devices, to improve network coverage in rural and inland areas, and to introduce new forms of data connectivity, such as machine-to-machine (M2M).[52] Even some of Africa's most "frontier" mar-kets, those that rank in the bottom twenty countries in the world for ICT infrastructure and affordability, have recently shown remarkable uptake of ICTs, suggesting that growing demand is likely to spur growth in ICTs even where the favorable factors are relatively lacking. Mobile penetration rates are among the highest on the continent in the Republic of the Congo, one of the region's poorest countries, and 3G networks have recently come online in Algeria, Cameroon, and the Democratic Republic of the Congo.[53]

In other countries, some of which have exhibited a perfect storm of rising incomes, infrastructural development, and local capacity, the ICT sector has already experienced levels of growth that rival more advanced re-gions.[54] Of Africa's emerging markets, Morocco provides an ideal example of a country with a well-developed ICT sector, with internet penetration nearing 50 percent of the population and mobile penetration surpassing 100 percent. For one thing, per capita income levels in Morocco are already relatively high by African standards, at $5,000 per year. More significantly, however, the government has created two public bodies tasked with facili-tating infrastructural development, private investment, and innovation in the sector. In addition to creating value-added services in e-governance, these bodies have simplified the regulatory and tax frameworks and re-moved significant tariff barriers to IT products. The result has been a re-markable level of competition in the mobile and internet services market, resulting in accessible and high-quality products at a relatively low cost.[55]

Despite much variation across countries, the current patterns in Africa point to substantial potential for ICT growth, particularly in countries characterized by rising income levels, infrastructural investment, e-government services, and especially the development of innovative ICT solutions across economic sectors. As in Morocco, growth in individual ICT service subscribers is now progressing more slowly in the more mature markets like Egypt and South Africa, yet the eventual revenue potential in these countries remains relatively higher than in those countries that do not yet share these favorable factors of income, infrastructure, and innovation.[56]

Opportunities

In order to identify specific opportunities for investment in Africa's ICT sector, we rely on data from the World Economic Forum's Global Information Technology Report series. Since 2001, the report has provided an annual evaluation of countries' performance on various indicators related to ICT in order to identify and compare countries' capacity to use technologies effectively. The report produces a Network Readiness Index, which provides both a composite score (1–7) and a global ranking for each country based on an in-depth assessment across four main categories and fifty-three sub-indicators of ICT performance. More specifically for our purposes, the Index provides a way of directly and empirically comparing African markets according to the various drivers of ICT growth identified in the previous section, such as infrastructure, affordability, political environment, and innovative capacity.

Although the mean level of network readiness is lower in sub-Saharan Africa than in any other world region, there is a significant amount of variation across the continent.[57] Some of Africa's top-performing markets receive scores that rival the more advanced economies—Mauritius, for example, ranks forty-ninth in the world and scores higher than China, and South Africa ranks just above Romania and Bulgaria. Moreover, when the North African countries are added to the region, Africa's mean network readiness becomes relatively similar to that of other developing regions, such as Latin America and Asia, since three of the five North African countries rank in the top ten in Africa: Morocco, Tunisia, and Egypt.

The ten most network-ready countries in Africa are listed in figure 4.1, in descending order, along with a comparison of their current mobile phone and internet penetration rates.[58] Not surprisingly, the highest penetration rates—when including both mobile and internet technologies—are currently located in those countries with the highest readiness scores: South Africa, Morocco, and Tunisia. All three countries report a proportion of internet users in the population more than twice as high as the regional average of 25 percent. In other countries, such as Ghana, Côte d'Ivoire, and Senegal, the rate of mobile subscribers is relatively high by African standards, but internet use still lags significantly behind.

We use these data to distinguish between countries in which the market has matured, indicated by high levels of both mobile and internet penetration, and those in which substantial room for growth remains. Although all countries in Africa will continue to see growth in ICT over the coming years, including those that already have relatively high subscription levels, growth is occurring most rapidly in regions where penetration rates are comparatively low.[59] Thus, of the top ten network-ready countries, those that score below the African mean for either mobile phone (84.7 percent) or internet (24.5 percent) penetration are considered less mature and, thus, high-growth markets.

FIGURE 4.1. Comparison of mobile phone and internet penetration rates per 100 people (2016) across top ten African countries on the Network Readiness Index.

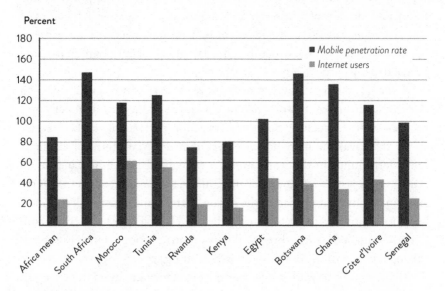

Source: Networked Readiness Index ranking from World Economic Forum (Baller et al. 2016), mobile phone and internet penetration rates from World Development Indicators (2014).

Table 4.1 provides a two by two classification of these ten countries according to the existing market size, as well as relative network readiness. The top five scoring countries on the Network Readiness Index are considered prime for ICT investment, whereas the next five scorers are considered "Tier II" opportunities, which might still exhibit some challenges for investors. A country like Ghana, for example, the eighth most network ready country in Africa, scores relatively high on rubrics such as ICT skills, political and business environment, and product and service affordability, but is marked by remaining infrastructural gaps (figure 4.2). We selected one country from each of the four categories in table 4.1, and from four different subregions within Africa, for a detailed discussion of the potential opportunities for investors.

TUNISIA

Along with South Africa and Morocco, Tunisia's ICT sector is already one of the most mature on the continent, with internet penetration reaching 56 percent and mobile penetration over 125 percent in 2016 (see figure 4.1).

TABLE 4.1. Classification of the top ten network-ready African countries according to ICT market growth potential and readiness scores.

	Prime Readiness	Tier II Readiness
Mature market	South Africa Morocco Tunisia Kenya	Egypt Botswana
High growth market	Rwanda	Ghana Côte d'Ivoire Senegal

Source: Networked readiness ranking from the World Economic Forum.

Note: The top five countries are considered "prime" for network readiness, while countries ranking six through ten are classified as "tier II." Market maturity is differentiated according to mobile and internet penetration rates. Countries with higher than 76.3 percent mobile phone penetration and more than 21.2 percent internet penetration are considered mature markets.

FIGURE 4.2. Comparison of four indicators across top ten network-ready African countries (2016).

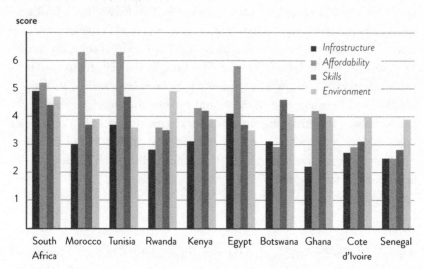

Source: World Economic Forum (Baller et al. 2016).

The level of infrastructure development for ICTs—a common shortfall in the region—is among the highest in Africa, with notable improvements in recent years. Broadband internet bandwidth, for example, nearly tripled between 2009 and 2012.

Much of this positive development has occurred as a result of the Tunisian government's eagerness to promote ICT investment and growth. In 2013, it worked with Orange Tunisie and Tunisiana telecom companies to progress plans for installation of a submarine data transmission cable that will connect the country with Europe (Didon). The government has also been proactive in encouraging the uptake of cloud computing services in areas such as education. The Ministry of Education's National Centre for Education Technologies established a data center that provides high-tech training modules for universities and various centralized curricula for the public educational sector, with plans to include a digital library.[60]

This commitment to state-of-the art learning is already reflected in the impressive level of ICT skills exhibited among the Tunisian workforce, as well as in the uptake of cloud technologies among SMEs. The private sector is increasingly conscious of the potential of Tunisia's ICT market, with foreign companies such as Microsoft, Google, Oracle, OVH, and HP investing heavily in advertising campaigns, as well as establishing domestic cloud operations to compete against local providers like Tunisia Telecom and Axelaris.

BOTSWANA

Studies have indicated that initial financial outlay is relatively high for companies working in Botswana's ICT sector, likely owing to the geographical limitations of working in a landlocked country with a heavily rural population.[61] Such costs being passed on to the consumer, the market is currently hindered by low affordability of ICT products and services (see figure 4.2). Despite high costs, however, the Botswanan population is rather wealthy by African standards (table 4.2), so the uptake of mobile phone services has been remarkably high compared to countries at similar levels of development—on par with that of South Africa, the region's largest ICT market (see figure 4.1). This indicates that a high level of demand exists for ICTs among the population. Moreover, high mobile penetration rates in this case might be indicative of multi-SIM ownership among an upper stratum of the population, as in Nigeria, such that ICT uptake could continue to increase rapidly if affordable solutions are found to reach rural populations.[62]

Although a 2007 study concluded that the shortage of high-skilled personnel in Botswana posed an acute threat to the development of the digital economy, the government's commitment to promoting the sector over the past 10 years has resulted in notable gains.[63] Specifically, the government laid out a National ICT Vision encompassing three primary goals: enabling growth in the industry, achieving universal access to services, and making the country a regional hub in the sector.[64] More recent analyses indicate that businesses no longer consider ICT knowledge or education as a hindrance to working in the country.[65] In fact, as an indicator of local capacity, the technical skills of the workforce in Botswana are now among the highest in Africa (see figure 4.2),[66] behind only Tunisia, and the ICT services sector has grown to represent nearly 14 percent of total service exports. Moreover, Botswana's market performs relatively well in terms of the environment for ICT investment (see figure 4.2), although several studies have found that more progress is needed in the areas of e-government services and in clarifying the ICT legal framework.[67]

TABLE 4.2. Key indicators across the top ten network-ready African countries.

Country	Network readiness Score[a]	Mobile subscriptions (per 100 ppl)	Internet users (%)	ICT service exports (% total)	GDP per capita (current US$)	GDP growth (%, 5-year average)
South Africa	4.2	147.13	54	17.51	6,160.73	1.62
Morocco	3.9	117.68	61.76	20.33	3,007.24	3.35
Tunisia	3.9	125.25	55.5	12.90	3,490.82	2.34
Rwanda	3.9	74.86	20	2.55	748.39	6.98
Kenya	3.8	80.44	16.6	12.66	1,507.81	5.38
Egypt	3.7	102.20	44.95	10.45	2,412.73	3.37
Botswana	3.5	146.16	39.36	13.96	7,595.60	4.15
Ghana	3.5	135.80	34.67	—	1,641.49	6.11
Côte d'Ivoire	3.4	115.85	43.84	12.60	1,662.44	8.90
Senegal	3.4	98.54	25.66	—	1,033.07	5.32

Source: Data from World Development Indicators, 2016 figures. Note that the small island nations (Mauritius, Seychelles, Cape Verde), Nambia, and The Gambia were excluded from the sample due to missing data across some measures used for evaluation. GDP growth is an average of annual percent growth between 2012 and 2017.

[a]*Ranges from 1 to 7, from World Economic Forum (Baller et al. 2016).*

GHANA

Beyond the major urban and industrial centers, broadband infrastructure remains relatively limited in Ghana, although there are expansion projects underway—one funded by Danida, for example, will add 600 km to the fiber network in East Africa.[68] This has facilitated beneficial uptake of ICTs among the business community, which is concentrated in the urban centers, but uptake in other areas has lagged.[69] Thus Ghana's ICT market is currently underdeveloped and unsaturated, as local and pan-African companies tend to dominate—such as MTN, Net Solutions Ghana Limited, Internet Ghana, and South African companies Dimension Data and Internet Solutions—although these often act as intermediaries for global players, especially in the provision of cloud-computing services.[70] Moreover, even SMEs that do use ICTs tend to rely on the internet for e-mail and maintaining a business website, rather than fully integrating technology into their business operations in order to maximize efficiency.[71]

While significant infrastructural gaps continue to hinder investment and uptake of ICTs, Ghana's regulatory and business environment for ICTs is remarkably favorable by regional standards (see figure 4.2). A subsidiary of Vodafone, the National Communication Backbone Company, has sole ownership of the country's main broadband fiber network, which stream-lines the process of access and expansion licensing.[72] Moreover, the govern-ment has prioritized cloud computing as part of its e-government program, and it is building several data storage centers to host and coordinate data that will ultimately serve a network of more than a thousand sites.[73] Given the pro-ICT position of the Ghanaian government, analysts have con-cluded that effective partnerships between the public and private sectors will present prime opportunities to develop the necessary infrastructure and build economies of scale in Ghana's ICT market into the future.

There are a number of reasons to be optimistic about the prospects for future growth in Ghana's ICT market. For one thing, the Ghanaian popu-lation has already exhibited a high willingness to invest in ICTs, even at current income levels—mobile penetration rates are higher than in even more advanced markets like Egypt, Tunisia, and Morocco (see figure 4.1).[74] This is perhaps due to the fact that ICT goods and services are already notably affordable in the country—more so than regional neighbors like Côte d'Ivoire and Senegal (see figure 4.2). And as the Ghanaian economy continues to grow at one of the most rapid rates on the continent (see table 4.2), this signals enormous potential for growth in consumer markets, as only 6.35 percent of Ghanaian workers currently use the internet for com-merce.[75]

RWANDA

The major challenges facing Rwanda's ICT sector today are in infrastruc-ture and human capital. Like Botswana, Rwanda faces geographic con-straints to connectivity due to its landlocked location. More than any other country analyzed, there is also a notable lack of ICT literacy and awareness at the local level, as well as a deficiency of skilled and trained workers to support innovation in the industry (see figure 4.2).[76]

Despite this, Rwanda represents perhaps the most appealing opportu-nity for ICT investment in Africa today. The Rwandan government has shown a commitment to developing the sector since the adoption of the National Information Communications Infrastructure policy in 2000, which was further integrated as a priority in its Vision 2020.[77] Tangible results of the program include the effective integration of ICTs into the country's health sector and the digitization of various services such as business registration, corporate tax filing, visas and national IDs, and corruption monitoring.[78]

Developing the necessary infrastructure was the major priority of the program between 2005 and 2010, and although there is still a long way to go, Rwanda's ICT infrastructure is well on the way to improving as a result of two projects recently negotiated by the government. Three submarine cable companies (SEACOM, TEAMS, and EASSy) have financed a project to extend a fiber-optic cable network countrywide, and a South Korean telecom giant (KT Corp) is investing $140 million to deploy a 4G broadband network. During this period, Rwanda exhibited one of the fastest growth rates in internet use on the continent—8,900 percent, more than three times higher than the average in Africa.[79]

At the same time, though, its current levels of internet and mobile phone penetration remain relatively low compared to the other top network-ready African countries (see figure 4.1). Given that Rwanda's recent economic growth rates are second only to Côte d'Ivoire (see table 4.2)—although starting from a much lower base—this signals growth potential in the consumer market for ICTs in Rwanda that is higher than any other country in the sample. Moreover, the current stage of the National Information Communications Infrastructure (2016–2020) is focused on encouraging private sector investment, which helps to explain why Rwanda's ICT environment is ranked so favorably according to the World Economic Forum (see figure 4.2), as well as the World Bank's Doing Business Report.[80]

Challenges and Risks

Studies on the inhibitors to investment in Africa's ICT sector typically highlight three major categories of challenges: infrastructure, regulatory frameworks, and local markets.[81]

First, despite marked improvements over the past decade, the relative deficiency of network infrastructure at country and regional levels is considered the primary obstacle to ICT investment. There is significant variation across countries, as some—especially South Africa and Morocco—have achieved impressive levels of development of land-based network infrastructure. Elsewhere, fixed broadband and cable infrastructure has often lagged behind, and this problem has been compounded in the short term as wireless technologies like 3G and LTE have become increasingly affordable and filled some of the networking gaps.[82] Without additional investment, these tower-based and satellite networks will be unable to transmit massively increasing quantities of data. Moreover, given the rapid growth in ICT traffic resulting from price wars in countries like Ghana and Kenya, existing providers have occasionally become overwhelmed and breached acceptable broadband congestion levels, resulting in sanctions.[83] These regulatory risks can increase the base cost of expanding ICT networks in certain countries. For example, MTN was fined $5.2 billion after failing to register SIM cards in 2015, amounting to 37 percent of its revenues and almost double its annual profits. The fine was eventually reduced to $1.7 billion, but the company suffered reputational drawbacks in the aftermath of the regulation challenge.

While Africa's urban and coastal areas are now remarkably well connected due to infrastructural investment and innovation, there is a substantial geographical barrier to internet access in rural areas and landlocked countries. For example, while the average monthly price of fixed broadband access in coastal countries is already relatively high at $206, it is more than double that in the average landlocked African country: $438.[84] Even countries that have benefited from access to submarine cables often lack the domestic infrastructure needed for cross-country distribution through subnational hubs.[85] In this context, the economies of expansion into more remote markets are compounded for private investors by the lower densities, penetration rates, and incomes of unintegrated populations.[86]

Second, despite the benefits of a liberalized market to the sector, there are notable gaps in government policies relating to ICT, particularly in their implementation. Even in attempting to implement their own national e-government projects, public sector ICT projects often fail to overcome regulatory and political barriers, with less than 20 percent of all e-government projects succeeding past the start-up phase.[87] Redundancies have been created by the absence of public infrastructure sharing initiatives, and some governments, including Tanzania and Egypt, have even introduced or raised taxes on telecom companies in recent years.

In fact, there is often a direct conflict that occurs between the process of social liberalization, which is facilitated by ICT networks, and governments, which often have an incentive to manipulate and censor ICTs in order to maintain political control. Although this problem might be limited to the more extreme cases of antidemocratic regimes, however, ICT stakeholders working across the continent often point to certain similarities, such as the relative weakness of intellectual property protection and the bureaucratic red tape associated with registering a new business. These barriers are particularly detrimental to the ability of SMEs to become competitive in the sector.[88] At the regional level, moreover, there has been little success in attempts to coordinate and harmonize frameworks in order to boost interconnectivity on the continent, resulting in a notable lack of cross-border broadband integration.[89]

Finally, the relative immaturity of the market means that local ICT knowledge is relatively lacking in Africa. The vast majority of African consumers are familiar with the internet, exhibiting demand for the same kinds of popular sites and services as in developed countries—such as Facebook, Google, and YouTube—but also, increasingly, for locally developed content.[90] However, a small minority of Africans has access to a personal computer, with most users relying on internet cafes or smartphones, and the high cost of bandwidth in such terminals leads to underuse.

A recent study of Rwanda showed that the absence of ICT literacy and awareness is hindering increased penetration, even as cost and access improve, and resulting in underutilization of e-government services.[91] More broadly, the African region is characterized by poor technical awareness at all levels of the value chain—from suppliers and distributers to users[92]—not only due to the lack of experience with ICT products and services but also to education gaps. The substantial investment in submarine and terrestrial network fibers, for example, will generate massive demand for trained and skilled personnel in both the public and private sectors, yet there are few ICT educational and training programs on the continent today. This gap reduces the prospects for innovation and prevents the emergence of the entrepreneurs of the future.[93]

Challenges related to infrastructure, regulations, and local ICT knowledge have inhibited optimal levels of investment to date. However, the barriers to growth are diminishing with the rapid increase in consumer demand—at the individual, business, and governmental levels—for ICT services in Africa, particularly as suppliers learn to adapt to the challenges of the environment.

Strategies for Effective Investment

Unlike in other areas of the economy, development of Africa's ICT sector has been driven since its inception by private companies, and the private sector will be responsible for the majority of the investment in infrastructure needed to sustain growth in the future.[94] Given the high costs associated with entering and remaining competitive in the sector, as well as the price wars that have started to occur as the market matures, African telecom companies have increasingly focused on controlling and reducing operational costs as the primary means of remaining competitive. Those companies that have remained competitive in Africa's ICT sector in recent years have employed a handful of concrete strategies, specifically, focusing the business model on data connectivity and diversifying the services provided.[95]

DATA

For the largest telecom operators working in Africa, non-SMS data have already become a substantial contributor to annual net revenues; they are now roughly 14 percent for Vodacom and 7 percent for Safaricom, for example, and average more than 15 percent for companies working in Africa's most advanced markets. In light of the existing—and rapidly increasing— demand for smartphones and mobile internet devices in the region, the major concern for ICT providers is securing the necessary infrastructure to serve increasing levels of data traffic, either through direct investment or subscriber acquisition.[96] There are now 4G networks in thirty-two African countries, with thirty-six new networks launched between 2014 and 2016 alone.[97]

Given the high profitability of data provision, companies should work to secure large shares in markets that are likely to support substantial use of data, such as wealthy segments of the population or lucrative company contracts. Given the high levels of development of data connectivity infrastructure in the continent's urban economic centers—now reaching levels of refinement and quality of the world's more advanced economies—cloud services for businesses offer a promising avenue for operators to offer large data storage, security, and information technology maintenance services, especially in helping SMEs compete in a globalized economy.[98]

As a means of reducing costs while increasing access to broadband, sharing of wireless towers and submarine cables has become increasingly common among telecom companies. Of the roughly 170,000 towers across Africa, a substantial portion are already shared, and there is increasing regulatory pressure from proactive governments to incentivize sharing, such as in Ghana, Kenya, and Nigeria. The Tunisian government, for example, brokered a deal between its two largest telecom operators for a shared investment in a private submarine cable, and last year it launched a public consultation into new policies that could increase sharing of fiber-optic networks.[99] Meanwhile, many providers are relying on multiple types of network technologies (e.g., 3G and WiMAX, cable and data) to reach subscribers in different locations.

DIVERSIFICATION

Mobile money services have been extremely successful in increasing penetration rates for both mobile providers and formal financial products, especially in East Africa, although there is enormous potential for the same pattern to be replicated across the continent in the near future. Mobile-only banks have already emerged in South Africa (TYME), for example. A number of other economic activities could replicate the same model over the coming years, such as microfinance, mobile insurance services, or retail partnerships—MTN has already formed partnerships to roll out services in each of these fields.[100] Given the declining price of SMS, telecom companies should seek out opportunities for achieving incremental margins by bundling services with adjacent sectors, either through building strategic partnerships or by directly acquiring smaller companies.

Building off the mobile money model, various industries are seeking innovative partnerships with telecom companies in order to access the next frontier of global consumers in Africa. For example, international advertisers have recognized the potential of Africa's emerging markets, with conglomerates like Coca-Cola and Unilever seeking new opportunities to target consumers through mobile applications and browsers.[101] Meanwhile, tech firms like Nokia and Google are already opening research and development labs in Africa. And while the majority of content demanded in Africa is produced abroad—which contributes to the higher price of broadband services—the demand for and availability of local content are increasing rapidly. There are relatively few local IXP (internet exchange point) networks that would facilitate such exchange, especially in West Africa, but the African Internet Exchange System, a project launched by the African Union, seeks to increase the proportion of intra-African internet traffic exchange to 80 percent by 2020.[102]

Increasing spending on entertainment among Africans with discretionary income could be captured by ICT companies that move into developing new forms of content, such as gaming apps, live broadcasting, and news services. The large telecom company MTN has had notable success moving directly into media offerings in gaming (MTN Play) and social networking (MTN Pulse). Although the media market has traditionally been dominated by international and South African providers—along with an extremely diverse and fragmented range of localized sources—it is now shifting toward regional entertainment hubs, supported by rapidly growing demand for African-produced content among consumers. Countries like Nigeria and Zimbabwe have started to develop their own film industries, known respectively as Nolly- and Zollywood, which receive substantial airtime on pan-African television station Voxafrica. Beyond direct production of content, moreover, bundling of mobile broadband services with film and television providers could bring a range of entertainment to the small screen at little additional cost to the subscriber.

Ultimately, Africans could come to view their mobile phones as their primary service provider for various aspects of daily life. A prime example of this opportunity lies in the rollout of electronic public services initiatives, as telecom providers could serve as a vital link between citizens and their governments in areas such as health, education, and even voting.[103] On the other hand, the increase of service bundling among ICT companies has, in some of the more saturated markets, resulted in a tariff innovation battle whereby companies increasingly offer free incentives in order to hook new subscribers into the market. Rapidly increasing competition in some countries—such as Kenya (2008–09), Ghana (2010), and Nigeria (2012)—led to price wars that caused the bottom to fall out of mobile services. Ultimately, these "freebies" can have a disruptive impact on the market, especially by distorting prices, if not carefully considered and researched.[104]

Given the remaining challenges related to local skills, much of the non-core functions of ICT businesses are often outsourced to other regions.[105] However, the challenges related to infrastructure cannot be avoided if the sector hopes to meet growing demand from consumers and businesses. Finding innovative solutions to the cost of increasing data flows could help businesses increase penetration into rural markets, a growing necessity given the saturation of urban areas. Although LTE networks are increasing cost-efficient coverage, mobile devices that are affordable to most African consumers remain 3G reliant. A number of innovations in network infrastructure and mobile products are being developed with the goal of reaching new populations, such as Vodacom's solar chargers. However, given the financial outlays that will be necessary to develop the needed infrastructure, and especially to improve local and international data connectivity, companies must be flexible and creative in reducing costs and maintain the ability to scale up as costs allow.

Looking to the Future

As Africa emerges as a major player in the world economy, the momentum displayed in the ICT market is projected to continue over the coming decades. In direct terms, the ICT industry is growing and creating jobs, with multinational companies increasingly looking to Africa as an opportunity for growing economies of scale in the future, especially the advantages offered by the region's new technology parks. Amazon, Microsoft, and Huawei, for example, are planning to open data centers in Cape Town within the next few years, underscoring the importance of the African markets for multinational technology companies. Meanwhile, the ecosystem for tech start-ups is impressively rich, with more than three hundred tech hubs active in Africa to date, and mobile platforms have become the standard instrument for creating and disseminating localized, innovative business solutions.[106]

Indirectly, and perhaps more significantly, the ICT sector is intimately connected with growth across various other areas of the economy.[107] Although infrastructure is viewed as one of the primary challenges to realizing ICT growth objectives, ICTs themselves provide an opportunity to leapfrog infrastructure constraints to growth in other sectors. Already, mobile money initiatives have generated exponential increases in the proportion of people integrated into formal financial markets, and this pattern is leading to a new wave of mobile banking services, such as mobile-only banks, mobile insurance products, and microfinance. Africa's mobile advertising market is already maturing by following this model, with potential for billions of dollars in increased revenues over the next few years.[108] With income levels rising among Africa's rapidly growing population, e-commerce will facilitate increased consumer spending, and millions more people on the continent will soon be able to afford ICT devices for personal use, such as computers and smartphones.

The growth potential in the African market for smartphones is particularly promising. Although smartphone penetration is 33 percent, it is increasing rapidly, and smartphones are likely to account for the majority of new mobile purchases over the next few years, especially in mature markets like South Africa, Kenya, and Nigeria. Although the availability of second-hand devices from Europe and the Middle East drove the initial increase in demand, retailers are now recognizing the growth potential, with increasing competition among producers like Huawei and Microsoft to produce a durable and affordable smartphone for the African market; the recently released Nokia 215 sells for just $29.[109] There are roughly 300 million new mobile internet subscribers expected by 2020,[110] and as a result, data will account for a growing proportion of revenues for telecom companies over the next decade—quickly replacing SMS—while increasing traffic on the continent will create an urgent need for improved local and international connectivity infrastructure.

In this light, the next challenge for African governments and private investors will be to improve broadband access beyond urban areas in order to incorporate rural and unintegrated communities. Roughly two-thirds of all private investment in infrastructure over the past 10 years has been targeted toward the ICT sector, and the result has been a substantial increase in satellite, tower, submarine, and terrestrial fiber networks across the continent. Yet remaining gaps mean that internet connectivity is still too expensive, too slow, or even unavailable outside major cities and coastal areas.[111] Much work remains to be done by African governments in targeting public resources and incentives toward achieving universal access and improving technological literacy, including removing excess taxation, developing ICT education and training (including free e-education services), building data storage centers and technology parks, and even providing subsidies for particularly hard to reach populations.[112]

Beyond the benefits to businesses and the broader goal of economic growth, information and communication technology plays a central role in the process of social development. Due to its role in accelerating inclusive and sustainable forms of development, mobile connectivity has been highlighted as essential to achievement of the Sustainable Development Goals (SDGs) of the United Nations, which seek to eradicate poverty and inequality in the world. As services become increasingly affordable, mobile phones are connecting families and communities across geographic divides, providing handheld entertainment, enhancing access to government services like health care, and creating opportunities for entrepreneurship among segments of the population that traditionally lacked such options. As the region comes online over the next decade, Africans are likely to view their mobile devices as the gateway to most of their daily needs and activities, and in this way, ICTs represent perhaps the greatest force improving quality of life on the continent.

FIVE

Africa's Manufacturing and Industrialization Transformation and Potential

Among policymakers and scholars alike, a robust manufacturing sector is broadly understood as a fundamental path to economic growth and development.[1] The key boon of manufacturing is that it absorbs large swaths of workers and places them into productive and decent-paying jobs. Consumption and job creation in the manufacturing sector contribute between 20 and 35 percent as a share of GDP at the peak, indicating the sector's critical role in economic development.[2] Throughout history, this exact recipe has transformed France, Germany, Japan, the United Kingdom, and the United States into some of the world's wealthiest nations. Most recently, a new age of industrialization has helped make China one of the world's fastest-growing economies boasting the largest middle class, with other Southeast Asian countries following closely behind. These are all examples of how industrialization can generate rapid structural change, drive development, and alleviate poverty and unemployment.

However, this narrative seems to exclude many African nations. Despite their manufacturing potential and promising trajectories, most African countries continue to have a relative dearth of factories. Furthermore, manufacturing-to-GDP ratios in most African countries have remained stagnant in recent years; African manufacturing has thus driven limited employment creation to date.[3] This limited industrial development represents a missed opportunity for economic transformation and the development of quality employment that alleviates poverty.

The silver lining is the potential. Business-to-business spending in manufacturing in Africa is projected to reach $666.3 billion by 2030, $201.28 billion more than it did in 2015.[4] Irene Yuan Sun, author and consultant at the McKinsey & Company, considers Africa to be "the world's next great manufacturing center,"[5] potentially capturing part of the 100 million labor-intensive manufacturing jobs that will leave China by 2030.[6] This trend creates a huge opportunity for the continent, not only for countries such as Egypt, Nigeria, and South Africa (all regional outperformers in the Global Manufacturing Competitiveness Index), but also for newer players, such as Ethiopia, Morocco, Rwanda, and others (all of whom have recently adopted policies enabling manufacturing and industrial development).

Today, leaders are increasingly realizing that manufacturing is a major factor in helping Africa attain its goals of achieving the next stage of economic development. The African Union has put the sector front and center in its Agenda 2063. African governments are seeking new and innovative ways to attract investment and nurture industry, implementing strategies that involve targeted investment in infrastructure, improved regional integration, and the establishment of special economic zones (SEZs) for priority subsectors.

However, for Africa to reach its manufacturing and industrial potential, the public and private sectors must take steps to increase Africa's economic complexity, diversity, competitiveness, and productivity. This chapter explores some of the key structural constraints that have prevented Africa's manufacturing sector from maturing and from launching the same kind of economic modernization process witnessed in other developing regions. It also conducts a cross-national comparison of the manufacturing sector in Africa, providing illustrative examples of countries that are experiencing four unique trajectories of industrial development and identifying specific opportunities in each country based on the size and level of competitiveness of its manufacturing markets. Finally, with special attention to current major transformations, the chapter draws conclusions about the future of the manufacturing sector in Africa.

The chapter ultimately offers business leaders an accessible overview of Africa's biggest opportunities in the manufacturing sector, discussing trends and perspectives by 2030. It provides policymakers with some options likely to attract private investors, accelerate manufacturing and industrial development, and contribute to growth and poverty alleviation, facilitating the fulfilment of the Sustainable Development Goals and the African Union's Agenda 2063. While policy solutions are likely to differ across countries, manufacturing will be central to Africa's ability to meet its development goals.

Evolution of Manufacturing and Industrialization in Africa—Facts and Trends

Modern industry contributes significantly to the accumulation of physical and human capital. It provides relatively well-paid jobs for large numbers of unskilled or undereducated workers—particularly those who are not integrated in the formal economy—which increases household income and, hence, domestic demand. In this way, industry generates substantial backward and forward linkages with other sectors, providing a wealth of opportunities for suppliers, distributors, retailers, and business services.[7] For example, the inputs needed for different kinds of industrial production generate demand for agriculture, mining, and other raw materials, as well as for energy and information technologies, while they increase the supply of products for consumer markets, construction, and other sectors. Moreover, in macroeconomic terms, a strong manufacturing sector is argued to improve a country's external account balance by decreasing imports and diversifying exports, thereby increasing resilience to external shocks as compared to reliance on primary commodities.[8]

Though African manufacturing grew in the immediate postindependence period, largely shaped by state-led and protectionist policies, by the mid-1980s, a series of external shocks—including oil price increases, commodity price decreases, real interest rate rises, withering public coffers, and the limitations of domestic markets—were major factors in industrial decline in the region. Though structural adjustment reforms like privatization of state-owned enterprises and trade liberalization, along with foreign aid, restarted African manufacturing in the 1990s, increased competition from foreign products and new pressures on African currencies, such as devaluations,[9] made these gains short-lived. By 2006 the share of manufacturing in GDP had declined to roughly 10 percent—the same as it had been in the mid-1960s.[10] Since the late-1990s, economic growth rates in Africa reached impressively high levels (even during the 2008–2009 global financial crisis). Yet, until recently, growth in manufacturing has lagged behind that growth except in just a few exceptional markets.[11] In 2017, manufacturing's share of sub-Saharan Africa's total GDP was just under 10 percent and stagnant, even if some countries are doing better than others (figure 5.1).

Due to natural resource wealth in Africa, much of the region's industrial production remains centered on resource-based manufacturing. Resource-based manufacturing accounts for approximately half of total MVA and manufacturing exports. Investment in manufacturing has also been uneven, with almost 70 percent of the continent's manufacturing activities now concentrated in just four countries.[12] In fact, most of Africa's total MVA is driven by the higher level of industrial development in North and South Africa.[13]

Despite these trends, manufacturing in Africa grew 3.5 percent annually from 2005 to 2014—faster than it had in the rest of the world. Some countries, such as Nigeria and Angola, have experienced an increase in output of over 10 percent per year.[14] As a result, the value of production in sub-Saharan Africa has increased, from $75 billion in 2005 to over $130 billion in 2016. Moreover, manufacturing exports have increased even more rapidly than total output, at a compound annual growth rate of 9.5

FIGURE 5.1. Share of manufacturing value added in selected African countries.

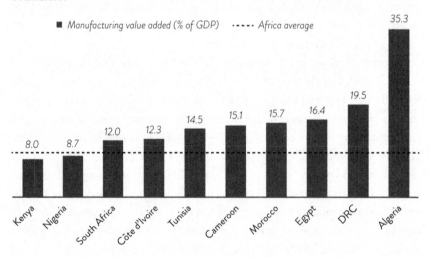

Source: World Development Indicators. All data are from 2017. Burundi, Eritrea, Comoros, Libya, Madagascar, Mali, Mauritania, Sudan, Somalia, South Sudan, and Chad are omitted from Africa average calculation due to lack of data.

percent, with shipments of heavy manufactures—such as transport vehicles, appliances, electronics, and industrial equipment—expanding by an impressive 14 percent.[15] Along with upstream and downstream sectors like construction and extraction, manufacturing is now among the top sectors for investment flows into Africa, accounting for 22 percent of total foreign direct investment (FDI) in 2015.[16]

Thus there is still significant room for growth in African manufacturing within the continent. The share of intra-African exports as a percentage of total African exports has increased from about 10 percent in 1995 to about 17 percent in 2017.[17] To support that growth, African regional bodies and governments are breaking down trade barriers, improving financial structures, and investing public resources in much-needed infrastructure—especially transport and energy networks and the internet.[18]

The proposed AfCFTA is key to this strategy. Its single continental market for goods and services, as well as a customs union with free movement of capital and business travelers, will accelerate continental integration. By promoting intra-African trade, the AfCFTA will also foster a more competitive manufacturing sector and promote economic diversification. The removal of tariffs will encourage companies to benefit from the economies of scale and expand their production and distribution markets. If successful, Africa's manufacturing sector is predicted to double in size, with annual output increasing from $500 billion in 2015 to $1 trillion in 2025 and creating an additional 14 million stable, well-paid jobs.[19] The AfCFTA is already the world's largest free-trade area in terms of the number of countries, covering more than 1.2 billion people and over $4 trillion in combined consumer and business spending. The potential for the AfCFTA is big for both structural transformation and poverty alleviation in Africa. Some studies show that by creating a pan-African market, the AfCFTA could increase intra-Africa trade by about 52 percent, resulting in an increase of African manufacturing exports. Right now, on average, manufacturing represents only about 10 percent of total GDP in Africa, lagging behind other developing regions. A successful AfCFTA could play a large role in reducing this gap.

The Status of Key Drivers and Policy Constraints for Manufacturing in Africa

While most developing regions' industrialization has started to plateau, Africa contains a wealth of favorable factors—particularly the availability of low-cost labor and an abundance of natural resources and raw materials— that signal a revolution in manufacturing is imminent. A recent survey from the Global Manufacturing Competitiveness Index indicates that the most crucial drivers of growth and investment in manufacturing are, in descending order, human capital (talent and productivity), cost, supplier networks, and domestic demand.[20] This section addresses the role of each of these factors as a determinant of industrialization, as well as discussing their current and future trajectories with empirical data from Africa.

HUMAN CAPITAL

At its most basic level, and particularly for labor-intensive subsectors, industry is only as healthy as the population that makes up its labor supply. The quality of a country's workforce, or its stock of human capital, is related to the country's flexibility, productivity, and ability to innovate.[21] Illiteracy, low education levels, and poor health conditions among the population hinder an individual factory's productivity and its ability to absorb new technologies, creating a negative impact on the diversification of manufactured goods in the whole economy. Moreover, only through continuous innovation, either in formal product development or management process improvement—which both need quality human capital—can growth be achieved over the long term.[22]

The evidence supports the impact of human capital stock on manufacturing growth in Africa. For example, an estimated 40 billion work hours are lost each year in Africa due to something as simple as a lack of fresh running water in the household.[23] Obstacles like this, combined with the cost and limited availability of safe medicines or health facilities, make disease and illness constant constraints on the productivity of the African workforce.[24] Education and experience are particular constraints to growth among small- and medium-sized enterprises (SMEs). In Ghana, for example, owners and workers of SMEs have, on average, 5 years of work experience—just half that of owners and workers in large firms.

At the same time, however, *The Economist* recently concluded that

Africa "is well on its way to developing the human capital that is required to industrialize."[25] Standards of education on the continent are improving, and the share of the population completing a primary education has risen continuously over the past 40 years—although it has remained roughly 20 percent lower than the global average. This is crucial because a number of studies have found that more-educated entrepreneurs and managers in Kenya and Zimbabwe have firms that grow more rapidly.[26] Moreover, many emerging markets in Africa already rank much higher in terms of innovative capacity than their education indicators would predict, such as South Africa and Kenya (33rd and 34th in the world for innovation, respectively). Others, like Morocco (129th in the world), still have a long way to go, and improvement in its innovative capacity will hinge on progress in education.[27]

To tap the full potential of Africa's human capital, policymakers should adjust education curricula to ensure that skills are adapted to the market. Policymakers should revisit curricula to focus on skills acquisition. They should also build capacity for entrepreneurship and self-employment through three main streams: (1) business training at an early age and regular skills upgrading with advancing age; (2) better promotion of science, technology, engineering, entrepreneurship, and mathematics; and (3) vocational and on-the-job trainings.

In addition, policymakers should also favor the continental migration of highly skilled workers as an immediate solution for pressing human capital needs.

COST

Cost effectiveness is widely viewed as the primary constraint on growth in manufacturing for firms of all sizes, but particularly for SMEs.[28] For example, Radelet and Sachs (1998) have produced a wealth of research linking shipping costs to a country's prospects for growth in manufactured exports, as well as to its overall economic growth. These transport costs are largely determined by structural constraints, such as access to seaports, but also by macroeconomic policies, bureaucratic red tape, and the quality of infrastructure.[29] Thus governments play a substantial role in determining the costs of doing business in any country. However, due to weak capacity, governments in many developing countries cannot reduce the costs of doing business. Therefore, firms will always seek to find ways to compensate for high transport costs in order to compete in world markets, which can result in managers paying lower wages or focusing on e-commerce.[30]

Like other developing regions, Africa has long been associated with substantial gaps in port, road, and power infrastructure. On the other hand, Africa is an increasingly cost-effective location for manufacturers, especially in light of current demographic trends.[31] The population living on the continent will be larger than that of either India or China by midcentury, with approximately 1.2 billion people, and Africa's share of the global working-age population (15–64 years) is projected to double to roughly 20 percent by 2050.[32] Meanwhile, improvements in bureaucratic and tax regulations, increasing public (and private) investment in infrastructure, and the wave of technology sweeping across the continent are all helping reduce the cost of doing business in Africa.

In particular, the exponential growth in mobile technologies has enabled African businesses to leapfrog previous technologies in order to access consumers and improve business-to-business networks. While a tiny fraction of African households are connected with the traditional landline telephones for communication, the penetration of smartphones is expected to increase rapidly, from 18 percent in 2015 to 50 percent in 2020.[33] In fact, there are parts of Africa that still lack running water or electricity but already have reliable access to the internet.[34] This mobile ecosystem is estimated to contribute at least 7 to 8 percent to Africa's GDP in the coming years, as the recent rise of e-commerce, e-banking, and mobile and internet communication is helping to facilitate business-to-business transactions along the supply chain.[35]

In terms of the role of governments, many countries in Africa are working to establish special economic zones (SEZs)[36] to empower manufacturing companies to capitalize on higher-quality infrastructure, tax benefits, protection from import competition, and duty-free movement of goods. Given country-level differences in natural endowments, these zones encourage countries to nurture certain industrial subsectors in order to take advantage of their own competitive advantage and drive growth.[37] Countries as diverse as Ethiopia (since 2015), Zambia (2006), and Nigeria (1992) have exhibited strong political commitment to implementing their SEZs, although there has been variation in terms of coordination and resource mobilization. For example, in all three countries, SEZs are part of national development strategies, and an SEZ policy framework and dedicated institutions for managing the SEZ program are in place. However, only in

Ethiopia and Zambia, SEZs have been consistently inaugurated at the head of state and government level and are regularly visited and promoted by high-level government officials. In Nigeria, however, coordination challenges occur between the federal and state levels of government.

SUPPLIER NETWORKS

A third factor affecting growth in manufacturing relates to the quality and availability of inputs in the local market, such as raw materials and equipment. Although there is significant variation across countries, the African region as a whole has a wealth of natural resources that are vital inputs for various manufacturing subsectors. One example is coltan, which is used in the production of electronic goods and is rich in the Democratic Republic of the Congo, Rwanda, and Mozambique.[38] However, as in other developing regions, the legacy of late twentieth-century protectionist industrialization policies—whether oriented toward producing for export or import substitution—has caused the sector to remain relatively insulated, despite increasing attempts to scale back trade barriers since the 1990s.[39] As a result, the availability of specialized machinery and equipment is relatively limited, and producers are often forced to rely on imperfect substitutes or import the necessary inputs at extra expense.[40]

Contrary to common perceptions, however, Africa's business-to-business market is already relatively well developed and growing rapidly, which signals that beneficial supply networks do exist currently. Domestic companies spent roughly $2.6 trillion in 2015, half of this on materials, and the total expenditure is expected to rise to $3.5 trillion by 2025.[41]

Moreover, recognizing that backward integration—whereby a country sources foreign inputs for its own production—is among the largest contributors to increasing productivity and value added in exports, many African countries are seeking to increase the size of the supply market by easing trade restrictions.[42] Increasing integration into international trade networks allows countries to overcome the constraints of the domestic labor force by importing technologies of innovation and encouraging knowledge transfer. Additionally, it increases countries' ability to specialize—since necessary inputs can be sourced from neighboring markets, rather than being produced domestically—which is viewed as an essential determinant of growth in manufacturing for small and underdeveloped economies.[43]

As mentioned earlier, the proposed AfCFTA is an effort taken by African countries to create a continental market and bolster an international negotiation block. One of the AfCFTA's goals is to "expand inter-Africa trade through better harmonization and coordination of trade liberalization and facilitation regimes and instruments across Regional Economic Communities (RECs) and across Africa in general."[44] Analysts predict that with the facilitation of the AfCFTA, the rapid expansion of intracontinental and regional trade over the next several decades, which accounts for just 11 percent of all African trade currently, will lead to a significant decrease in transit costs and an increase in the availability of intermediate inputs for production.[45]

DOMESTIC DEMAND

The limited size of the domestic market for manufactured products is viewed as a significant constraint to growth in developing countries. Where income levels are low, household consumption is limited to basic subsistence needs, so all but the most essential manufactured products are exported to distant, wealthier markets.[46] At the same time, however, income levels and household spending patterns are improved by growth in manufacturing more than any other individual economic sector, since it helps to create a large number of stable and well-paying jobs among previously poor and underemployed demographic groups.[47]

Income levels in Africa have already started to rise substantially, with household consumption projected to grow by an impressive 3.8 percent to reach nearly $2.1 trillion per year by 2025; in some countries, such as Nigeria and Tunisia, incomes are increasing even more rapidly. Moreover, in the next 20 years the majority of Africa's rapidly growing population will live in sprawling urban areas; thus nearly 600 million people on the continent will have daily access to formal markets and retail outlets.[48] This increasingly young and cash-conscious population is further generating a huge and untapped market for affordable, durable telecommunications goods—especially smartphones, but also tablets and computers—and most of the resources necessary to make these products are already extracted in Africa.

Because of these trends, most countries will experience rapid growth in demand for manufactured products in the near future, with the largest increases likely to occur in the processed food and beverages industry: analysts predict that revenues will increase in this subsector by $120 billion over the next decade. Meanwhile, "affluent" consumers are expected to spend an additional $200 billion per year from now until 2025, with approximately one-in-five Africans spending more than 70 percent of their income on discretionary items by 2025, signaling growing demand for electronics, appliances, and labor-intensive goods like clothing and footwear.[49] The latter subsector alone is estimated to increase revenue streams by $27 billion by 2025.[50] Meanwhile, because cement is necessary for factory construction and other infrastructural projects, revenues from cement production are likely to grow by up to $72 billion by 2025.[51]

In summary, the current trends in cost effectiveness, supply networks, and domestic demand indicate that Africa is poised for rapid industrialization in the coming years. In the near future, the region will possess a more productive and cost-efficient workforce, improved transport infrastructure and regulations, larger and more developed supply networks, and consumer markets to support a range of manufacturing subsectors. In Côte d'Ivoire, for example, the impressive projection of about 7 percent annual GDP growth through 2020 is attributed to an approximately 10 percent increase in the value of household consumption, growing access to markets across the Economic Community of West African States (ECOWAS), increasing public investment in infrastructure and agribusiness, and a shift in the workforce from farming (currently 70 percent of the workforce) to formal employment. [52]

Key Players in Africa

Due to the large amount of capital that is necessary for entering and operating in Africa's manufacturing sector, foreign businesses have tended to dominate the market since the colonial period. In absolute terms, foreign direct investment (FDI) in manufacturing has been relatively low but has begun to increase rapidly in recent years. In fact, manufacturing is now the "top business function in the region by capital investment," receiving roughly one-third of total FDI to the region, which is second to only the oil and gas sector.[53] Moreover, despite the common perception that foreign manufacturers tend to avoid investing in sub-Saharan Africa, FDI has continued to increase steadily over the past two decades, even as MVA has stagnated.

Many of the current FDI trends are occurring due to rising wages in East Asia, as many Asia-based companies are increasingly shifting manufacturing opportunities to Africa.[54] FDI from Chinese firms has increased by nearly 200 percent in recent years, with a 106 percent increase in project numbers in 2016. In addition, African production for Chinese markets has increased by a compound annual growth rate of 20 percent per year since 1980, with the vast majority of this growth occurring over the last decade.[55] Singapore's Tolaram, for example, has ratcheted up interest in West Africa and currently has full ownership of the newly developing Lagos Free Trade Zone in Nigeria, while several SEZs under development in Zambia are funded by Malaysian and Japanese companies.[56]

Despite rapidly increasing investment interest from the East, the primary source of manufacturing FDI in Africa has traditionally come from Europe and the OECD countries, especially the former colonizers (tables 5.1a, b). France was the number one source of FDI into Africa in 2014, with investment capital valued at $18.3 billion, and remained among one of the top ten source countries in 2015 and 2016. Combined with the United Kingdom and Italy, the major colonial powers accounted for roughly 30 percent of the value of all FDI into Africa in 2015.[57]

Like the increasing interest from Asia, new Western investors are turning to Africa due to its growing, youthful, and affordable workforce.[58] For example, Bosch recently launched its first foray into Africa with seven pilot projects, and European retailers H&M (Sweden) and Primark (Ireland) already source much of their clothing materials from countries like Ethiopia. FDI from the United States was up by nearly 50 percent in 2014, with ninety-seven investment projects, and has been the most of any single country since 2014. American conglomerate General Electric is constructing a quarter-billion-dollar factory in Nigeria to produce electrical gear, and even luxury producers are starting to acknowledge opportunities for small-scale production in Africa, such as New York's Madecasse chocolatier, which recently increased its workforce in Madagascar by 650 employees.[59]

At present, intra-African investment is becoming an increasingly significant source of FDI in the region—accounting for almost 40 percent of total manufacturing investment in Rwanda, for example. South African companies have traditionally been the largest source of intra-African investment, with $4.8 billion and nearly seven thousand new manufacturing jobs created in 2014. Morocco is the fastest-growing investment investor, but it remains seventh overall among African countries.[60] Unlike foreign investors, African manufacturers more often target their operations toward production for the African market. For example, South African Seemhale Telecoms has plans to produce cheap and durable mobile phones, while

TABLE 5.1A. Major sources of foreign direct investment in Africa's manufacturing sector in 2015.

Country	Size of investment (US$ billions)	Market share in Africa (%)	Number of investment projects in 2015
United States	6.8	10	93
France	5.7	9	53
United Kingdom	4.9	7	76
United Arab Emirates	4.2	6	45
Germany	2.6	4	37
China	2.3	3	32

Source: The Africa Investment Report. 2016. FDI Intelligence, 6.

TABLE 5.1B. Major sources of foreign direct investment in Africa's manufacturing sector in 2016.

Country	Size of investment (US$ billions)	Market share in Africa (%)	Number of investment projects in 2016
China	36.1	38.4	66
United Arab Emirates	11.0	11.7	35
Italy	4.0	4.3	20
United States	3.6	3.9	91
Japan	3.1	3.3	27
United Kingdom	2.4	2.5	41
France	2.1	2.2	81

Source: EY Attractiveness Program Africa "Connectivity Redefined." 2017. Ernst & Young, 20.

Kenya's Mobius Motors is doing the same with cars.[61] On the other hand, small-scale African artisans—such as Kenya's Ali Lamu, which produces specialized handbags and textiles—are capitalizing on tourism and the internet to access new export markets.[62]

FDI in Africa's manufacturing sector tends to be concentrated in just a handful of countries, and the total level of accumulated FDI is dominated by a few substantial investments (figure 5.2).[63] Two-thirds of the value of African manufacturing production is located in Egypt, Morocco, Nigeria, and South Africa; this figure increases to more than 80 percent when Angola, Côte d'Ivoire, Democratic Republic of the Congo (DRC), Ghana, Kenya, Tunisia, and Zambia are included.[64]

Many of these countries' economies are more often associated with mining and resource extraction, and as such, manufacturing activities have developed around the production of equipment and other industrial inputs necessary to support those sectors. In fact, the most rapid growth in manufacturing over the past decade has occurred in Angola (18.3 percent per year) and Nigeria (11.8 percent)—two notable resource-dependent coun-

FIGURE 5.2. Comparison of top foreign direct investment recipients, 2000 and 2017.

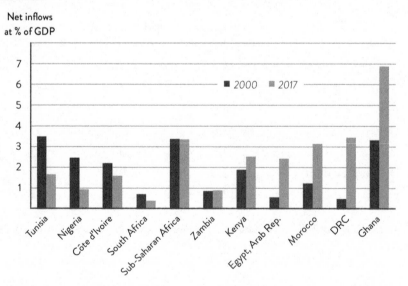

Source: World Development Indicators. Data for Tunisia, Côte d'Ivoire, sub-Saharan Africa, and DRC are 2016, not 2017.

tries. Angola's manufacturing sector, with its industrial share of GDP nearly doubling since the mid-2000s and $16 billion in FDI reported in 2014, is now the fifth largest on the continent in output, having recently surpassed Tunisia. Companies from Portugal, its former colonizer, have traditionally dominated Angola's FDI, and heavy manufacturing still makes up 40 percent of the country's imports bill. The government recently recognized the potential for production growth via diversification and import substitution as part of its Plano Nacional de Desenvolvimento. As part of the plan, beginning in early 2015, cement imports were banned, and domestic production capacity for cement was expanded to 8 million tons per year (with prior demand at just 6.5 million tons).[65]

The DRC is another extractive-based industrializer on the continent whose manufacturing accounts for more than 16 percent of its GDP, among the highest on the continent. However, light and heavy manufacturers account for just 3 percent of total export revenues, meaning that most of its domestic factory output is used for servicing domestic needs. Factory production has contributed little to economic growth because of poor linkages with local markets and overwhelming reliance on imports.

There are a growing number of successful industrial markets in Africa that are not directly related to extraction, such as leather in Ethiopia, garments in Lesotho, automobiles in South Africa, and pharmaceuticals in East Africa.[66] Already a major player in manufacturing on the continent, Egypt experienced the largest absolute increase in FDI in 2014, with nearly $18 billion in new investments and fifty-one new manufacturing projects planned—a 42 percent increase since 2013. Although, the rate of increase in investment was even higher in Morocco (59 percent), Mozambique (67 percent), and Ethiopia (100 percent) for similar periods.

In fact, some of Africa's frontier markets for manufacturing have exhibited the greatest gains in FDI since 2000. Meanwhile, a number of well-known multinational producers have set up shop in Ghana, including Unilever (consumer goods), PZ Cussons (health care products), Fan Milk (beverages), and Mahindra (vehicles). Even many factories that had been previously dormant, such as the Volta Aluminum Company, have relaunched production. With substantial opportunity for growth into the future, many of these midsize markets are already rapidly climbing the rankings among the top manufacturing countries in Africa.

Opportunities: Key Sectors and Countries

As we have described, Africa's competitive advantage in manufacturing is currently being driven by its demographic makeup and resource abundance. Therefore, prime opportunities for investment are currently concentrated in industries that are either labor intensive or require inputs of raw materials that can be sourced locally, such as minerals and agricultural products. Thus the manufacturing subsectors that have benefited the most from the rise in FDI in recent years include software (up 72 percent), auto components (133 percent), industrial and business machinery (378 percent), and chemicals production (2,000 percent).[67] At the same time, growth in manufacturing in the coming years will be driven by increasing linkages among African countries and with the rest of the world and growing consumer markets on the continent. Analysts predict that the fastest growth over the next decade will occur in agroprocessing (projected revenue increase of $122 billion), cement production ($72 billion), and clothing and footwear ($27 billion) subsectors.[68] For companies looking to invest in Africa, therefore, consumer-facing and infrastructure-related industries look to be among the most valuable in terms of annual revenue by 2025.[69]

In terms of variation across countries, investment opportunities are largely shaped by structural factors such as resource endowments and the size of the domestic market—in terms of both consumer demand and labor supply. In addition, though, the favorability of manufacturing investment is often affected by the national policy on investment climate. South Africa, for example, has had marked success in attracting investment since adopting its Industrial Policy Action Plan, which seeks to coordinate various ministries and policy areas and to subordinate trade and other economic goals to the exigencies of industrialization.[70] The Zuma administration created a number of SEZs in order to spur employment and bolster investment in specific, targeted subsectors, especially steel (Saldanha) and automotives (Gauteng and Eastern Cape).[71]

In order to compare and highlight some specific manufacturing investment opportunities, we first provide an overview of the ten largest manufacturing markets in Africa—in terms of the current value of manufacturing output—across key indicators of market competitiveness.[72] Figure 5.3 compares countries' scores for the pay versus productivity of the labor force,[73] quality of electricity supply, and quality of transport infrastructure, which is an average of the individual scores for the quality of roads, railroads, ports, and air transport infrastructure. Not surprisingly, those countries that score best across all three variables are also those with the largest and most well-developed manufacturing sectors to date, namely South Africa, Egypt, Tunisia, Morocco, and Kenya. At the same time, though, several frontier markets exhibit strong foundations for manufacturing investment, especially in terms of the value of the workforce.

Using these data, we classify country cases in terms of the relative size of the manufacturing market and its competitiveness. The threshold for the size of the manufacturing market is drawn at about $10 billion in annual output, while countries are considered to have highly competitive markets for investment if the average score across the three indicators summarized in figure 5.3 is greater than or equal to three. The two-by-two categorization of these ten countries is provided in table 5.2. In the subsequent discussion, we select one country from each box—specifically, Morocco, Kenya, Zambia, and Nigeria—in order to discuss specific opportunities for investment in light of the unique structural and policy-related dynamics of each case.

FIGURE 5.3. Global Competitiveness Index scores on key indicators for manufacturing investment.

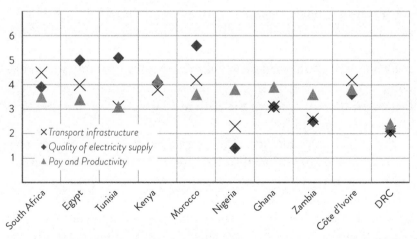

Source: Global Competitiveness Index 2017–18, World Economic Forum. Data for Côte d'Ivoire are from 2016–17.

TABLE 5.2. Comparison of current market size and competitiveness of Africa's ten largest manufacturing countries.

	Large market	Small market
High competitiveness	Egypt South Africa Morocco	Tunisia Kenya Côte d'Ivoire Ghana
Low competitiveness	Nigeria	Zambia DR Congo

MOROCCO

Manufacturing already accounts for more than 15 percent of GDP and provides 10 percent of formal employment in Morocco, with roughly one-third of the sector concentrated in textiles. Some of the more traditional subsectors—including food, fertilizer, steel, and textiles and clothing—have struggled in recent years due to declining demand from the EU and increasing competition from Asian imports. While the manufacturing sector has exhibited real annual growth of only 2.4 percent in the past 10 years, growth in production volume has outpaced the rest of the North African region, and a few emerging subsectors have expanded rapidly as foreign investors have hastened to take advantage of Morocco's low wages and free trade zones.[74] In response to positive reforms in bureaucratic regulations, such as reducing the length of time commercial disputes run through the courts, Morocco shot up the African FDI ranks from fourteenth in 2006 to third in 2015.[75]

Specifically, the aeronautics industry grew by 15–20 percent per year between 2008 and 2013. More than 100 aeronautics companies now operate in Morocco, many of which are concentrated in the Midparc Casablanca Free Zone, including Boeing and Bombardier. The government has also responded to calls from the industry for investment in the human capital needed to support innovation and engineering by launching the Institut des Metiers de l'Aeronautique in 2011.

The production of automobile components was a traditionally strong subsector for the country—combining with electronics to account for 10–15 percent of manufactured exports. The government has recently further incentivized a shift toward automotive assembly by offering fiscal and tax incentives in certain free zones. The Greater Tanger-Med Industrial Platform contains six free trade zones connected by road and rail to the Tangiers port—already one of the busiest ports in Africa, with a capacity of 8 million containers per year and ongoing expansion projects. The French car manufacturer Renault took advantage of these opportunities by opening a $1.5 billion factory in Tanger Automotive City in 2012,[76] in addition to its older factory in Casablanca founded in 1959.[77] Other car manufacturers investing in Morocco's automotive industry include Japan's Nissan and India's Tata. Now, Morocco is the second-largest car producer in Africa, after South Africa, producing 156,000 vehicles in 2013.[78]

KENYA

Industrial manufacturing is relatively strong in Kenya compared to countries at similar levels of economic development. Growing by an average of 4 percent per year over the past decade, it now accounts for nearly 20 percent of economic activity and provides 12.5 percent of all formal jobs in the economy, about 280,000 jobs. The most striking growth in production rates has occurred in dairy, chemicals, and fabricated metals production, all of which expanded by more than 50 percent between 2010 and 2013.[79] Other notable sectors include textiles, pharmaceuticals, furniture, leather goods, and motor vehicles, for which Kenya is the prime supplier to the rapidly urbanizing East African market.[80]

Investors in Kenyan manufacturing have already benefited from SEZs, where downtime caused by electricity and other power interruptions are significantly less frequent than in other areas of the country. Almost 20 percent of all manufacturing jobs are located in export processing zones (EPZs),[81] where Kenya's largest subsector—food and consumer goods processing—tends to operate. This includes especially flour and maize mills, meat and produce canning, sugar refining, and beer and soft drink production.

The government has also expressed a commitment to reclaiming Kenya's place as the region's top textiles producer by establishing three new SEZs: one near the Mombasa port, one at the new Lamu port, and one in Kisumu near Lake Victoria. Beyond Kenya's relatively high-skilled workforce and capacity for innovation, added incentives for global textile firms investing in Kenya's SEZs include deferment on value-added tax and duty-free imports.

In partnership with the United Nations Industrial Development Organization (UNIDO), the Kenyan government recently launched a program to strengthen its pharmaceutical industry.[82] The program helps funnel resources toward building production capacities and ensuring that the production of pharmaceuticals meets World Health Organization (WHO) good manufacturing practice (GMP) quality and safety standards.[83] The program is part of a broader strategy to improve local manufacturing infrastructure and to develop a high-quality manufacturing sector.

According to the World Economic Forum, Kenya is ranked fourth in Africa in terms of its competitive advantage on the international market, after the Seychelles, Ghana, and Zambia.[84] Kenya's MVA per capita is already 50 percent higher than that of neighbor Tanzania and more than twice as high as Uganda and Rwanda. Kenya is also ranked the second highest in Africa (forty-first in the world in 2017, following South Africa which is ranked thirty-ninth in 2017) in terms of innovation and sophistication, an indication of a relatively highly skilled labor force.[85] Between 1990 and 2014, the share of its working-age population increased from 47 percent to 56 percent, and it is projected to have roughly 40 million available workers by 2030—up from 25.5 million currently.[86] In light of these expected trends, many analysts predict that Kenya will remain one of the top manufacturing exporters in the region over the medium to long term.[87]

ZAMBIA

Although it is a landlocked country, Zambia ranks third on the continent, behind the Seychelles and Ghana, in the competitiveness of its manufactured goods in the world market. Its manufacturing sector grew by roughly 30 percent between 2009 and 2013. In addition, despite the overwhelming attention to Zambia's natural resource wealth (i.e., copper deposits), by 2013 the manufacturing sector received 25 percent of all FDI into Zambia. Currently, roughly two-thirds of the sector is involved in agroprocessing and production of consumer goods, while the rest largely focuses on producing inputs for the local industrial sector.[88]

The government has actively sought to diversify its export portfolio by providing tax incentives for investment in priority sectors and launching a

Multi-Facility Economic Zone (MFEZ) program in 2005. Now the area around the capital Lusaka hosts six MFEZs, which eliminate value-added tax payments on manufacturing inputs and either discount or defer corporate tax payments. As of March 2015, eleven different companies pledged to invest $120 million in the Lusaka South MFEZ, the first government-run MFEZ pilot project with an area as large as 2,100 hectares.[89] Further plans are underway to improve the country's industrial investment climate as part of a 5-year development plan—the "Revised Sixth National Development Plan"—in which a total of eleven SEZs are either in operation, under development, or being reviewed for approval.[90] In order to capitalize on the incentives offered by the SEZs, companies are required to prove that their activities will contribute to the diversification of the Zambian economy.

NIGERIA

The automotive industry in Nigeria is also expanding rapidly. Although nearly all of the automobiles sold in the country are imported—and just one company, Toyota, dominates 70 percent of the market—Nigerian automakers have exhibited a large increase in sales over the past few years, and the first domestically produced cars reached the market in 2015. With its New Automobile Industrial Policy Development launched in 2013, the government now seems committed to promoting this domestic industry by raising import tariffs, improving industrial infrastructure, and investing in vocational training. Companies that have since expressed plans to invest in Nigeria include Nissan, Skoda, and Mercedes-Benz.[91]

Another promising opportunity is in the Lagos Free Trade Zone (LFTZ), first launched in 2002, which intends to be a trade and logistical hub for all of West Africa, especially the ECOWAS member states. It has since expanded from 215 to 850 hectares, and became fully operational in 2018, with a particular focus on petroleum refining, petrochemicals, and agroprocessing. Companies are required to invest at least $1 million in share capital to get access to the zone, which offers exemptions from taxes at all levels of government and from import/export licensing requirements. The first company to set up shop was palm oil refiner Raffles Oil with $30 million invested since 2012, and then packaging company Insignia with roughly $20 million. At least five more manufacturing companies already have plans to become capital shareholders in the LFTZ.[92]

Industrialization has been one of the major catalysts of growth in Nigeria, and it is a priority strategy for the government in shifting away from its overreliance on volatile primary commodity exports, especially oil. Overall, the manufacturing sector currently accounts for 9 percent of GDP, more than expected in past projections, with an impressive annual growth rate of 18 percent between 2011 and 2013. Important subsectors include food, beverages, cigarettes, and textiles. Like Kenya, Nigeria's pharmaceutical sector is also booming due to WHO certification of local manufacturers, with four companies now producing medicines for the world market.[93]

Recurrent Challenges

Despite the recent, surprising expansion of its manufacturing sector as just described, MVA per capita in Nigeria is still among the lowest in Africa. The problems experienced by manufacturers working in Nigeria are indicative of the challenges of investing in manufacturing elsewhere in Africa—specifically, the quality of human capital, infrastructure gaps, and policy and regulatory failures.[94] In this section, we discuss some of these obstacles to doing business in Africa's manufacturing sector and describe some empirical variation in these constraints across the continent.

First, although an abundance of low-cost, underemployed labor exists already, Africa's workforce is perceived to be lacking in skills and efficiency, a major hindrance to investment, especially in more specialized forms of production. Only two-thirds of 15- to 24-year-old persons in Africa have completed a primary education, which is roughly 20 percent less than the world average, with fewer than one in five students continuing beyond primary school.[95] Secondary and tertiary enrollment rates are even lower, and schools at all levels face issues of low quality. As a result, only ten African countries are ranked in the top half in the world for "Pay versus Productivity" in the World Economic Forum's Global Competitiveness Index. Uncoincidentally, these are the countries that have the most developed education systems in the region, namely Kenya, Mauritius, Rwanda, and Seychelles. For others—notably Egypt, Morocco, Namibia, and South Africa—the marginal value of labor is low compared to the average wage.[96] Unable to locate sufficiently qualified workers in the local labor market, many companies have resorted to importing foreign workers or else investing in intensive training courses.[97]

Second, although spending on infrastructure has more than doubled since the turn of the century, amounting to $80 billion in 2015,[98] gaps in energy infrastructure continue to result in frequent power outages in many countries. The African Development Bank estimates that electricity costs three times more in Africa than in comparable developing regions, and most manufacturers operating in West and East Africa have to rely on expensive backup generators as a primary energy source, which adversely affects their profit margins.[99] At the same time, weak transportation networks hinder manufacturers' ability to capitalize on regional economies of scale. According to the World Bank, the number of railroads by total kilometers has actually declined since the 1980s, and only a minority of roads on the continent are paved or traversable year-round. Despite its population of 1 billion people, the continent currently has just 64 ports.[100]

In the immediate postindependence period, Africa was largely comparable to East Asia in the quality and penetration of its roads, electricity, and telecommunications infrastructure. By the end of the century, it had fallen behind in every category. The region as a whole now lags 20 percent behind the average for low-income countries across all infrastructure indicators, with only five African countries above the global median for electricity supply and only ten for the quality of transport infrastructure.[101] The few countries that rank in the top ninety in both categories—Morocco, Tunisia, Namibia, Seychelles, and Mauritius—are also those with the highest MVA per capita in the region. Access to utility services continues to pose a challenge even in many SEZs, although some countries are ratcheting up efforts to address these problems either by privatizing the electrical sector (Nigeria) or by building massive hydropower plants (the DRC, Ethiopia, Zambia) or solar/wind farms (Morocco).[102]

Finally, burdensome port and tax bureaucracies in Africa have contributed to the highest direct and indirect costs of international trade in manufacturing in the world. It can take as many as 51 days and seven different documents to export a container from Zambia, compared to 10 days and four documents from Morocco.[103] FDI agencies and other government ministries in African countries have been unable to effectively address issues of overlapping jurisdictions and uncoordinated personnel practices in order to improve the investment environment.[104] Much of this is due to a lack of political commitment, since industrial, tax, and trade regulations offer significant opportunities for corruption.[105]

Effective Strategies for Investment

In light of the preceding discussion, any investor looking toward Africa's manufacturing sector should consider the following factors: those related to the structure of a country's economy and those related to a country's policies. In order to reduce costs related to transport, import tariffs, and exchange rate fluctuations, investors should first consider where manufacturing inputs can be sourced locally. According to KPMG, "Africa has a wealth of mineral and agricultural resources that could be used as manufacturing inputs that give African manufacturers a competitive edge in years to come."[106] However, local suppliers lack quality and availability, with only a handful of African countries performing well on cross-national indicators on the quality and the quantity of local suppliers in the World Economic Forum's Global Competitive Index. Specifically, among the largest manufacturing markets, Côte d'Ivoire, Kenya, Morocco, and South Africa score highest across both indicators (figure 5.4), and a few smaller markets also perform relatively well in cross-national comparisons, such as Mauritius, Senegal, The Gambia, and Mali. However, many resource-rich manufacturing countries are also among the lowest ranked in terms of quality of governance and infrastructure, the burden of tax and trade regulations, and corruption, such as the DRC and Angola. In other words, it is hard to address supply- and policy-related constraints facing manufacturers at the same time in Africa.

Many governments in Africa have worked hard to grow their manufacturing sectors by reducing policy-related constraints, and even by implementing policy measures specifically intended to improve their attractiveness to investors, such as import restrictions for priority industries.[107] In Nigeria, for example, cement manufacturers have benefited from increased import duties and even the cessation of new import licenses in the sector. On the other hand, since Nigeria continues to be constrained by its political and regulatory environment—especially high levels of corruption, poverty, and bureaucratic red tape—investors might do well to look toward a similar, though more investor-friendly, policy climate in neighboring Ghana. Ghana has many challenges of its own, such as a recent bout of fiscal volatility caused by increasing government spending. However, it is currently ranked sixty-seventh in the world for its business climate according to the World Bank. Not to mention that its recent discoveries of gas deposits and development of processing facilities are likely to offset power shortages and

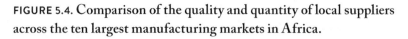

FIGURE 5.4. Comparison of the quality and quantity of local suppliers across the ten largest manufacturing markets in Africa.

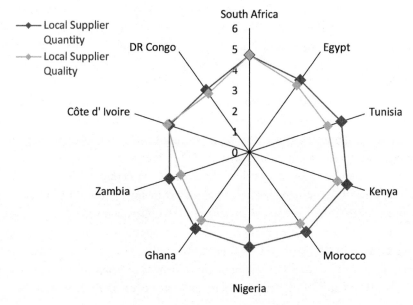

Source: Global Competitiveness Index 2017–18, World Economic Forum. Data for Côte d'Ivoire are from 2016–17, the most recent year available.

reliance on electricity imports, making it one of the most promising places for investment in Africa.[108]

In addition, the SEZs are considered a manageable and realistic option to overcome some of the policy-related constraints in developing countries in the short term. Due to its notable success in attracting investment and creating jobs, the concept of the SEZ as part of a national industrial development strategy has been adopted from the Chinese model. As China's experience shows, it is important that each SEZ model be adapted to the local context (i.e., endowments) and to a country's specific development goals. The government should also actively engage in monitoring, infrastructural support, and long-term planning and revision. Moreover, since the size of country-level consumer markets is relatively constrained in Africa, as compared to China, more regional integration will be necessary in order to create a comparable context for growth in manufacturing.[109]

At present, even in light of the cross-country variation described here, the best investment advice for manufacturers looking to invest in Africa is to identify optimal SEZs for the relevant subsector. These SEZs will be the first and priority recipients for government investment in infrastructural improvements; they have substantially lower barriers related to the time and cost of importing and exporting; and they confer initial tax benefits that help to offset start-up costs. For example, downtime related to electricity outages is much less frequent in Kenya's SEZs than it is for companies operating elsewhere in the country. It also takes the country fewer days to reestablish power and internet connections and to move goods across neighboring borders.[110] Identifying upcoming SEZs as they are in the planning and development phases will allow producers to benefit from a first-mover advantage and effectively scale up in the nascent market.

In this way, the strongest foundations for investment will be located in countries that demonstrate the necessary flexibility, coordination, and, especially, political commitment to full implementation of business-friendly regulations in SEZs, as well as simultaneous integration into regional economic communities (RECs). Such commitment appears relatively strong in South Africa and Zambia, where authority over SEZs has often been elevated to the highest levels of government. The commitment is less strong in Nigeria, again, where confusion between the national and state levels of government has led to coordination issues. However, a Federal Government Committee on Free Zone Reforms has been created in Nigeria in order to suggest policy recommendations for overcoming coordination issues and improving the administrative efficiency of SEZs.[111] It will remain to be seen whether such commitment exists in Ethiopia, where it has only recently established its first SEZ —the Chinese-managed "Eastern Industrial Zone (EIZ)," which is located 35 km southeast of Addis Ababa in Dukem, Oromia, and is connected to the capital, the Djibouti port, and other economic centers by both road and railway.[112]

Looking to the Future

A substantial amount of room remains for growth and expansion in Africa's manufacturing sector, and as the cost of labor is rising in other developing regions, the World Bank has suggested that these manufacturing jobs could migrate to Africa in the coming decades. Business-to-business spending in manufacturing in Africa will reach $666.3 billion by 2030, an increase of $201.28 billion from 2015. With the exception of a handful of countries,[113] however, industrialization in Africa remains a challenge, as the necessary economic and political foundations for the sector are just starting to take hold. In light of the region's relative deficiency of factories to date, some analysts have reached pessimistic conclusions about the potential for industrialization and, by extension, economic modernization in Africa.[114] Worryingly, exports of low-technology manufactured goods—a sector in which the region should have a comparative advantage on the world market—actually declined between 2000 and 2010. Meanwhile, resource extraction–related industry continues to dominate the sector, depressing per capita value added in manufacturing and making the macroeconomic climate vulnerable to commodity price shocks.[115]

On the other hand, Africa's manufacturing output is now keeping pace with the impressive rates of growth observed across the rest of the economy, as manufacturing's share of GDP has remained relatively constant in recent years, between 10 and 14 percent (see figure 5.1).[116] Many countries are also making significant progress in improving the climate for doing business, across a range of indicators relevant to manufacturing. Currently, sub-Saharan Africa has the largest share of countries that are making progress among all world regions, according to the World Bank, with forty-five out of forty-six countries measured improving their business regulatory environments over the past decade.[117] Citing these trends, some have suggested that Africa is likely to soon emulate the remarkable growth story of East Asia.[118]

Given its unique socioeconomic and demographic conditions, however, the Asian growth model cannot simply be transplanted in Africa. In the foreseeable future, the potential for Africa's manufacturing sector will be driven by the growing size of its low-cost workforce, its rapidly expanding and urbanizing consumer market, its untapped agricultural and resource endowments, growing economies of scale created by increasing integration of the RECs, and increasing public spending in education and infrastructure.[119] In order to address the remaining, nonstructural constraints that can be improved through political commitment, African Union member states have committed themselves to substantial public investment in infrastructure, specifically a high-speed rail network, oil and gas pipelines, information and communications technology broadband cables, and sea- and airports. All of this is part of the regional project to drive industrialization and to increase intra-African trade from 11 percent to nearly 50 percent of total trade by 2045.[120]

Moreover, the potential for the AfCFTA to facilitate structural transformation in Africa is big. Given the AfCFTA's market size of 1.2 billion people and over $3.4 trillion of cumulative GDP, a successful AfCFTA could increase the growth of the manufacturing sector and its value added given in Africa.[121] Some studies show that by creating a pan-African market, intra-Africa trade could increase by about 52 percent, resulting in an increase of African manufacturing exports.[122]

Ideally, this structural transformation of industry will proceed hand in hand with the region's other impending revolution—namely, in agriculture. Increasing productivity in both sectors has the potential to compound exponentially as part of a complementary value chain, with domestically manufactured chemicals and machinery feeding into agricultural production and agroprocessing plants, which provide the food and energy to meet growing African and global demand. Even beyond the agroindustry feedback loop, and in more technical and high-value manufacturing, US computer conglomerate IBM has recently suggested that Africa's capacity to leapfrog technologies has generated a market for African developers of computer software and smartphone apps.[123]

Across all subsectors and countries, Africa's industrial revolution appears imminent. Regional integration and transport infrastructure development could double the African-produced supply to local markets and increase revenues by $326 billion per year for manufacturers of consumer goods alone.[124] Given current patterns, Egypt, Nigeria, and South Africa are likely to be among the world's twenty-five largest economies in the next decade—becoming similar in size to Turkey or the Netherlands. A number of other African countries will continue to experience rapid industry-driven growth: Angola, Ethiopia, Ghana, Kenya, Mozambique, Tanzania, and Zambia, among others.[125] If interested parties are successful in pushing through investment-oriented reforms and in tapping the growing demand from African businesses and consumers, Africa's manufacturing output has the potential to surpass $1 trillion per year by 2025, with roughly half that production remaining on the continent and the rest exported to other world regions.[126]

SIX

Africa's Oil and Gas
Transformation and Potential

The discovery of the Jubilee Field off the coast of Ghana in 2007 drastically reconfigured the estimations of oil and gas potential all along Africa's Atlantic coastline. Soon after, offshore prospecting and development began in countries previously untouched by the hydrocarbon economy: Benin, Côte d'Ivoire, Guinea, Liberia, Sierra Leone, and others. In 2012, Togo was revealed to possess large oil reserves in its Dahomey Basin, which is part of the larger Atlantic Transform Margin that extends from waters belonging to Ghana eastward to Togo, Benin, and Nigeria.[1] More recently, enormous reserves of natural gas have been discovered in the waters off Tanzania and Mozambique, leading prospectors to shift their attention toward the potential of East Africa for the first time.

In many ways, the landscape of Africa's oil and gas sector is undergoing significant changes. Until recently, the sector was dominated by the exporting countries in North Africa and Nigeria. Now, Angola is poised to overtake Nigeria as Africa's top producer of crude oil within a decade, having exhibited the most rapid growth in fuel production on the continent over the past decade. Meanwhile, major industry analysts predict that Mozambique might soon emerge as the third-largest exporter of natural gas in the world.

Although oil and gas reserves have often been labeled as a curse in Africa, due to their association with corruption and political instability, the contribution of some multinational natural resource corporations to governance failure and corruption,[2] and the lack of linkages to other productive sectors of the economy, we will discuss whether this need be the case in the future given the diversity of institutions across the region, and the strategies to turn the potential curse into a blessing, as done by Norway, for example. While Diamond (2015) points out that some weak and fragile African states, such as Equatorial Guinea, may struggle to effectively manage oil and gas rents for positive economic and social gains, other major discoveries have occurred in countries that have made substantial gains in political accountability in recent years, such as Kenya and Ethiopia. It remains to be seen whether the governments of these countries will be able to use their newfound resource wealth to the benefit of the broader economy.

Background Facts and Trends

The first discoveries of crude oil and gas in Africa occurred in 1957–58 in Algeria, Gabon, and Nigeria, and oil production on the continent officially began in the 1960s. Except for a brief slowdown in the early 1980s caused by a dip in oil prices, total production has increased gradually from 2.2 million barrels per day (bpd) in 1965 to over 10 million bpd by 2006.[3] Over the first few decades, petroleum companies primarily focused on oil extraction in North Africa and the Gulf of Guinea since initial explorations in East Africa were deemed inadequate for development.[4]

ENDOWMENTS

There have been two major waves of exploration successes since the 1990s, when improvements in Africa's political and economic environment began to make the region more appealing to foreign oil companies. The first was a series of deepwater discoveries off the coasts of Nigeria and Angola in the 1990s, which exposed approximately 16 billion barrels of oil. At the turn of the century, it was thought that Africa possessed roughly 10 percent of the world's remaining crude oil reserves and 8 percent of natural gas reserves. Since then, however, almost 30 percent of all new discoveries of oil and gas worldwide have been located in Africa. This recent wave of discoveries has revealed new basins in Mauritania (2001), Uganda (2006), Kenya (2007), Mozambique and Tanzania (2010), Sierra Leone and Liberia (2010 and 2012), and Kenya (2012).[5] As a result, proven reserves of oil on the continent have increased by approximately 150 percent, from 53 billion barrels in 1980 to over 130 billion barrels at the end of 2013.[6] Over the full 30-year period, total rents from oil exports have nearly tripled, from $27.2 billion to $75.3 billion, and natural gas rents have massively increased, from just $694 million in 1985 to $14.3 billion in 2015.

Since oil and gas are geographically determined endowments, the sector is dominated by a handful of countries, five of which are among the top thirty oil-producing countries in the world.[7] While at least twelve countries in Africa have proven oil reserves of more than 500 million barrels, the region's four Organization of the Petroleum Exporting Countries (OPEC) member states are estimated to possess over 80 percent: Libya (48.5 billion barrels), Nigeria (37.1 billion barrels), Angola (12.7 billion barrels), and Algeria (12.2 billion barrels).[8]

ECONOMIC RELIANCE

In general, Africa's major fuel exporters tend to be heavily reliant on the oil and gas sector in economic terms. In the region's top-ten producers, oil revenues totaled $254 billion between 2011 and 2013 alone—an amount equivalent to 56 percent of those countries' total public revenues.

In comparison with other developing regions, however, especially the Middle East and central Europe, Africa's economy is not as heavily dependent on oil. In fact, since the region experienced its enormous economic boom over the past 10 years, the total GDP share of oil rents has decreased from about 11 percent to just over 2 percent (figure 6.1), even as the total volume of oil rents increased by more than 10 percent.

Import and Export Trends

Fossil fuels are expected to continue supplying the majority of the world's energy needs in the coming decades, with the African Development Bank predicting an increase in consumption by 57 percent over the next 10 years.

Sub-Saharan Africa remains a net exporter of hydrocarbons, with the total annual value of fuel exports now exceeding that of developing Latin America (figure 6.2). Renewed interest from the world's major oil consumers has driven much of this trend. For example, due to recent efforts by the United States to diversify its oil imports, sub-Saharan Africa now provides the US with more oil than Saudi Arabia—approximately 18 percent of total US oil imports.[9] Oil exports to the US are even expected to increase to

FIGURE 6.1. Comparison of dependence on oil rents as share of total GDP across developing regions.

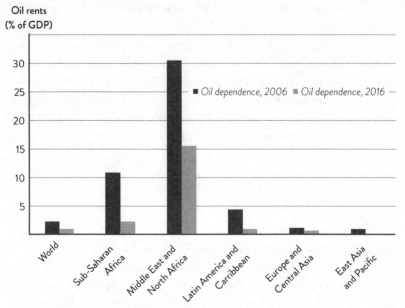

Source: Data from World Development Indicators (2017). High-income countries are excluded from all regions, except the "world average" category.

25 percent over the next decade. At the same time, China is projected to surpass even the US as a destination for African oil exports, with Chinese officials seeking to increase their country's reliance on African crude oil to 40 percent of total oil imports by 2025.[10]

A few years ago, energy analysts were predicting that Africa will be able to increase its oil production by between 25 and 40 percent in the coming decade.[11] However, due to the decline in the spot price of oil and gas since 2014—as well as production interruptions caused by the political instability and conflicts in Libya, Sudan, Egypt, and Algeria—Africa's fuel exports are currently declining.[12] In 2013, the continent's net oil exports decreased from an average of over 6 million barrels per day (bpd) over the previous 5 years to 5.2 million bpd, and gas exports reached 80.9 billion m³ in the same year, after having peaked at 111.4 billion m³ in 2008.[13]

Notably, the vast majority of recent energy discoveries in Africa have been in gas, leading industry analysts to predict that the region's largest future gains will be in natural gas production.[14] Natural gas resources in

FIGURE 6.2. Comparison of change in fuel exports and imports across developing regions, 2000–2016.

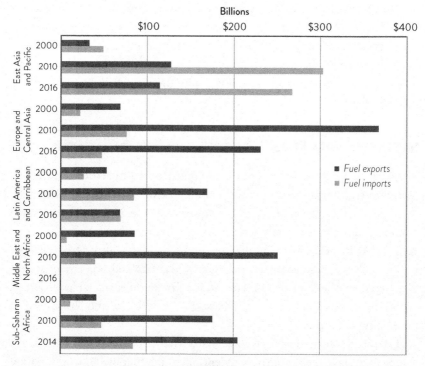

Source: All figures calculated from World Development Indicators (2017). Note that data are missing for the Middle East and North Africa region in 2016 due to political instability. High-income countries are excluded from all regions for comparative purposes.

West Africa possess more growth potential than in North Africa, which has already been producing large volumes of gas over a longer period. Algeria was the first country in the world to export liquid natural gas (LNG) with the construction of its Arzew plant in 1964, and Libya followed soon after in 1971. Nigeria is now the largest single LNG producer in Africa, exporting 22.4 billion m³ in 2013, while Angola just became the region's newest gas exporter.[15] At present, roughly three-quarters of Africa's natural gas is produced in North Africa, with a further 23 percent from West Africa—primarily Nigeria and Equatorial Guinea—although the International Energy Agency projects annual increases in West African gas production to average 5.6 percent per year through 2040.[16] Currently, most of the region's exports are in the form of LNG, with the remaining 45 percent of gas exports traveling via pipeline, mostly to Europe.

The largest increase in energy consumption worldwide is expected to occur within Africa itself—more than a 63 percent increase by 2035 according to the US Energy Information Administration.[17] By this time, especially if commodity prices rebound to their pre-2014 levels, cumulative investments in energy production and exploration in Africa are projected to reach $2 trillion.[18]

Importance of the Sector in Terms of Economic Development

The wave of recently discovered oil and gas deposits in Africa has the potential to transform the economic—and political—landscape of the continent, especially since so many major new reserves seem to be concentrated in countries not traditionally associated with hydrocarbons, such as Ghana, Kenya, Mauritius, Senegal, Tanzania, and Uganda. In order to drive economic growth, these countries must actively create and implement strategies to reduce the tendency for economic reliance on extractable resources, especially oil, to dampen the prospects for growth and modernization in developing countries.

Literature on the resource curse states that dependence on natural resource exports makes countries susceptible to fluctuations in world market prices of primary commodities. The boom-and-bust cycles of oil prices can enhance the volatility of economies that rely on fuel exports by increasing inflation and national debt and distorting exchange rates.[19] Furthermore, this volatility itself has a negative impact on the potential for foreign investment in productive sectors of the economy, such as manufacturing. Moreover, oil rents provide governments with revenues that replace taxation as the primary source of funding, creating an accountability gap between political leaders and their populations. Absent the need to rely on tax revenue, there is little incentive for officials to provide the kinds of public goods that contribute to development more broadly, such as education, health care, and a robust national infrastructure.[20]

However, in recent years, a number of scholars have started to question the logic of the resource curse argument, particularly its failure to operate in a systematic way beyond the Arab Gulf states.[21] For example, Haber and Menaldo (2011) argue that, rather than a curse, resource rents are actually a necessity for governments in weak, poor states where the masses are not yet a good source of tax revenue.

Analyses of Africa's oil and gas producers have shown that the hydrocarbons sector has minimal positive linkages with the wider economy. In Angola, one of the largest oil exporters on the continent, the sector employs less than 1 percent of the total workforce, and many of the region's oil-producing states have some of the highest levels of income inequality in the region—including Angola, Equatorial Guinea, Gabon, and Nigeria—and international efforts at diversification have yielded few results. At the same time, according to KPMG, large portions of the populations in these countries view the low cost of fuel, maintained through economically distorting fuel subsidies, as "the only benefit of living in an oil-rich nation."[22]

On the other hand, looking at variation across Africa, the empirical evidence is mixed regarding the relationship between resource wealth and economic development. In 2016, countries with a sizeable GDP share of oil rents exhibited just as much variation on levels of per capita income as non–oil producers. Similarly, when we examine Africa's most recent economic boom (2006–2010), the oil-producing countries at the beginning of the period did not appear prone to higher or lower growth rates—in fact, Angola experienced the highest average annual growth rate of the entire region, at 12.6 percent.

In the past, attempts to set aside surplus oil revenues as a stopgap during bust cycles have met the challenges of governance: Nigeria's Excess Crude Account (ECA), for example, lacks an appropriate legal framework for the allocation of needed revenues and has been crippled by corruption and mismanagement.[23] As a potential solution to these challenges, Diamond (2015) has proposed a more radical approach that involves directly allocating revenues from fuel exports to the population as taxable income, which could help to "catapult developing countries into genuine economic and social development" (295).

Given that notable oil and gas discoveries have recently occurred in African countries that have already made relatively significant gains in improving the quality of governance and accountability, there is potential for a positive feedback loop to emerge between growth in the hydrocarbons sector and in the economy more broadly if governments can build sustainable linkages between hydrocarbons' extraction and other sectors. There is also the potential to reduce the links between natural resources and inequality through further improvements to governance and accountability, including to the provision of licenses, to taxation, and to the limitation of illicit financial flows.[24]

Key Drivers of Growth

Given the lack of direct linkages between hydrocarbons and other sectors of the economy, growth in the oil and gas industry is largely driven by underlying structural conditions, which can often have unpredictable and competing effects. Eighteen of the forty largest discoveries of oil and gas deposits between January 2015 and July 2016 were located in Africa. While some of these new deposits are in countries already exporting hydrocarbons on the continent—such as Angola, Egypt, and the Republic of the Congo—many are in new and surprising markets (table 6.1). Moreover, fifteen of the African discoveries were gas, suggesting that the future trajectory for growth in the sector might depend on developing capacity for extraction, refinement, and transport of LNG, and increasing demand for its use as an energy source within Africa.

The decline in the world price of oil and gas has lowered expected returns from investment, particularly in these new frontiers, which tend to lack existing infrastructure. Combined with the shift in global norms toward a focus on renewable energy sources, the potential for long-term sectoral growth in countries known to have large reserves might be more constrained than in the past. However, given the current rate at which energy consumption is increasing—both across the world and within Africa—growing demand for carbon-based fuel is likely to continue for at least the foreseeable future.

COMMODITY PRICES

Given the large increase in the world market price of oil and gas starting in the late 1990s, the recent sharp decline came as a surprise to sectoral analysts.[25] Despite rebounding quickly after the global financial crisis, the world market price of crude oil fell by half between 2008 and 2015. The price of natural gas, on the other hand, never experienced a recovery period and still stands at less than one-third of its 2008 level.

While this trend has been an economic boon to some of the region's fuel importers, it has had a negative impact on the region's major exporters.[26] Since 2010, the annual growth rate in sectoral productivity among Africa's largest fuel exporters—Algeria, Angola, Nigeria, and Sudan—has decreased from 3.9 to 1.4 percent.[27] Moreover, with market prices at their current levels, there is a reduced likelihood that some of Africa's current

TABLE 6.1. Largest new discoveries of oil and gas in Africa, 2015–2016.

Country	Location	Year (ranking)	Operating company	Oil/gas	Estimated size (million BoE*)
Egypt	Zohr Phase 2	2015 (1)	Eni	Gas	2,214.6
Mozambique	Area 6	2016 (1)	Petronas	Gas	1,198
Mauritania	Ahmcyim	2015 (2)	Kosmos Energy	Gas	1,096.9
Egypt	Zohr Phase 1	2015 (3)	Eni	Gas	989
Angola	Katambi	2016 (2)	BP	Gas	705.4
Mozambique	Area 4	2016 (3)	Eni	Gas	544.3
Egypt	Zohr (LNG)	2015 (6)	Eni	Gas	298.4
Angola	Zalophus	2016 (7)	Cobalt Internat'l	Gas	248.1
Tanzania	Mdalasini	2015 (12)	Statoil	Gas	162.9
Angola	Block 19	2016 (12)	BP	Oil	162.2
Angola	Zalophus	2016 (13)	Cobalt Internat'l	Cond.†	148.5
Angola	Katambi	2016 (17)	BP	Cond.	139.5
Angola	Block 19	2016 (18)	BP	Gas	136.5
Tanzania	Mnazi Bay	2016 (19)	Maurel & Prom	Gas	136.1
Congo-Brazzaville	Nkala Marine	2015 (15)	Eni	Gas	134.1
Egypt	Nooros	2015 (17)	Petrobel	Gas	84.3
Tanzania	Mbakofi	2015 (18)	Dodsal Resources	Gas	83.1

Barrel of oil equivalent.
†*Condensate*

Source: Rystad Energy. Ranking number represents the global ranking in terms of the size of the deposit in the calendar year of the discovery.

importers with recently discovered deposits—such as Kenya, Mozambique, Tanzania, and Uganda—will be able to transition into net exporters in the near future.[28]

Companies working in the industry continue to cite the current market price of oil as the primary impediment to doing (and growing) business in the sector in the near future, resulting in an estimated $300 billion in deferred final investment decisions.[29] The number of operating oil rigs in Africa has decreased by 7 percent since the start of the global commodity dip (although this is less than the global average of 26 percent).[30] Many companies have also expressed their intention to cease exploration activities in deepwater formations off the coast of Angola, Gabon, and the Republic of the Congo, which are too expensive for profitable extraction operations under current market conditions.[31]

Even if demand for hydrocarbons continues to increase over the long term as expected, a corresponding increase in supply therefore remains wholly dependent on whether market prices rebound. As long as prices remain low, existing projects are prone to cancellation—as many already have been in the Gulf of Guinea, especially Nigeria and Ghana, where extraction is relatively expensive compared to North Africa—and future investment is likely to be put on hold.[32]

FUEL CONSUMPTION

Despite rising global awareness of climate change and an increasing emphasis on moving toward renewable energy sources, an explicit priority in recent African development programs, one notable impact of the sharp decline in the price of oil and gas is an increase in fuel consumption, particularly among the world's poorest consumers.[33] Currently, Africa accounts for roughly 10 percent of all oil and gas exports worldwide, but only 4 percent of global energy consumption. However, the growing gap between growing demand and supply of energy within Africa represents a "new frontier" for the sector. Since 2000, Africa's consumption of oil and natural gas has increased by 45 percent—much more rapidly than the change in domestic production (figures 6.3 and 6.4). Yet more than two-thirds of African households still lack reliable access to electricity, while 34 billion m³ of the natural gas that is produced on the continent is flared (or combusted)—an amount equal to nearly half of the region's current gas consumption.

As Africa approaches its period of rapid economic transformation and modernization, household energy consumption will be enhanced by the rise in income levels and purchasing power, while the rise of industry will generate business-to-business markets for fuels. Given that the majority of new hydrocarbon discoveries in Africa are gas, the construction of gas-fired power stations presents an opportunity to increase the profitability of these new energy discoveries while also capitalizing on the worldwide shift toward a lower-carbon economy.[34]

Looking beyond Africa, global energy consumption is projected to grow at an increasingly rapid rate. As figure 6.5 illustrates, total worldwide consumption is estimated to increase by roughly two-thirds of its current level by 2040, nearly doubling the growth rate witnessed over the past 25 years.

Even as the world finds new solutions to meet its energy needs, such as solar and wind farms, hydrocarbons will continue to serve as the primary source of fuel for the foreseeable future, particularly in the developing world, which will account for the bulk of the increase in energy consumption in the coming decades (figure 6.5).

INVESTMENT CLIMATE

Beyond consumption needs, there are a number of reasons to remain optimistic about the prospects for Africa's energy sector in the near future. Energy production in Africa is already relatively cost competitive when compared to other regions, even at low world market prices.

Moreover, the increasing willingness of African governments to act as development partners and create a favorable environment for investment in the sector makes investing in the region attractive. A number of governments have initiated promising reforms of their regulatory, fiscal, and licensing systems in recent years. Interventions in Angola, Egypt, and Ni-

FIGURE 6.3. Change in consumption and production of oil in Africa, 1985–2018.

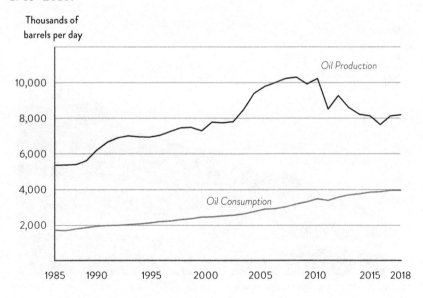

Source: BP Statistical Review of World Energy, 2019.

FIGURE 6.4. Change in consumption and production of natural gas in Africa, 1985–2018.

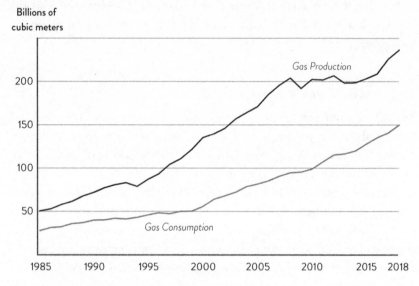

Source: BP Statistical Review of World Energy, 2019.

FIGURE 6.5. Growth in combined world energy consumption, by region, 1965–2017.

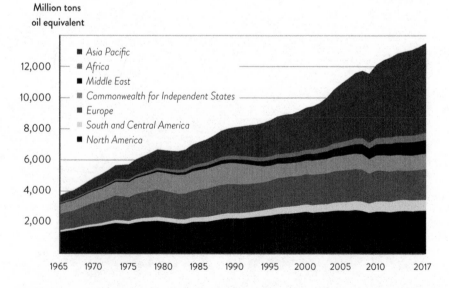

Source: Networked readiness ranking from the World Economic Forum.

geria, for example, aim to improve efficiency, transparency, accountability, and contract enforcement.[35] One particularly noteworthy target would be to incentivize investment in oil refineries, since this is an existing infrastructure gap that raises transit costs and limits profitability.[36] Recognizing these changes, companies working in Africa's oil and gas sector have identified improvements in legal and regulatory efficiencies and in extractive and distribution infrastructures as the leading drivers of investment in the near future.[37] With governments and the private sector working together to redress remaining gaps, such as in infrastructure and electrification, the supply of African energy to African markets alone is estimated to more than double in the next 10 years.[38]

Key Players

Large western multinationals have historically been major investors in Africa's oil and gas and will continue to play a large role in the sector. However, African companies and nontraditional partners are beginning to play a larger role as demand for energy continues to increase worldwide.

WESTERN MULTINATIONALS

Historically, the development of the oil and gas industries in Africa has required massive external investment in infrastructure and technologies. In particular, the "upstream" components of the oil business—exploration and production—continue to involve large foreign investors. As a result, large, well-known multinational corporations are heavily active in Africa's oil economy (table 6.1).

By 2007, ExxonMobil (US)—the world's largest oil corporation and one of the biggest private foreign investors in Africa—was extracting nearly 800 million barrels per day from its African rigs, and it has committed a further $24 billion to exploration and development in recent years.[39] Roughly 20 percent of the total oil production of Italy's Eni comes from its African operations, and it has plans to invest approximately $25 billion more in Africa's oil and gas sector, representing 60 percent of the company's planned future investment.[40] Over the past 10 years, investment from BP (United Kingdom) and ChevronTexaco (United States) has contributed to Angola's emergence as a major oil-producing and exporting country—roughly $8 billion from BP alone. Other major players include Royal Dutch Shell, operating in fourteen African countries; China's Sinopec, operating in nine African countries; France's Total, in eight African countries; and Malaysia's Petronas and Norway's Statoil, both operating in three African countries.

Despite these developments of oil- and gas-related infrastructure in Africa, many Western multinationals' involvement has been criticized for feeding corruption and political instability.[41] In 2011, for example, Shell and Eni purchased a western Nigerian oil field for $1.1 billion, and rather than going to the Nigerian treasury, the funds knowingly went directly to a company owned by Nigeria's then oil minister.[42] Many of these companies have worked to block legislative reforms that would improve transparency and oversight of the industry and make questionable activities more difficult. For the past 20 years, France's TotalFinaElf (ELF) has been accused of political meddling to influence policy in oil-rich countries like Gabon and Angola.[43] Rarely have there been any legal ramifications, so it is apparent that the legal systems require more mechanisms to check these issues of political tampering with the oil and gas sector.[44]

DOMESTIC COMPANIES

While the large multinationals dominated Africa's oil and gas scene in the early decades of its development, the role of African national oil companies (NOCs) has become increasingly more important in recent years. The centralized, and often patronage-based, system of domestic economic planning in the region has resulted in blurred lines between public and private corporations, particularly in the energy sector, with most oil-producing countries having a majority—or fully—state-owned NOC.[45]

- *Nigerian National Petroleum Corporation* (NNPC). Founded in 1977 with headquarters in Abuja, NNPC sold around one million barrels per day as of 2015, almost half of Nigeria's total production.[46] Nigeria currently produces the most oil by volume in Africa, but the NNPC has recently come under fire for failing to remit $20 billion in oil revenues to the Nigerian treasury over a 2-year period. The state-owned company is also responsible for managing joint ventures between the government and foreign multinationals for offshore exploration and production.

- *Sonatrach* (Algeria). Established in 1963, its primary output is natural gas, but it is also the largest producer of oil among the African NOCs and the eleventh largest oil consortium in the world. Revenues reached $76.1 billion in 2012, over 30 percent of Algeria's GNP. It boasts a diversified business program, engaging in exploration, extraction, transport, refinement, and petrochemistry, and employs 120,000 people as of 2010.

- *Sonangol* (Angola). Established in 1976 with headquarters in Luanda, the Angolan parastatal has a global portfolio, with contracts in Asia, South America, and Iraq.[47] The company has been responsible for the development of sizeable public works projects and servicing public debt with revenues from oil sales. It recently partnered with Eni on public infrastructure projects with the goal of developing a major oil refinery.[48]

- *Sasol Limited* (South Africa). Founded in 1950 and based in Johannesburg, the company is a major African company despite the fact that South Africa has relatively small domestic oil reserves, as it has oil exploration and production operations on six continents. The company employs 34,000 people with revenues of $21.78 billion to date.

- *National Oil Corporation* (Libya). Founded in 1970 with headquarters in Tripoli, it produces crude oil, natural gas, and petrochemicals. Combined with a number of small subsidiaries, it represents roughly 70 percent of the country's oil production. One of these subsidiaries, The Arabian Gulf Oil Company (Agaco), now operates independently. Oil reserves in Libya were estimated at 46.42 billion barrels in 2010, the most on the continent.

- *Sudapet* (Sudan). Headquartered in Khartoum since 1997, the state-owned Sudan National Petroleum Corporation no longer produces oil, but it oversees the Sudanese Ministry for Energy and Mining's profits from concessions to foreign companies. Sudan has the sixth-highest volume of proven oil reserves in Africa: 5 billion barrels as of 2010.

Other relevant African NOCs include the Ghana National Petroleum Corporation (GNPC), the National Petroleum Company of the Congo (SNPC, Congo-Brazzaville), Vegas Oil and Gas (Egypt), Entreprise Tunisienne d'Activites Petroliere (ETAP, Tunisia), Madagascar Oil, and Petro Gabon.

NEW PARTNERS

Since the end of the Cold War, Africa has become central to the interests of the world's most rapidly developing and increasingly energy-reliant economies, such as Brazil, India, Malaysia, and South Korea. For example, the International Energy Agency predicts that India will need to import 90 percent of its petroleum supply by 2025 in order to keep up with projected energy consumption. Its Oil and Natural Gas Corporation (ONGC) has begun to seek deals across the African continent in recent years, and it successfully secured a memorandum with Angola in 2010.[49]

Chinese national oil companies in particular have invested generously in Africa over the last decade. The largest, Sinopec, currently has operations in at least nine African countries, with others focused on oil extraction in Nigeria (CNODC), Ethiopia (ZPEB), and Sudan (CNBC). Chinese officials recently referred to oil as "the crux of the Sino-Angolan relationship." The two countries have developed a mutually beneficial trade arrangement whereby Angolan oil is exchanged for bilateral loans and infrastructure projects built and paid for by the Chinese government.[50] For example, in 2014, China's export investment bank loaned $2 billion to Angola's Sonangol for the development of an oil refinery.[51]

The strategy of using the oil trade to fill gaps in infrastructure, as well as in governance more broadly, is becoming increasingly common in other oil-rich African countries as well. The Nigerian government, for example, agreed to grant certain oil concessions only after commitment of $7 billion in investments, specifically earmarked for the rehabilitation of two power stations and the provision of weapons to combat rebel forces in the Niger Delta.[52]

Opportunities

All along Africa's western coastline south of Nigeria—from Cameroon and Gabon to Angola—the vast majority of oil reserves are located offshore, mainly in deepwater, pre-salt formations. Because the technical and capital requirements of exploration and production in these conditions are particularly high, the decline in world oil prices has led analysts to predict a suspension of exploration and extraction projects, especially new drilling. Angola's Sonangol, for example, has cut spending on exploration over the past 2 years.[53]

If oil prices remain low for the foreseeable future, offshore exploration off the West Coast of Africa is likely to be too expensive for continued investment, especially the deepwater reserves of Angola, Gabon, and the Republic of the Congo. The investment environment in North Africa also remains relatively unfavorable under current market conditions, particularly since production costs for the recently discovered shale deposits would be substantially higher than for conventional oil and gas due to the costs of hydraulic fracturing and horizontal drilling. Out of seventeen Algerian shale blocks on offer in a licensing round in September 2014, only one bid was made.[54] Recent projections about the future of Africa's oil and gas sector have, therefore, been less optimistic than in the past due to current market conditions.

On the other hand, recent discoveries of large reserves of hydrocarbons in Africa, especially in natural gas and including new and underexplored locations, mean that the long-term prospects for investment in the sector are bright. Table 6.2 lists the top fifteen African countries by remaining proven reserves of crude oil and natural gas, respectively, as well as estimated quantities.

Many of these countries already have well-developed energy sectors and a high GDP reliance on fuel exports, indicating that infrastructures already exist for exploration, extraction, and distribution. Although initial start-up costs for investing in these countries might be comparatively low, the scale of new discoveries and low level of market saturation in other countries point to opportunities to gain extensive market share for investors willing to devote capital toward needed infrastructure. Figure 6.6 provides a comparison of Africa's ten largest fuel exporters by annual value of exports and the general quality of infrastructure. In light of these findings, we analyze four particularly exciting opportunities for future investment: Algeria, Ghana, East Africa, and, more tentatively, Nigeria.

ALGERIA

Of the five largest oil and gas producers in Africa, Algeria presents the most attractive investment opportunity in terms of the quality of existing infrastructure. By African standards, it scores particularly highly on

TABLE 6.2. Largest proven reserves of oil and natural gas in Africa.

Top 15—crude oil reserves	Quantity (billions bbl)	Top 15—natural gas reserves	Quantity (billions m³)
Libya	48.36	Nigeria	5,110
Nigeria	37	Algeria	4,500
Algeria	12	Mozambique	2,832
Angola	8.4	Egypt	2,186
Sudan	5	Libya	1,505
Egypt	4.4	Angola	308
South Sudan	3.75	Cameroon	135.1
Uganda	2.5	Congo, Republic of	90.61
Gabon	2	Tunisia	65.13
Congo, Republic of	1.6	South Sudan	63.71
Chad	1.5	Namibia	62.29
Equatorial Guinea	1.1	Rwanda	65.63
Ghana	0.66	Equatorial Guinea	36.81
Tunisia	0.4	Gabon	28.32
Cameroon	0.2	Côte d'Ivoire	28.32

Source: CIA World Factbook, January 1, 2016.

indicators related to the business costs of crime, violence, and terrorism, as well as corruption levels, according to the World Economic Forum's Global Competitiveness Index (2017). Although it has fallen in the World Bank's Ease of Doing Business Index rankings owing to political instability over the past few years, the size of its remaining reserves and the high likelihood of a return to political order point to positive prospects for investment in the near future. Algeria possesses the second-largest known quantities of proved natural gas reserves in Africa (4.5 trillion m³) and the third-largest reserves of crude oil (12 billion bbl), coming in just behind Nigeria in both categories (see table 6.2).

In addition, a 2013 report published by the U.S. Energy Information Administration (EIA) revealed that Algeria has almost 20 trillion m³ of recoverable shale gas reserves, the third highest in the world—after China and Argentina—and more than four times the country's proven reserves of

FIGURE 6.6. Market opportunity comparison of Africa's top oil and gas exporters.

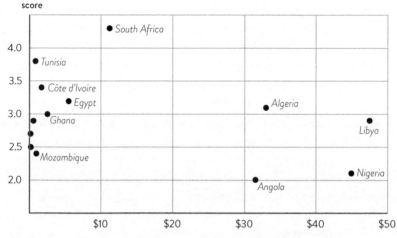

Source: Fuel export value figures from World Development Indicators (2015). Note that Sudan is excluded due to missing data. The latest figures available for Libya are from 2010. World Economic Forum figures are from the 2016 report.

conventional gas.[55] The national company Sonatrach already has extensive plans to invest and develop the shale sector, and the Algerian government has been active in attracting investment in its energy sector since production levels started declining in recent years. In 2014, thirty-three blocks with high shale potential were offered to foreign bidders, resulting in at least five contracts between Sonatrach and foreign companies.[56] Algeria is also thought to possess noteworthy reserves of shale oil. The commercial viability of these newly identified oil and gas reserves has yet to be determined, though, as it will be necessary to drill hundreds of test wells in order to precisely verify their potential.[57]

GHANA

In Ghana, production recently launched at the Tweneboah, Enyenra, and Ntomme oil fields and the Sankofa gas project is likely to result in a twofold increase in total fuel production in the coming years.[58] Oil extraction in

Ghana already has a lower break-even price than in Nigeria, at $67/barrel (bbl) compared to $80/bbl, and analysts predict that this will make Ghanaian oil profitable within the next year. Tullow Oil estimates that operating costs in the Jubilee Field averaged just $10 per barrel in 2014, and it has plans to maintain its ongoing extractive operations in Ghana despite the current world market for oil.[59]

Recognizing the importance of the energy sector to economic stability and growth, with oil and mining combining for 66 percent of total exports, the Ghanaian government has made significant strides toward improving the attractiveness of investing in its energy sector.[60] A Gas Master Plan (2016–2014) was approved in June 2016, which contains a broad outlook for increasing leverage over the country's gas assets. A new petroleum law—the Extractive Industries Transparency Initiative—has also improved the process of obtaining licenses and contracts for oil and gas concessions.

Despite these moves in the right direction, challenges remain in the effective implementation of proposed policies and effective management of resource extraction. The Public Interest and Accountability Committee intended to oversee the sector suffers from budgetary shortfalls and remains heavily reliant on donor support. Oil companies working in Ghana continue to complain about the increasing burden of direct and indirect taxation, rising inflation and interest rates, and currency instability, much of which has been caused by the government's growing fiscal deficit.[61]

EAST AFRICA

Beyond Sudan, previous exploration for hydrocarbons in East Africa had revealed a few minor deposits in Tanzania and Mozambique deemed insufficient to warrant development, leading oil and gas companies to focus largely on North Africa and the Gulf of Guinea.[62] However, in 2006, Tullow Oil and Heritage discovered the largest onshore deposit of oil in Africa on the border of Uganda and the Democratic Republic of the Congo—over 2 billion barrels.[63] Since then, and with further discoveries of natural gas in Mozambique and Tanzania, East Africa has emerged as a promising frontier for oil and gas production.[64] The Comoro Islands, for example, remain largely unexplored, though the first permits were granted to a number of small energy companies in 2014.[65]

Large discoveries of natural gas in the offshore territories of Tanzania and Mozambique in the past few years have led the two countries to be dubbed Africa's newest "lion cubs."[66] Mozambique's proven gas reserves have included one of the most significant hydrocarbon discoveries of the last decade and increased from 126 billion m³ in 2013 to 2.8 trillion m³ in 2014, with the Rovuma Basin alone containing roughly 175 trillion cubic feet. This finding poises Mozambique to become the fourth-largest LNG exporter in the world after Qatar, Australia, and the US. According to the IMF, however, an estimated $24 billion will be necessary in infrastructure developments in order to extract, transport, and process the natural gas. Anadarko and Eni have since announced plans to build four train lines to transport LNG by 2020, with a combined capacity of 27 billion m³ per year. In a further signal of the potential for returns on investment, a report by Standard Bank estimates the internal rate of return on Anadarko's Area 1 concessions in Mozambique at 12.2 percent based on current gas prices.[67]

Despite enormous potential, the primary challenge to growth in East Africa's energy sector is geography and infrastructure given the nascence of the discoveries.[68] Estimates of commercially viable oil reserves in Uganda have recently increased to as much as 6.5 billion barrels,[69] but the proven oil reserves in Uganda and Kenya are isolated and far inland, in the Hoima and Turkana districts, respectively, as much as 1,300 km from the coast. In recent years, the governments of the two countries have been active in attracting investors and engineers to advance their respective pipeline projects that will connect inland extractive regions to the coast, and it is expected that this development will soon allow these countries to become oil exporters.[70] According to recent reports, Tullow Oil and its partners have already started extracting oil in Lokichar and rely on trucking exports to Mombasa as a temporary measure until the pipeline is completed.[71] In Tanzania and Mozambique, new LNG plants will need to be built before the extractable resources are viable for distribution, requiring as much as $24 billion in infrastructure investment. Anadarko and Eni have plans to build four trains to transport LNG by 2020, with a combined capacity of 27 billion m³, with further plans for several more trains to be constructed by 2025.[72]

East African governments have worked to improve the climate for investment in oil and gas. Tanzania, for example, passed three laws in July 2015 in order to stabilize the legal and institutional climate: the Petroleum Act, the Extractive Industries Transparency and Accountability Act, and the Oil and Gas Revenues Management Act.[73] However, lack of experience and the absence of clear petroleum sector legislation have led to disputes, for example, between the Ugandan government and Tullow Oil in 2010.[74]

NIGERIA

Nigeria is the largest fuel exporter by value in all of Africa, and the size of its remaining reserves of oil and natural gas are second and first in the region, respectively. In fact, some industry analysts claim that the reserves of natural gas could be more than three times the current estimate of 5.1 trillion cubic meters.[75] Moreover, while the quality of infrastructure is relatively low and improvements needed in power supply, pipelines, and refineries, the cost of offshore oil drilling in Nigeria remains particularly low and free from the risks associated with the lack of security in many parts of the country.

On the other hand, due to its heavy reliance on fuel exports and the decline in the world market price for oil, the Nigerian economy is in a period of recession—it shrank by 0.36 percent in the first quarter of 2016 and by 2.06 percent in the second.[76] This, combined with the threat of attacks by nonstate armed groups on oil facilities, resulted in a decline in oil production volumes by 17.5 percent between 2015 and 2016.[77] Although fuel rents represent less than 4 percent of Nigeria's total GDP, oil exports account for 90 percent of the country's foreign exchange earnings and 80 percent of government revenue, suggesting that there are likely to be substantial spillover effects across the economy—as well as in the development and maintenance of much-needed infrastructure—if commodity prices do not rebound. Nigeria's "break-even" price of $80 per barrel of oil is almost twice the current level, at which the country stands to lose $45 billion per year in oil revenues.[78] Net portfolio investment inflows declined from $26.4 billion to $1.1 billion between 2012 and 2014. One of the largest companies working in the region, ConocoPhilips, sold its entire Nigerian operations in 2013 for $1.79 billion citing the economic outlook.[79] Some analysts fear a full reversal of capital flows in the near future, which could lead to further devaluations of the naira, and Nigeria's removal from the JP Morgan Government Bond Index.[80]

Nigeria has also faced substantial problems with corruption linkages in its oil and gas industry and, as a result, has been held up as a prime example of the oil curse phenomenon in Africa. According to the World Economic Forum's most recent *Global Competitiveness Report* (2017), Nigeria receives one of the lowest scores in the world for "Ethics and Corruption"—2.16 out of a possible 7. Its national oil company, the Nigerian National Petroleum Corporation (NNPC), was worth roughly $41 billion as of 2013 and accounted for the largest revenue stream for the federal government, selling 1 million barrels of oil per day, or half of the total production of the country. However, in 2014 the NNPC came under accusations from the central bank that $20 billion of its sales revenues over 2 years remained unaccounted for in treasury receipts.[81] This has been attributed to faulty crude-for-refined-product swap deals with private oil companies that were brokered by former President Goodluck Jonathan, reportedly to avoid domestic fuel shortages.[82]

Observers are more optimistic about the future of transparency and anticorruption measures under current president Muhammadu Buhari, particularly in tackling NNPC performance.[83] Already, a former oil minister is under investigation for involvement in the mishandling of funds, as are some private purchasing companies, and Buhari's administration has earmarked an estimated $10 billion from NNPC sales to be transferred to Nigeria's state governments, many of which are in a state of fiscal crisis.[84] Moreover, the recent passage of the Petroleum Industry Bill—which had lingered in parliament since first being introduced in 2003, creating uncertainty that hindered new investment—seeks specifically to increase transparency and improve governance of the NNPC.[85]

Challenges

Through a survey of businesses working in the industry, Pricewaterhouse-Coopers (PwC) reveals the most commonly cited challenges of developing an oil and gas business in Africa. Some of these issues have dramatically increased in salience in recent years, especially domestic taxation requirements and host governments relations. Others—such as the regulatory framework, corruption, infrastructure, and local capacity—have remained relatively constant over time. The following sections deal with the major challenges in turn, as well as the issue of political conflict and violence in the oil-producing states, before identifying strategies for mitigating risk and doing business effectively in Africa's oil and gas sector.

REGULATORY ENVIRONMENT AND UNCERTAINTY

Political instability, poor contract enforcement, and fears about expropriation of concessions are frequently cited as hazards of doing business in Africa. Indeed, many examples exist: Madagascar's transitional government threatened to reclaim major oil fields, which has impeded foreign investment; a tax dispute between the Ugandan government and Tullow Oil recently resulted in the repossession of an oil field; and the DRC government has awarded the same oil concession in its Virunga National Park to several different companies in recent years, even under public scrutiny from environmental activist groups.[86] In Algeria, an unfavorable hydrocarbon law and presidential decree passed in 2005 and 2006, respectively, were directly responsible for a 20 percent decline in production over the next 5 years.

Many energy companies working in Africa have reported difficulty in obtaining government permission and contracts for new projects. In countries that have only recently discovered hydrocarbon potential, like Mozambique, the bureaucracy does not yet exist to handle the intricacies and scale of oil and gas projects, and governments often lack a complete understanding of the risks incurred by various players.[87] In Uganda, a moratorium was recently imposed on new licensing until a revised oil bill could be passed by parliament.[88] Recent reports indicate that investment in oil refineries has been particularly hampered by uncertainties about government intentions to deregulate the downstream sector of production.[89]

CORRUPTION

The issue of bureaucratic and regulatory uncertainty is closely linked to levels of corruption, a problem especially pronounced in Africa's hydrocarbon sector. Analysts highlight the risks of corruption at several stages of the process, such as in the awarding of licenses, negotiation of terms of the contract, and transfer of revenues.[90]

Nowhere has this problem been better illustrated than in Nigeria, where the national oil company NNPC failed to remit $20 billion in oil revenues to the government treasury over a 20-month period in 2013–14, when oil prices were at an all-time high. Angola's Sonangol has also been associated with suspicious budgetary shortfalls of $4.2 billion in the process of bankrolling public works projects and servicing public debt with off-the-books transactions.[91]

The problems of bribery, favoritism, and misappropriation of funds often result in unforeseen costs for oil companies, which reduce the profitability of investment, especially because illegally secured contracts are unenforceable and subject to expropriation. Beyond the commercial costs, there are also reputational and legal risks. Investigation of NNPC's revenue with-holdings has exposed a number of the world's largest commodity trading houses, banks, and multinationals.[92]

TAXATION REQUIREMENTS

Another challenge related to the bureaucratic and regulatory framework that exists in many African countries is in taxation. In many cases, the burden of taxation might prove favorable for investing in the energy sector, as many governments have been willing to grant tax credits for companies' development of infrastructure necessary for oil and gas production. On the other hand, a lack of bureaucratic coordination and technical expertise has resulted in fragmented and uncoordinated oversight of the extractive sector.

In Ghana, businesses have complained about increasing direct and in-direct taxes in recent years, which have resulted from improvements in the legal and institutional framework related to oil taxation.[93] A new Transfer Pricing Unit has been established in order to target misrepresentation of the value of internal transfers in multinational corporations, a common strategy of tax avoidance.[94] Reforms seeking to improve bureaucratic coordination, oversight, and transparency are increasingly common in Africa, and this trend has the potential to increase the tax burden on energy companies.

INFRASTRUCTURE

Gaps in the infrastructure that are necessary for oil and gas production exist at every stage. Companies working in Africa have pointed to an unre-liable power supply as the most pressing obstacle to growth, even more so than access to credit, bureaucratic red tape, and corruption.[95] Power outages often require the use of private backup generators running on gasoline or diesel fuel in order to avoid costly production stoppages.

Infrastructure improvements currently account for at least 13 percent of investment needs, or more than 20 percent if expansion of the distribution and domestic retail network is addressed, as hoped.[96] Despite promising onshore discoveries in Uganda, Kenya, and the DRC, for example, a pipe-line will be necessary to transport the extracted crude oil for either export or domestic refinement.

Notably, there are no refineries operating in the region since the recent closure of the Mombasa refinery.[97] More generally, increases in oil refinement capacity have not kept pace with that of oil extraction in Africa. In 2010, 10.2 million barrels of crude oil were produced each day on the continent, but refining capacity only existed for 3.2 million bpd.[98] For this reason, most oil-producing countries export crude oil only to import refined oil for domestic consumption at a higher cost.

As of 2015, there were only forty-nine operative refineries on the continent, with only one new refinery, in Lagos, expected to be completed by 2025. Although investment in existing refineries is projected to increase capacity by just 23 percent over the next decade, a relatively meager figure, the resulting increases of 40 percent in oil output and $20 billion to $40 billion in profits—depending on oil prices—is substantial.[99] The current gap between production and refining capacity is particularly wide in Nigeria and Angola, which signals a significant opportunity for investors willing to build refineries to reduce their overall distribution costs and tap into local and regional markets.

Yet, as figure 6.7 shows, the capacity of Africa's refineries increased from 2005 to 2015, even as throughput has declined, particularly since 2010. Thus, even at current levels, existing oil refineries in Africa are operating well below full efficiency.

LOCAL CAPACITY

The scale required by oil and gas production generally surpasses local capacity in Africa, but is also due to lack of education, skills, and access to credit. In most contexts, the hydrocarbon industry lacks linkages to other sectors of the domestic economy and provides very little employment for local residents. Despite representing over 30 percent of GDP in Angola, for example, the oil sector employs less than 1 percent of the Angolan workforce.[100]

PwC estimates that improvement in local content and skills development will be the second-highest driver of investment in the industry over the next few years.[101] There have been a few examples of energy companies and African governments partnering to provide tuition for tertiary education in subjects related to oil and gas management, engineering, and innovation. In light of recent offshore gas discoveries in Tanzania, recent legislation requires that any license holders prepare and file a "credible plan for investment in local capacity building" in order to develop a domestic basis for its gas sector.[102]

FIGURE 6.7. Comparison of African oil refinery capacity versus throughput, 2000–2015.

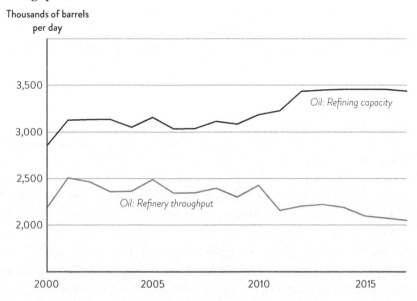

Source: Figures from BP Statistical Review of World Energy, 2018.

CONFLICT AND VIOLENCE

Africa's traditional oil-producing countries are also some of the most heavily afflicted by political conflict and violence, although the extent to which the conflict is linked to the oil sector varies from country to country. Investment and production in Nigeria have been affected by violence in the Niger Delta, the region with the country's largest proven onshore oil reserves, to the extent that the International Energy Agency (IEA) projects that Angola will overtake Nigeria as Africa's top producer of crude oil over the next 10 years.[103] Despite a ceasefire in 2009, Niger Delta militants attacked an oil pipeline in February 2010 and, by the second quarter of 2016, oil output in the region had declined to 1.69 million barrels per day.[104]

Oil and gas infrastructure have also come under attack by militant groups in North Africa, particularly since the onset of the Arab Spring. An attack on the Amenas gas facility in Algeria led to an estimated 3.7 billion m³ decrease in the country's gas production in 2013, and the Greenstream pipeline transporting gas from Libya to Europe was closed for most of 2011 due to the civil war.[105] More generally, the violence and political unrest in North Africa was cited by ConocoPhillips in its decision to sell its Algerian concessions in December 2012, as well as those by Shell and Chevron to halt exploration and production in several areas of Libya. In contrast, foreign investment in Egypt has been relatively unaffected, since its top-producing oil and gas regions—the offshore Nile Delta and the Western Desert—are located far from the urban centers of political conflict.[106]

Effective Business Strategies

Recently, in light of current market conditions, Tullow Oil announced its plans to limit further capital expenditure in West Africa to its existing "high-margin" oil production facilities in order to stabilize and guarantee long-term profits. At the same time, however, it also plans to reallocate resources toward exploration, focusing on "high-impact, low-cost" opportunities in East Africa, especially Kenya.[107] Tullow is a notable success story of a small, regionally focused firm growing and competing effectively against large, multinational petroleum companies by understanding and navigating the challenges of investing in Africa.

Thus there are a number of strategies for mitigating risk and doing business effectively in Africa's hydrocarbons sector. For one thing, the most successful companies are proactively forming partnerships with governments and employing teams specifically focused on government relations. These legal and diplomatic experts help ensure that companies manage regulatory risk and meet taxation requirements, and they also encourage governments to improve bureaucratic coordination and draft effective, transparent, and enforceable oil and gas policies, particularly where these sectors are newly developing. An advisory team from three different oil companies recently helped the government of Angola draft a memorandum of understanding, which has reduced investment uncertainty by formally detailing a new framework for production, transport, and refinement.[108]

The recent wave of oil and gas discoveries also increases the options available to companies about where to invest in Africa. The risk of violence and political stability is much lower in Ghana and in East Africa when compared to the traditional oil-producing countries. Moreover, although the governments of the new hydrocarbon-producing states often lack existing technical and human capacities for managing the sector, there is greater opportunity for potential investors to impact these countries' frameworks for regulation, taxation, and contract enforcement as they are developing.[109]

Some countries have also shown a willingness to actively attract and maintain investment. In 2014, the parliament of Mozambique amended its petroleum law to provide tax breaks for the offshore field operated by Anadarko and Eni in order to ensure that project development would continue.[110] Companies like Tullow Oil and Heritage are already taking advantage of the favorable business environments offered by Kenya, Mozambique, Tanzania, and Uganda, among others. Eventually, these kinds of geographical shifts in Africa's energy sector could have a knock-on effect, incentivizing countries like Nigeria to effectively implement regulatory reforms and ensure a secure business environment in order to avoid losing investment.

Incrementally diversifying into low-carbon technologies will also help energy companies remain profitable despite the volatility of world oil prices. This strategy will be particularly important with growing constraints on carbon-based fuel production worldwide, as well as attempts to reduce fossil fuel reliance in the West. In November 2015, Royal Dutch Shell, traditionally a multinational oil company, became the world's largest trader in LNG with the purchase of BG Group.[111]

According to Alex Vines of Chatham House, several independent companies have had success by striking an initial find, which they then sell to a major multinational or national oil company with the infrastructural and investment capacity to fully develop the site. This strategy has been lucrative for Kosmos Energy in Ghana, Heritage Oil in Uganda, Triton Energy in Equatorial Guinea, and HyperDynamics in Guinea, for example.[112] Others have used finds to grow their capacity incrementally, such as Tullow and Anadarko, which are now relatively established companies. Tullow even succeeded in using its preemption rights in Uganda, along with a commitment to the government to build an oil refinery, to prevent Eni from buying Heritage in 2010.[113]

Finally, Chinese companies have had astounding success doing business in Africa in recent years. China has now overtaken Europe as the main source of foreign direct investment on the continent. This rapid growth in the investment presence of Chinese companies has revealed three specific strategies for growing an effective business in Africa:[114]

- *Backward and vertical integration.* Companies such as Sinopec and China National Offshore Oil Corporation (CNOOC) have expanded into upstream assets to secure resources and commodities as well as downstream activities like retail, petrochemicals, and power generation.

- *Partnerships and joint ventures.* Chinese corporations have recognized the technical and administrative gains to be made by linking up with established firms, both multinationals and African NOCs. This strategy has also facilitated access to the political and economic elite in countries with which China has historically had limited relations. Sinopec's joint venture with Sonangol in Angola is one example.

- *Parent satellite investments.* This strategy involves the selective use of listed satellite companies or subsidiaries in order to acquire resources, as well as a willingness to use unlisted parent companies when deemed more appropriate, such as securing a contract more rapidly. The vast majority of Chinese multinational corporations in all sectors continue to be under the control of a parent company in China.

Looking to the Future

Despite plummeting oil prices and pessimism about investment in fossil fuels in the near future, the prospects for the oil and gas sector in Africa remain positive. Compared to other oil-producing regions, African countries offer international oil companies an environment of relative freedom in which to invest and operate, and most of these countries are not (yet) bound by OPEC quotas or restrictions. Africa's crude oil is considered to be of a particularly high quality, and a wave of recent discoveries suggests that the next two decades will offer a high proportion of successful exploration projects. The continent's commercially viable reserves of oil and gas are much more extensive than previously thought.[115] Many of these recent discoveries have been in previously unexplored and untapped areas of the continent, and the vast majority have been gas reserves, which is particularly noteworthy as the global energy market shifts toward lower-carbon alternatives.

Prior to the recent decline in world oil prices, the OECD estimated that $1.25 trillion would be invested in Africa's energy sector through 2030, particularly focused on upstream exploration and infrastructural development. Unfortunately, however, investment has been stunted in recent years in response to the low price of oil. According to Bloomberg, the number of rigs in Africa peaked at 154 in February 2014, when oil prices were at their highest, before dropping to 125 one year later.[116] An estimated $300 billion has been lost due to deferment of final investment decisions over the past 2 years, as operators are waiting to see when and if the commodity price of oil is likely to rebound to its pre-2015 levels.[117]

Even before oil prices plummeted, a forecasting model from the African Futures Project predicted that oil and natural gas production on the continent would peak sometime around 2030, with Nigeria and Libya projected to have the highest and latest peaks.[118] However, there are a number of reasons to remain optimistic about the prospects for investment in Africa's energy sector.

The recent discoveries in East Africa are an indication that oil and gas reserves on the continent might be much larger than previously thought, and they present exciting new prospects for potential investors. As early as 2014, the IEA predicted that the focus of new gas projects would shift away from Nigeria and toward the east coast, particularly the offshore reserves in Mozambique and Tanzania, which could provide a 75 billion m^3 boost to annual output in the region—projected to reach 230 billion m^3 by 2040. If initial projections continue on pace, Mozambique could soon become the third-largest exporter of natural gas in the world.[119] It will require large initial investments before production comes online in these countries, including the completion of pipelines and natural gas liquefaction plants. However, the proximity to Asia and the Middle East, as well as both governments' stated commitment to increase domestic demand for gas, improves the prospects for long-term profitability of these countries' oil and gas sectors.[120]

In fact, domestic demand for gas is likely to increase significantly in the coming years, with some projecting natural gas to triple its share of the total energy use in Africa by 2040. In Algeria, for example, gas exports are expected to decline over the next 2 years despite the recent discoveries of proven gas reserves, largely due to rising domestic consumption.[121] There is an ongoing push to fill the gap between supply and demand in electrification, as less than one in three people in sub-Saharan Africa currently have access to electricity.[122] By 2035, the EIA projects that demand for electricity in Africa will grow by an average of 2.6 percent each year, and that 40 percent of electricity supply will come from natural gas–fired plants.[123] This points toward a substantial upsurge in Africa's consumption of natural gas and vast potential for increasing profits in the coming years, since much of the natural gas that is currently extracted is wasted in flaring.

On the other hand, compared to the billions of dollars in capital investment needed to commercialize East Africa's newly discovered reserves, on-shore and shallow offshore oil production in West Africa has potential for immediate profitability. For this reason, many analysts predict that West Africa is the region that will continue to receive large-scale investment if market conditions continue.[124] In light of the relatively high break-even price required by oil production in Nigeria, as well as the risks related to insecurity and corruption, investors are likely to shift attention toward new prospects in the region. Substantial offshore discoveries of both oil and gas have been made off the coast of Senegal, for example, which is a model of political and economic stability in Africa.[125] Jubilee Field also holds a wealth of potential, especially since the Ghanaian government appears committed to bureaucratic transparency and coordination in order to fa-cilitate investment.

According to Professor Jean Batou of Lausanne University, "We all know oil resources are becoming increasingly rare. The last major reserves of oil in Africa will become increasingly important. Pre-positioning oneself with a view to exploiting these resources is vital."[126] Even as the world tran-sitions toward a low-carbon and renewable energy system, global demand for affordable, reliable energy will continue to increase over the foresee-able future. The most successful companies working in Africa's oil and gas sector in the coming decades will be those that manage to adapt and in-novate, especially by taking advantage of new discoveries in previously un-explored areas, by diversifying with the goal of shifting toward natural gas production, and by tapping into domestic markets. Resource wealth need not be a "curse" to economic and political development if the recent, un-tapped discoveries of oil and gas lead to effective and transparent partner-ships between private corporations and African governments underpinned by initiatives such as the Extractive Industries Transparency Initiative in Ghana. Ideally, these partnerships will contribute to filling existing in-frastructure gaps and building coordinated, rationalized energy policies, which will guarantee that the rents from Africa's resources have positive spillover effects with other, vital economic sectors.

SEVEN

Africa's Tourism Transformation and Potential

The tourism industry is playing an increasingly important role in the global economy, contributing 5 percent of GDP, 30 percent of service exports, and 235 million jobs. Indeed, each year, approximately one billion people travel internationally. Given these trends, the travel and tourism industry has significant potential in Africa, notably due to the continent's richness in natural resources and its potential to further develop cultural heritage (e.g., music). However, despite a few countries, such as Seychelles and Mauritius, where the tourism sector's share of the economy is particularly large, tourism in Africa is still at an early stage of development and strongly connected with more general and long-standing development challenges, including infrastructure as well as health and hygiene.

Most countries in the region are aware of the potential role of tourism as an economic opportunity and development catalyst and have drafted strategic plans to develop the sector. For example, The Gambia, Kenya, South Africa, and Tanzania are all putting significant efforts into advancing travel and tourism development. Botswana, Mauritius, Rwanda, and South Africa are particularly working hard to improve their business environment for tourism investment.

The African Union and subregional communities have also put tourism at the top of their agendas. For example, the African Union has endorsed the continent's Tourism Action Plan (TAP) developed by the New Partnership for Africa's Development (NEPAD), now African Union Development Agency (AUDA). The TAP recognizes tourism development among priority sector strategies of AUDA across Africa and aims to make Africa the destination of the twenty-first century. The fifteen members of the Economic Community of West African States (ECOWAS) have introduced a visa policy that enables free movement of people across member states, offering a larger market to international travelers.

While improvements have been achieved in various areas, especially at the local level, to fully tap Africa's potential in the tourism industry, much needs to be done by both the public and the private sectors. This chapter starts with an overview of tourism development in Africa and explores some of the key constraints that have prevented this sector from maturing. It identifies important stakeholders and potential opportunities for its future development and provides illustrative examples of countries representative of different trajectories of tourism development. Finally, with attention to current major policy reforms, the chapter draws conclusions about the future of the tourism sector in Africa.

The chapter aims to offer business leaders an accessible overview of Africa's biggest opportunities in the tourism sector, discussing factors that need to be considered when making an investment. It also aims to advise policymakers on areas that need to be improved and policy options that could be taken to attract private investors.

Background Facts and Trends

Since the 1950s, the market for international travel and tourism has exhibited uninterrupted growth. After the end of the Cold War, the sector accelerated more rapidly than the global economy, with an average annual growth rate of 4.1 percent between 1995 and 2010.[1] During this period Africa experienced its initial boom in tourism. Africa's tourism-based revenues increased by more than 50 percent in the 1990s—from $2.3 billion to $3.7 billion[2]—while the total number of international arrivals on the continent ballooned by roughly 300 percent, from 6.7 million in 1990 to 26.2 million in 2000.[3]

These trends have continued into the twenty-first century, bolstered by a period of impressive economic growth and improvements in political stability and openness across the continent. In fact, during the global financial crisis of 2007–2008, Africa was the only region in the world that continued to experience growth in the tourism industry: arrivals in the region increased by 3.7 percent in 2008–2009, compared to the net *decline* of 4.3

percent in the rest of the world.[4] The African Development Bank (AfDB) estimates that, in 2015, Africa received 62.5 million visitors, contributed 9.1 million direct travel and tourism jobs, and generated $39.2 billion in international tourism receipts.[5]

While the international tourist arrivals on the whole continent increased by nearly 36 million between 2000 and 2017, the sub-Saharan region has experienced the lion's share of this growth (24.7 million).[6] For one thing, prior to the turn of the century, North Africa already had a relatively well-developed tourism industry. In 1995, the five northern countries (Morocco, Algeria, Tunisia, Libya, and Egypt) received nearly as many international visitors annually as the forty-eight sub-Saharan countries combined—10.5 million versus 13 million, respectively. Second, since 2011, perceptions of political instability and insecurity associated with the Arab Spring and terrorism have made the region a less popular destination. Thus, as illustrated in figure 7.1, while sub-Saharan Africa's tourism continues to grow, the size of the sector in North Africa is on the decline.

There is marked variation within the sub-Saharan African region as

FIGURE 7.1. International tourism arrivals in sub-Saharan Africa and North Africa, 1995–2016.

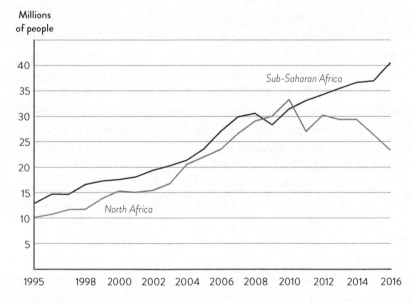

Source: World Development Indicators, 2018.

well, with East and Southern Africa attracting the vast majority of visitors; in those countries, most international tourists arrive from Europe and the United States. Unsurprisingly, then, in terms of GDP share, the tourism markets of East (4.5 percent) and Southern Africa (3.0 percent) are relatively well developed compared to the western (2.1 percent) and central (1.7 percent) ones.[7] In terms of the number of arrivals, Africa's most popular destinations in 2017 were, in decreasing order, Morocco, South Africa, Egypt, Tunisia, Algeria, and Zimbabwe. By value of tourism receipts, the most popular destinations were, in decreasing order, South Africa, Morocco, Egypt, Nigeria, Ethiopia, and Tanzania.

At the same time, in comparison with other world regions, Africa's tourism industry remains relatively underdeveloped. Of the 1.2 billion people traveling internationally in 2016, only 58 million arrived in Africa—roughly 5 percent of the world's inbound tourism.[8] Despite more than doubling over the past 20 years, the sector continues to lag behind other developing regions in terms of the number of tourists received per year (figure 7.2). Moreover, the size of sub-Saharan Africa's market in terms of the export share of receipts—defined as spending by international incoming travelers, including payments to national carriers for international transport—from tourism has remained relatively stagnant over the past two decades, as the industry has grown at a similar rate to that of the region's economy as a whole.

Thus, looking to the future, there is substantial room for growth in Africa's travel and tourism market, particularly in light of current sectoral growth patterns, as international tourists are increasingly interested in developing countries as travel destinations. The emerging market share of world tourism increased from 32 percent in 1990 to 45 percent in 2017.[9] Analysts predict that the majority of international travelers, an estimated 57 percent, will prefer emerging and developing countries as their destination of choice by 2030, especially driven by the growth in the adventure and nature tourism subsectors.[10]

Given that the economic and political environment in Africa continues to improve, many of the benefits of this promising trend in emerging and developing countries are likely to accrue to the African continent, specifically. In fact, now, Africa's tourism industry is growing faster than its economy as a whole and, unlike in other economic sectors, the majority of countries in sub-Saharan Africa—at least 33 of 48 countries—have demonstrated the capacity and political will to improve and expand their tourism sector by incentivizing investment, attracting finance, and easing restric-

FIGURE 7.2. Comparison of the number of tourists visiting developing regions each year, 1996, 2006, and 2016.

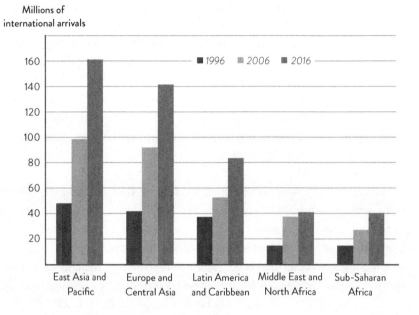

Source: World Development Indicators, 2018. Note that high-income countries are excluded from all regions.

tions on movement.[11] If current trends continue unabated, the number of arrivals on the continent is expected to reach 85 million by 2020 and 134 million by 2030.[12]

Importance of the Sector to Africa's Growth

In all of the world's emerging economies, tourism is one of the primary industries driving growth and job creation. Even a decade ago, tourists were already spending $295 billion every year in developing countries—which amounts to roughly three times total overseas development assistance to the developing world in 2007—and interest in underexplored and "off the beaten path" travel destinations continues to rise. This signals enormous potential for tourism-driven development in Africa's emerging markets over the long term.

As the sector became incorporated into the debate about global dependency in the 1970s and 1980s, a number of scholars were skeptical of the potential for tourism to have a positive impact beyond strict measures of growth and export earnings.[13] Many argued that the nature of tourism relies on small and short-term investments from foreign visitors, which are volatile and prone to extreme shocks during times of political or health crises, and which often exacerbate problems of cultural appropriation and environmental degradation with few direct benefits for local communities.[14] Opponents of this negative viewpoint to its failure to acknowledge the flexible specialization of the tourism industry, as well as variation in states' abilities to capitalize on gains from tourism. They are also skeptical of local ownership in the sector and the strength of linkages between production and consumption.[15]

In general, scholars and policymakers agree that encouraging the development of a robust tourism industry has a direct, positive impact on economic growth by promoting investment in diverse, productive sectors across the economy, such as in construction, infrastructure, local manufacturing, and consumer markets.[16] The macroeconomic benefits of tourism include an increase in foreign exchange earnings, state revenues, and domestic consumption.[17] Numerous case studies have demonstrated the ways in which this mechanism has played out in middle-income countries over the past 40 years, such as in Spain[18] and Greece,[19] yet the positive effects on growth are potentially even higher in low-income countries.[20]

There are a number of mechanisms to account for tourism's positive contribution to the economy. For one thing, tourism provides much-needed diversification of countries' export earnings away from a dependence on agricultural and primary commodities, thereby contributing to broader patterns of economic modernization. Meanwhile, in comparison to other economic sectors, such as manufacturing, the tourism industry requires relatively low levels of inputs of capital and expertise—resources that tend to be scarce in developing economies—thereby creating an abundance of space for small- and medium-sized enterprises (SMEs) to thrive. Given the relative absence of large corporations as domestic investors in many of the world's emerging markets, and especially those in Africa, SMEs are poised to serve as vital drivers of economic growth and the increase in the number of Africans with discretionary income.[21]

There are also substantial benefits from tourism that accrue at the local level, including improvements in income distribution, regional development, and employment opportunities for remote and low-skilled workers, which have both direct and indirect impacts on poverty levels.[22] Compared to other sectors, tourism also provides a disproportionately high number of jobs for women, who are often difficult to integrate into the formal economy in developing countries. A recent study by the UN World Tourism Organization (UNWTO) concluded that, in the global hotel and restaurant industry, women often outnumber men and receive equal pay. In sub-Saharan Africa, where women are significantly more likely to be poor and employed in the informal economy, women manage a majority of all hospitality businesses; in Ethiopia, Lesotho, and Mali, they manage at least 80 percent of them.[23]

In addition, Fayissa, Nsiah, and Tadasse (2008) have found strong support for the causal relationship between tourism receipts and economic growth, and Lee and Chang (2008) have shown that sub-Saharan Africa saw a larger growth from tourism between 1990 and 2002 than any other non-OECD region. One African country in particular, Mauritius, has capitalized on its shift toward a tourism-dependent economy in order to reduce dependence on its agricultural staple—sugar—and has consequently achieved rapid economic growth.[24] In terms of social development and poverty alleviation, Briedenhann and Wickens (2004) have shown the effectiveness of South African communities in achieving indigenous ownership and capitalizing on the tourism boom through clustering and cooperation.

As of yet, however, the trend does not seem to bear out across the African continent in terms of variation in levels of economic development. Although the region's largest tourist markets are also on the higher end of the spectrum in terms of income levels, there is too much variation among countries with relatively small tourism industries to reach a clear conclusion. Much of this is likely due to the fact that the tourism industry has only recently begun to take off in Africa and still remains relatively underdeveloped and concentrated in a handful of key markets. Where significant growth has occurred in Africa, as in Morocco and Tunisia, Bouzahzah and El Menyari (2013) have shown that it might be more an effect of increasing levels of economic development rather than an independent driver of growth.

However, many African countries that have previously been considered unattractive tourist destinations due to political instability, violence, or health crises have already managed to transform their images through successful tourism campaigns. For example, Rwanda features its population of endangered mountain gorillas, Mozambique its beaches, and Ethiopia its ancient cultural attractions from the Abyssinian period.[25] It remains to be seen, though, whether these countries will experience the expected economic boom from tourism in the coming years, as has been the case in

Mauritius. From the perspective of African governments and development organizations, though, the positive role of tourism is clear—it represents a vital pathway to overcome challenges of development related to foreign exchange earnings and central government debt.[26] The World Bank and UNWTO predict that tourism will be one of the main drivers of economic growth in Africa over the coming decade. An increasing number of countries, then, have made tourism a central pillar of their economic development and reform programs over the near future, such as Kenya's Vision 2030, Tanzania's Vision 2025, and Uganda's Vision 2040.[27]

Key Drivers of Tourism Growth in Africa

Despite market challenges related to the recent decline in oil prices and political instability and violence in North Africa, arrivals are expected to continue increasing by as much as 5 percent each year, and the region is projected to increase its share of the global tourism market from 5 to 7 percent by 2020.[28] In fact, the *Travel and Tourism Competitiveness Report 2015* by the World Economic Forum found that Africa's travel and tourism industry is remarkably resilient to economic shocks and well equipped to continue offering positive investment opportunities, even in countries that have relatively low levels of wealth and human capital.[29]

Indeed, Africa's emerging markets are currently characterized by opportunities for new economic partnerships, diversifying market linkages, and increasing foreign investment and access to international capital. As a result of these processes, the continent exhibits an increase in people with discretionary income who have more interest in domestic travel, while improvements in development and stability are making the region substantially more attractive to international visitors than in the past. In this light, market analysts agree that the tourism industry provides one of the best opportunities for capitalizing on the rise of Africa in coming years.

In the future, growth in Africa's tourism industry will primarily be driven by two factors: globalization and infrastructure.

GLOBALIZATION

Globalization is leading to the increase in the movement of people everywhere. As in other sectors, there has been a surge of interest in Africa from China. More and more Chinese travelers are choosing to visit the "magic continent," most frequently during their October national holiday.

South Africa, Kenya, Zimbabwe, and Angola have especially benefited due to being granted Approved Destination Status[30] for outbound Chinese tour groups since 2004. As a result, the number of Chinese visitors to South Africa quadrupled between 2003 and 2005. The World Tourism Organization predicts that China will be the world's largest source of tourists by 2020, and an expansion of the special status to more countries—beyond the twenty African countries—will allow Africa to profit from this trend.[31]

Another opportunity for the hotel and restaurant industry lies in the rapid growth of business-related travel on the continent, particularly because business travelers tend to be more affluent and less seasonal than leisure tourists. There has been a surge of discoveries of minerals and hydrocarbons in Africa in recent years, and most mining companies tend to book long-term hotel accommodations for their employees. In recognition of these trends, the Industrial Development Corporation invested more than $8 billion in ten African countries in 2015 in developing not only mining capabilities but also tourism and related infrastructure, such as the Park Inn in Cape Town, South Africa.[32] Meanwhile, global players like Accor, Starwood, Intercontinental, and Kempinski are planning to increase their investment in African cities that have the most potential to develop dynamic business activities.[33]

Intra-African travel is also projected to increase dramatically over the next few decades, as increasing average income levels and job security are contributing to the emergence of a stable and growing population with discretionary income on the continent. The governments of Kenya, Zimbabwe, and Ghana have already started promoting domestic travel through marketing campaigns and the improvement of transport infrastructure. Meanwhile, more than 10 million Africans already travel across regional borders every year. South Africa dominates intraregional travel, accounting for 47 percent of visitors, but other regions (e.g., East Africa) and countries (e.g., Nigeria and Zimbabwe) are poised to increase their market share. There is potential for keen investors to capitalize on this trend by creating low-cost tourism services that cater to the African market, especially for those who travel repeatedly for business or to visit family.[34]

In global terms, tourist demand is increasing most rapidly in the nature and adventure, culture and history, and health and wellness subsectors. Given these trends, the potential for expansion of the tourism market is especially high in Africa due to its abundance of natural assets, such as beaches, wildlife, cultural heritage, and adventure opportunities.

Countries that are serious about making themselves targets for tourism investment are those that are seeking to initiate reforms in wildlife conservation and visa and permitting restrictions. Recognizing their value as an attraction to affluent safari travelers, some African governments have adopted creative policy solutions to save the dwindling populations of elephants and rhinoceroses, among others. For example, in Uganda, with the help of conservation groups, state-funded projects include the construction of fences made of beehives to prevent elephants from encroaching onto local farms, or painting the horns of live rhinoceroses bright pink to deter poachers.[35] Governments should adopt new and creative policies for all kinds of problems related to the conservation of land and wildlife to increase the profitability of tourism.

Reducing restrictions on visa and permits to enter countries helps facilitate freer movement of people, thus enabling the tourism sector. For example, Rwanda has profited from implementing relatively simple and inexpensive visa requirements compared to its neighbor, the Democratic Republic of the Congo (DRC), in order to attract visitors interested in the mountain gorilla population that straddles the border between the two countries. In response to stagnating tourism growth rates in recent years, the government of Mauritius recently relaxed its visa requirements for more than thirty African countries, thus increasing its revenues from intraregional travel.[36] It borrowed the idea from the East African Community, where the tourism market has benefited immensely from the freedom of movement granted to citizens of Kenya, Tanzania, and Uganda.

INFRASTRUCTURE

Improvements in public goods provision go hand-in-hand with infrastructure investment. In contrast with medium-income countries, where levels of social development (e.g., health services) and GDP per capita seem to determine tourism growth, low-income countries have been shown to become travel destinations only when they achieve adequate foundations of infrastructure and education.[37]

Necessary investments include power and water supply, waste management, and transport.[38] One factor that will contribute substantially to the growth in Africa's tourism market will be the increase in airline travel. Although it is currently home to 15 percent of the world's population, sub-Saharan Africa has just 4 percent of the world's scheduled airline seats, and air travel tends to be more expensive than in other developing and emerging regions.[39] In fact, air travel in Africa is twice as expensive as that in Latin America and four times that in the United States. In addition, it is often characterized by unreliable service and complex itineraries.

Due to the high cost of airfare and utilities and a heavy reliance on imported goods and services, tours in sub-Saharan Africa are estimated to cost travelers 25 to 35 percent more than those in other parts of the world. In addition, it is more expensive to develop hotels in countries with higher import duties and weaker infrastructure—such as Angola, Ghana, and Nigeria—causing these high costs to be passed on to consumers.

So far, substantial progress has been made in certain areas. For example, improved air access to tourist destinations in Africa is being driven by factors that include implementation of the Yamoussoukro Decision (YD), low-cost carriers (LCCs), and airline network cooperation.

Also called the Open Skies for Africa initiative, the YD was signed by forty-four African countries in 1999, agreeing to liberalize intra-African movement, such as by allowing non-national airlines to land and take passengers to a third country—known as the fifth freedom of the air.[40] As a result, a country like Nigeria, which does not have its own national airline, has seen a massive increase in traffic volume and reduction in the cost of air travel. New direct routes have emerged as well, such as the Lagos-Casablanca route, which has cut travel time down by more than 75 percent.[41]

Progress has also been made with airlines that do not provide most traditional services and thus charge lower fares, referred to as LCCs. Other emerging regions have improved economic efficiency and interconnectivity using LCCs. For example, a new Johannesburg-Lusaka route was created in 2006 via partnership between an LCC, kulula.com, and Zambian Airways, which increased traffic volumes in the region while bypassing new state permitting and air service agreements. Small charter flights with low overhead help travelers access remote destinations that are otherwise difficult—or even dangerous—to reach by road. In the past, these kinds of flights have been prohibitively expensive in Africa due to political and regulatory intervention, but there is evidence that this situation is changing.[42]

Finally, in 2016, Ethiopian Airlines and RwandAir announced a new partnership that grants each airline the right to operate freely in the other's market space, taking advantage of the "fifth freedoms" initiative. Passengers can now use either provider's hub to reach a third destination or country more easily. Ethiopian Airlines has become a dominant force on the continent by pursuing this strategy, and it has similar alliances with Malawi Airlines and Togo's ASKY.[43]

Key Players

In Africa, as in other emerging markets, the development of a market for tourism has required substantial amounts of foreign direct investment (FDI) to build up the necessary infra- and superstructures, such as hotels, charter services, and airline access.[44] For example, in South Africa, primary foreign direct investors come from European countries such as France, Germany, the Netherlands, the United Kingdom, and the United States. These countries are also the primary markets of international visitors to the region, suggesting a strong correlation between countries interested in visiting and sources of direct investment. Different investment markets exhibit variation in their preferences for different subsectors of tourism—for example, French companies tend to focus their investment on wineries, U.K. and U.S. investors build up safari and adventure tourism, and German buyers prefer holiday homes.[45]

At the moment, the majority of investment continues to come from individual developers, and there are relatively few tourism consortiums operating on a large scale in Africa. However, Tourvest Holdings, a South Africa-based tourism group with operations extending across the continent, and major international hotel chains like Intercontinental are already planning to increase their investments in Africa.[46] From 2012 to 2016, in terms of investment of hotel chains (regional and international) in Africa, both the number of hotels and rooms in the pipeline roughly doubled, increasing from 177 to 365 and from 34,326 to 64,231, respectively.[47] Table 7.1 shows the top hotel chains that invested in Africa in 2018.

If the investors, consultants, lenders, and other parties involved can make these deals come to fruition, the pipeline of the future will bring about much-needed expansion of Africa's hotel industry and tourism sector.[48]

Opportunities Presented by the Tourism Industry

At present, there are just ten countries in Africa that receive $1 billion or more per year in tourism revenues, signaling enormous potential for market growth across the continent (figure 7.3 and table 7.2). Indeed, the region's natural endowments as well as untapped cultural and historical resources

TABLE 7.1. Top hotel chains investing in Africa, 2018.

Hotel chain	Hotels under construction	Rooms under construction	Change in 2017
Hilton	24	6,687	17%
Radisson Blu	25	5,473	2%
Marriott	16	3,438	14%
Fairmont	8	2,977	66%
Hilton Garden Inn	17	2,818	31%
Sheraton	9	2,013	18%
Four Points	13	2,006	−8%
Swissôtel	4	1,961	65%
Meliá Hotels & Resorts	6	1,935	−21%
Golden Tulip	9	1,662	251%

Source: W Hospitality Group (2018), "Hotel Chains Development Pipelines in Africa." https://w-hospitalitygroup.com/wp-content/uploads/2018/06/W-Hospitality-Group-Hotel-Chain-Development-Pipelines-in-Africa-2018-2.pdf, 24.

offer numerous opportunities to attract visitors. At the same time, however, in light of the relatively low income levels of most Africans, industry growth presently depends to a large extent on attracting visitors from other world regions. Beyond the potential for capitalizing on natural and cultural endowments, therefore, the strongest candidates for investment are those countries with well-developed travel infrastructure, relatively open international movement policies, and an attractive environment for starting a tourism-related business.

As of 2011, the primary countries receiving tourism-focused foreign investment in Africa were South Africa ($6.1 billion), Kenya ($404 million), Ghana ($270 million), and Uganda ($165 million).[49] As figure 7.3 shows, however, some of the region's largest markets for tourism have exhibited declining tourism revenues in recent years, especially the North African countries and South Africa. Meanwhile, a handful of frontier markets are becoming increasingly attractive destinations for tourists and investors alike by recognizing the potential for tourism-driven development, incentivizing investment in the sector, and building up necessary travel infrastructures. Table 7.3 summarizes the global ranking of Africa's top tourism markets across various indicators of tourism market competitiveness: Morocco, South Africa, Kenya, and Mauritius seem to offer particularly promising investment opportunities.

MOROCCO

Morocco has been called the "new star of emerging markets among overseas property developers" for a number of reasons.[50] Not only has the country been less affected by the political turmoil related to the Arab Spring compared to its neighbors, but the government has also actively and strategically prioritized the tourism industry as a tool of development—initially as part of its Vision 2010, later updated and included in its Vision 2020.[51] In general, the goal of the program is to increase the number of annual visitors to Morocco from 4.3 million in 2000 to 20 million by 2020. In 2013, Morocco surpassed Egypt as the primary tourist destination in North Africa. It now receives more than 10 million visitors each year—the second most on the continent, behind South Africa.

TABLE 7.2. Summary of key tourism indicators for top African markets.

	Annual tourism receipts (US$ billions)	GDP share of tourism (% total exports)	Arrivals, millions	Air passengers, millions	Hotels in the pipeline
Angola	0.63	2	0.40	1.48	—
Egypt	3.31	10	5.26	11.84	18
Ethiopia	2.14	36	0.87	8.24	—
Kenya	1.62	16	1.27	4.85	8
Mauritius	1.82	35	1.28	1.59	—
Morocco	7.92	23	10.33	7.74	31
South Africa	8.81	10	10.04	19.74	13
Tanzania	2.16	23	1.23	1.18	—
Tunisia	1.71	10	5.72	3.61	12
Uganda	0.77	16	1.32	0.05	9

Source: World Development Indicators, 2018, Africa Tourism Monitor (2015). All data are from 2016.

TABLE 7.3. World ranking on travel and tourism competitiveness indicators, 2017.

Country	Prioritization of tourism	Business environment	International openness	Price competitiveness	Natural resources	Cultural resources	Air transport infrastructure	Ground/sea infrastructure
South Africa	59	21	110	43	23	19	46	59
Morocco	35	49	91	47	47	41	63	60
Egypt	37	78	102	2	97	22	58	82
Tanzania	45	102	64	34	8	86	106	102
Ethiopia	115	118	97	64	69	70	11	90
Tunisia	48	66	76	9	94	83	85	95
Kenya	21	70	70	74	15	77	72	70
Mauritius	4	24	59	116	102	109	56	27
Uganda	99	87	69	60	44	79	121	117
Angola	140	136	141	13	106	122	114	140

Source: World Economic Forum *Travel and Tourism Competitiveness Report 2017*. Note that figures for Angola are from the 2015 report.

FIGURE 7.3. Growth in tourism-related revenues in Africa's largest markets, 1996–2016.

International tourism receipts
(current USD billion)

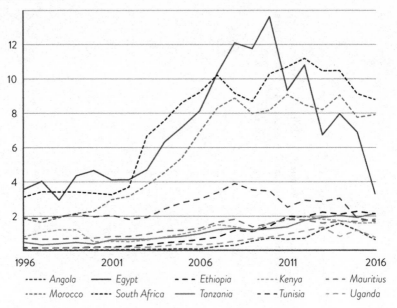

Source: World Development Indicators, 2018.

The impact of government-led tourism development has been twofold. First, as part of a broader global trend labeled Riad fever, foreign capital investment has flocked toward Morocco's historical centers—especially Marrakech, Fez, Meknes, Casablanca, and Rabat—many of which have medinas that have been classified as United Nations Educational, Scientific, and Cultural Organization (UNESCO) World Heritage Sites.[52] Second, the government has sought to extend its tourist attractions beyond the cultural centers to include coastal beach resorts. Notably, a multilateral agreement was signed in December 2006 liberalizing international air travel between Morocco and the European Union member states.[53]

As a result, the combination of natural and cultural resources, as well as the friendly business environment, make Morocco exceptionally appealing for tourism investors.[54] At the same time, however, Morocco does not exhibit the same degree of price competitiveness as some of its North African counterparts, and there remains substantial room for improvement in areas that could benefit from direct policy reform, such as international openness (see table 7.3).[55]

KENYA

With just over 1 million visitors per year and less than $2 billion in annual revenues (see table 7.2), there is enormous room for expansion in Kenya's tourism sector. Like neighboring Tanzania, Kenya is a particularly attractive market for investment in light of its natural attributes; it is ranked fifteenth on the measure that evaluates natural capital, especially its popular safari parks and UNESCO World Heritage sites. And, although there is substantial room for improvement, it also scores much better than its east African neighbor, Tanzania in the quality of its travel-related infrastructure and the environment for doing business in tourism (see table 7.3).

Perhaps most significantly, the Kenyan government has actively prioritized the tourism sector as a driver of growth (twenty-first worldwide). Roughly 7 percent of the annual government budget is allocated toward developing the tourism industry, including effective marketing campaigns and policy reforms that have improved efforts at conservation and environmental sustainability.[56]

MAURITIUS

Until recently, the small island nation of Mauritius had been largely dependent on exports of its agricultural staple crop, sugar. Due to progressive and forward-thinking policy planning by the government, however, its economy has since diversified into specialized markets—especially textiles and services.[57] Today, Mauritius is one of the largest African markets for tourism receipts by volume, receiving more than 1 million visitors every year—roughly the same as Kenya. Now, tourism is one of the country's primary industries, accounting for more than 30 percent of total export earnings—about $1.68 billion in 2015—and 16 percent of government investment.

Recognizing the importance of the sector, the Mauritian government scores higher than any other country in Africa for its prioritization of tourism (fourth worldwide, see table 7.3) and has generated a relatively well developed ground and sea travel infrastructure. However, there is much room for improvement in air infrastructure, the primary means of reaching the country, as well as in the business environment for investing in tourism.[58] In addition, Mauritius has faced increasing pressure on environmental sustainability and conservation in recent years. With damage to its marine life and a number of species under threat, it dropped in the global rankings of travel and tourism competitiveness from twenty-fourth in 2015 to fifty-fifth in 2017.

SOUTH AFRICA

The tourism sector boomed as the country hosted the 2010 World Cup, generating an enormous project in the construction of stadiums with the capacity to hold major events, festivals, and conferences, with the potential to attract further business and entertainment-related travel in the future. Although the size of the sector has declined from its peak during the World Cup, South Africa's tourism sector remains the largest on the continent by volume, with total revenues valued at more than $9 billion in 2015. The "Big 7" wildlife marketing campaign has been extremely effective, which promotes both the "Big 5" animals common to many safari-promoting countries—lions, leopards, elephants, rhinos, and buffalos—with the addition of whales and great white sharks. According to the World Economic Forum, South Africa now receives the highest global ranking (fifty-third) among all African countries for averaged natural (twenty-third) and cultural (nineteenth) resources (see table 7.3).

Although the South African economy has suffered setbacks in recent years, with inflation rates outpacing per capita income growth, the resulting weakness of the rand against major international currencies has been a positive development in terms of price competitiveness, which is already among the most favorable on the continent.[59] From the perspective of investors, according to the World Economic Forum's *Travel and Tourism Competitiveness Report* (2017), South Africa's tourism business environment (twenty-first in the world) is "characterized by little red tape and modest administrative burden and relatively good infrastructure compared to neighboring countries." Domestic hospitality businesses have thrived in the country, the largest of which—Tourvest Holdings—now has operations extending across the African continent.[60]

On the other hand, however, the most significant barrier to growth in

South African tourism is its existing travel restrictions: It is ranked 110th in the world for international openness (see table 7.3) and, even more worrisome, there are indications that border regulations could become even more stringent with the passage of new immigration laws in the near future. This is in spite of recent reforms in the visa application process that improved access to Africa for travelers from China, with the goal of creating a substantial boom in the volume of Chinese tourists to the country, according to South Africa's minister of tourism. Meanwhile, there is substantial room for improvement in the degree to which the government prioritizes conservation of its valuable natural resources, with only 6.5 percent of total land currently protected. A clear and progressive policy position that prioritizes the interests of the tourism sector will be a significant determinant of South Africa's ability to remain competitive and to continue attracting high levels of tourism-related FDI in the future.[61]

Challenges and Risks to the Proliferation of Tourism in Africa

Some of the primary challenges to investing successfully in Africa's tourism sector include infrastructure and institutions, environmental and security risks, and economic risks.

INFRASTRUCTURE AND INSTITUTIONS

African ministries for tourism tend to be underfunded, requiring donors or investors to step in and fill the gaps. In some cases, donor-driven development can be extremely effective—for example, an "anchor development" site in Tunisia received initial stimulus from Western donors, which ultimately led to the buildup of a destination that now receives 7 million tourists each year and accounts for 7.5 percent of annual GDP.[62]

Although there is some variation, even the more developed African destinations face problems related to unsafe roads, inadequate water supply and sanitation, poor access to hospitals and other emergency services, expensive and inconsistent electricity, and inadequate construction procedures. Indeed, one of the major challenges for tourism businesses in Africa, especially those working in more remote destinations like safari lodges, is how to ensure safe, reliable, and affordable access for clients. While domestic movement is most often restricted by the quality of roads and public transit infrastructure, as noted earlier, international access is often constrained by complicated and expensive visa procedures, as well as poor development of the aviation industry.

On the other hand, tendencies for bribery and corruption in the public sector can often lead to mismanagement of funds. In the DRC, spontaneous changes in fees can cause the cost of landing an aircraft to fluctuate from $1,000 to over $12,000 with little warning. Almost 75 percent of tourism companies operating in Kenya have reported having to make "informal payments" in order to facilitate business, a trend that is common across the region.[63]

ENVIRONMENTAL AND SECURITY RISKS

In the absence of effective coordination and management of environmental conservation policies, the natural assets that bolster Africa's potential for tourism development are likely to deteriorate. The continent is facing a widespread problem of deforestation and the potential extinction of its most popular wildlife species due to habitat loss and poaching. Despite some recognition and collaboration by African governments to address these problems, most countries in the region perform well below the international average in terms of environmental sustainability.[64]

Many businesses are finding creative solutions to these problems. One of which is the use of solar panels, which reduces contributions to carbon emissions, while also limiting reliance on unreliable electricity supply chains and lowering operational costs.[65] The tourism industry is responsible for about 5 percent of anthropogenic carbon emissions in Africa, and the share is growing. Given that climate change will pose a major impediment to the global tourism industry in the coming decades, the rise of ecotourism is a promising pathway to building positive feedback loops between tourists and environmental preservation.

Other risks for tourism businesses operating in Africa are political instability and insecurity. This problem has been most acutely illustrated in North Africa in recent years, where international news coverage of events related to the Arab Spring and several terrorist attacks on tourist destinations has led to a substantial decline in international arrivals, especially in Tunisia and Egypt.

The U.S. State Department has issued more travel warnings for countries in Africa than any other world region over the past two decades. Although the most frequent offenders are not considered major tourist destinations—Algeria (13), the DRC (10), Burundi (12), and Chad (9)—fears that insecurity might spill across borders often lead travelers to avoid the region altogether. The impact can also be direct: a travel warning issued in 2014 for Kenya, which prohibited U.S. government employees from visiting the shore, caused significant decline in the country's coastal tourism industry. Media coverage of events like the 2014 Ebola crisis often contribute to negative public perceptions of the continent.[66]

ECONOMIC RISKS

Related to the problems of lack of infrastructure and economic mismanagement is the high cost of doing business in Africa, which is particularly acute in the tourism sector due to the importance clients give to the price-value ratio. Within the region, it is more expensive to develop a hotel in countries with higher import duties and weaker infrastructure for construction projects—such as Angola, Ghana, and Nigeria —and these high costs are passed on to consumers. Where travelers face higher costs, they expect a higher quality of experience, but many tourist destinations and attractions in Africa remain poorly managed. Most international hotel chains are run as local franchises and thus rely on domestic capital and local staff, which necessitates improvements in local capacity.[67] The low quality of customer service is often attributed to the lack of education levels in the region in general, and the absence of hotel and restaurant management training courses in particular. This could hinder the further development of the industry by potentially driving consumers away.

African countries use less local content than countries in other developing and emerging regions; countries like Tanzania import most of their hotel furniture from China. Contrast this with the Dominican Republic, which fulfills over 90 percent of its local tourism needs domestically. Improving the profitability and appeal of tourism in Africa will require the development of local value chains, including manufacturing of large-scale and craft products and access to loans for small- and medium-sized businesses.

Business Strategies

Investing successfully in Africa's tourism industry requires identifying optimal locations for future growth in the first place. Research shows that the primary determinants for investors looking toward Africa's tourism market are infrastructure, government policy that enables a prosperous tourism sector, national and macroeconomic climate, competitiveness, and natural endowments.

Although tourism is mostly restricted to the private sector, the most lucrative countries for investment are those in which governments have explicitly targeted tourism as a sector to empower through policy reform. These countries are also the most likely to facilitate improvements in transport, utilities, and capital and land availability that will promote rapid growth in the sector. Savvy investors can capitalize on a first-mover advantage by partnering with tourism ministries to target investment funds as they become increasingly available toward developing infrastructure around destinations with a high potential for growth, such as cultural attractions, beaches, or national parks.

Many tourism-focused governments are actively seeking to streamline the investment process by consolidating and providing information for potential investors related to accessing finance, zoning regulations, and tax breaks. For example, Tanzania held an investment promotion forum in 2002 that directly resulted in over $100 million in tourism investment over the following 2 years.[68]

In addition, strong linkages between the public and private sectors are necessary to enable businesses to enter and operate effectively in the tourism industry, as coordination is required across multiple sectors, such as infrastructure, finance, education, and transport. Effective strategies depend on visa requirements, marketing, and local content creation.

VISA REQUIREMENTS

One of the most important strategies for the promotion of tourism is a country's current visa regulations. In contrast to other regions, African countries are not as visa-open vis-à-vis each other. For example, while visitors from North America need visas to travel to 45 percent of the countries on the continent, the figure is 55 percent for African travelers who themselves live on the continent.[69]

However, there is significant variation across the continent. The average "openness" score—which measures the extent to which a given country requests a visa from foreign visitors—of the top ten countries in Africa is double that of all countries combined (0.861 vs. 0.425), and 75 percent of the most "visa-open" countries are located in East or West Africa.[70] East

Africa allows free movement of citizens within the region and has a favorable protocol for foreigners' eligibility to obtain visas on arrival. The smaller, landlocked or island African countries also tend to have less restrictive requirements in order to promote trade. It is not surprising that seven of the ten most "tourism-ready" economies in sub-Saharan Africa are also among the most visa-open countries. In contrast, Central and North Africa are considered the most closed regions on the continent.

The African Union's Agenda 2063 includes a proposal to remove visa requirements for travel within the continent. Some governments have taken a more progressive and strategic approach to this concept than others. Growth in tourism will therefore be substantially improved where travel restrictions are eased, and potential investors should keep an eye on the potential for reform in targeted countries. Investors that have favorable partnerships with the public sector should advocate visa reform to promote tourism, including visa-on-arrival policies, regional blocs or bilateral reciprocity visas, and multiyear or multientry visas. Countries like Rwanda and Uganda have already had success in attracting tourists by easing their visa requirements in comparison to neighboring countries with more restrictive policies.

Other policy interventions that would ease the visa process include reducing the cost, the number of documents required, and processing time, as well as creating an online system for information and applications. Right now, only thirteen African countries currently offer electronic visas (eVisas): Côte d'Ivoire, Egypt, Gabon, Guinea Bissau, Kenya, Lesotho, Nigeria, Rwanda, São Tomé and Príncipe, Sierra Leone, Uganda, Zambia, and Zimbabwe.[71]

MARKETING

Building an effective tourism business in Africa requires creative solutions to accessing clients. The continent's electronic connectivity boom is one trend that is lowering costs and increasing access to domestic customers—15 percent of hotel room bookings in Africa are now made via mobile phone, and this figure is growing rapidly.[72] On the other hand, there is much room to increase online travel booking within Africa—in 2016, only 16 percent of travelers made their travel bookings through online travel agencies.[73]

After initial development, destination promotion is critical for attracting clients and financing. Some destinations are already ripe for positive marketing, such as those with particularly attractive endowments. Certain submarkets are highly receptive to different kinds of endowments, such as untouched beaches, active volcanoes, big game, or a variety of bird species. Specific trends indicate that investors are most likely to acquire or develop property after they have already visited a destination, signaling the potential for tourism marketers to impact FDI and develop a positive feedback loop in order to grow the industry. Successful promotions are those that emphasize the attractive elements of a country's political and business climates, as well as specific endowments that set a destination apart from competitors. For example, South Africa has benefited from promoting its "Big 7": lions, leopards, rhinos, elephants, buffaloes, whales, and great white sharks.

Building a positive image about the country is especially important where political violence, civil war, famine, or disease has occurred.[74]

LOCAL CONTENT CREATION

Over the long term, working successfully in Africa's tourism market will depend on maintaining effective partnerships with the public sector and developing linkages with the local community. Since the profitability of tourism is reliant on an enabling policy environment and well-developed infrastructure, companies are advised to create positive feedback loops in order to maintain government commitment to supporting the industry, such as facilitating government access to economic rents that derive from tourism. It is also vital to identify and invest in the natural resources and cultural heritage sites on which tourism is dependent, as their preservation requires collaboration between the private and public sectors.

Supporting a basis for tourism also requires gaining support from the local community, which makes visitors feel welcome and contributes to the authentic experience that many travelers are looking for. Where collaboration with the local community has been poorly managed, the tourism industry has been associated with contributing to sociocultural crises, such as the spread of disease, rising crime rates, income inequalities, prostitution, and exploitation.[75]

Effective partnerships also emerge when businesses directly engage the local community in their activities, such as creating cultural experiences for visitors or investing in education and training exercises to increase local employment in the industry.[76] The rise of the "voluntourism" sector also means that many travelers are interested in contributing to projects that benefit the surrounding community.[77]

Looking to the Future

Africa is poised to capture the lion's share of future growth in global tourism due to its unique history and natural endowments. Beach and safari tourism, two of the most popular subsectors for international travelers, are already central features of the most developed tourist destinations on the continent, namely East and Southern Africa, and they are rapidly spreading to other regions. The nature and adventure tourism market is also becoming more saturated due to unique offerings like dune-boarding in Namibia, volcano trekking in the DRC, camel expeditions in Mali, lemur tracking in Madagascar, and whitewater rafting on the Nile in Uganda. In fact, this submarket is currently experiencing the most rapid growth in worldwide travel, and the relative underdevelopment of the tourism industry in Africa makes the region particularly appealing to these kinds of travelers.

In addition, diaspora tourism, a unique subsector of African tourism, offers descendants the opportunity to visit historic sites and memorials and to experience the culture of their ancestors. Cultural heritage tourism is also one of the fastest-growing markets worldwide; roughly half of all international leisure travel has a cultural component. This sector has enormous potential in Africa due to its rich traditions in music, dance, art, and architecture, and it has already contributed to the development of burgeoning tourism markets in Cape Verde, Ethiopia, and Mali.[78]

When businesses are planned and managed wisely, tourism can enhance a sense of pride among local communities, generate economic activity and direct employment for locals, and preserve resources, historic sites, and traditional activities. All of this contributes to a positive feedback loop that bolsters the long-term sustainability and profitability of investment in Africa's tourism market.

At the moment, Africa's emerging economies are transitioning away from reliance on commodities and agriculture and toward sectors that offer more growth potential, such as services. This strategy has placed tourism squarely at the center of many countries' plans for future development. Even in the absence of high levels of education and vocational training, tourism provides relatively high levels of employment for women and young people, the demographic groups most in need of opportunities in Africa's formal sector over the next few decades. The industry also creates a large amount of space for small- and medium-sized enterprises, which are poised to be key drivers of economic growth on the continent with the projected rise of an African population with discretionary income.[79]

Countries that recognize these advantages are already working to create more favorable policy and infrastructural environments for individuals and businesses interested in investing in tourism. In this light, the most favorable opportunities for rapid growth in the coming years are likely to be countries that invest heavily in the development of transport services and utilities, improve access to finance and tax breaks, and ease their zoning regulations and visa requirements.

The tourism industry is also at the center of the objectives of NEPAD and the African Union Agenda 2063. Over the next 10 years, the World Travel and Tourism Council predicts that tourism will create at least 3.8 million new jobs on the continent—increasing the size of the industry by roughly 30 percent—and generate $33.5 billion in direct investment from the United States alone.[80] Long-term projections estimate that arrivals on the continent will continue to grow by an impressive 4.4 percent through 2035—from 120 million to 280 million domestic and international travelers each year. All these signal enormous potential for returns to investment in tourism in the coming decades, and Africa is getting ready to reap the benefits.

EIGHT

Africa's Banking Transformation and Potential

The banking sector plays a crucial role in the rise and viability of Africa's emerging markets. Well-functioning financial systems are vital contributors to economic growth and development, offering savings, credit, payment, and risk management products to a diverse range of people.[1] Without inclusive, functioning financial systems, the poor must rely on their own savings to pursue opportunities, which reinforces inequality and slows growth.[2] At present, the sector remains relatively small and underdeveloped, with a high degree of market concentration and low penetration rates, and measures of financial depth in Africa continue to lag behind the rest of the world, including those of other developing regions. Beyond a handful of notably fragile markets, however, the foundations for profitable investment have improved dramatically over the past two decades. Measures of financial depth are continuing to rise, while progress in governance quality has improved the macroeconomic and regulatory climate. In fact, Africa's banking market was the only one in the world to manage the global financial crisis of 2008–2009 without a major setback.

While significant challenges remain, there is an abundance of remaining capacity for investment and increased market competition in the sector, especially in less saturated markets. Most foreign investors tend to assume that finance in Africa is a high-risk, low-reward venture. However, substantial variation exists across African countries, not only in terms of the market's capacity for growth but also in the potential risk to investors. Many forward-looking African governments are ramping up efforts to implement regulatory policies in compliance with the Basel III guidelines for best financial practices, and some have sought innovative solutions to attract investors, such as the offshore financial centers established in Mauritius and Botswana. Meanwhile, integration of the regional economic communities (RECs) is helping to rationalize and coordinate regulations—as in the creation of regional bodies for supervision and technical assistance—and to facilitate cross-border financial transfers, thereby increasing market size.

While international investors have been wary, African companies have been extremely successful in capturing the banking market, especially in comparison to other economic sectors. These regional and "Pan-African" banks have shown a high capacity for innovation and a willingness to quickly expand across borders as regulatory conditions become favorable. Partnerships between commercial banks and telecom companies have led to a rapid expansion of mobile financial services, which significantly enhances financial inclusion while reducing operating costs. In Kenya, the M-Pesa and M-Kesho initiatives for mobile transfers and deposits have been so successful that roughly one-in-four people have used financial products on their mobile phones to date.

This chapter examines the development of Africa's banking sector and its prospects for the future. In the process, we highlight a few frontier markets that have substantial capacity for growth in banking but are differentiated based on their potential risk to investors: namely, Botswana, Mauritius, Rwanda, and Tanzania. We also draw on the success stories of banking groups that have expanded out of the region's largest banking markets—especially those from Kenya and Nigeria—in order to reveal lessons for effectively entering the market and thriving in Africa.

In the coming decades, most African countries will experience rapid growth in banking, and this financial development will play a vital role in the region's ability to launch an economic transformation, as financial intermediaries will be necessary to fill the capital gap needed to fund projects in manufacturing, infrastructure, mining, agriculture, and other priority sectors. As the region develops, however, economic and cultural shifts will lead to a massive increase in demand for banking services. As such, investors in banking will stand to gain more than those in perhaps any other sector from the rise of Africa.

Background Facts and Recent Trends

In the 1980s, nearly every country in sub-Saharan Africa found itself in a state of financial crisis—the result of two decades of state-centric economic management, public spending, and mounting interest from international loans. In order to avoid insolvency and total economic collapse, the World Bank and International Monetary Fund conditioned any additional loans on the acceptance of a series of structural adjustment reforms. Although implementation of the reforms varied from country to country, the universal goal of the reform package was to achieve macroeconomic stability, specifically through liberalization and reduction of the state's presence in the economy.

In the banking sector, specifically, this meant a reorientation away from the monopoly held by state-owned banks and toward private, commercial competition—in many cases, full-scale privatization. In the two decades between 1990 and 2010, the share of total assets held by state-owned banks declined by roughly half in Africa's middle-income countries and threefold (from 30 to 10 percent) in the lower-income countries. Meanwhile, foreign-owned banks increased their asset share from 40 percent in both groups to 70 percent in middle-income and 60 percent in low-income countries.[3]

Although the neoliberal agenda pushed by the international financial institutions met with much criticism and resistance, the health of Africa's financial sector has improved markedly as a result of these reforms.[4] While one-in-three African countries suffered from a full-scale banking crisis in the mid-1990s, only one major crisis has been recorded on the continent since 1998. Most African banking systems are now stable and exhibit decent levels of liquidity.[5] Meanwhile, in many countries, financial liberalization has proceeded hand-in-hand with improvements in interest and exchange controls, regulatory frameworks, and contract enforcement mechanisms.[6] For example, most African governments have implemented a minimum risk–weighted capital adequacy ratio of 8 percent, although the actual ratio tends to be even higher.[7] Private citizens' access to banking services has also increased dramatically across Africa since the turn of the century, and the standard indicators of financial development have exhibited marked improvement in at least 80 percent of African countries, showing that the positive trends are not driven by just a few outliers.[8]

The financial sector in Africa now includes a robust variety of actors and creditors, including private- and state-owned banks, development finance organizations such as the African Development Bank and the International Finance Corporation, sovereign wealth funds (particularly in natural re-source–rich countries such as Angola, Botswana, and Libya), and, more re-cently, private equity and venture capital funds.[9] Private equity and venture capital provide particularly promising sources of funding for innovative African businesses in large markets, such as Egypt, Kenya, Nigeria, and South Africa, while development finance organizations and international lenders, such as China, France, and the United States, provide an impor-tant source of funding for large public sector projects.

The largest and most developed financial sectors on the continent are located in Kenya, Nigeria, North Africa (excluding Libya), and South Afri-ca.[10] With the exception of Egypt, these countries' GDP shares of domestic credit to the private sector—a standard indicator of financial depth—have improved since 1990, with the rates in Morocco and South Africa now sur-passing those of even more developed world regions (figure 8.1).

Although the general trend is positive, however, there has been substan-

FIGURE 8.1. Domestic credit to the private sector as share of GDP in Africa's five largest banking markets, 1990–2016.

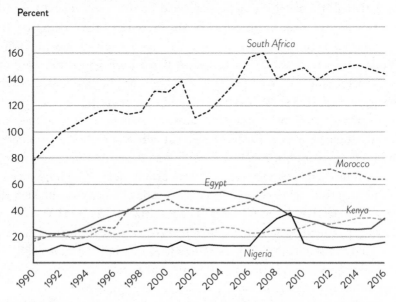

Source: World Development Indicators.

tial variation across the continent.[11] Significant progress has been made in North and Southern Africa in areas like regulatory oversight and record keeping: approximately 9 percent of adult citizens are registered in a public credit history system in North Africa and 7 percent in Southern Africa, compared to just 3 percent and 1 percent in West and East Africa, respectively.[12] Both the value of banking assets and the contribution of the banking sector to these regions' GDP are substantially higher than in the rest of Africa. Measures of financial depth, specifically the bank account penetration rate and the GDP share of private sector credit, also indicate that markets in North and Southern Africa have reached a higher level of maturity. On the other hand, the average return on equity to shareholders is highest for banks working in West and Central Africa, indicating a relatively high degree of profitability for investing in these less developed and saturated markets (table 8.1).

Even where the processes of liberalization and improved governance have progressed, most African countries' financial systems continue to be characterized by high levels of concentration.[13] Although competition has intensified noticeably in the past 10 years,[14] the banking sector remains small in both absolute and relative terms,[15] and finance in Africa is largely a short-term endeavor—60 percent of loans have a maturity of less than

TABLE 8.1. Regional comparison of Africa's banking sector.

Region	Value of assets (US$ billions)	Average return on equity (%)	Share of assets (% GDP)	Contribution to regional GDP (%)	Domestic credit (% GDP)	Account penetration (% pop)	Number of banks
North Africa	$571	12.7	44	51	48.1	28.5	125
West Africa	$168	23.8	13	31	20.3	13.7	211
Central Africa	$20	28.3	2	19	—	—	69
East Africa	$62	13.9	5	31	21	21.1	200
Southern Africa	$459	12.5	36	75	43.1	36.7	176

Source: Derreumaux P. et al. (2013, p. 16), Nyantakyi (2015, p. 3), the European Investment Bank, the CIA, and Global Financial Development.

1 year, less than 2 percent have a maturity of 10 years or more, and 80 percent of all deposits take the form of immediate, sight deposits.[16] Moreover, while the mean interest margin in Africa is similar to that of Latin America, there is more variation in interest margins in Africa than in any other world region—an indication of high levels of intermediation inefficiency caused by operating costs and default risk.[17]

Meanwhile, a minority of Africans take advantage of the increased availability of formal financial services. A comparison to other world regions shows that only 30 percent of people in Africa had a bank account in 2017, while the global average is closer to 67 percent (figure 8.2).[18] The banking penetration rate falls below 10 percent of the population in much of Francophone Africa—specifically in Chad, Madagascar, Mali, Niger, Senegal, and the Democratic Republic of the Congo (DRC).[19] The rate of bank branches per capita tells a similar story: a country like Benin has less than one bank branch for every 100,000 adults, compared to seven in Bolivia and eleven in Malaysia.[20]

Thus the current figures indicate that there is still a long way to go before the maturity of Africa's banking sector catches up with the rest of the world; yet there are a number of reasons to be optimistic about the future of

FIGURE 8.2. Percentage of respondents who report having an account at a bank or other financial institution by region, 2011 and 2017.

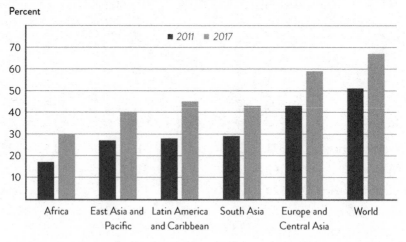

Source: World Bank Findex Survey. For comparability purposes, high-income countries are excluded from all regions except the world average.

Africa's banking sector. Unlike in other economic sectors, private African companies have become major players in the banking industry, expanding beyond national borders to create regional networks, many even continental networks. These "Pan-African" Banks (PABs) have filled the gap left when many foreign companies exited during and after the debt crisis, often becoming even more important than the major European and American banks in their role as domestic lenders to the private sector. Meanwhile, with the creation of the regional economic communities (RECs), regional banking commissions have emerged to improve supervision and risk management and to facilitate cross-border flows of capital.[21]

Moreover, banks in Africa have been more effective at taking advantage of mobile banking technologies than anywhere else in the world. In East Africa, an impressive 22 percent of adults now use mobile banking, and only in West Africa is the rate of mobile banking usage on the continent lower than the 3 percent observed in the Organization for Economic Cooperation and Development (OECD) countries.[22]

In spite of its problematic history, analysts now consider the foundations of Africa's banking sector to be healthy and robust. The positive recent trends described here have been driven by rapid rates of economic growth on the continent. Although the unprecedented levels of growth witnessed in the period leading up to the global financial crisis are not likely to be repeated, economists project that economic growth in Africa will continue to outpace the rest of the world, including other emerging markets.

Importance of the Sector

The strength of the banking sector is a major determinant of any country's prospects for long-term economic development, for a number of reasons. First, as providers of commercial credit, banks mobilize domestic savings for investment in productive sectors, such as industry and agriculture. Moreover, they act as guarantors and mitigate risk, thereby facilitating inflows of foreign capital and increasing the long-term time horizons of potential investors. By acting as financial intermediaries, therefore, banks contribute to capital accumulation, technological innovation, and productivity gains.[23] This role of effectively channeling resources into productive investment is commonly argued to be a necessary prerequisite for economic growth.[24]

Over the past half century, the correlation between financial and economic development has been well established.[25] In a series of papers by King and Levine (1993), for example, financial system development is found to account for 20 percent of the difference in economic growth rates between the fastest- and slowest-growing countries (1960–1989), while others have shown various measures of financial depth to have a negative relationship with poverty levels (Honohan 2004) and income inequality.[26]

This literature has sparked a debate about the precise mechanism through which banks are assumed to catalyze growth, or even whether a directly causal relationship exists at all.[27] It is possible that the correlation between financial depth indicators and growth rates is indicative of the effect of growth on the financial sector, as rising income levels lead more people to save, invest, and seek access to credit. Several convincing studies have found evidence for bidirectional causality between financial and economic growth; however, the independent effect of financial depth on growth is shown to be relatively more important at early stages of development—in other words, financial development is a significant determinant of growth potential in developing countries.[28] Not only are banks found to be essential to the health of the economy in emerging markets, but an underdeveloped financial sector is understood to impede growth potential and jeopardize the sustainability of any short-term economic gains, even triggering crises and leaving countries in a "poverty trap."[29]

Beyond the academic debate, from the perspective of international policymakers and, increasingly, African governments, the dearth of commercial credit is viewed as one of the most significant structural impediments to achieving the increases in agricultural and industrial productivity that will be necessary to make Africa's "revolution" a reality. Although many African states have recently undertaken costly reforms and public spending initiatives in order to establish the necessary conditions to achieve economic growth, such as investment in education, sufficient levels of market entry and business growth will be impossible without banks to act as lenders and financial intermediaries. In contrast, the few African countries that have exhibited the foundations of a strong financial sector for decades are now the region's most well-known economic success stories, such as Mauritius. In South Africa, for example, the average annual GDP share of domestic private credit throughout the 1980s was nearly 70 percent, which more than doubles the average on the continent today.

Currently, measures of financial depth in Africa are low compared to the rest of the world, specifically in terms of the GDP share of private sector credit and bank account penetration rates. Much progress has been made in financial development over the past two decades, however, and these gains are not restricted to the economic outliers like Mauritius and South Africa.[30] The pattern of financial deepening in Africa has been most observable since the late 1990s, when the wave of privatization, liberalization, and macroeconomic stabilization began to have positive effects on the banking sector. As figure 8.3 shows, the bank account penetration rate increased almost 12 percentage points between 2008 and 2015, and the GDP share of liquid asset liabilities increased slightly. And despite a recent downturn, the GDP share of private sector credit increased noticeably in the 2000s, which parallels the region's most rapid period of economic growth.

In fact, Africa's growth rates were the highest of any region in the world over this period, and, perhaps even more significantly, analysts predict that they will continue to outpace the global average for the foreseeable future. Although the economic outlook is positive, though, Africa's economic transformation remains in its early stages—the point at which growth and deepening of financial intermediation is crucial. The literature suggests that, at the moment, development of the banking sector is playing a central role in the rise of Africa's emerging markets in the interna-

FIGURE 8.3. Financial deepening trends in sub-Saharan Africa, 2000–2016.

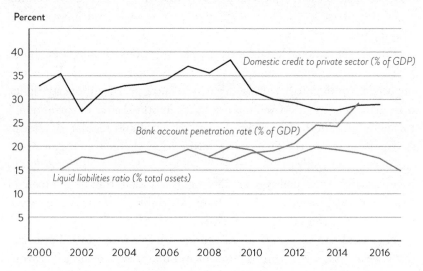

Source: World Development Indicators. Note: Data exclude high-income countries.

tional economy. At the same time, as the process of modernization starts to gain momentum over the next decade, a positive feedback loop is likely to emerge, whereby the banking sector will continue to serve as one of the most important foundations *and* one of the largest benefactors of Africa's economic transformation over the next 50 years.[31]

Key Drivers of the Sector

Commercial banks in Africa are relatively profitable compared to the rest of the world, in terms of both returns on assets and interest margins.[32] This has often been attributed to the high-risk environment in which banks operate due to poor economic performance and weak legal institutions of African states, which have also contributed to concentration of the banking sector and, consequently, large market power for a handful of banks.

In light of these conditions, what kinds of factors are driving the transformation of Africa's banking sector and impacting returns on investment? Previously, in the 1990s and 2000s, Africa's financial market was transformed by the process of privatization and general improvements in stability and governance on the continent, which resulted in an increasingly consolidated and stable banking landscape.[33] Presently, growth in Africa's banking sector is being driven by new and unique dynamics. We highlight two factors with major potential to transform the sector in the coming years: the changing financial regulatory environment, and innovation in banking products.

First, at the national level, the nature of institutions has long been shown to impact development and growth of the financial system.[34] Especially important are the quality of the legal system, respect for property rights, management of inflation and interest rates, and the degree of corruption.[35] Levine et al. (2000), for instance, find that legal and regulatory reforms can spur growth in the financial sector by strengthening mechanisms for accounting and contract enforcement, while La Porta et al. (1998, 2000) have shown that the quality of creditor rights is a significant determinant of financial development, since it constrains the ability of executives to expropriate resources from external investors.

Historically in Africa, these institutional mechanisms have been relatively weak, as compared to the rest of world and even to other developing regions. Since the program of structural adjustment reforms launched in the 1980s and 1990s, however, the sector has shifted massively away from state control and toward the private sector, which has dramatically strengthened its asset base and improved strategies for managing risk.[36] Meanwhile, the African state has renewed its focus on the legal framework supporting private finance, such as contract enforcement and accounting regulations.[37] According to a survey conducted by the Financial Stability Institute in July 2014, at least sixteen African countries (of thirty-three surveyed) had made progress implementing policies to conform with the Basel II guidelines for financial regulation, and two countries—Morocco and South Africa—had begun implementation on the latest round of Basel III principles (table 8.2).[38]

The institutional financial environment is being transformed not just at the national level but also through the process of subregional integration in Africa. The rise of regional economic communities (RECs) and monetary zones, such as the Economic Community of West African States (ECOWAS) and the West African Monetary Zone (WAMZ), is con-

TABLE 8.2. Comparative summary of Basel accords on systemic financial regulation.

	Basel I (1988)	Basel II (2006)	Basel III (2010)
Requirements	Capital to risk-weighted assets ratio: > 8%	Context-specific minimum capital ratio Disclosure requirements for capital adequacy of banks Effective disclosure requirements	Minimum ratio of loss-absorbing capital to all assets Minimum liquidity ratio Stronger supervisory requirements for cross-border exchange Additional requirements for systematically important banks

Source: Financial Stability Institute.

tributing to the coordination of financial regulations, increasing market size, and protection against macroeconomic stability.[39] The rise of the Pan-African Banks (PABs), which have capitalized on opportunities to expand across borders caused by the increasing integration of the RECs, is a prime example of the benefits of regionalization to the growth prospects of Africa's banking sector. Although much progress remains to be made in the area of supervision and regulation of cross-border finance, the PABs have themselves encouraged improvements in oversight and accounting practices in host countries in order to harmonize banking norms across borders. In this way, Africa's regional integration and financial deepening have been complementary processes in recent years.[40]

Second, product innovation is helping to revolutionize financial services in Africa, especially by improving access to traditionally "unbanked" and difficult-to-reach populations, such as those living in rural areas or working in informal economic sectors.[41] New products include branchless banking through kiosk agents, post office savings banks, financial cooperatives, and especially microcredit services. Although the success rates of microfinance initiatives (MFIs) as part of the goal of improving household livelihoods have been varied,[42] MFIs have been shown to have substantial positive spillover effects in developing economies, particularly by increasing the availability of information about borrowers in public registries.[43] In light of the positive results, donors are increasingly willing to partner with banks to provide new banking services and facilities to populations previously accustomed to using nonbank financial intermediaries. The result of this trend has been a notable improvement in financial literacy and in the number of potential customers considered creditworthy.[44]

At the same time, mobile and internet banking has spread across Africa faster than anywhere else in the world.[45] These technological innovations have reduced barriers to financing and credit, particularly for small- and medium-sized businesses, thereby encouraging both entrepreneurial activity and financial deepening at the country level.[46] From the banks' perspective, the shift toward digital services in Africa has increased profit margins by reducing the need to build and staff bricks-and-mortar branches[47]— perhaps an explanation for the relatively low branch-per-capita ratio observed in the region today.

In just 4 years between 2007 and 2010, the number of mobile banking subscribers in Africa increased from less than 1 million to nearly 12 million people, while the number of mobile phone users more generally (potential clients) reached nearly half a billion.[48] As figure 8.4 illustrates, the number of private citizens who use mobile phones to pay bills or to send and receive money is substantially higher in sub-Saharan Africa as compared to the global average, even including the wealthy OECD countries. Mobile phones now serve as virtual debit cards, sales and purchase terminals, peer-to peer transfer servers, and internet banking devices.[49] In light of the continued spread of mobile phones—especially smartphones—in the near future, increasing convergence between Africa's banking and telecommunications sectors has the potential to contribute upwards of 0.5 percent per year to Africa's total GDP.[50]

There is significant variation in the use of mobile banking and mobile money services across the continent, however—the rate is highest in East Africa (22 percent), and significantly lower in northern (7 percent), southern (6 percent), and West Africa (2 percent).[51] A study by David-West and Iheanachor (2016) suggests that three primary supply-side constraints in the areas of business and regulatory environment, operation, and physical

FIGURE 8.4. Mobile money services uptake in sub-Saharan Africa versus the global mean, 2011.

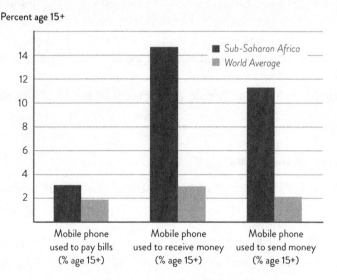

Source: World Bank Findex Survey.

access have prevented the uptake of mobile money outside of East Africa. In Nigeria, for example, lack of policy cohesion on financial innovation, high fees on financial services, low ownership of mobile devices among vulnerable populations, low awareness of digital financial services, and a lack of distribution agents in rural areas have all contributed to low take-up.[52] Conversely, in Kenya, the Central Bank played a progressive role, which allowed for the spread of mobile money while reassuring the market of its oversight; furthermore, mobile money operator Safaricom built a distributed network of agents across the country.[53]

The formerly government-owned national banks in Uganda and Zambia, now being fully privatized, have survived as commercial enterprises by effectively capitalizing on mobile banking transactions.[54] The most notable African success story for the uptake of mobile banking technology has been in Kenya, where the M-Pesa mobile payment system was launched in 2007 and is now used by 17 million people with more than 40,000 agents across the country.[55] The system allows customers to send and receive money cheaply and without needing to have a formal bank account, which is still viewed as a costly luxury in many rural and informal marketplaces. Kenya's Central Bank was a key partner in the initiative, facilitating its success through the appropriate modification of existing regulations, such as helping to push through a policy reform allowing third parties to conduct financial services on banks' behalf.[56] Building on this model, a new partnership between Equity Bank and Kenya's leading telecommunication company, Safaricom, has led to the development of M-Kesho, a mobile deposit account intended for customers without access to a bank branch.[57] More than one in ten Kenyans now use mobile banking services to pay bills, and nearly one in four use their mobile phones to send or receive money.[58]

Key Players in the Sector

From the end of the colonial period through to the financial crisis of the 1980s, the major players in Africa's banking sector were the big European and American multinationals, as well as the national, state-owned banks of each country. Much of the foreign banking presence was associated with the former colonial powers and their geostrategic and linguistic spheres of influence on the continent. For example, Société Générale has roughly 1,000 bank branches operating in sixteen different African countries, primarily in Francophone West, Central, and North Africa and Madagascar.[59] Similarly, the major UK brand Barclays had—until recently—operations in twelve countries in southern and East Africa, especially Ghana, Kenya, Mozambique, South Africa, and Tanzania.

However, in 2016 Barclays announced plans to abandon its African holdings and fully exit the continent, in a move that reflects a broader trend of international withdrawal from Africa's banking sector since the 1990s.[60]Along with the wave of privatization of the national banks as part of the international financial institutions' structural adjustment package, these patterns have changed the landscape of competition in the sector, as a number of African-based banks have successfully managed to consolidate their holdings and expand across borders, filling the gap left by the multinationals and the state-owned banks.[61] In general, the most successful companies have tended to originate from the region's largest economies and most developed financial markets. South Africa (36 percent) and Nigeria (9 percent) together account for nearly half of the total assets held by the region's largest 100 banks, and together with North Africa (41 percent), for more than 85 percent of the total.[62]

This section provides a brief overview of the histories, operations, and future plans of some of the largest African commercial banks (table 8.3).

STANDARD BANK/STANBIC

Established in South Africa in 1862 and based in Johannesburg, Stanbic is now the largest African banking group by assets and earnings, and it has a presence in at least twenty African countries.[63] China's Industrial and Commercial Bank is the largest shareholder, with 25 percent of shares, and China is the second-largest region by ownership share after Africa.[64]

ECOBANK

Originating in Nigeria in 1985, the bank's success was facilitated by financial support from ECOWAS and technical support from New York's Citibank, which managed the company for its first 4 years. More recently, it has been bolstered by an alliance with Nedbank, which became the largest shareholder of Ecobank's parent company ETI in 2008. Currently based in Togo, Ecobank has expanded its presence to at least one new country in Africa each year since 1997.[65] It now claims the broadest geographic foot-

TABLE 8.3. Overview of major banks and banking groups operating in Africa.

Bank Name	Country of origin	Asset value (US$ billions)	Presence in Africa (number of countries)
Standard Bank (Stanbic)	South Africa	$89.3	20
Ecobank	Nigeria	$22.6	36
Nedbank	South Africa	$63.8	8
Attijariwafa	Morocco	$46	11
Groupe Banque Centrale Populaire	Morocco	$27	7
Bank of Africa/BMCE	Morocco	$25	15
United Bank for Africa	Nigeria	$13.5	20
Guaranty Trust Bank	Nigeria	$9.1	10
Diamond Trust Bank	Kenya	$2.7	4
Kenya Commercial	Kenya	$6.2	6
Equity Bank	Kenya	$6.2	6
Oragroup	Togo	$3.6	12

Source: Data from the 2018 annual reports of each financial institution, except Attijariwafa, Groupe Banque Centrale Populaire, and Bank of Africa/BMCE, for which data is from 2017 annual reports.

print in Africa with branches in thirty-six countries, and it ranks among the five largest banks in at least eighteen of these countries.[66] Besides formal banking, it also incorporates specialized subsidiaries that are active in microfinance, securities, and leasing operations.

NEDBANK

Founded in Amsterdam in 1888, the Netherlands Bank of South Africa was established as a South African company in 1951. Cross-border expansion started in 1997 with acquisitions in Lesotho, Malawi, and Swaziland. Nedbank later became the majority shareholder of the Commercial Bank of Namibia and Zimbabwe's MBCA Bank Limited, and since 2014 it is the largest single shareholder of ETI in Togo, a major pan-African banking group. Largely due to the size of the South African economy, Nedbank's external operations make up a relatively small share of the total—less than 3 percent of all deposits, assets, and loans.[67]

ATTIJARIWAFA BANK

A merger led to the establishment of Attijariwafa in Morocco in 2004, and since then it has expanded across northern and western Francophone Africa. Its international subsidiaries account for 24 percent of branches in the bank's network, 24 percent of revenues, and 17.6 percent of loans. Activities include leasing and real estate, asset management, securities brokerage, insurance, and money transfer services.[68]

GROUPE BANQUE CENTRALE POPULAIRE

The GBCP is an integrated cooperative of banks operating as a credit institution under the supervision of a management committee, which has been traded on the stock exchange since 2004. The group coordinates financial policy across its regional bank members and manages surplus, while the regional institutions carry out day-to-day banking operations. A strategic partnership was reached with the Atlantic Financial Group in 2012, which led to the extension of GBCP's responsibility for the financial, operational, and strategic management of the Atlantic Bank network to seven new West African countries.[69]

THE BANK OF AFRICA/BMCE

Established in Mali in 1892, the Bank of Africa now operates in fifteen countries in Africa.[70] Its activities also include insurance, brokerage and investment, and leasing and real estate finance. Its principal shareholder (73 percent) is BMCE Bank, the second-largest bank in Morocco.[71]

UNITED BANK FOR AFRICA

Started in Nigeria in 1948 as British French Bank Limited, a subsidiary of Paris's Banque Nationale de Credit, UBA was incorporated following Nigerian independence in 1961 and was the first Nigerian bank to undertake an initial public offering (IPO) in 1970. This perhaps helps to explain the diversity of its shareholder structure, as its largest shareholder has less than 8 percent ownership. It later merged with Continental Trust Bank, Standard Trust Bank, and Trade Bank. UBA began expanding beyond Nigeria in 2007 with the establishment of UBA Cameroon, and just 3 years later it had expanded to nineteen new countries.[72] UBA has recently restructured itself from a universal banking model to an organization that provides corporate, commercial, consumer, and international banking; cash management; and trade and treasury services through what it calls a Monoline Commercial Banking Model.

GUARANTY TRUST BANK

GTBank was incorporated in Nigeria in 1990 as a limited liability company, and in 2002 it began expanding to other countries through a series of acquisitions and Greenfield start-ups. Today, it has a presence in ten African countries, including both Angolophone and Francophone, West and East Africa. Its operations outside of Nigeria are relatively small, constituting just 8.7 percent of the group's assets. GTBank's main activities include retail banking, equipment leasing, corporate finance, money market services, and foreign exchange services. The group also owns Guaranty Trust Bank Finance BV of the Netherlands, which it uses to secure funds from international financial markets. Its largest single shareholder is South Africa's Stanbic, through Stanbic Nominees Nigeria Limited, with a 22.33 percent stake.

DIAMOND TRUST BANK

Founded in 1946 in Kenya, Diamond Trust Bank (DTB) now includes subsidiaries in Burundi, Tanzania, and Uganda, and focuses on the small- and medium-sized enterprise sector. Its flagship company, Diamond Trust Bank Kenya, is licensed by the Central Bank of Kenya. DTB has grown significantly in recent years; between 2015 and 2018, its total assets increased by 39 percent and its total customer deposits increased by 48 percent. In the same period, the market share of DTB Kenya rose from 4.1 percent to 6.7 percent.

KENYA COMMERCIAL BANK

The largest and oldest bank in East Africa, KCB has subsidiaries in all East African Community (EAC) countries and South Sudan. Driven primarily by trade finance activities, cross-border expansion started in 1997 with the creation of a subsidiary in Tanzania, and KCB now operates in six countries. Its cross-border operations reported nearly $1 billion in assets, $800 million in deposits, and $360 million in loans in 2014.[73] Along with groups like Equity Bank and I&M Bank Limited, Kenyan banks have expanded rapidly in recent years and now tend to dominate the financial sector in East Africa.[74]

EQUITY BANK

Founded in Kenya in 1984, Equity Bank became a microfinance institution and eventually a commercial bank in the 1990s. Its focus is on small- and medium-sized enterprises and innovative financial services, such as mobile banking. The rise of the EAC facilitated increased integration and trade, leading Equity Bank to expand across borders with the acquisition of Uganda Microfinance Limited, and it soon spread to South Sudan, Rwanda, and Tanzania through subsidiaries. Though new, these cross-border subsidiaries now account for 10 percent of assets and 4.4 percent of the group's profits.[75]

ORAGROUP

Financial BC Geneve was created in Geneva in 1985, expanding to Benin in 1988 as Financial Bank Benin, and soon to many other countries, including Chad (1992), Gabon (2002), Guinea (2002), and Togo (2003). The group was restructured in its current form as Oragroup in 2009 following investment from Emerging Capital Partners, which involved divesting its microfinance business activities. Its foreign operations consist of majority or whole ownership of subsidiaries, such as Banque Togolaise de Developpement and the Banque Regionale deSolidarite Group, which has a presence in all eight West African countries.[76]

The regional and Pan-African Banks (PABs) discussed here have been among the most successful at filling the gaps left by some of the major European and American banks, and they are now emerging as the region's primary providers of syndicated loans and financers of infrastructure development.[77] Despite the rise of the PABs, however, Africa's financial sector is still characterized by a relative dearth of competition. The five largest banking groups account for roughly 85 percent of total assets in the region,[78] and of these groups, less than ten have ongoing operations in seven or more countries.[79] On the other hand, the quality and availability of financial services in Africa have improved markedly over the past two decades as these companies have helped to harmonize banking norms and to transfer best practices and innovations across the continent.[80] Thus the PABs promise to be the major drivers of financial innovation, integration, and inclusion across Africa in the coming years.[81]

Opportunities for Investment

Given the massive improvements in macroeconomic and political stability in Africa, foreign investors seem increasingly interested in government bonds and equity markets. In this case, prime opportunities exist where the financial market is already relatively large and liquidity levels are high, conditions only met in countries like Kenya, Mauritius, Nigeria, and South Africa.[82] By African standards, these countries exhibit relatively high levels of bank account and ATM penetration, as well as domestic private credit (table 8.4). Thus financial deepening is already well underway, and, as a result, the banking sector in each country is relatively well saturated. While the outlook for the sector is stable, therefore, the rate of growth is likely to lag behind those countries that have strong foundations but where competition is currently low.

While the outlook for the sector is generally positive across Africa, there is wide variation in the prospects for investment across countries due to differing levels of development, political commitment and stability, and policy climate. For example, countries whose economic futures are overly reliant on primary commodities—such as Nigeria and Angola—have been adversely affected by the recent decline in oil and gas prices, which is likely to dampen foreign investment and, by extension, prospects for the financial market.

Thus there are two major determinants structuring opportunities for investment in Africa's banking sector, which vary across countries. First is the capacity for growth in the sector. Countries with high growth capacity are those that have relatively low levels of financial depth, as measured by the proportion of the population with a formal bank account or the GDP share of private sector credit (see table 8.4). Second, we distinguish countries based on the potential risk or volatility of investment. Countries whose economic growth potential—and macroeconomic climate more generally—is overly dependent on world commodity prices, particularly hydrocarbons, are classified as high risk. On the other hand, countries that have

TABLE 8.4. Country comparison of selected banking indicators, circa 2016.

Country	Commercial bank account holders (%)	Commercial bank branches (per 100,000)	ATMs (per 100,000)	Mobile account holders (%)	Domestic credit to private sector (GDP share, %)
South Africa	69	10	69	19	144
Nigeria	44	5	17	6	16
Kenya	55	5	9	73	33
Mauritius	82	20	45	6	96
Angola	29	10	19	—	21
Botswana	49	8	31	24	32
Rwanda	38	6	6	31	21
Tanzania	19	2	6	39	14

Source: World Bank Findex Survey.

made significant strides toward rationalization of their legal and regulatory climates or integration into a regional economic community are associated with more promising investment prospects and, hence, lower risk.

The two-by-two matrix is presented in table 8.5. The selection of categorized countries includes Africa's largest banking sectors, as well as a few frontier markets that are particularly promising. Here, we focus on the opportunities available in these frontier countries, emphasizing the ways in which each country presents an opportunity for investment, depending on the potential investors' capacities and willingness to incur risk.

RWANDA

Profits for banks operating in Rwanda increased 146 percent in 2014, and the country has markedly outperformed its neighbors in sectoral growth in recent years. The trend was driven by an increase in banking penetration rates, with assets growing by 28 percent and deposits by 27 percent. Moreover, overall profitability nearly doubled with returns on equity increasing from 7.3 percent in 2013 to 14.3 percent in 2014, and interest margins grew from 9.9 percent to 13.2 percent. Many of these figures reflect the fact that

TABLE 8.5. Categorization of market opportunities for investment in banking.

	High-risk market	Low-risk market
High growth capacity	Rwanda Angola	Botswana Tanzania
Low growth capacity	Nigeria Egypt	South Africa Kenya Mauritius Morocco

Source: Author.

Rwanda's banking market is starting from such a small foundation—its assets are worth just 0.6 percent of that of South Africa, and it accounts for just 4.2 percent of banking assets in the East African region.

On the other hand, these patterns are indicative of massive potential for sustained and rapid growth in finance over the coming years, as there are a number of reasons to believe that prospects for the sector—as for the country's economy as a whole—are strong. While the size of the formal banking sector is relatively small in terms of branch and ATM penetration, the proportion of the population with a formal bank account is above average by African standards, which indicates high demand for banking services (see table 8.4). Moreover, the Rwandan government has shown a commitment to maintaining strong banking fundamentals as part of its drive to industrialize, attract investment, and improve employment levels, such as by effectively keeping inflation rates below 5 percent. Meanwhile, regional integration into the East African Community (EAC) is improving cross-border integration and coordination, while facilitating trade and increasing economies of scale. As a result, economic growth in Rwanda is projected to remain above 5 percent per year over the near future, among the highest projections on the continent, and many of the benefits of this growth are likely to accrue to its banks.[83]

TANZANIA

The banking sector in Tanzania is already large by African standards, yet it exhibits a high capacity for growth due to the extreme fragmentation and underdevelopment of the market.[84] More than thirty banks are licensed to operate in the country, and the three largest—FBME Bank, CRDB Bank, and National Microfinance Bank—account for roughly half of total banking assets. Most of the remaining banks are subsidiaries of major international banks, such as South African PAB Stanbic, Standard Chartered, Barclays, and Citibank.[85] There has been a strong drive in recent years by medium-sized enterprises to capture a larger market share in Tanzania, which has contributed to a declining concentration of assets and increasing market diversification, yet the smaller banks tend to be less efficient and have difficulty offering competitive prices and terms.[86] There is therefore ample opportunity for investors to enter the Tanzanian market and consolidate a business through acquisitions, either of exiting multinationals, such as Barclays, or of struggling, fledgling local banks.

The asset base of Tanzania's banking sector has already grown by more than 700 percent since 2005, with growth in deposits growing much faster, suggesting rapidly increasing demand for banking services. Meanwhile, the proportion of mobile phone users (33 percent) is higher than in almost any other country on the continent—more than twice as high as the rate in well-developed South Africa, for example (see table 8.5)—and the penetration of mobile money transfers has already started to catch up with neighboring Kenya.

In terms of the regulatory climate, the Tanzanian government has lagged behind many others in the region in terms of updating its policy framework to comply with the most recent rounds of the Basel accords, and its legal system suffers from weak land tenure rights. On the other hand, it is one of only a handful of countries to achieve almost full implementation of the initial Basel guidelines (ca. 1988) and to have a system of national depositor insurance in place. Furthermore, the central bank has been a progressive driver of financial deepening and increased inclusion in the country, with plans in place to establish a credit bureau in the near future. Moreover, although the Tanzanian economy is not currently dependent on hydrocarbons, substantial offshore reserves of natural gas have recently been discovered, as well as on- and offshore oil deposits. While development of the energy sector will likely depend on the trajectory of oil prices, there is an enormous potential for infrastructural and industrial project finance deals once investment starts to take off.[87]

BOTSWANA

The financial sector in Botswana is supervised by a central bank that maintains clear, stable, and technocratic policy guidelines, which has contributed to an impressively healthy and professional regulatory environment. The government of Botswana, considered one of the most stable and democratic in Africa, has demonstrated a commitment to maintaining macroeconomic stability and to its strategy of economic diversification through industrialization. Finance has been specifically prioritized by the government as part of the country's shift away from economic reliance on diamond mining and other commodities.[88] In a display of commitment and willingness to innovate, the government has established an offshore financial services center, modeled on that of Ireland, which is starting to attract some major regional financial institutions. In this light, as well as the country's integration into the Southern African Development Community (SADC), the risk associated with investing in Botswana is low.

Yet there are just ten banks currently licensed and operating in Botswana, four of which account for 82 percent of total assets: South Africa's Standard Bank and First National, and the UK's Barclays and Standard Chartered.[89] These data signal enormous room for growth in the sector. Moreover, these large banks report high profitability and efficiency for their Botswanan operations—specifically, roughly 30 percent return on equity and cost-to-income ratios between 40 percent and 65 percent. As a result, Botswana's banking industry already provides relatively sophisticated consumer services—the country is among the top three in Africa for bank account (52 percent) and mortgage penetration (9.6 percent), for example.[90] Given these conditions, Botswana is a case of a relatively mature and profitable banking market that exhibits potential for steady growth and continued profitability, and the imminent exit of Barclays from its African holdings would present a prime opportunity for acquisition by a savvy investor.

MAURITIUS

Though small, the island nation of Mauritius has a modern and well-developed financial market. The seventeen banks licensed to operate in Mauritius have $36 billion in total assets and, unlike in many other African countries, offer extensive credit to the private sector, with over 60 percent of bank assets valued as loans. Moreover, the vast majority of adult citizens have a formal bank account, 17 percent a credit card, and 15 percent a home mortgage—rates even higher than those in South Africa, the region's largest banking sector.

The major constraint to growth capacity in Mauritius is in the size of the domestic market, as the limited number of corporations operating in the country means that corporate debt is relatively low and concentrated. To address this, the government has attempted to develop the sector's capacity as an offshore financial center, capitalizing on its proximity and access to the other markets of the SADC region, by offering beneficial tax incentives to companies officially domiciled in the country. As a result, Mauritius is increasingly becoming a target for holding companies of banks that operate across Southern Africa. Its central bank is also developing progressive policies, such as a macroprudential oversight framework, a formal deposit insurance plan, and a financial intelligence institution, and is considering a risk-weighted assets framework. These patterns are signs of a sophisticated and professional regulatory climate that aligns with contemporary (post–financial crisis), international financial norms.[91]

Challenges

To date, growth in Africa's banking sector has been constrained by the small size of domestic markets, low income levels, and poor governance—specifically, the weakness of formal regulatory frameworks, oversight, and judicial enforcement mechanisms.[92] Obviously, the rapid economic transformation taking hold on the continent indicates that these conditions are starting to change: regional integration and rising income and employment levels are dramatically increasing the size of markets. Meanwhile, political and economic governance indicators point to marked improvements in contract enforcement, creditor rights, and macroeconomic stability across much of the continent. In the wake of the global financial crisis—which demonstrated the cost associated with the absence of a transnational operational framework—many African governments have attempted to become compliant with the Basel II/III guidelines, an international baseline for optimizing financial regulations.

Yet progress in implementing reforms and in improving de facto oversight and enforcement continues to vary greatly across countries.[93] Although the cases of focus for this study have done better than most across Africa in terms of the uptake and implementation of Basel guidelines, most still lack depositor insurance, which is a major impediment to increasing financial inclusion and penetration rates (table 8.6). Differences in accounting standards and levels of implementation of the Basel accords have complicated banks' ability to monitor and assess their own financial situation, especially in terms of cross-border exposures.[94]

At the level of regional governance, even where economic integration has contributed to increasing market size, the pace of change has often been

TABLE 8.6. Overview of financial policy reforms in case study countries.

Country	Implementation of Basel I guidelines	Uptake of Basel II/III guidelines	Depositor insurance?
South Africa	Near complete	Basel III	No
Nigeria	Majority	Basel II in progress	Yes
Kenya	Majority	Parts of Basel II/III	Yes
Angola	Very little	No Basel II	No
Botswana	Near complete	Basel II in progress	No
Rwanda	Near complete	Basel II in progress	No
Tanzania	Near complete	No Basel II	Yes
Mauritius	Majority	Basel II	No

Source: Column two indicates the degree to which the country is compliant with the initial Basel framework of 2006. Column three indicates whether the government has begun to implement policies in compliance with the more recent Basel II or III frameworks, based on a survey from the Financial Stability Institute. See Mecagni et al. 2015 ("Evolving Banking Trends in Sub-Saharan Africa," *International Monetary Fund,* p. 29); original sources are IFRS.org (Jurisdiction Profiles, April 2014) and PricewaterhouseCoopers report *IFRS Adoption by Country* (April 2013); FSI Survey on Basel II, 2.5, and III implementation (Financial Stability Institute, July 2014); Standards and Codes Database; Demirgüç-Kunt et al (2015); IMF Financial Sector Assessment Program and Technical Assistance reports.

disappointing. The establishment of the regional securities of the West African Economic and Monetary Union (WAEMU), for example, has led to financial deepening and an increased market for government securities, yet domestic banking systems in the region have largely remained unaffected due to conflicting responsibilities. Oversight is carried out by the regional body, but licensing and resolution remain within the jurisdiction of national authorities.[95] Much more progress has been made on financial integration within the common monetary area of Southern Africa, though this is largely due to the dominance of South African–based banks in the region.[96]

The rise of the PABs has brought the need for coordinated financial oversight mechanisms and regulatory frameworks into even starker relief.[97] Several PABs currently operate in the WAEMU as unregulated holding companies. On the other hand, a recent public investigation of Ecobank by the Nigerian Central Bank in 2014, as well as a subsequent report published by the International Monetary Fund, has demonstrated that norms of transparency and disclosure are likely to change in the near future, which will increase the onus on banks to record and report financial data. Currently, however, such data are extremely limited and constrained by national-level secrecy laws.

Beyond governance issues, the technical infrastructure necessary to support a healthy financial sector is lacking in Africa. South Africa's Industrial Development Corporation published a white paper in 2013 pointing to information and technology (IT) and the major operational challenge for banks working in the country, even though South Africa's financial system is perhaps the most developed on the continent.[98] The absence of a single, clear and consistent IT architecture to govern transactions, especially across borders, has led to coordination problems and exceedingly high transaction costs. Meanwhile, the sector lacks a coordinated, online database on individual and corporate credit and savings history.

These infrastructural gaps mean that current costs of entering the banking market and of doing business in Africa are relatively high.[99] Specifically, overhead costs for banks working in Africa are roughly three times as high as compared to the high-income OECD countries, and account for as much as 6 percent of total assets in West and Southern Africa.[100] As a result, bank account fees and minimum balances tend to be much higher in Africa than in other regions compared to income per capita.[101] In light of high operational costs and uncertainty, the resulting lack of competition means that

Africa's banking sector tends toward oligopoly, with just a handful of banks accounting for the vast majority of total assets. This small number of banks tends to compete over access to the small strata of high-income individuals and enterprises, while small- and medium-sized enterprises are limited in their access to credit. Further, most private individuals in Africa lack any access to formal banking services, which tend to be too expensive for rural households and people employed in informal sectors.[102]

Overall, the absence of a savings-and-loan culture, financial literacy, and credit history registers means that borrowers viewed by banks as creditworthy are exceedingly scarce, and monetary policy and governance reforms are unlikely to impact this perverse incentive structure.[103] As a corollary, the small amount of commercial lending that does exist is generally short-term in nature, with roughly two-thirds of all loans reaching maturity in 1 year or less. Meanwhile, loan-to-deposit ratios are generally low despite high levels of private demand for credit—an indication of intermediation inefficiency.[104] The result is disproportionately high levels of liquidity and assets held in government securities.[105]

Finally, in some extreme cases of political or macroeconomic fragility, the monetary system may be perceived as too volatile to support long-term contracting and savings. Such cases often report particularly high levels of nonperforming loans—in the past 5 years, the rate of nonperforming loans as a share of the total has been higher than 5 percent in Gabon, Ghana, Rwanda, Sierra Leone, Swaziland, and Uganda, to name a few.[106] Countries characterized by especially high levels of unemployment and illiteracy, low life expectancy, violent conflict, and state failure tend to experience capital flight, resulting in weak financial development.[107] Where political and economic risk is especially high, moreover, the threat of repatriation of assets and hyperinflation constrains incentives for foreign investment. For example, the Zimbabwean government continues to debate whether its "indigenization" policy applies to foreign-owned banks, which has led to divestiture.[108]

Many African countries facing such conditions over the past few decades have resorted to "dollarization," or the use of foreign currency—typically the US dollar—as a medium of exchange or unit of value.[109] As a result, foreign currency now makes up more than 30 percent of total deposits in the DRC, Liberia, Mozambique, Sierra Leone, Tanzania, Uganda, and Zimbabwe. As one example, the DRC resorted to dollarization in response to rampant inflation of the Congolese franc during its civil war in the late 1990s; the

US dollar is still used as the primary medium of exchange and valuation in formal markets, and recent attempts to de-dollarize have proven unsuccessful. Confidence in the franc has never recovered, and the balance of assets in the DRC's extremely small banking market is mostly government-issued securities with limited loan exposure—even the largest banks report loans at less than 50 percent of total assets. Despite its enormous natural resource wealth, commercial credit to the private sector is currently lower in the DRC than any other SADC country, at 5.2 percent of GDP.[110]

Despite the impact of a strong financial sector on the overall economy, there are still some sector-specific risks and structural hindrances to strengthening the sector. Such risks include the small size of domestic markets, low income levels, and poor governance in the form of weak regulatory frameworks and oversight. While some African countries are increasingly becoming compliant with the Basel II/III guidelines, there remains a variation in terms of implementation, which poses a challenge to both investors and financial inclusion. These risks also increase the cost of doing business in Africa.

Effective Business Strategies

Despite the infrastructural constraints and high costs associated with investing in Africa's banking sector, the potential for market expansion is enormous. With necessary political commitment, integration of the regional economic communities is likely to progress and continue to grow the economies of scale that will stimulate investment by harmonizing financial regulatory frameworks in the subregions and eliminating constraints on cross-border transfers.[111] At the same time, multilateral supervisory colleges are being established at the regional level, aimed at improving the collective and coordinated oversight of banking groups through ongoing collaboration and exchange of information.[112] Given these positive developments, those banks that already have a presence on the continent will be primed for aggressive expansion into newly integrated, low-saturation markets in order to capitalize on first-mover advantages.[113]

The most successful banking groups working in Africa have used a series of acquisitions to progressively expand their portfolio into new markets as institutional conditions become favorable—Greenfield investments have been less common.[114] For example, Morocco's major banking groups expanded their presence across Francophone Africa by acquiring existing groups, such as BMCE becoming the majority shareholder in Bank of Africa in 2010. Others have taken advantage of the withdrawal of some of the European Banks, as with Attijariwafa's purchase of Credit Agricole's African holdings in 2008.[115] Between 2006 and 2010, the seven largest PABs nearly doubled their number of subsidiaries, from fifty to ninety operations; Ecobank alone added fifteen new subsidiaries during this 5-year time period.[116] This rapid expansion of the Pan-African Banks (PABs) over the past 15 years provides lessons in the optimal strategies for leveraging investment in order to build scale across markets.

Nigerian banks have been particularly successful at expanding into new frontiers, especially after a policy change in 2004 raised the minimum capital requirements for banks to $210 million (from $17 million) and led to consolidation of the domestic market. UBA has been the most expansive of the banking groups beyond Nigeria, with subsidiaries in nineteen different African countries. Between 2004 and 2008, Nigerian banks were responsible for a 20 percent increase in bank branches in neighboring Ghana, 26 percent in Sierra Leone, and 35 percent in The Gambia.

Although Nigeria's financial sector was the hardest hit in Africa by the global crisis of 2008–2009—causing some banks that had previously survived consolidation and expanded to other countries to fail, such as Oceanic Bank— the Central Bank of Nigeria (CBN) has worked to strengthen its oversight and risk management frameworks, and the sector has since stabilized and regenerated. Nigeria's banking sector is now the second largest in Africa, with assets and profits both accounting for roughly one-quarter of the total on the continent, and its five Tier 1 banks have reported annual growth in profits of nearly 10 percent—or more, in the case of Ecobank—in recent years.[117]

Those Nigerian banking groups that survived and effectively expanded have relied on a few common strategies. They first focused on directly adjacent markets and members of the West African Monetary Zone— especially Ghana—before expanding further to Francophone countries and to other regions. Second, given their relatively high capacity to raise capital at home,[118] Nigerian banks leveraged opportunities for financing trade between Nigeria and its regional partners and contributing to the financial base for foreign investment in the new host markets. In the process, the banks themselves have acted as major contributors to the emergence of the regional financial market and to improving regulatory coordination. The CBN now requires that banks reach a memorandum of understanding with any host country prior to expansion; to date, thirty-eight such MOUs have been proposed, and fifteen have been formally signed. Moreover, a supervisory college has been established for the WAMZ, which has strengthened oversight and information exchange and allowed the CBN to serve as a technical resource for host country supervisors.[119]

The Central Bank of Kenya has played a similarly positive role in the expansion of Kenyan PABs in recent years. It has established supervisory colleges for its major regional players—Kenya Commercial Bank (KCB), Equity, and Diamond Trust Banks—and plans to introduce more, and has also entered into MOUs with supervisors in host countries.[120] As a result, Kenyan banks have been the most successful at expanding across the East African Community (EAC) since KCB started its Tanzanian operations in the late 1990s, and even more significantly, these Kenyan operations have proved more efficient, with lower spreads and overheads, as compared to other foreign banks that have invested in the EAC thus far.[121] There are now at least eleven Kenyan banks operating in other EAC countries, with roughly 300 bank branches. [122]

One of the most impressive illustrations of innovation in banking has emerged from business partnerships between Kenyan commercial banks and telecom companies. It started with the creation of the revolutionary M-Pesa[123] service in 2007, via the country's largest mobile phone company, Safaricom, which allows customers to send and receive money via short message service (SMS) using even a rudimentary mobile phone. Mobile transactions cost as little as one-sixth that of formal bank transactions, with no membership fees or minimum balances, and there are thousands of M-Pesa agents in informal kiosks around the country, all of which make the service much more accessible for the majority of Kenyans than the standard commercial banks. Although only 19 percent of Kenyans have access to a formal bank account, the use of mobile transfers has skyrocketed over the past decade—nearly 73 percent of people in the country had a mobile money account per 2016 data (see table 8.4), and roughly one-third of these mobile money users are counted among the previously "unbanked" population. The total deposit base increased by an average compounded rate of 40 percent between 2007 and 2012, which represents an enormous increase in demand for banking services with little additional cost to the banks. A more recent initiative, M-Kesho, is a mobile money account that has arisen out of a similar bank-telecom partnership in order to encourage savings, which has the potential to incorporate an additional 20 million Kenyans in formal banking services in the coming years.

Similar to the Nigerian story, the success of the Kenyan banks has been attributed to their relatively high levels of capitalization and technical experience as compared to other commercial banks working in the region, which they have used aggressively in order to expand into new markets as institutional conditions improve, especially by being the first to jump on policy changes among EAC member states as they are made and implemented. Many Kenyan banks, such as Equity Bank and KCB, have been the first to apply innovative banking models in new host countries, especially agency (i.e., kiosk) banking and mobile money transfers, which has contributed to a rapid increase in the size of the market for banking services.[124] Now that all of the major banking players in the region have joined the M-Pesa partnership, Safaricom has plans to continue expanding the service throughout the EAC, and the service has been approved for international transactions by a number of major regulatory bodies, such as the UK's revenue and customs agency (Her Majesty's Revenue and Customs).[125]

Although Africa's banking sector presents a number of challenges, there are few direct barriers to entering the market, and the marked success of Nigerian and Kenyan banks—both domestically and in expanding across borders—highlights a number of lessons to interested investors. First, given the high start-up costs associated with banking, it is important to take advantage of opportunities for acquisitions as they arise, such as the exit of foreign conglomerates like Barclays or of medium-sized enterprises in fragmented markets like that of Tanzania. Second, investors should keep an eye on countries as they progress with implementation of the Basel guidelines and with integration into RECs. These institutional changes will improve returns on investment by upgrading legal frameworks to meet international regulatory and enforcement frameworks, increasing financial record-keeping and information flows, improving electronic and telecommunications infrastructures, strengthening macroeconomic governance institutions, and increasing the size of financial markets.[126] Finally, given the need to find innovative solutions to increase financial inclusion and penetration, investors should target countries with high levels of mobile phone usage—such as Tanzania—and work aggressively to forge partnerships in order to roll out mobile banking products.

Looking to the Future

Presently, Africa's banking sector is relatively small, concentrated, and underdeveloped, though with significant variation across the continent. Although the demand for private credit exists, the share of assets held as liquid or government securities tend to be significantly higher than that as loans. Thus the market currently suffers from an inefficiency—a gap between supply and demand—which is exacerbated by the lack of technical infrastructure, information and oversight, and contractual frameworks.[127] However, major transformations are taking place in Africa, which are helping to close this gap.

The banking climate in Africa is first being improved through efforts to harmonize financial regulatory frameworks, to integrate payment and transfer systems, and to promote cross-border operations within the REC subregions.[128] While progress on this front is likely to be constrained by political commitment at the national level, one institution that will have a major impact on financial deepening across the continent is the African Development Bank (AfDB). Its primary goal is to eradicate poverty in Africa, both by mobilizing and allocating foreign investment and by providing technical assistance to governments and banks.[129] With 81 member countries—54 in Africa and 27 non-African donors—the AfDB has theoretically authorized $100 billion in capital for investment in development projects, and it is increasingly likely to impact the regulatory environment affecting banking through its partnerships with African governments and the RECs. Thus the development of strong and coordinated institutional frameworks, buttressed by the necessary infrastructural foundations, will be a major factor in Africa's financial deepening in the coming decades.[130]

Second, in the immediate future, innovative approaches to banking services—such as mobile money and microfinance—will continue to rapidly increase penetration and inclusion rates across the continent. In Nigeria and Kenya, for example, 20 million customers are expected to be incorporated into the formal banking system via mobile money services over the next few years.[131] Over time, initiatives like M-Kesho and various microcredit programs will contribute to the emergence of a savings-and-loan culture, first in the most developed banking markets, but eventually in the frontier markets as well.[132] As trust and integrity are built in the sector, along with a stronger capacity for innovation and experimentation, growth in banking is likely to gain even more momentum.[133]

The latest figures indicate that the 200 largest banks in Africa are worth approximately $1.3 billion in total assets, with $45 billion in annual net revenues,[134] yet the growth prospects in the major banking markets remain among the highest globally, and many "frontier" markets exhibit substantial remaining capacity.[135] In this chapter, we have distinguished these markets according to their potential risk to investors, based on their unique trajectory of policy reform and regional integration, as well as whether their macroeconomic outlooks are impacted by commodity prices. For risk-averse investors looking for markets with substantial growth potential, Botswana and Tanzania offer particularly promising prospects. The case of Rwanda is one of rapid growth, particularly in recent years, yet whether or not these growth rates will be sustained depends largely on the political will of the leadership, as well as whether or not prioritized, capital-intensive sectors, such as manufacturing, receive commitment from corporate investors.

In light of the patterns described in this chapter, those banking groups that already have a strong network on the continent will be poised for expansion, especially by capitalizing on first-mover advantage in these frontier markets.[136] Research shows that foreign investors tend to be less willing to take on the risk associated with Africa's financial market, as only a handful of foreign banks have entered the market over the last three decades. On the other hand, those international banking groups that have been working in the region since the end of the colonial period tend to be satisfied with their investments, and are even planning future expansion, which demonstrates that the risks are manageable and rewarded with returns on investment.[137]

Thus foreign investors would be wise not to overlook the potential of Africa's banking sector, particularly in light of the changes sweeping across the continent. A number of lessons have been highlighted for potential investors in light of the success stories of the pan-African banking groups that have expanded beyond the more developed markets of Nigeria and Kenya. Specifically, the most successful commercial banks must rely on innovative solutions to reaching previously unbanked populations while also keeping start-up and operational costs low, such as through mobile banking initiatives and effective partnerships with telecom companies and central banks.

Given the early stage of Africa's economic development more generally, banks will be crucial in their role as financial intermediaries by channeling resources—both domestic savings and, increasingly, cross-border capital—toward industrial and infrastructural projects. In order to raise the capital needed for credit to the private sector, however, increasing rates of bank penetration, financial inclusion, and subregional integration are vital. As income levels continue to rise and a savings-and-loan culture takes hold across the continent in the coming decades, however, a positive feedback loop is likely to emerge. In other words, while banking represents perhaps the most important sector driving the rise of Africa today, it stands to be the largest benefactor of economic growth in the coming decades as operational costs decline and profitability continues to increase.

NINE

Africa's Infrastructure and Construction Transformation and Potential

Across economic sectors, the infrastructure deficit is often perceived to be the primary impediment to investment and growth in Africa. Issues related to unreliable power supply, lack of access to telecommunications networks, and weak transit and trade networks increase the perceived cost and risk of doing business in Africa in areas as diverse as manufacturing, retail, tourism, and mining.[1] Thus policymakers and analysts alike view development of the construction industry—particularly growth in the number and size of projects that contribute to a robust and sustainable infrastructural foundation—as key to Africa's achievement of its short- and long-term development goals.

Although the quality of infrastructure in Africa is commonly perceived as lagging behind that of other developing world regions, there has been significant progress made over the past decade, in particular. While continuing to trail the world average in terms of the economic share of infrastructural development, the African region has caught up with its developing counterparts in Latin America and Central Europe since 2000. Moreover, there is a substantial amount of variation in the degree to which infrastructural development has been prioritized and, therefore, in the short-term growth potential for the construction sector across countries. Despite the central role of infrastructure as a pillar of the African Union's *Agenda 2063*, some African governments still lack the political will or the revenue capacity to allocate sufficient resources toward much-needed infrastructure projects, or to adequately incentivize the private sector to fill the remaining gap. In other cases, however, African governments have taken an aggressive approach to infrastructural development, which has contributed to substantial investment and growth in the domestic construction sector.

Despite major setbacks related to political turmoil and economic uncertainty in Ethiopia, for example, its government recently implemented a particularly progressive development program by regional standards: the Growth and Transformation Plan (GTP). Combined public and private investment in the build-up of Ethiopian infrastructure is now second highest in Africa, after Algeria, and its infrastructure stock increased by an impressive annual average of 15 percent between 2002 and 2012. One noteworthy component of the program includes the government's goal of becoming carbon neutral by 2025, which has resulted in current construction of mega-projects that include the largest geothermal energy farm in Africa, valued at $4 billion, and a 6000 mega-watt hydropower dam, the Grand Ethiopian Renaissance Dam (GERD).[2] According to industry analysts, the construction industry has been the single largest beneficiary of the GTP, with an estimated $20 billion in construction contracts available each year.[3]

In light of Africa's remaining economic challenges and the ambitious goals of the regional development banks, public commitment to addressing the infrastructural deficit will need to be substantial. The World Bank estimates that filling the major existing gaps in infrastructure will require an additional $90 billion in investment per year through 2020, and where governments cannot meet the resource needs, private capital flows will need to be effectively incentivized and channeled toward priority targets.[4] Africa's GDP growth rates are currently projected to remain well above the global mean, at 5 to 6 percent annual growth over the coming years, yet much of this potential remains dependent on whether key infrastructural development goals are funded, constructed, and maintained.[5]

This chapter examines the current state of African infrastructure and the vital role of the sector in determining future development trajectories in the region. While the quality of infrastructure is a significant determinant of investment and growth in other economic sectors, the most developed, resource-rich countries in Africa are not necessarily those with the largest economic concentration in construction and infrastructural buildup at the moment. Instead, we find that growth in the infrastructure sector is currently determined by rapid structural transformations—such as urbanization and the needs of other high-growth sectors, such as manufacturing, mining, and agriculture—and by political will, especially in encouraging partnerships with the private sector for infrastructure-related projects. With this in mind, we identify those countries in Africa that appear to have the strongest growth potential over the coming decade, in order to explore some variation in existing opportunities for investment, namely in Nigeria, South Africa, Kenya, Tanzania, and Mozambique. Finally, we identify the remaining political and technical challenges to doing business in Africa's construction sector, as well as some precise strategies for sustainably and effectively overcoming the infrastructure gap in Africa.

Background Facts and Trends

At the end of the colonial period, the level of development of infrastructure in sub-Saharan Africa lagged far behind that of the rest of the world. General infrastructure in areas such as roads, railroads, and power supply was most effectively built up only in colonies with large settler populations—especially South Africa, Kenya, Zimbabwe, and, to a lesser extent, Namibia and Angola.[6] Elsewhere on the continent, construction projects focused largely on building up the necessary infrastructure to support the extractive industries that would export commodities and other raw materials to Europe and the Americas.[7] Thus a substantial amount of investment was needed to launch Africa's postcolonial industrialization and development projects in the 1960s and 1970s. Throughout this period, the bulk of this investment was state led with funding from the major international financial institutions, specifically the World Bank and International Monetary Fund.

By the 1980s, however, the high levels of spending sustained over two decades had placed extreme pressure on African coffers and, facing an imminent debt crisis, governments were forced to reduce their investments in infrastructure, as in all other areas of government consumption. Although this transformation would ultimately create more space in the sector for private investment, Africa would lag far behind the rest of the world in infrastructural development for the subsequent two decades. Although the region had been exceeding the global mean in the period leading up to the early 1980s, infrastructural investment in Africa declined rapidly from 1982 to 1983, and despite much volatility throughout the 1990s, it largely stagnated around just 15 percent of GDP from 1985 to 2005.

To place this in a comparative perspective, other developing regions managed to sustain much higher GFCF rates throughout this period. In 2000, the GFCF rate of sub-Saharan Africa was less than half that of East Asia, and more than 20 percent lower than that of Latin America or Central Asia. Since roughly 2005, however, investment in African infrastructure—even south of the Sahara—has rapidly begun to pick up the pace. In 2015, the GDP share of gross fixed capital formation in sub-Saharan Africa matched that of Latin America and Central Asia, and it lagged only 3 percentage points behind the global mean. Between 2014 and 2015 alone, the value of ongoing construction projects in Africa increased by roughly 15 percent, from $325 billion to $375 billion, with the largest beneficiaries of this investment being transport (37 percent) and energy and power (28 percent).[8]

Much of this trend has been driven by increasing interest from a range of new sources of financing and contracting. Although the African state has largely taken a backseat in terms of direct funding of infrastructure and construction projects (11–15 percent of projects in 2015–2016), the majority of projects (71 percent) are still primarily government owned. Yet private investors are becoming increasingly important players in the sector, as an estimated 20 to 30 percent of all construction projects on the continent now fall entirely within the private domain, with a further 13 percent funded through private-public partnerships (PPPs), especially in subsectors focused on energy, power, and mining.[9] PPPs are rapidly becoming prominent in the sector, in terms of both value and quantity, as a strategy for encouraging private investment while maintaining state ownership and management. This trend has generated an increasing market share for domestic private firms, especially in the building of projects, and together with a wave of new foreign investment—including companies from East Asia, Australia, the United Arab Emirates, and Israel, for example—this serves as an indication of the increasing maturity and capacity of Africa's construction market.[10]

When it comes to financing large-scale infrastructural projects, however, the international and African development finance institutions remain especially important.[11] The World Bank Group, the European Investment Bank, and the G7 countries are still among the most important donors to African infrastructural development,[12] while China has become increasingly central to the buildup of infrastructure across the continent, both through PPPs and through lending from the Exim Bank of China and the China Development Bank. Together with China, African development finance institutions—such as the African Development Bank and the Development Bank of Southern Africa—currently fund roughly half of all infrastructure megaprojects on the continent.[13]

While the business of building is on the rise across Africa, significant regional variation remains. Most notably, North Africa has experienced much higher levels of infrastructural development over the past fifty years as compared to sub-Saharan Africa, with the exception of a few outliers. The Middle East and North Africa region exhibits impressively high GFCF rates, which currently surpass the world average as well as that of other developing regions—with the exception of East Asia—despite recent political and economic setbacks related to the Arab Spring and declining oil prices.[14] In fact, the number of major construction projects in the region increased by nearly 50 percent between 2015 and 2016, while the value of relevant investment roughly doubled, signaling a renewal of confidence in the region.[15]

Throughout the 1990s, the GFCF share of GDP was highest in Central Africa (figure 9.1), although infrastructural investment in the region declined significantly from about 2000 and, unlike in North Africa, the sector has not recovered from the downturn in global commodity prices, which led to a number of large mining construction projects being halted. Central Africa now accounts for less than 10 percent of all infrastructure projects in Africa (table 9.1). Moreover, roughly half of all projects in the region, both by number and by value, are located in Cameroon, with a further one-third located in the Democratic Republic of the Congo, signaling a significant dearth of infrastructural development in the other seven countries in the region.

Surprisingly, West Africa currently has the largest infrastructure and construction sector in Africa, both by total value ($120 billion) and by number of projects (92). Unlike in Eastern and Southern Africa, where investment has declined in recent years, the sector is continuing to grow in West Africa, with the number of projects increasing by 16.4 percent between 2015 and 2016. However, roughly three-quarters of all projects in the region are concentrated in just three countries: Nigeria (with 38 ongoing projects valued at $73 billion), Ghana, and Senegal.[16]

Thus, in addition to the variation across Africa's subregions, there is substantial variation in levels of investment in and development of the sector across countries within regions, with most regions dominated by one or a few major powerhouses. Impressive investment levels in countries

TABLE 9.1. Regional comparison of the current state of the infrastructure and construction sector in Africa.

Region	Share of total African projects (%)	Number of projects	Value of sector (US$ billions)	Government ownership (%)	Top construction subsectors
North Africa	14.7	42	$76.1	66.7	Transport Real estate
West Africa	32.2	92	$119.8	78.3	Transport Real estate Energy & power
East Africa	15	43	$27.4	86	Transport Energy & power
Central Africa	8.4	24	$7	87.5	Transport Energy & power
Southern Africa	29.7	85	$93.4	60	Transport Real estate Energy & power

Source: From Deloitte 2016. North Africa comprises Algeria, Egypt, Libya, Morocco, South Sudan, Sudan, Tunisia, and Western Sahara. West Africa includes Benin, Burkina Faso, Cape Verde, Côte d'Ivoire, The Gambia, Ghana, Guinea, Guinea-Bissau, Liberia, Mali, Mauritania, Niger, Nigeria, Senegal, Sierra Leone, and Togo. Central Africa includes Cameroon, Central African Republic, Chad, the Democratic Republic of the Congo (DRC), Equatorial Guinea, Gabon, the Republic of the Congo, and São Tomé and Príncipe. East Africa includes Burundi, Comoros, Djibouti, Eritrea, Ethiopia, Kenya, Rwanda, Seychelles, Somalia, Tanzania, and Uganda. Southern Africa comprises Angola, Botswana, Lesotho, Madagascar, Malawi, Mauritius, Mozambique, Namibia, South Africa, Swaziland, Zambia, and Zimbabwe.

like Ethiopia (39.2 percent) and Tanzania (34.5 percent), for example, are glossed over by poor performance in countries like Burundi (16 percent), Malawi (11.3 percent), and Somalia (8 percent), which face substantial challenges to investment owing to geographic constraints or political crisis.

The regional leaders tend to be countries in which the government has prioritized infrastructure as a top development goal.[17] For example, South

FIGURE 9.1. Subregional comparison of gross fixed capital formation, 1995–2016.

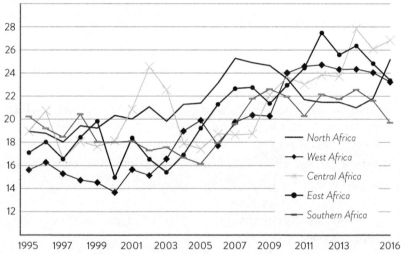

Source: World Development Indicators (2017). Note that Equatorial Guinea is excluded from the sample due to extreme outlier figures in the 1990s, owing to the relatively small size of the national economy in comparison to investment in oil projects. Average is unweighted.

Africa, largely as a result of progressive policymaking, now has the most ongoing projects of any country in Africa (41)—almost equal to all of North or East Africa—and accounts for roughly half of all infrastructure and construction activity in the Southern African region.[18] South Africa is widely considered the most developed country in Africa across a range of infrastructural indicators, including railway, telecommunications, and electricity networks. Even here, however, with 86 percent of the population reporting access to electricity and only 20 percent of the country's road network paved, additional investments will be necessary in the coming years.[19] Elsewhere, remaining infrastructure gaps are even more significant, especially in Africa's landlocked countries and inland, rural areas, and in these countries, the current GFCF rates generally continue to lag behind those of the already more developed markets.[20]

The current upward trends in infrastructural investment are projected to continue into the future. Significantly, analysts highlight that more than one-third of all construction projects receiving funding in 2015 represented new ventures.[21]

Importance of the Sector

Due to its role in facilitating and impacting every economic sector in various ways, an effective and robust infrastructure is universally viewed as essential to development and modernization. Although the last two decades of research have found little evidence for the impact of infrastructural investment on growth in developed economies, where infrastructural stocks and construction markets are already mature,[22] there is a strong consensus about the positive effect in developing countries.[23] The role of infrastructural investment has been identified both in terms of general, overarching mechanisms, which apply broadly across economic sectors and across the population, and in more specific ways, depending on the type of infrastructure in question.

At the macrolevel, cross-national indicators related to human and physical capital have a positive relationship with the quantity and quality of infrastructure.[24] For one thing, public spending on infrastructural improvements has been shown to increase confidence in potential investors, thereby facilitating capital flows and improving countries' balance of payments.[25] Moreover, public spending on infrastructure associated with the distribution of basic services—such as clean water, education, roads, and power supply—has both a direct and a long-term impact on growth by improving the quality and productivity of a country's workforce and, therefore, social development.[26]

Beyond public spending, a robust construction sector has been shown to contribute significantly to higher employment and income levels,[27] indicating that private investment in infrastructure also contributes directly to economic growth and wealth creation.[28] In fact, a handful of recent studies have argued that the overwhelming focus on government spending has underestimated the true impact of infrastructural improvement on GDP per capita and growth rates.[29] The construction industry generally accounts for at least half of gross domestic capital formation, and where robust, it generates enormous opportunities for productive employment and rising income levels among the poorest segments of society.[30]

In studies focusing on specific subtypes of infrastructure, transit investment has been shown to facilitate trade and allow countries to capitalize on economies of scale, while reducing internal economic disparities between urban and rural areas within countries.[31] Improved transit networks increase profit margins for businesses by reducing the cost of transporting goods and services, and therefore have significant spillover effects into other sectors, such as manufacturing.[32] Other studies have shown the quality and capacity of ports (Portugal-Perez and Wilson 2012; Wilson et al. 2003) and of telecommunications networks (Chakraborty and Nandi 2011; Datta and Agarwal 2004; Röller and Waverman 2011; Zhan-Wei Qiang and Pitt 2003) to have a direct, positive relationship with export levels and with GDP per capita.[33] In addition to transportation, energy infrastructure is a significant determinant of the cost of doing business, and as such, unreliable power supply undermines industrialization by impeding investment in manufacturing and other sectors that require constant energy inputs.[34]

Current measures of the quality of transport and energy infrastructure across developing regions lend support to the consensus that Africa lags significantly behind comparable markets. Developing countries in East Asia, Latin America, and Central Asia have more efficient and well-developed ports than those in Africa,[35] and double or more the quantity of rail lines constructed by area. Trade and transportation costs—which are highest in Africa's rural and landlocked areas—are viewed as one of the main drivers of poverty and food insecurity in Africa.[36] In addition to ports and railroads, Buys et al. (2006) and others have argued that a quality, paved road network is essential to allowing Africa to catch up with other developing regions and effectively compete in the global economy.[37]

Second, while other developing regions have achieved near universal access to electricity, even surpassing the global mean of 85.3 percent, just 41.9 percent of Africa's population has reliable access to electrical power. Data from the Infrastructure Consortium for Africa reveal that electricity gaps pose the greatest challenge for most African countries, even more so than transit costs, and these gaps have a direct, negative impact on investment in sectors like manufacturing, mining, tourism, and agriculture.[38]

At a country level, a gross fixed capital formation (GFCF) of roughly 30 percent of GDP is considered to be the necessary baseline for creating an environment conducive to growth.[39] Unfortunately, only ten of the fifty-four countries in Africa met this requirement in 2015,[40] and an even greater number exhibited GFCF rates of less than half this minimum level—less than 15 percent of GDP in Angola, Central African Republic,

Egypt, Guinea, Guinea-Bissau, Malawi, Nigeria, Sierra Leone, Somalia, South Sudan, Swaziland, Sudan, and Zimbabwe. However, infrastructural investment is not strongly correlated to the level of development of African countries, as measured by GDP per capita. Although a positive correlation exists, there is a significant amount of variation in the sample; a large number of relatively low income and less developed countries in the region have managed to direct a significant proportion of public and private investment toward infrastructural development, which bodes well for these countries' short-term growth prospects.

In sum, Africa's infrastructural deficit is viewed as the single most significant impediment to unlocking the region's growth potential due to its role in impeding private investment, access to natural resources, international trade, and regional market integration.[41] A study conducted by Calderón and Servén (2010) attempted to quantify this drain, arguing that infrastructure shortages undermine economic growth rates in Africa by as much as 2 percent per year, despite the region's impressive growth rates since the early 2000s. Thus policymakers and scholars working on Africa agree that the infrastructure and construction sector will remain of central importance to the achievement of the region's economic and social development goals over the next fifty years.

Key Drivers

Although the entire African region is considered to be relatively infrastructure deficient to date, much of the cross-national variation in the quality and quantity of infrastructure has been attributed to the resource capacity and degree of commitment of African governments. Presently, however, the widespread improvement of political indicators on the continent, as well as increasing regional integration and influence of development institutions, has resulted in a common acknowledgment of the need to prioritize infrastructure as a foundation for development. In the coming years, growth in the infrastructure and construction sector will likely be impacted by the economic sectors that drive development and determine infrastructural needs, which vary across countries, as well as the pressures generated by the demographic changes that are sweeping across the continent as a whole.

STATE CAPACITY

Where income levels are high, states are presumed to garner greater tax revenues from their population, generating the resources needed to fund and implement high-cost initiatives, such as infrastructure projects. Thus wealthier countries are expected to have a higher capacity to meet infrastructure priorities.[42] However, wealth and development levels are not good predictors of current resource commitment to infrastructure in Africa.

Rather than the capacity of the state, what seems to matter more in Africa is the nature of the regime, since less-democratic states are more likely to concentrate investment in public goods toward co-ethnic communities and exacerbate problems like food and water insecurity and rural-urban divides.[43] For example, Milner (2006) has applied this logic to the spread of telecommunications infrastructure, showing that autocratic governments often constrain the development of infrastructures that might produce a threat to their hold on power. Adequate levels of political representation and accountability, on the other hand, tend to rationalize investment and result in more favorable and equitable infrastructural development outcomes.

SECTORAL PRESSURES

In addition to political factors, variation in the quality and quantity of infrastructure is being impacted by the different economic sectors that drive development across countries, both over the past few decades and looking to the future. Over the last 10 years, the commodity boom has driven massive growth in the construction sector in order to facilitate exploitation and exportation of natural resources, such as oil, natural gas, and minerals, in more endowed African countries.[44] A recent report by the New Partnership for African Development (NEPAD and United Nations 2015) acknowledges that Africa's resource-hungry trade partners have been directly responsible for much of the construction of infrastructure needed for commodity exports since the early 2000s.[45] In fact, a direct, causal relationship has been observed between the two sectors, as the recent dip in world commodity prices led to a subsequent slowdown in construction projects. In some places, like Cameroon and Ghana, major projects have been halted while investors wait to see whether the commodity market will rebound to previous levels. On the other hand, major discoveries of oil and gas reserves over the past few years—such as in Uganda, Kenya, Tanzania, and Mozambique—have stimulated new interest and investment in building the foundations needed for exploration and, eventually, extraction. These countries are largely deficient in the relevant infrastructures and thus exhibit enormous potential for growth in construction, particularly since the East African regional organizations and individual governments have lent strong support to raising and channeling the estimated $60 billion to $70 billion needed to expand transport and logistics.[46]

As part of their short- and medium-term development programs, most African governments have started implementing initiatives ensuring that needed domestic and international infrastructure projects will be adequately facilitated and incentivized in the coming years. Relevant measures take a variety of forms, from directly allocating funding toward projects to forging PPPs and granting tax concessions for businesses that invest in substantial construction projects. For example, tourism has contributed significantly to growth in the construction sector in recent years in countries such as Kenya, Tanzania, and Uganda, where the needs of the tourism industry—especially roads, airports, and real estate—have been prioritized as part of forward-looking development policy.[47] Following from this logic, countries that have prioritized industrialization, like Rwanda, will need to build and improve electricity and telecommunications networks, while those seeking to modernize and expand their domestic agricultural sectors will likely favor large-scale irrigation projects.

Of particular note is the region's shift toward renewable energy sources. Population growth and economic modernization are likely to boost energy demand by an annual average of 5.7 percent through 2040, with a projected five- to sixfold increase in energy consumption. To date, the entire continent possesses power-generating capacity comparable to that of the United Kingdom, with few pipelines and limited local transmission networks.[48] To keep pace with growing consumption—and to shift African economies away from a reliance on price-volatile, imported petroleum—a central goal of the regional development organizations is to ensure that renewables generate more than 40 percent of power capacity by then.[49] This signals the potential for enormous investment in the construction of hydropower plants and solar and wind farms—resources that are notably abundant in the region. In fact, hydropower already accounts for 20 percent of power-generating capacity in Africa, which is higher than any other world region, even though current systems are relatively small and inefficient.

DEMOGRAPHIC PATTERNS

Africa is the second-fastest urbanizing continent in the world, after Asia; its urban population has nearly doubled over the past 20 years, from 240 million urbanites in 1995 to 470 million in 2015.[50] Already, the continent is home to three cities with populations over 10 million people—Lagos, Kinshasa, and Cairo—and six more "mega-cities" are projected to emerge over the next decade,[51] with a majority of the population expected to reside in urban areas by 2035. These changes will generate increasing demand for housing development and basic utilities like clean water, sanitation, electricity, and telecommunications networks.[52] In most African countries, demand already outstrips supply for these services.

Meanwhile, in many parts of Africa, especially East Africa, the number of people with discretionary income is growing at a rate faster than any of the world's other emerging markets, including India. Economic growth rates are estimated to remain at 5 to 6 percent over the next two decades, and as a result, per capita income among the rapidly growing population will soon reach $10,000 per year. In the next 10 years, this increasingly robust class will begin to view access to basic infrastructure—especially electricity and other utilities, internet and mobile phone networks, and domestic and international transportation—as necessities rather than luxuries.[53] Meanwhile, the imminent retail boom will generate pressures for the construction of office space, real estate developments, malls, and warehouses.[54]

Particularly noteworthy is the growing demand for improved commercial transportation networks, especially roads, but also air- and seaports. Traffic in the region has already started to increase at an exponential rate, placing enormous pressure on existing hubs and networks. On East Africa's Northern Corridor, traffic increased by 50 percent between 2013 and 2015, and it is projected to increase by a further 250 to 300 percent by 2030.[55] Recognizing the need to facilitate the movement of people and goods in the region, the Kenyan government has invested heavily in the construction of a new commercial railway line connecting Nairobi with Mombasa on the coast and Malaba on the Ugandan border.[56]

PRIVATIZATION

At the same time, though, the demographic changes just described make it exceedingly difficult for governments, especially those in resource-poor countries, to maintain and increase infrastructural investment at a level that keeps pace with pressures related to urbanization and changing living standards.[57] The limited resources and inefficiencies of the public sector mean that private investment is often necessary to effectively address infrastructure gaps and meet construction needs. Closing just half of the commercial and industrial real estate gap between Nigeria and that of India or Indonesia, for example, will require an additional investment of $645 billion—a commitment that likely exceeds the capacity of the Nigerian government alone.[58] Partnerships between the private and public sectors are becoming an increasingly popular solution to raising the necessary funds for infrastructure construction, while allowing the government to maintain its control over project prioritization.

Over the next few decades, therefore, growth in Africa's infrastructure and construction sector will be determined by the gap between existing quantity and quality of infrastructure and the demand generated by growth in other economic sectors, and particularly by the degree to which the private sector steps in to fill the resource gap left by cash-strapped governments in these priority areas. Given the pressing need for infrastructural improvements in order to bolster development goals in other industries, the construction sector is projected to soon overtake other major economic sectors in terms of GDP share in Africa's emerging markets. Africa's Programme for Infrastructure Development (PIDA) has identified fifty-one priority infrastructure projects and programs across the continent, which will necessitate roughly $68 billion in investment through 2020, although the long-term projection of infrastructure needs to meet development goals through 2040 is closer to $360 billion.[59] Across the continent, achieving the development and prosperity goals laid out in the Agenda 2063 will necessitate expansion of the construction industry as the continent develops an increasingly integrated and modernized infrastructural foundation.

Opportunities

Based on the relative size of the infrastructure and construction sector according to the current annual volume of fixed capital formation (table 9.2), we identify the ten largest African countries according to market size. The large construction sectors are located in the six countries that currently produce more than $40 billion per year in land and building improvements. The other four countries in the top ten by market size are identified as Tier II markets, with between $9 billion and $30 billion in gross fixed capital formation per year.

Second, countries are categorized according to their short-term growth potential, derived from growth patterns in GFCF over the past 5 years. Countries that maintained at least 3 percent average annual growth in GFCF between 2011 and 2016 are identified as having high growth potential in the short term. Among the largest African markets, a decline in infrastructure and construction investment since 2011 has been witnessed in those countries that have been adversely affected by political turmoil and the decline in the world price for hydrocarbons—especially Sudan (–3.1 percent growth), Angola (–1.06 percent), Egypt (0.5 percent), and, to a lesser extent, Morocco (2.1 percent). As such, future investment and growth in the building industry in these countries will likely depend on

TABLE 9.2. Current data on gross fixed capital formation (GFCF) in Africa's ten largest infrastructure and construction markets.

Country	Total GFCF (current US$ billions)	Economic share of GFCF (% GDP)	Percent annual growth in GFCF (2011–2016)
Nigeria	71.33	14.83	2.86
Algeria	68.23	42.90	10.65
South Africa	57.74	19.54	2.57
Egypt	48.17	14.48	2.45
Morocco	31.29	30.20	3.19
Ethiopia	28.83	39.84	23.44
Tanzania	15.87	33.51	10.51
Sudan	17.85	18.68	–1.94
Kenya	12.19	17.28	5.13
Angola	8.01	8.40	N/A

Source: World Development Indicators (2017). Most recent data for Nigeria are from 2015.

the degree to which these factors rebound. On the other hand, as expected, countries with positive growth trajectories correlate well with those places that allocate a large share of the economy toward investment in infrastructural development.[60] In fact, only Nigeria has a fixed capital formation GDP share that is lower than the regional average for Africa, likely owing to the relative size of the Nigerian economy as a whole; others, such as Algeria and Ethiopia, greatly exceed the 30 percent baseline suggested by Deloitte (2016) as necessary to encourage investment and achieve growth.

Table 9.3 outlines this classification of African countries according to the size of the infrastructure and construction market and short-term growth potential. Beyond the ten largest and most mature construction markets, moreover, we have included a few frontier markets that—despite the small size of the construction sector at the moment—have been identified by analysts as likely to exhibit enormous growth in the coming years. This list of small-sector markets is, therefore, not exhaustive, as it contains all African countries not classified as large or tier II construction markets. Although currently exhibiting low volumes of capital stock, each of the countries included—Zambia, Ghana, and Mozambique—has reached the 30 percent GDP share threshold for GFCF identified as conducive to high growth potential over the past 5 years, which signals an upward trend for capital stock in the near future. A few small-market, low-growth countries are also listed for illustrative purposes, being classified as such due to their weak GFCF growth trajectories over the 2011–2016 period.

In this section, we have selected five high-growth cases, two each from the large- and medium-sized market categories and one small-market country, to describe some of the major factors driving growth and to highlight specific opportunities for future investment: namely, Nigeria, South Africa, Kenya, Tanzania, and Mozambique.

NIGERIA

Although Nigeria produces the largest volume of fixed capital formation ($72 billion in 2015) in the region, infrastructure and construction's share of the total economy is relatively low, at just 14.8 percent of GDP (see table 9.2).[61] Yet two factors point to a positive growth trajectory for the sector in the coming years. First, although GFCF in Nigeria increased by 3.24 percent per year, on average, between 2011 and 2016, this relative slowdown followed a period of rapid and impressive growth for the industry, averaging roughly 30 percent per year between 2005 and 2010 (figure 9.2).

TABLE 9.3. Classification of countries by current size of construction sector and immediate growth potential.

	High growth	Low growth
Large construction sector	Algeria Nigeria South Africa	Egypt
Tier II market size	Ethiopia Tanzania Kenya	Morocco Sudan Angola
Small construction sector	Zambia Ghana Mozambique	Somalia Burundi Central African Republic

Source: Author.

Second, since Nigeria's infrastructure lags substantially behind that of the other major emerging markets in Africa (table 9.4), there is substantial need for increased investment in the sector in order to meet the demands of other, rapidly growing sectors. Nigeria's economy as a whole is projected to triple by 2030—with compound annual growth of more than 7 percent per year—making it one of the top twenty economies in the world. In the process, an estimated $839 billion in investment will be needed to achieve growth potential in other sectors, especially targeted toward energy and transit networks. As a result, a recent report on Nigeria by the McKinsey Global Institute projects that infrastructure and construction will soon surpass even the oil and gas industry to become the third-largest contributor to the country's economy, with 16 percent of GDP.[62]

Recognizing the enormous deficiency of Nigeria's infrastructure across indicators, the government has adopted a progressive position to encourage investment in building and construction.[63] Although the government has been constrained in recent years by budget shortfalls owing to the decline in world oil prices and by coordination issues across its multiple layers of administration, the recent National Integrated Infrastructure Master Plan has attempted to synchronize the approach to infrastructural development, earmarking roughly $3 trillion in federal funding through 2043. The benefits of the plan will accrue primarily to the energy sector ($1 trillion),

TABLE 9.4. Comparison of case study countries across current indicators of infrastructure and construction inputs.

Country	Transport infrastructure quality	Railway density	Road density	Electricity and telecom infrastructure quality	Electricity production (kwh per capita)
Nigeria	2.4	3,528	—	1.8	3,468
South Africa	4.8	20,500	29.7	3.6	104,066
Algeria	2.9	4,175	4.8	3.6	30,586
Ethiopia	3.3	—	3.8	2.2	1,410
Tanzania	2.9	4,582	9.1	2.5	2,452
Kenya	3.7	1,917	27.7	3.0	4,352
Zambia	2.6	1,273	8.9	2.2	16,866
Ghana	2.9	953	24.4	2.8	9,764
Mozambique	2.6	3,116	3.8	2.4	12,348

Source: Scores for the quality of transport and electricity and telecommunications infrastructure from the World Economic Forum 2017 Competitiveness Report, scaled from 1 (worst) to 7 (best). Data on road and railway density from World Data Atlas. Figures included are from the most recent year available and excluded if earlier than 2000. Road density is the ratio of the length of the country's total road network to the country's land area (km). Rail density is the total length (km) of railway route available for train service. Note that figures for railway density for Nigeria, Ghana, Zambia, and Tanzania are from 2005.

transport ($775 billion), real estate development ($350 billion), telecommunications ($325 billion), and agriculture ($400 billion).[64]

At the same time, however, substantial involvement of the private sector will be necessary in order to meet future demands on national infrastructure. In this light, the government has worked to initiate a number of large, high-priority, fundamental projects—such as the Nigeria-Algeria natural gas pipeline—that are the most likely to incentivize private investors to contribute in the future. For example, Dangote Group's plan to construct a petrochemicals refinery in southern Nigeria has been attributed to the

FIGURE 9.2. Change in GDP share of fixed capital formation in Africa's largest infrastructure and construction markets, 1995–2016.

(% of GDP)

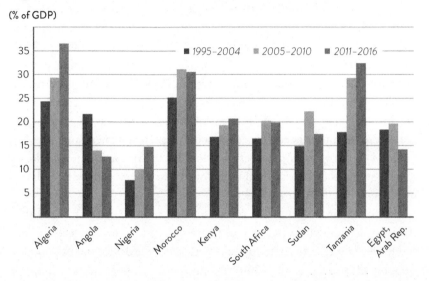

Source: World Development Indicators (2017). Ethiopia is excluded due to missing data.

Nigerian government's breaking ground on a second Niger Bridge, which will improve cross-country transport.[65] Moreover, Nigeria has served as an example to the rest of Africa in the use of public-private partnerships (PPPs) in order to encourage investment. Chinese firms now dominate in the country's expansion of transit networks, securing a number of high-profile recent contracts like the Nigerian Coastal Railway ($12 billion, China Railway Construction Corporation) and the Lagos-Kano Railway ($8.3 billion, China Civil and Engineering Construction Company).[66] The PPP model is understood to create attractive opportunities for private investment while allowing the government to manage and channel resources toward priority sectors and development targets, as in Nigeria's ambitious goal of becoming the flight hub for the West African region.[67]

SOUTH AFRICA

The quality of South Africa's transit, power, and telecommunications infrastructure is the highest in the African region according to the World Economic Forum (see table 9.4). In light of the relative maturity and saturation of the market, considered the highest on the continent, GFCF growth rates have been slightly lower as compared to countries seeking to aggressively close the infrastructure gap, averaging 3.8 percent per year since 2011. However, although it lags slightly behind Nigeria and Egypt in terms of gross fixed capital formation, totaling roughly $64 billion in 2015, the private sector accounts for a much greater share of building projects in South Africa compared to other African countries, where government ownership continues to dominate.[68] Thus, given the attractive environment for investment—particularly in terms of the impressive levels of domestic production of inputs needed for construction, such as cement and steel (see table 9.5)—the growth prospects for South Africa's construction industry remain stable and positive, and much of this future growth will be driven by planned infrastructure projects.[69]

In 2012, the South African government released its National Infrastructure Plan, identifying eighteen Strategic Integrated Projects as central to the country's short-term social and economic development program. Roughly 80 percent of the $360 billion value of these projects will accrue

TABLE 9.5. Domestic production of construction inputs in Africa's top high-growth markets.

Country	Cement production (metric tons)	Steel production (metric tons)
Nigeria	1,754	100
South Africa	12,348	7,254
Algeria	11,399	440
Ethiopia	1,300	0
Tanzania	2,602	0
Kenya	5,059	20
Zambia	480	0
Ghana	2,000	25
Mozambique	969	0

Source: Data on cement and steel production from Banks's Cross-National Time Series Dataset (Banks, Arthur S. and Wilson, Kenneth A., 2016. Cross-National Time-Series Data Archive. Databanks International. Jerusalem, Israel). Most recent figures available for each country.

to the power and transportation subsectors, with plans to increase nuclear energy generation (to 9,600 MW), the import and distribution of natural gas, and the proportion of paved roads from the current level of 20.6 percent.[70] Other notable construction opportunities include the government's plan to modernize the country's educational infrastructure, with $767.8 million earmarked for 510 new schools through 2023, as well as a number of industrial zones and social housing developments.[71] For example, in one of the largest real estate deals secured by a Chinese firm in the region, property group Shanghai Zendai is responsible for the construction of a $7 billion, 1,600-hectare "mini-city" on the edge of Johannesburg.

A particularly noteworthy development is in the South African government's role in leading Africa's shift toward renewable energy, with the goal of roughly doubling the share of renewables in total energy production by 2030 (from 12 percent to 21 percent).[72] This policy is likely to drive growth in the country's construction industry in the coming years, and international energy firms have been particularly keen to invest in the South African market as a result. SolarReserve has 238 MW of solar energy projects under construction—including the Jasper Power Project, one of the largest ongoing infrastructure projects on the continent—while Sener and Acciona secured the contract to build the Kathu thermal solar plant that will soon supply power to 80,000 homes.[73]

KENYA

In terms of volume, the infrastructure and construction sector is relatively small in Kenya compared to the largest markets in Africa, at just $12.2 billion in gross fixed capital formation in 2015. However, as a share of the national economy, GFCF in Kenya is the seventh largest on the continent, and even more striking, it has exhibited steady growth over the past decade, averaging an impressive increase of 5.1 percent per year since 2011 (see table 9.2). In fact, growth in the construction industry, which accounts for an estimated 5 percent of total GDP, has been identified as one of the primary drivers of Kenya's rapid economic growth rates over the past decade.[74] Yet, while the quality of Kenya's existing infrastructure is relatively high compared to its neighbors, substantial gaps remain in areas such as rail transit and electricity production per capita (see table 9.4), for example, and much of the current growth trajectory in the sector is attributed to the government's willingness to aggressively prioritize these areas for investment.

Infrastructural development is the central focus of the second and current phase (2012–2017) of Kenya's "Vision 2030" program. Specifically, reducing the price of electricity and telecommunications and improving transport efficiency are viewed as the foundations to the economic pillar of the program, which aimed to achieve a GDP growth rate of 10 percent per year by 2018.[75] While working to increase government spending by 25 percent, much of which will accrue to infrastructure projects, the government has also specifically earmarked roughly KES 263 billion ($2.5 billion) to be allocated to the energy, information and communications technology, and transit sectors. In 2015, moreover, the Central Bank of Kenya sold a KES 24 billion ($260 million), 12-year maturity infrastructure bond in order to directly finance projects in energy and transport construction.[76]

A number of substantial projects are already underway as a result of this ambitious policy stance. Several megaprojects have been launched in order to increase energy production, including the 960 MW Lamu coal-fired power station, nine solar power plants, and the commissioning of the largest geothermal plant in the world in 2014. The potential for geothermal energy is particularly noteworthy in Kenya, as East Africa's Rift Valley might have the potential to power as many as 150 million homes; the World Bank's investment of $400 million is helping Kenya to meet its objective of 5,000 MW of geothermal production by 2030.[77]

As a flagship project of Kenya's Vision 2030, the LAPSETT Corridor is likely to spur enormous growth in the construction industry in the coming years, directly injecting as much as 2–3 percent of GDP into the economy and contributing to economic growth more broadly by facilitating domestic and international trade. Various components of the project—estimated to cost roughly $23 billion—include the construction of a new port at Lamu, oil pipelines, an oil refinery, three airports, and an express railway line linking Nairobi to Kenya's ports, Juba (South Sudan), and Addis Ababa (Ethiopia), as well as modernization of existing road networks.[78] World Bank funding ($165 million) is also helping to finance the upgrade of several key road corridors in northern and western Kenya. Meanwhile, the Chinese government has financed the construction of the $3.2 billion Standard Gauge Railway connecting Nairobi to the largest port of Mombasa, Kenya's largest infrastructure project since independence, which opened in May 2017 a full 18 months ahead of schedule.[79]

TANZANIA

The current size of the construction industry in Tanzania is now roughly similar to that of Kenya by volume, yet, since roughly 2005, it has been growing faster than perhaps any other country in Africa apart from Algeria (see figure 9.2). In terms of GDP share, GFCF in Tanzania has increased by an average of more than 10 percent per year since 2011 and now represents roughly 35 percent of the total economy (see table 9.2), signaling prime potential for the sector's growth trajectory to continue over the next decade.[80] Already, the Bagamayo Port project in Tanzania is receiving the largest investment by value in the East African region—much larger than Kenya's Standard Gauge Railway. Other major ongoing projects include the construction of three new double-circuit electricity transmission lines totaling roughly 800 km in length and connecting major Tanzanian urban centers to electricity networks in Kenya and Zambia.[81]

Despite impressive expansion in the sector over recent years, though, the quality of Tanzanian infrastructure remains relatively low to date, particularly in terms of domestic energy production, road networks, and port quality. The figures presented in table 9.4 show that, although Tanzania's rail network is relatively well developed by regional standards, road density is roughly one-third that of neighboring Kenya, with just over half the production of kilowatt hours per capita. Several promising discoveries of substantial natural gas reserves over the past few years, both onshore and offshore, have generated much interest from international investors, including some of the largest multinational oil companies.[82] Building a robust energy sector—including prospecting, drilling, and refining for export—will require filling these remaining infrastructure gaps, suggesting enormous potential for targeted investment in building capacity for energy production and transit and trade over the coming years.

MOZAMBIQUE

Although its construction sector is relatively small by regional standards, a 2014 report by Deutsche Bank identified Mozambique as one of the top three destinations in Africa for foreign investment. Current growth in the sector is being driven by recent discoveries of offshore natural gas reserves, which are potentially the third largest on the entire continent behind Nigeria and Algeria, as well as particularly rapid expansion of a domestic middle class and urbanization.[83] Moreover, the country's position as a potential gateway to landlocked, developing neighbors like Zambia, Zimbabwe, and Malawi means that infrastructural development in Mozambique is viewed as a priority across Southern Africa.

Currently, the vast majority of investment in infrastructure, as much as 95 percent, is targeted toward energy and transit,[84] and the figures presented in table 9.4 suggest that remaining gaps in these sectors will require further prioritization in order to catch up with neighboring countries like South Africa and Tanzania. Already, there are eighteen large construction projects ongoing in Mozambique, worth a combined $24 billion, the vast majority of which—as much as 95 percent—is targeted toward energy and transit infrastructure. The Mepanda Nkua dam and hydroelectric power station on the Zambezi River, for example, is one of the largest ongoing projects on the continent, valued at $3.1 billion and financed by the Export-Import Bank of China. Other substantial projects include upgrades of railway and ports and the construction of new airports and road networks, much of which is being driven by partnerships between private investors and regional development banks.

More than one-third (37 percent) of ongoing projects are considered new ventures, which signals enormous potential for the future trajectory of the sector.[85] In fact, the value of investment in Mozambique's infrastructure is expected to increase by at least $8 billion over just the next few years.[86] If investment continues at current rates, unhindered by recent fears that the government might default on repayments of loans for completed megaprojects, Mozambique has the potential to become one of Africa's top exporters of coal and liquid natural gas by 2020. According to a recent report from Deloitte, "Mozambique is undoubtedly a market warranting close observation, as it continues en route to become a sustained high growth zone."[87]

Remaining Challenges and Strategies for Effective Investment

Although the growth trajectory in Africa's construction sector is generally positive, its current level of infrastructural quality is the lowest of any world region, which points to a number of interrelated challenges in overcoming existing gaps and barriers to investment. Broadly speaking, these challenges can be grouped into three main categories: political, technical, and sustainability related. Beyond describing each of these obstacles in turn, we also address the strategies needed to overcome them, to achieve positive returns on investment in Africa's construction industry, and to effectively develop much-needed infrastructure in the region.

POLITICAL

Although there is a broad consensus among policymakers and African leaders about the central role of infrastructure in achievement of the region's development goals, including its key position in the African Union's Agenda 2063, the level of political will to channel resources and investment toward construction varies across countries. In terms of GDP share of gross fixed capital formation, a common measure of an economy's commitment to infrastructural development, the latest figures range from more than 30 percent in a few highly motivated countries—namely Algeria, Ethiopia, and Tanzania—to less than half that level in countries such as Somalia, Zimbabwe, Guinea, and the Central African Republic.[88]

Unfortunately, however, the construction sector is a common target of opportunities for corruption in Africa, even in countries that have made substantial progress on this front over the past decade, which limits the transparency and competitiveness that would most efficiently drive growth.[89] In Kenya, a 2015 report by the Ethics and Anti-Corruption Commission concluded that major infrastructure projects, including the Standard Gauge Railway ($3.2 billion) and a major oil pipeline project ($500 million), have been unfairly awarded to Chinese companies through irregular selection mechanisms.[90]

Moreover, governments that have been unable to ensure peace and security throughout their territories have seen major infrastructure projects targeted by terrorist and armed groups. In southern Nigeria, for example, oil infrastructure has been the target of attacks by an armed group known as the Niger Delta Avengers, while Al-Shabaab has increasingly looked toward high-profile economic targets in Kenya. Uganda recently announced its intention to divert a major oil pipeline through Tanzania in order to avoid this potential threat. Thus political instability often results in unforeseen budgetary outlays, such as toward added security, and increases the perceived risk of investment—in recent years, potential investors have abandoned plans in countries like Mozambique, Ethiopia, the DRC, and Burundi for this reason.[91] Unfortunately, much of the continent's potential for hydropower generation is concentrated in countries characterized as unstable or politically fragile, such as the DRC, Zimbabwe, Niger, and Sudan.

TECHNICAL

The technical requirements of engineering works are generally difficult to meet in Africa. There is a significant lack of commercial credit to private construction companies in the region, owing largely to banks' perceptions that construction firms lack liquidity and the short-term nature of most of the private sector loans in the region.[92] Due to the inability of most African governments to fund large-scale infrastructure projects directly, international financial institutions and development banks often have to fill the capital gap, which the World Bank has estimated to amount to as much as $200 billion over the next 3 years.

Moreover, very few African countries have developed a domestic industrial sector to produce the quantity or quality of inputs needed for major construction projects, such as steel and cement. As table 9.5 indicates, of the most promising high-growth markets for construction, only Algeria, South Africa, and (to a lesser extent) Nigeria, Kenya, and Ghana record any domestic production of construction materials, and even this is generally not sufficient to meet demand. In most cases, inputs need to be imported from other countries and—as growth in construction precedes and outpaces that of industrialization—other world regions, which further inflates the cost of any project. This problem is particularly severe in landlocked countries, where the cost of moving goods, especially heavy materials needed for construction, is relatively high, which is itself largely attributed to the poor quality of existing transit infrastructure.

SUSTAINABILITY

The capital requirements for meeting short- and medium-term priorities are enormous—in the energy sector, for example, private sector financing needs to increase by an estimated seven to ten times from current levels in order to fund the major projects that have already passed the planning phase.[93] Yet the long-term viability of infrastructure projects is dependent on constant upkeep, modernization, and expansion. In order to meet current trade forecasts for 2020, existing transit corridors need to expand by between 100 and 200 percent from current levels over the next few years, yet the economic growth projections for Africa suggest that future traffic increases will require further increase by factors of 6 to 10 percent per year through at least 2040.[94]

This problem is further exacerbated as project costs continue to rise, particularly due to the increasing price of oil and steel, the weakening of many local currencies, and the higher cost of imported workers, as most African countries are characterized by a lack of domestic skilled labor. The construction of Kenya's Standard Gauge Railway, for example, required the import of more than 10,000 workers from China in order to manage and build the rail line and to train locals in maintenance and operations.[95]

STRATEGIES MOVING FORWARD

In light of these challenges and the ambitious nature of current infrastructure objectives, it will be necessary to build effective partnerships between the public and private sectors and to achieve efficient political coordination between governments for projects that cross borders, such as roads, railroads, oil pipelines, and electricity transmission cables.

Given the current infrastructure-related impediments to growth in the construction industry itself, analysts suggest that resources be prioritized toward projects that will minimize the financial cost of investment in other projects, including in other sectors beyond construction. This entails first targeting the most efficient regional transit corridors, such as road networks and airports to serve landlocked hubs, especially as traffic from landlocked countries to coastal areas is projected to increase greatly over the next three decades.[96] As a step in the right direction, the Business Working Group—formed by Africa's development partners in order to accelerate the implementation of PIDA's Priority Action Plan projects—has developed a methodology to identify projects that should be accelerated according to criteria that the private sector considers fundamental requirements for future investment.[97]

In the meantime, African governments must continue to work toward harmonizing and rationalizing their legal and policy frameworks in order to encourage private investment, including in large, international projects and in subsectors previously dominated by the public sector, such as railways.[98] At the national level, one important priority will be to address the prevalence of non–cost recovery tariffs, which impede cross-border flows of electricity and other energy produced, as well as imports of needed construction inputs.[99] Moreover, this goal will best be served by taking a regional approach to infrastructural development, as large, foundational projects should be prioritized and coordinated at the level of Africa's increasingly integrated regional economic communities.[100]

Looking to the Future

According to Africa's Programme for Infrastructure Development (PIDA), "Closing the infrastructure deficit is vital for economic prosperity and sustainable development."[101] Building robust and well-functioning infrastructure for energy, transit, and information and communications technology will be vital if Africa is to achieve its goal of economic integration, especially by linking major hubs for production and distribution, as well as increasing the region's global competitiveness and foreign investment flows by reducing the cost of doing business in the region.[102] This role has been recognized across a range of reports from private analysts, regional development organizations, and African governments in recent years. Yet the World Bank estimates that the capital requirements needed to immediately overcome the deficit by 2020 could amount to more than $350 billion,[103] and, in the meantime, the region (as a whole) stands to lose an estimated 2 percent in potential GDP gains every year until the gap is filled.[104]

Despite the remaining challenges, however, there is already a growing number of megaconstruction projects launched across infrastructural subsectors on the continent, some of which are already at advanced stages of completion, such as the hydropower projects Ruzizi III and Sambangalou Dam and the Nigeria-Algeria Gas Pipeline. In June 2014, an African Union financing summit in Dakar identified sixteen infrastructure projects for short-term prioritization which are intended to have a substantial impact on the region's development trajectory.[105] Some of these have been launched as part of individual countries' sustainable development programs, such as the Dar-es-Salaam Port Expansion in Tanzania or the Grand Ethiopian Renaissance Dam.[106] Other megaprojects cross the borders of two or more African states, and will require coordinated efforts on the part of multiple governments, international institutions, and private stakeholders. These include the Dakar-Bamako Rail Modernization, Abidjan-Lagos Road Corridor Modernization, and the North African Transmission Corridor.

Remaining funding shortfalls needed to fully complete these short-term, high-priority projects are currently estimated at $68 billion, with an additional $300 billion needed to complete second-tier priority projects through 2040. As a result of these budgetary requirements and the time-intensive nature of current building goals, privatization has accelerated in a sector traditionally dominated by government works, as much of the capital investment will need to come from the private sector and be facilitated through partnerships with the state.[107] Those African countries that have achieved substantial gains in infrastructural stock over the past decade, such as Morocco and Nigeria, have done so by building effective partnerships between the public and private sectors.[108] Recent PIDA meetings have focused on ways of extending this strategy to other countries, as well as to facilitate long-term private sector infrastructural projects that cross state borders—such as regional energy and transit corridors—which has previously been impeded by a lack of regulatory coordination across countries.[109]

Therefore, while many economic sectors will accrue spillover benefits from the improvements in infrastructure currently underway in Africa—especially those sectors that rely heavily on transport networks and power and water supply, such as manufacturing, agriculture, and mining—the construction industry stands to be the largest direct beneficiary. If adequately funded, these projects promise to improve the integration of regional markets, to grow economies of scale across priority sectors, to facilitate trade, to improve social development and human capital, and to increase interest from private investors in a variety of industries. Thus, perhaps more than any other sector, the trajectory of Africa's infrastructure stock will be the foremost determinant of the region's prospects for industrialization, modernization, and sustainable development over the coming decades.

CONCLUSION

Seizing the Tremendous Business Potential of Africa by 2050

With its tremendous business potential, Africa is rising to the top agenda of global business leaders. Since 2000, the continent has contained many of the world's fastest-growing economies. This book has covered eight key sectors and highlighted the opportunities, challenges, drivers, key players, and potential of each of these sectors. By doing so, the book has provided business and policy leaders with insights related to the transformation of African economies and their tremendous business potential. It has also provided the strategies to identify and seize opportunities in specific sectors, astutely preventing and managing risks, and effectively creating high values and generating globally competitive high returns.

The following sections discuss the tremendous business potential of Africa by 2050. Although very conservative evidence-based projections for 2050[1] are critical resources for leaders in business, policy, and academia, it should be acknowledged that specific estimates for such a long horizon will need regular updates given the fast pace of change brought by the Fourth Industrial Revolution (4IR), globalization 4.0, and the continuously evolving nature of the global political economy and continental sociopolitical and security dynamics, among others.

By 2050 and with a successfully implemented African Continental Free Trade Area (AfCFTA), Africa is projected to have about 2.53 billion people and $16.12 trillion of combined consumer and business spending. Sub-Saharan Africa alone is expected to reach $29 trillion in cumulative

GDP by 2050. A 2011 article in the *Harvard Business Review* highlighted that "the continent is home to many of the world's biggest opportunities. The trick is deciding where and how to seize them" (Chironga et al. 2011).

In 2050, 2.53 billion Africans will need critical products and services, such as food, beverages, pharmaceutical products, health care services, education, security, and many other important products and services. Food and beverages alone will represent at least $1.85 trillion of total spending. Reaching billions of customers in Africa and abroad will require effective agriculture and food processing; well-organized distribution channels including transportation, wholesalers, and retailers; and well-educated professionals supporting an effective value chain. Corporations should prioritize the countries and cities with the highest (optimal) population and spending relevant to their sectors.

By 2050, household consumption could reach about $8 trillion. Three sectors will generate more than 50 percent of the consumer spending: food and beverage ($1.85 trillion), housing ($1.44 trillion), and hospitality and recreation ($1.2 trillion). Other important sectors include health care ($623 billion), financial services ($516 billion), telecommunications ($131 billion), other services such as education and transport ($1.08 trillion), and other consumer goods ($1.3 trillion).

Special attention should also be paid to households' growing purchasing power. By 2050, 59 to 79 percent of Africans will live above the poverty line, increasing their flexibility to purchase higher-value goods and expand their general consumption. The tremendous potential of African countries is therefore not only correlated to population growth but to income growth as well.

By 2050, business spending could reach $8.2 trillion. Four sectors will represent about 80 percent of the business spending: construction, utilities, and transportation ($1.8 trillion); agriculture and agriprocessing (1.7 trillion); wholesale and retail ($1.5 trillion); and manufacturing ($1 trillion). Other important sectors include banking and insurance ($640 billion), resources ($494 billion), telecommunications and IT ($190 billion), and others ($930 billion).

By 2050, the AfCFTA will boost intra-African trade and industrial development, creating unique continental market opportunities for businesses and jobs for Africans, and putting the continent in a stronger position to negotiate with global trade partners. Along the way, infrastructure development (transport, electricity, water, information and communications technology) and a conducive business environment will be critical to unlock Africa's business potential and reach people where they are and meet their demands. As mentioned in the introductory chapter and the subsequent sectoral discussions, infrastructure development that can accommodate larger markets and the introduction of 4IR technologies cannot happen without strong financial resources and services supported by accountable, effective governance, a strong banking and insurance sector, and public-private partnerships that will encourage the success of small and medium enterprises. The Fourth Industrial Revolution and the AfCFTA may work in tandem to increase the market supply of value-added goods traded within and from the continent, and contribute to job creation.

In conclusion, although this book has mostly focused on eight sectors systematically accessed in their dedicated chapters (consumer markets and distribution, agriculture and food industries, information and communications technology, manufacturing and industrialization, oil and gas, tourism, banking, infrastructure and construction), it is important to note that all the sectors have contributed to the stronger virtuous circle and economic performance observed in the past couple of decades. Most of the challenges also constitute unique opportunities for innovative policymakers and creative entrepreneurs to unlock Africa's potential. For example, workers should be fed (food and beverage sector), have a shelter (housing), be in good health (health care, hospitality, and recreation), be skilled (education), be able to communicate (transportation and information and communications technology), and have access to finance to develop other initiatives (banking and insurance). Technologies will help the continent leapfrog the world into the Fourth Industrial Revolution, moving beyond the digital revolution using a fusion of technologies that integrates the physical, digital, and biological spheres. The responsibility to create a conducive environment for business, trade and investment, and continental integration lies with policymakers, who should speed up and scale up the process. Finally, corporations must definitively explore seizing the tremendous business potential of Africa and should start expanding before the competition becomes too stiff. Africa is the last frontier of markets and offers one of the highest returns for courageous investors.

Notes

Chapter 1

1. Schwab 2018.
2. Woetzel et al. 2018.
3. Woetzel et al. 2018.
4. Amâncio 2017.
5. International Monetary Fund 2018.
6. International Monetary Fund 2018.
7. International Monetary Fund 2018.
8. Mo Ibrahim Foundation 2018.
9. Kaufmann and Kraay 2018.
10. World Bank 2018.
11. Jayadev et al. 2015.
12. For example, the African Development Bank considers people to belong to the middle class when they have an income ranging from $2 to $20 (350 million people in 2011), while Kharas (2010) uses cutoffs from $10 to $100 a day (or 32 million people), among others.
13. Signé 2011.
14. Chen and Nord 2018.

Chapter 2

1. Deloitte 2013.
2. Spivey L. et al. 2013.

3. Bughin et al. 2016, 8.

4. *How Consumer Products & Retail Companies . . .* 2016, 3.

5. Kuranga 2012.

6. World Bank 2012.

7. Foster et al. 2016. The service reduces the high costs and risks previously associated with commodity trading and increases the accessibility and profitability of commodity markets for buyers and sellers at all tiers, including small farmers.

8. Foster et al. 2016.

9. Second only to the East Asia and the Pacific region among developing countries over the period from 2000 to 2010, for example.

10. Household final consumption expenditure, formerly referred to as private consumption, "is the market value of all goods and services, including durable products (such as cars, washing machines, and home computers), purchased by households. It excludes purchases of dwellings but includes imputed rent for owner-occupied dwellings. It also includes payments and fees to governments to obtain permits and licenses. Here, household consumption expenditure includes the expenditures of nonprofit institutions serving households, even when reported separately by the country." For comparability, figures are in current US dollars (World Development Indicators 2017).

11. However, Angola's growth rates have been damaged by declining world oil prices since 2013.

12. KPMG 2016, 9. Other countries with over 10 percent CAGR in this period include Nigeria (23.4%), Ghana (15.8%), Ethiopia (15.6%), Sudan (15%), Kenya (12.2%), Uganda (12.2%), and Cameroon (10.1%).

13. Leke and Barton 2016.

14. EIU 2010.

15. Karuri 2016; Hatch et al. 2011, 3.

16. Bughin et al. 2016, 10.

17. The market for alcohol has suffered setbacks in recent years, with imports stagnating in 2012 and declining in 2014. Guinness Nigeria, as one example, reported an 11 percent drop in total revenues in 2013–14. However, the market for nonalcoholic beverages has been one of the fastest growing among packaged foods, at 19 percent per year, and beer still remains the single largest beverage subcategory in Africa (KPMG 2016, 9).

18. Dihel 2011.

19. Dihel 2011; Mugai 2015.

20. Chenery et al. 1986; Deng et al. 2008.

21. Tisdale 1942; Allen 2000; O'Brien 1996; Matsuyama 1992.

22. The direct causal effect is mitigated in a perfectly open economy, where international trade can affect the cost of agricultural products (Matsuyama 1992), as well as in countries that engage in price setting and distort the value of domestic produce (see Bates 1980).

23. Matsuyama (2002).

24. Kuranga 2012, 8.

25. Deloitte 2013.

26. *How Consumer Products & Retail Companies* . . . 2016, 4.

27. Hatch et al. 2011, 3; Kuranga 2012, 8.

28. Deloitte 2013; Kuranga 2012, 8.

29. Deloitte 2013, 2–3.

30. Business Sweden 2016, 4.

31. Hattingh et al. 2012, 2.

32. Leke and Barton 2016.

33. Bain & Company 2012, 1.

34. Business Sweden 2016, 5–6.

35. Sassi and Goaied 2013; Kpodar and Andrianaivo 2011; Steinmueller 2001.

36. Deloitte 2013, 2–3.

37. Foster et al. 2016.

38. Spivey et al. 2013.

39. Foster et al. 2016.

40. Nielsen 2015, 5.

41. Mugai 2015.

42. Business Sweden 2016, 5–6.

43. KPMG 2016, 8.

44. Dihel 2011, 1.

45. Hach et al. 2011, 3.

46. Foster et al. 2016.

47. Spivey et al. 2013.

48. Meacham et al. 2012.

49. *How Consumer Products & Retail Companies.* . . . 2016, 4.

50. PwC 2012, 11; Martins 2007, 1.

51. XCOM Africa 2009, 2.

52. KPMG 2016, 8.

53. Foster et al. 2016.

54. Business Sweden 2016, 6; KPMG 2016, 8.

55. KPMG 2016, 9.

56. KPMG 2016, 9.

57. See, for example, Business Sweden 2016, 7.

58. KPMG 2016, 9.

59. KPMG 2016, 9.

60. Business Sweden 2016, 5.

61. KPMG 2016, 10.

62. KPMG 2016, 15.

63. KPMG 2016, 15.

64. Invest in Morocco 2017.

65. Dihel 2011, 1.

66. KPMG 2015, 13. Other countries in the top five according to the analyses cited include Seychelles, Ghana, and Zambia.

67. Business Sweden 2016, 5.

68. Spivey et al. 2013.

69. XCOM Africa 2009, 2.
70. Dihel 2011, 5–6.
71. Foster et al. 2016.
72. Spivey et al. 2013.
73. *How Consumer Products & Retail Companies*... 2016, 2.
74. Dubai Exports Agency 2016, 5.
75. Foster et al. 2016.
76. Deloitte 2013, 4.
77. Kuranga 2012.
78. *How Consumer Products & Retail Companies*... 2016, 17.
79. Dihel 2011, 6.
80. Bughin et al. 2016, 16.
81. Dihel 2011, 9.
82. Spivey et al. 2013.
83. *How Consumer Products & Retail Companies*... 2016, 3.
84. Spivey et al. 2013.
85. Karuri 2016.
86. Hatch et al. 2011, 32.
87. Foster et al. 2016.
88. Spivey et al. 2013; Dihel 2011, 9.
89. Meacham et al. 2012.
90. Bughin et al. 2016, 7–8.
91. Spivey et al. 2013.
92. Spivey et al. 2013.
93. Dihel 2011, 1–2; XCOM Africa 2009, 3.
94. Foster et al. 2016.
95. Kuranga 2012, 8.
96. Hatch et al. 2011, 15.
97. Karuri 2016.
98. Meacham et al. 2012.
99. Hatch et al. 2011, 3; Leke and Barton 2016.

Chapter 3

1. Binswanger-Mkhize and Savastano 2017, 26.
2. Sheahan and Barrett 2017, 14.
3. Christiaensen, Demery, and Kuhl 2011, 239.
4. Bah et al. 2015, 37.
5. *Africa Agriculture Status Report* 2016, 19.
6. Schaffnit-Chatterjee 2014, 1.
7. Byerlee et al. 2013, 3.
8. Schaffnit-Chatterjee 2014, 10.
9. UNIDO 2016, 21.
10. Byerlee et al. 2013, 25.

11. *Africa Agriculture Status Report* 2016, 31.

12. Schaffnit-Chatterjee 2014, 25.

13. Jayne, Mather, and Mghenyi 2010.

14. African Development Bank et al. 2015, 37.

15. *Africa Agriculture Status Report* 2016, 2.

16. *Africa Agriculture Status Report* 2016, 17; Deininger, Xia, and Savastano 2015.

17. UNIDO 2016, 21.

18. AfDB 2016, 9.

19. Alemayehu 2014, 2.

20. *Africa Agriculture Status Report* 2016, 10; Byerlee et al. 2013, 27.

21. AfDB 2016, 5.

22. Byerlee et al. 2013, 16.

23. Sanghvi et al. 2011, cited in Van Rooyen 2014, 25.

24. Schaffnit-Chatterjee 2014, 15.

25. Byerlee et al. 2013, 16.

26. UNIDO 2016, 20; *Africa Agriculture Status Report* 2016, 4. See also Mellor 1976; Timmer 1988; Johnston and Kilby 1975; Lipton 2005; Vollrath 2007.

27. Schaffnit-Chatterjee 2014, 3. See Bates 1981.

28. Bates 1981; African Development Bank et al. 2015, 39–40.

29. *Africa Agriculture Status Report* 2016, 19.

30. Chamberlin and Ricker-Gilber 2016; Jin and Jayne 2013; *Africa Agriculture Status Report* 2016, 12.

31. Nomathemba 2010, 8–12.

32. Byerlee et al. 2013, 15. "Agribusiness denotes organized firms from small and medium enterprises to multinational corporations involved in input supply or in downstream transformation. It includes commercial agriculture that involves some transformation activities (even if they are basic). It includes smallholders and micro-enterprises in food processing and retail to the extent that they are market oriented – indeed these producers and enterprises make up the bulk of agribusiness activity in Africa today" (Byerlee et al. 2013, 3).

33. Alemayehu 2014, 18.

34. Alexandratos and Bruinsma 2012, 65; Bremner 2012, 2.

35. Van Rooyen 2014, 22.

36. Alexandratos and Bruinsma 2012, 69–72; Hubert et al. 2010, 39–40.

37. Bremner 2012, 2.

38. Hubert et al. 2010, 41.

39. Van Rooyen 2014, 22.

40. Byerlee et al. 2013, 68; Hubert et al. 2010, 42–43.

41. Byerlee et al. 2013, 48.

42. Alexandratos and Bruinsma 2012, 84; Hubert et al. 2010, 36.

43. Schaffnit-Chatterjee 2014, 7.

44. Hubert et al. 2010, 42–43.

45. Byerlee et al. 2013, 16.

46. UNECA 2010, 8.

47. *Africa Agriculture Status Report* 2016, 2.

48. Van Rooyen 2014, 20.

49. Cotula et al. 2009; Mhlanga 2010, 20–21.

50. UNCTAD 2009.

51. Borger 2008.

52. von Braun and Meinzen-Dick 2009; Borger 2008.

53. Borger 2008.

54. Mhlanga 2010, 21–22.

55. *Africa Agriculture Status Report* 2016, 26; Sasson 2012.

56. Mhlanga 2010, 35–36.

57. Mhlanga 2010, 35–36.

58. Mhlanga 2010, 39.

59. Mhlanga 2010, 37–40.

60. UNCTAD 2008.

61. *Africa Agriculture Status Report* 2016, 19.

62. UNIDO 2016, 27.

63. Schaffnit-Chatterjee 2014, 1.

64. African Development Bank et al. 2015, 19.

65. Schaffnit-Chatterjee 2014, 25; Alemayehu 2014, 7.

66. Mbabazi et al. 2015.

67. African Development Bank et al. 2015, 39–40.

68. Kowalski et al. 2015.

69. Mbabazi 2015.

70. PricewaterhouseCoopers 2007, 9.

71. Mhlanga 2010, 24.

72. Msuya 2007 and World Economic Forum 2009, cited in Mhlanga 2010, 24.

73. Bates 1981; African Development Bank et al. 2015, 39–40.

74. Dorosh et al. 2010.

75. World Bank 2007, cited in Mhlanga 2010, 24.

76. Mosoti and Koroma 2008.

77. PricewaterhouseCoopers 2007, 25.

78. African Development Bank et al. 2015, 39–40.

79. Schaffnit-Chatterjee 2014, 25.

80. PricewaterhouseCoopers 2007, 25.

81. Hubert et al. 2010, 41.

82. Mhlanga 2010, 20–21; Montpellier Panel 2014 quoted by *Africa Agriculture Status Report* 2016, 11–12.

83. Drechsel et al. 2001; Stoorvogel and Smaling 1990; Tittonell and Giller 2013.

84. *Africa Agriculture Status Report* 2016, 12.

85. *Africa Agricultural Status Report* 2016, 11.

86. Msangi 2012, 5.

87. *Africa Agriculture Status Report* 2016, 14.

88. UNIDO Statistics Unit 2013, 26.

89. UNECA 2010, 11.

90. Jayne et al. 2003, cited in UNECA 2010, 24.

91. Kelly et al. 2003, cited in UNECA 2010, 48.

92. UNECA 2010, 48.

93. Minde et al. 2008; UNECA 2010, 49–50.

94. Rohrbach, Minde and Howard 2003.

95. UNECA 2010, 60.

96. Alexandratos and Bruinsma 2012, 85.

97. AfDB 2016, 7.

98. Schaffnit-Chatterjee 2014, 1; Hubert et al. 2010, 38.

99. UNECA 2010, 58.

100. UNIDO 2013, 26.

101. *Africa Agriculture Status Report* 2016, 16.

102. PricewaterhouseCoopers 2007, 64–65.

103. PricewaterhouseCoopers 2007, 64–65.

104. Swinnen 2007 and McCoullough et al. 2008, cited in Van Rooyen 2014, 21.

105. UNIDO 2016, 21; Hughes 2009; Vermeulen et al. 2008.

106. Hubert et al. 2010, 38; Van Rooyen 2014, 21–22.

107. UNIDO 2016, 9.

108. *Africa Agriculture Status Report* 2016, 16.

109. Mhlanga 2010, 1.

110. Hubert et al. 2010, 42–43; Schaffnit-Chatterjee 2014, 1.

111. UNECA 2010, 1.

112. *Africa Agriculture Status Report* 2016, 16.

113. UNIDO 2016; African Development Bank et al. 2015, 37–38.

114. AfDB 2016, 6.

115. von Braun and Meinzen-Dick, 2009.

116. *Africa Agriculture Status Report* 2016, 19.

117. Van Rooyen, 2014, 19; Bremner 2012, 2.

Chapter 4

1. Apulu and Latham 2011, 51–52; Adeosun et al. 2009; Ashrafi and Murtaza 2008; Wangwe 2007.

2. Stefanski 2014, 11.

3. Ewing 2015, 11.

4. IST Africa 2012; Msimang 2011; Stefanski 2014, 11.

5. Adeya 2001, 12–13.

6. Adeya 2001, 12–13.

7. Deloitte 2014, 4–11.

8. GSMA Intelligence 2016, 2.

9. Soremekun and Malgwi 2013.

10. Jumia 2019; Rizzato 2017.

11. M&G Africa Writer 2016; Kenya National Bureau of Statistics and Communications Authority of Kenya.

12. Bankole and Mimbi 2015, 2.

13. GSMA Intelligence 2016, 2.

14. Silver and Johnson 2018.

15. GSMA Intelligence 2018, 3.

16. GSMA Intelligence, 2016 2; Cisco Systems 2017, 2–3; Rice-Oxley and Flood 2016.

17. GSMA Intelligence 2016, 3.

18. Deloitte 2014, 4–11; Tcheng et al. 2007.

19. GSMA Intelligence 2018, 18.

20. See Vu 2011.

21. Bresnahan et al. 2002; Buhalis 2003; Chowdhury and Wolf 2003; Obijiofor et al. 2000; Love et al. 2006; Apulu and Latham 2010, 2011.

22. Spanos et al. 2002; den Hengst and Sol 2001; Grace, Kenny, and Qiang 2003; Fink and Disterer 2006; Adeosun et al. 2009.

23. Apulu and Latham 2011; Irani 2002; Fulanteli and Allegra 2003; Maldeni and Jayasena 2009; Ongori and Migiro 2010; Chibelushi 2008; Jennex et al. 2004.

24. Datta and Agarwal 2004; Waverman et al. 2005; Sridhar and Sridhar 2006.

25. Di Battista et al. 2015, 4; Apulu and Latham 2011.

26. Bussotti 2015.

27. Calandro et al. 2010, 1–3.

28. Kwankam 2004; Mars and Scott 2015.

29. Qureshi et al. 2014.

30. Sambo and WHO 2014.

31. Bankole and Mimbi 2015.

32. Lee, Levendis, and Gutierrez 2009; Andrianaivo and Kpodar 2011.

33. Deloitte 2016.

34. See Pepper and Garrity 2015.

35. GSMA Intelligence 2016, 2; Matambalya and Wolf 2001.

36. Whether or not ICT contributes to economic growth might also depend on variance in country-level endowments, such as institutional quality, education and skills levels, and trade openness (Khuong 2005).

37. Heeks 1999.

38. Pepper and Garrity 2015, 33–34.

39. Grace et al. 2003; Andrianaivo and Kpodar 2011, 7–9.

40. M&G Africa Writer 2016.

41. Stefanski 2014.

42. PIDA 2014, 3.

43. Stefanski 2014, 3; see also Sassi and Goaied 2013.

44. GSMA Intelligence 2016, 2.

45. Deloitte 2014, 7.

46. Straub 2008; Ngwenyama and Morawczynski 2009; Sridhar and Sridhar 2008.

47. Deloitte 2014.

48. PIDA 2012, 8.

49. GSMA Intelligence 2016, 2.

50. Gillwald and Moyo 2014, 1.

51. Mirembe 2010, 6–17.

52. Deloitte 2014, 4.

53. GSMA Intelligence 2016, 2.

54. Soremekun and Malgwi (2013) show that ICT development has progressed more rapidly in North and Southern Africa, while the East and West have lagged behind.

55. Ewing 2015, 14.

56. Deloitte 2014, 4.

57. See Baller et al. 2016, figures 10, 15.

58. Note that the small island nations (Mauritius, Seychelles, Cape Verde), Namibia, and The Gambia were excluded from the sample, even though they rank in the WEF's top ten, due to the lack of some measures used for evaluation.

59. Deloitte 2014, 4.

60. Gillwald and Moyo 2014.

61. Duncombe and Heeks 1999. See also Adeya 2001, 14.

62. Sebusang and Maasupe 2003.

63. Mutula and Van Brakel 2007.

64. IST Africa 2012.

65. Asare et al. 2012.

66. Asare et al. 2012.

67. Nkwe 2012; Sebusang and Maasupe 2003; Moahi 2009.

68. Gillwald and Moyo 2014.

69. Afari-Kumah and Tanye (2009) found that ICT uptake was lagging in Ghana's education system, even at the university level.

70. Gillwald and Moyo 2014.

71. Akomea-Bonsu and Sampong 2012.

72. Akomea-Bonsu and Sampong 2012.

73. Akomea-Bonsu and Sampong 2012.

74. Owen and Darkwa 1999; Baller et al. 2016.

75. Quarshie and Ami-Nahr 2012. Kwapong (2007) has found that even relatively small differences in income levels determine willingness to purchase and use ICTs in different rural communities in Ghana.

76. See also Fortune of Africa n.d.

77. See Harrison 2005.

78. See Farrell 2007; Lwakabamba 2005.

79. Ben-Ari 2014.

80. Ben-Ari 2014.

81. Stefanski 2014, 6.

82. PIDA 2012, 91.

83. Deloitte 2014, 4.

84. M&G Africa Writer 2016.

85. Deloitte 2014, 4.

86. Deloitte 2014, 4.

87. M&G Africa Writer 2016.
88. InfoDev et al. 2010, 17.
89. Adeya 2001, 11; PIDA 2012, 91; M&G Africa Writer 2016.
90. PIDA 2012, 91.
91. Fortune of Africa n.d.
92. Adeya 2001, 11.
93. InfoDev et al. 2010, 17; Internet Society 2016, 1.
94. PIDA 2012, 8.
95. Apulu and Latham 2011.
96. Deloitte 2014.
97. GSMA Intelligence 2016, 2.
98. Deloitte 2014.
99. Lancaster 2017, 171; Gillwald and Moyo 2014.
100. Deloitte 2014, 21.
101. Deloitte 2014.
102. Lancaster 2017, 172.
103. UN 2018.
104. Deloitte 2014, 8.
105. Deloitte 2014.
106. GSMA Intelligence 2016, 2.
107. Ewing 2015, 9.
108. Deloitte 2014, 4–11.
109. Deloitte 2014, 4–11.
110. GSMA Intelligence 2016, 3.
111. Other studies have shown that, in addition to the urban-rural divide, a gender gap exists in ICT uptake, with fewer women and girls reporting access to the internet in Africa (Deen-Swarray et al. 2013; Kwapong 2007).
112. Internet Society 2016, 1; Ewing 2015, 9.

Chapter 5

1. Clark 1940; Lewis 1954; Chenery 1960; Kaldor 1966; Kuznets and Murphy 1966; Cornwall 1977.
2. Manyika et al. 2012.
3. Bhorat and Tarp 2016.
4. Signé 2018.
5. Sun 2017, 122–129.
6. John Page, interview with Brookings Cafeteria Podcast, January 22, 2016.
7. Kuznets and Murphy 1966; Tybout 2000; Ansu et al. 2016, 7; Rodrik 2012.
8. KPMG 2013, 1; Chang et al. 2016.
9. Noble 1994, A6.
10. Ansu et al. 2016, 1–2.
11. Outliers include Nigeria, Kenya, Tanzania, and Ethiopia; see ACET 2014, 38.
12. KPMG 2015, 6.

13. Taken as a whole though, the regional economic community of East Africa (EAC) surpasses the Southern Africa Development Community (SADC) in terms of manufactured goods' share of total trade, at 54 and 51 percent, respectively, and both substantially exceed the rates in the Community of Sahel-Saharan States (34%) and the Economic Community of West African States (26%). (Conde et al. 2015, 2–4).

14. Balchin et al. 2016, 7, 5; KPMG 2015, 6.

15. Bolaky 2011.

16. Foreign Direct Investment Intelligence 2016a, 8.

17. Songwe 2019.

18. African Union Commission 2015, 5.

19. Bughin et al. 2016, 1, 8–9.

20. Deloitte 2016, 1.

21. Nelson and Phelps 1966; Evenson and Westphal 1995; Keller 1996; Tybout 2000.

22. O'Regan et al. 2006; Narayanan 2001; Bessant and Tidd 2007; Prakash and Gupta 2008; Wheelen and Hunger 1999.

23. KPMG 2016, 4.

24. UNIDO 2015, 3.

25. The Economist Intelligence Unit 2016.

26. McPherson 1996; Mead and Liedholm 1998. Note that the findings apply to secondary education attainment, while primary education is shown to have no effect.

27. KPMG 2013, 8.

28. O'Regan et al. 2006

29. Tybout 2000; Brunetti et al. 1997; World Bank 1994.

30. O'Regan et al. 2006.

31. The Economist Intelligence Unit 2016.

32. ACET 2014, 14; Bughin et al. 2016, 36.

33. Ernst and Young 2014, 14; Bughin et al. 2016, 7; Business Sweden 2016, 3.

34. Ernst and Young 2014, 42.

35. Bughin et al. 2016, 7.

36. As per Foreign Investment Advisory Service (FIAS), SEZs are generally defined as geographically delimited areas administered by a single body, offering certain incentives (generally duty-free importing and streamlined customs procedures, for instance) to businesses that physically locate within the zone.

37. IPRCC and UNDP 2015, 10–11.

38. The Economist Intelligence Unit 2016.

39. Schiff and Valdez 1992; Erzan 1989; Ng and Yeats 1996; Tybout 2000.

40. Tybout 2000.

41. Bughin et al. 2016, 12.

42. Conde et al. 2015, 2–4.

43. Imbs and Wacziag 2003; Ernst 2002.

44. African Union n.d.

45. Ernst and Young 2014, 42; KPMG 2013, 4.

46. Conde et al. 2015, 4–5; Tybout 2000.

47. Kuznets and Murphy 1966; Tybout 2000; Ansu et al. 2016, 7; McMillan and Rodrik 2011.

48. ACET 2014, 14; Bughin et al. 2016, 36.

49. Bughin et al. 2016, 8.

50. Bughin et al. 2016, 16.

51. Bughin et al. 2016, 16.

52. Business Sweden 2016, 6.

53. Foreign Direct Investment Intelligence 2016b, 4.

54. The Economist Intelligence Unit 2016.

55. Ernst and Young 2014, 9, 18.

56. IPRCC & UNDP 2015.

57. Foreign Direct Investment Intelligence 2016a, 6.

58. Foreign Direct Investment Intelligence 2016a, 14.

59. The Economist 2014.

60. Foreign Direct Investment Intelligence 2016a, 6.

61. The Economist 2014.

62. The Economist 2014.

63. Balchin et al. 2016, 5.

64. KPMG 2015, 6.

65. KPMG 2015, 11.

66. UNIDO 2015, 6; KPMG 2013, 4.

67. Foreign Direct Investment Intelligence 2016a, 10.

68. Bughin et al. 2016, 9, 16; Balchin et al. 2016, 10.

69. Roxburgh et al. 2010, 1.

70. Ngulube 2014, 4.

71. KPMG 2015, 9.

72. The data come from the World Economic Forum's Global Competitiveness Index (2017–18), which scores countries from 1 to 7 on each indicator. Note that Angola is excluded due to lack of data.

73. According to the World Economic Forum, this indicator means to what extent pay is related to employee productivity.

74. KPMG 2015, 10.

75. Foreign Direct Investment Intelligence 2016a, 4.

76. "The plant is revolutionary in that it emits very little carbon dioxide by optimizing energy consumption and using renewable energy. Compared to other plants of similar size, the Tangiers plant emits 98 less carbons, consumes 70% less water, and has zero industrial liquid discharges." (KPMG 2013, 13).

77. Jacobs 2019, 439.

78. KPMG 2013, 13.

79. KPMG 2015, 12.

80. The Economist Intelligence Unit 2016.

81. EPZ is a type of SEZ.

82. UNIDO 2015, 6.

83. According to WHO, GMP is a system for ensuring that products are consis-

tently produced and controlled according to quality standards. It is designed to minimize the risks involved in any pharmaceutical production that cannot be eliminated through testing the final product.

84. KPMG 2015, 12.

85. KPMG 2013, 10.

86. The World Bank 2016, 21–22.

87. KPMG 2013, 10.

88. KPMG 2015, 16.

89. IPRCC and UNDP 2015, 35.

90. IPRCC and UNDP 2015, 33–34.

91. KPMG 2013, 11–12.

92. IPRCC & UNDP 2015, 32–33.

93. KPMG 2015, 7.

94. KPMG 2013, 2.

95. Ansu et al. 2016, 2–3; Filmer and Fox 2014.

96. KPMG 2013, 6.

97. IPRCC & UNDP 2015, 39–42.

98. Bughin et al. 2016, 24.

99. KPMG 2013, 2.

100. Economist Intelligence Unit 2016; Bughin et al. 2016, 24; KPMG 2016, 4.

101. Ansu et al. 2016, 2–3; Foster and Briceño-Garmendia 2010 ; KPMG 2013, 5.

102. KPMG 2013, 5.

103. Conde et al. 2015, 9.

104. Ansu et al. 2016, 18.

105. Africa has the highest level of corruption in the world, according to Transparency International's Corruption Perceptions Index.

106. KPMG 2013, 6.

107. Ansu et al. 2016, 18.

108. KPMG 2016, 5.

109. IPRCC and UNDP 2015, 57.

110. KPMG 2016, 9.

111. IPRCC and UNDP 2015, 39–42.

112. IPRCC and UNDP 2015, 20.

113. Namely, South Africa, Egypt, Morocco, and Tunisia.

114. Rodrik 2016.

115. Bolaky 2011.

116. The Economist 2014.

117. Ernst and Young 2014, 10.

118. Ernst and Young 2014, 21.

119. The Economist Intelligence Unit 2016; Ernst and Young 2014.

120. African Union Commission 2015, 5.

121. Signé 2017.

122. Luke and Sodipo 2015.

123. The Economist 2014.

124. Bughin et al. 2016, 16.

125. Angola, Kenya, Ghana, Tanzania, Zambia, Ethiopia, and Mozambique, among others; see Ernst and Young 2014, 21.

126. Bughin et al. 2016, 14.

Chapter 6

1. Brown 2014, 15.

2. Kimemia 2018.

3. African Development Bank and The African Union 2009, 46.

4. Chinese, Indian, and Malaysian oil companies started producing oil in Sudan in 1999, with production peaking at 470,000 barrels produced per day between 2000 and 2010, making Sudan the sixth largest African oil producer behind Nigeria, Angola, Algeria, Libya, and Egypt. See Augé 2015, 6.

5. Brown 2014, 27.

6. *Oil and Gas in Africa Sector Report* 2015, 2.

7. Nigeria, Angola, Libya, Algeria, and Egypt.

8. Other countries with notable oil reserves are Egypt, South Sudan, Gabon, Equatorial Guinea, Republic of Congo, Chad, Ghana, Uganda, and Kenya.

9. See Brown 2014, 30.

10. Vines 2012.

11. KPMG 2013, 18; Bughin et al. 2016, 75.

12. World Bank Group 2016, 4.

13. KPMG 2015, 2.

14. PwC 2016, 5.

15. The country's primary gas plant was shut down in 2015 due to a gas leak, but it is expected to start producing LNG in 2016 and to increase gas liquids capacity by 70 kb/d to 140 kb/d by 2021. *Choice to Change* 2016, 26. See also *Oil and Gas in Africa Sector Report* 2015, 6.

16. U.S. Energy Information Administration 2016, 46. The World Economic Outlook of 2008 put this figure at 3.5 percent per year for the continent as a whole, with natural gas production increasing from 215 billion m^3 in 2008 to a projected 452 billion m^3 in 2030.

17. Cilliers et al. 2011, 43–44.

18. IMF 2008; "The Race for Oil and Gas in Africa" 2016.

19. African Development Bank and the African Union 2009, 31.

20. Diamond 2015, 294–296; Ginsburg 1957; Auty 2001; Gylfason 2001; Ross 2001, 2012; Collier and Hoeffler 2005; Dunning 2008; Teorell 2010. The resource curse goes beyond the connection between oil dependence and underdevelopment to focus on political outcomes as well, especially the prevalence of corruption and the democratic deficit in resource-rich states; see Diamond 2015; Haggard and Kaufman 2016; and Dunning 2008.

21. Liou and Musgrave 2014.

22. KPMG 2013, 6.

23. KPMG 2013, 7. "Nigeria finally enacted the Sovereign Wealth Fund Act in May 2011 to invest windfall oil earnings in infrastructure development, to provide a stabilization fund, and to ensure savings for future generations of Nigerians. However, it has proven more difficult than hoped for Nigeria to move the sovereign wealth fund into the operational phase of its existence, and at present, the ECA is still actively used."

24. Odusola et al. 2017.

25. Baffes et al. 2015.

26. African Development Bank and the African Union 2009, 31.

27. Bughin et al. 2016, 28.

28. PwC 2016, 7, 22.

29. PwC, 2016, 15.

30. PwC, 2016, 7.

31. KPMG 2015, 18.

32. Baffes et al. 2015.

33. African Development Bank and the African Union 2009, 30–31.

34. Initiatives like the United States Agency for International Development's (US-AID's) Power Africa are attempting to increase Africans' access to electricity by adding over 60 million new electricity connections with 30,000 megawatts of new and cleaner power generation. Natural gas is positioned as a "bridging fuel" in the shift toward low-carbon energy, one that is particularly attractive to emerging economies where cost-effectiveness remains a top priority (PwC 2016, 6).

35. See PwC 2016, 6, 42.

36. Bughin et al. 2016, 75.

37. PwC 2016.

38. PwC 2016, 16.

39. Vines 2012, 22; "The Race for Oil and Gas" 2016.

40. Shaxson 2008; "The Race for Oil and Gas" 2016.

41. *Time for Transparency* 2004.

42. "Shell Knew" 2017; "Shell and Eni's Misadventures" 2015.

43. Alden and Davies 2006, 85; Astier 2003.

44. Henley 2003.

45. KPMG 2015.

46. Sayne et al. 2015, 2.

47. Vines 2012.

48. Sayne and Gillies 2014, 11; Gupte and Shaw 2016.

49. Vines 2012.

50. Zhao 2011.

51. Gupte and Shaw 2016.

52. Alden and Davies 2006, 92.

53. KPMG 2015, 18.

54. KPMG 2015, 18.

55. Shale is a precursor of oil called kerogen—a "teenage oil" of sorts that constitutes the building blocks of conventional oil—which is trapped in rock formations that

make it difficult to extract due to low porosity and permeability. Shale reservoirs are replete with clay and fissile, meaning they have split in layers containing clay stone, which may stretch horizontally for hundreds or thousands of miles. Smaller amounts of shale gas reserves have also been identified in Libya (3.4 trillion m^3), Egypt (2.6 trillion m^3), Tunisia, Morocco, and Western Sahara. South Africa potentially possesses the eighth largest reserves of shale gas in the world and the most in Africa south of the Sahara (10.9 trillion m^3). See Maugeri 2013.

56. U.S. Energy Information Administration 2016, 30.

57. KPMG 2015, 15.

58. Bekoe et al. 2016, 2.

59. Tullow Oil recently announced plans to limit its capital expenditure in West Africa to existing "high-margin" oil production in order to stabilize and guarantee long-term profits, while reallocating resources for exploration focusing on "high-impact, low-cost" opportunities in East Africa, especially in Kenya; see KPMG 2015, 18; KPMG 2015, 16.

60. Readhead 2016, 1.

61. Bekoe et al. 2016, 1–3.

62. Augé 2015, 6.

63. Vines 2012, 22.

64. KPMG 2015, 15.

65. Augé 2015, 23.

66. Brown 2014, 19; KPMG 2015, 15; NRGI 2016, 1.

67. KPMG 2015, 17.

68. KPMG 2013, 7.

69. KPMG 2015, 16.

70. Original plans proposed in 2012 envisioned a pipeline from Uganda's Lake Albert through Kenya's Lochichar and terminating at Lamu on the Kenyan coast. However, in 2016 the Ugandan government reached a competing deal with Tanzania to build a pipeline that will terminate at Dar es Salaam, and Kenya has suggested that it will build a separate pipeline connecting Lochichar to Lamu; see Augé 2015, 19; Senelwa 2016.

71. Perkin and Gupte 2016.

72. KPMG 2015, 17.

73. "The Petroleum Act, which is the central pillar of the legislation governing the sector, establishes the legal and institutional infrastructure. It is comprehensive in scope, applying to the sector's up-, mid- and downstream, and it addresses many of the key issues of petroleum sector governance, such as the institutional framework, competitive license allocation, the fiscal regime, local content, environmental management and the decommissioning of project sites. The Revenue Management Act establishes the rules for the spending and saving of extractive revenues to ensure that both current and future generations will benefit. It builds on many of the lessons learned from other resource-rich countries and addresses some key challenges of non-renewable resource revenue management: revenue volatility, exhaustibility of revenue and the risk of waste through misuse and corruption. The TEITA act establishes transparency and disclosure requirements to enable stakeholders to monitor the sector, thereby helping ensure

that it operates in the best interests of all Tanzanians. The act includes provisions regarding revenue disclosure, contract transparency, local content/social investment disclosure, environmental reporting and establishes the institutional infrastructure to facilitate enhanced transparency." NRGI 2016, 1.

74. KPMG 2013, 7.

75. KPMG 2015, 5.

76. Gupte 2016.

77. U.S. Energy Information Administration 2016, 46.

78. KPMG 2015, 10

79. Brown 2014, 13.

80. PwC 2016, 22; KPMG 2015, 13.

81. Sayne et al. 2015, 2.

82. Sayne and Gillies 2016, 7.

83. Sayne et al. 2015, 3.

84. Sayne and Gillies 2016, 10; Sayne et al. 2015, 37.

85. "Passage of the Petroleum Industry Governance Bill" 2017.

86. Brown 2014, 20.

87. PwC 2016, 8.

88. KPMG 2015, 16.

89. KPMG 2015, 4.

90. Sayne and Gillies 2016, 2.

91. Sayne and Gillies 2016, 10–11.

92. Sayne et al. 2015, 2.

93. Bekoe 2016, 3.

94. Readhead 2016.

95. International Energy Association 2014, 1–4.

96. According to PwC 2016.

97. Augé 2015, 18.

98. KPMG 2015, 4.

99. Bughin et al. 2016, 75.

100. KPMG 2013, 6.

101. PwC 2016.

102. NRGI 2016.

103. International Energy Agency 2014, 2.

104. Vines 2012, 21; Eklavya, 2016.

105. KPMG 2015, 4–5.

106. Brown 2014, 11–12.

107. Statement to Bloomberg on January 15, 2015, quoted in KPMG 2015, 16.

108. KPMG 2015, 16.

109. PwC 2016, 8.

110. KPMG 2015, 17.

111. PwC 2016, 28.

112. However, the Ghanaian government has challenged an attempt by Kosmos to sell its assets in Jubilee Field to ExxonMobil for $4 billion.

113. Vines 2010, 22.
114. Alden and Davies 2006, 86–88.
115. Brown 2014, 29–30.
116. KPMG 2015, 15.
117. PwC 2016, 15.
118. Cilliers et al. 2011, 44.
119. KPMG 2015, 8.
120. International Energy Agency 2014, 3.
121. KPMG 2015, 14.
122. PwC 2016, 3.
123. Cilliers et al. 2011, 51.
124. KPMG 2015, 8.
125. PwC 2016, 19.
126. "The Race for Oil and Gas" 2016.

Chapter 7

1. World Bank 2011, 1.
2. Fayissa et al. 2008, abstract.
3. UNWTO 2018, 3.
4. World Bank 2011, 2.
5. AfDB 2016b, 4.
6. Calculated by the author based on data in UNWTO 2018, 3.
7. Average between 2011 and 2014, see UNCTAD 2017, 23.
8. UNWTO 2017, 12.
9. Calculated by the author based on data in UNWTO 2018, 3.
10. UNWTO 2017, 14.
11. World Bank 2013.
12. UNWTO 2016, 15.
13. For more on this debate, see De Kadt 1984.
14. Butler 1980; Britton 1982; De Kadt 1984.
15. Poon 1989, 1993; Urry 1990; Milne and Pohlmann 1998; Milne and Ateljevic 2001.
16. Sequeira and Nunes 2008.
17. Balassa 1978; Schubert et al. 2011.
18. Balaguer and Cantavella-Jorda 2002; Nowak et al. 2007.
19. Dritsakis 2004. Among case studies in Asia, the findings seem to be more mixed. Oh (2005) concludes that tourism growth, in fact, fails to demonstrate a causal link with economic expansion in the case of South Korea when tested against various lag selections, suggesting that the relationship between tourism and development might be more cyclical than previous studies have argued. This is echoed by Chen and Chiou-Wei (2009), although they find that even though a cyclical relationship holds for South Korea, the linear effect of tourism on growth holds in Taiwan. However, Kim et al. (2006) find evidence that the effect is also cyclical in Taiwan.

20. Lee and Chiang 2008; Eugenio-Martine et al. 2004. See also Sequeira and Nunes (2008), who find that tourism contributes to growth in countries of all income levels.

21. UNDP 2011, 4; AfDB 2016b, 13–17.

22. Ashley and Mitchell 2009. Ashley and Mitchell identify three key "pathways" in which tourism can benefit the poor: direct earnings through formal and informal employment, indirect and induced effects where tourism expenditures impact the non-tourism economy through supply-chain linkages, and dynamic impacts on the economy. See also Dieke 2003.

23. World Bank 2011, 3.

24. Durbarry 2004.

25. World Bank 2011, 4.

26. Sinclair 1998.

27. Okello and Novelli 2014, 54.

28. Mwiti 2014.

29. World Economic Forum 2015, 23.

30. ADS is an arrangement between the Chinese government and other countries, which allows Chinese tourists to visit partner countries in tour groups.

31. Ayenagbo 2015, 176.

32. Industrial Development Corporation 2016.

33. World Bank 2011, 7.

34. World Bank 2011, 8.

35. Jones 2012.

36. AfDB 2016a, 19.

37. Eugenio-Martin et al. 2004.

38. Christie and Crompton 2001, 26.

39. Mwiti 2014.

40. Schlumberger 2010.

41. Adeyeye 2016.

42. Shea 2017.

43. Adeyeye 2016.

44. Chen and Devereux 1999, 216–217; Snyman and Saayman 2009, 49.

45. Snyman and Saayman 2009, 52.

46. Industrial Development Corporation 2016.

47. AfDB 2016b, 44.

48. AfDB 2016b, 49.

49. Mwiti 2014.

50. Lee 2008.

51. Ernoul 2009; Minca and Borghi 2009; Scherle 2011.

52. Lee 2008.

53. Dobruszkes and Mondou 2013, 24.

54. UNWTO 2016, 11.

55. World Economic Forum 2017, 41.

56. World Economic Forum 2015, 19–20.

57. Durbarry 2004.
58. World Economic Forum 2017, 43.
59. Du Plessis and Saayman 2017.
60. Industrial Development Corporation 2016.
61. Snyman and Saayman 2009, 55–56.
62. Mwiti 2014.
63. Mwiti 2014.
64. World Economic Forum 2015, 19.
65. Industrial Development Corporation 2016.
66. AfDB et al. 2015, 42–43.
67. World Bank 2011, 6.
68. Christie et al. 2014, 6–8.
69. AfDB 2016a, 13.
70. AfDB 2016a, 13.
71. AfDB 2017, 12.
72. Industrial Development Corporation 2016.
73. "The Sun Rises on Online Travel" 2017.
74. AfDB et al. 2015, 42–43.
75. World Bank 2011, 6
76. Christie et al. 2014, 6.
77. Ashley and Roe 2002, 62.
78. World Bank 2011, 8.
79. AfDB 2016a, 18.
80. World Bank 2015, 1.

Chapter 8

1. Demirguc-Kunt and Klapper 2012, 2.
2. See, for example, Demirguc-Kunt and Klapper (2012), Demirguc-Kunt and Levine (2009), and Beck, Demirguc-Kunt, and Levine (2007).
3. Nyantakyi and Mouhamadou, 2015, 1; Mecagni et al. 2015, 16.
4. Kasekende 2010; Derreumaux 2013, 2.
5. Beck et al. 2011, 27.
6. European Investment Bank, 2015, 9.
7. European Investment Bank, 2015, 9.
8. European Investment Bank 2015, 12; Beck et al. 2011, 11–12.
9. Hogan Lovells 2018, 1.
10. Derreumaux 2013, 2.
11. Mlachila et al. 2013, 23–24.
12. Nyantakyi and Mouhamadou 2015, 3.
13. Mecagni et al. 2015, 13.
14. Léon 2015, 18.
15. Beck et al. 2011, 10.
16. Mlachila et al. 2013, 21–23; Beck et al. 2011, 12.
17. Oduor et al. 2011, 226–240.

18. Nyantakyi and Mouhamadou 2015, 3; KPMG Africa 2014.

19. Derreumaux 2013, 2; KPMG Africa 2014.

20. Beck et al. 2011, 12.

21. Derreumaux 2013, 2.

22. Nyantakyi and Mouhamadou 2015, 5.

23. Nyantakyi and Mouhamadou 2015, 2; King and Levine, 1993a; Levine 1997; De Gregorio and Guidotti 1995; Levine and Zervos 1998; Rousseau and Wachtel 1998; Beck et al. 2000.

24. De Gregorio 1996; Levine 1997; Levine and Zervos 1998; Rousseau and Wachtel 1998; Levine et al. 2000; Vaithilingam et al. 2006.

25. Goldsmith 1959; King and Levine 1993a, 1993b, 1993c; Jalilian and Kirkpatrick 2005.

26. Greenwood and Jovanovic 1990; Banerjee and Newman 1993; Galor and Zeira 1993; Clarke, Xu, and Fou 2002.

27. Demetriades and Hussein 1996; Odedokun 1996; Zingales 2003. For a comprehensive discussion of this debate, see DFID 2004.

28. Patrick 1966; Gurley and Shaw 1967; Jung 1986; Calderon and Liu 2003.

29. Berthelemy and Varoudakis 1996; Vaithilingam et al. 2006, 1.

30. European Investment Bank 2015, 5; Beck et al. 2011, 11–12.

31. European Investment Bank 2015, 9.

32. Flamini et al. 2009.

33. Mecagni et al. 2015, 12.

34. Zingales 2003.

35. Demirgüç-Kunt and Huizinga 1999; Saunders and Schumacher 2000; Athanasoglou et al. 2006.

36. Mlambo, Kasekende, and Murinde 2012.

37. DFID 2004, 16; Levine et al. 2000.

38. FSI Survey on Basel II, 2.5, and III Implementation (Financial Stability Institute, July 2014).

39. For the argument about benefits of financial regionalization, see Dieter 2000.

40. European Investment Bank 2015, 55; Mecagni et al. 2015, 8; Beck et al. 2011; Lukonga and Chung 2010.

41. Mlachila et al. 2013, 6.

42. Holden and Prokopenko 2001; Morduch 1999; Coleman 1999.

43. Hulme and Mosley 1996. See also Pitt and Khandker 1998.

44. KPMG Africa 2014. For a summary of MFI studies, see Littlefield, Morduch, and Hashemi (2003).

45. Mlachila et al. 2013, 6.

46. Mecagni et al. 2015, 34; Mlachila et al. 2013, 28.

47. Nyantakyi and Mouhamadou, 2015, 4.

48. Derreumaux 2013; Ondiege 2010, 1.

49. Ondiege 2010, 1; Ernst and Young 2014, 9.

50. Ernst and Young 2014, 9; European Investment Bank 2015, 71.

51. Nyantakyi and Mouhamadou 2015, 5.

52. David-West 2018.

53. Fengler 2012.

54. Beck et al. 2011, 16.

55. Nyantakyi and Mouhamadou, 2015, 5.

56. Mlachila et al. 2013, 28.

57. Mlachila et al. 2013, 28.

58. World Bank 2017.

59. Mattei 2013.

60. Arnold and Jenkins 2016.

61. Mlachila et al. 2013, 28–29; Mecagni et al. 2015, 23.

62. Derreumaux 2013.

63. KPMG Africa 2014.

64. IMF 2014, 79–80.

65. IMF 2014, 80.

66. Mlachila et al. 2013, 28–29.

67. IMF 2014, 79.

68. IMF 2014, 76–77.

69. IMF 2014, 77–78.

70. Mlachila et al. 2013, 28–29.

71. IMF 2014, 77.

72. IMF 2014, 78.

73. IMF 2014, 76.

74. Mecagni et al. 2015, 23; Thorsten 2013.

75. IMF 2014, 76.

76. IMF 2014, 80.

77. IMF 2014; European Investment Bank 2015, 9.

78. This is compared to closer to 70 percent in the other low- and middle-income countries in the world.

79. Mlachila et al. 2013, 28–29.

80. KPMG Africa, 2014.

81. Mlachila et al. 2013, 30.

82. Mlachila et al. 2013, 30.

83. Ernst and Young 2014, 41–42.

84. For example, the GDP share of credit to the private sector is roughly one-third of the regional average, at just 13 percent.

85. European Investment Bank 2015, 51–52.

86. Ernst and Young 2014, 37.

87. European Investment Bank 2015, 51–52.

88. European Investment Bank 2015, 48.

89. Bankscope, Bureau van Dijk.

90. European Investment Bank 2015, 42.

91. European Investment Bank 2015, 49.

92. Mlachila et al. 2013, 6; Andrianaivo and Yartey 2009; Beck et al. 2011; McDonald and Schumacher 2007; European Investment Bank 2015, 10.

93. KPMG Africa 2014.

94. Mecagni et al. 2015, 27–28.

95. IMF 2014, 7–8; Mecagni et al. 2015, 27–28.

96. Mlachila et al. 2013, 30.

97. Mecagni et al. 2015, 25.

98. KPMG Africa 2014.

99. Beck et al. 2011, 13–14.

100. Nyantakyi and Mouhamadou 2015, 7.

101. Beck et al. 2011, 13–14.

102. Mlachila et al. 2013, 21–23; KPMG Africa 2014.

103. Beck et al. 2011, 13–14.

104. Kamau 2011; Beck et al. 2011, 10.

105. KPMG Africa, 2014.

106. Mecagni et al. 2015, 12.

107. Beck et al. 2011, 14–15.

108. European Investment Bank 2015, 53.

109. Mecagni et al. 2015, 14.

110. European Investment Bank 2015, 49.

111. Mlachila et al. 2013, 30.

112. European Investment Bank 2015, 55.

113. Ernst and Young 2014, 43.

114. Greenfield investments refer to the strategy of a parent company to build and develop its business in a new market entirely from scratch, including construction of offices and necessary infrastructure, as well as staffing.

115. IMF 2014, 22.

116. IMF 2014, 22.

117. Ernst and Young 2014, 26.

118. In the African Business Survey, Nigerian banks ranked first through fifteenth of the "most capitalized businesses in Africa."

119. IMF 2014, 72–73.

120. IMF 2014, 70.

121. IMF 2014, 69.

122. European Investment Bank 2015; IMF 2014, 70.

123. "M" stands for mobile, while *pesa* means money in Kiswahili.

124. Ondiege 2013, 10.

125. Ondiege 2010, 8.

126. Vaithilingam et al. 2006, 8–9.

127. Mlachila et al. 2013, 21–23; Andrianaivo and Yartey 2009; Beck et al. 2011; McDonald and Schumacher 2007.

128. Mlachila et al. 2013, 30; Ernst and Young 2014, 43.

129. Ondiege 2013, 10.

130. Vaithilingam et al. 2006.

131. Ernst and Young 2014, 9.

132. Vaithilingam et al. 2006.

133. Mlachila et al. 2013, 31; Vaithilingam et al. 2006.

134. Derreumaux 2013, 2.
135. Ernst and Young 2014, 43.
136. Ernst and Young 2014, 43.
137. Ernst and Young 2011; Kouassi-Olsson and Lefilleur 2013, 15.

Chapter 9

1. In general, "infrastructure" refers to power, telecoms, transit networks, and systems for water sanitation and sewage. The broader concept of "soft infrastructure" also applies to trade and customs procedures, legal mechanisms, regulatory environment, and other informal institutions that are not dependent on the construction industry and, therefore, beyond the scope of this study; see Estache and Garsous 2012, 1; Ismail and Mahyideen 2015, 7.
2. Deloitte 2016, 20.
3. V.e.n.t.u.r.e.s Onsite & Construct East Africa 2015, 3, citing a report by Access Capital.
4. Deloitte 2016, 16.
5. AECOM 2016, 35.
6. See, for example, Jedwab et al. 2015 and Good 1976.
7. Acemoglu et al. 2000.
8. Deloitte 2015, 2.
9. Deloitte 2015, 2.
10. Deloitte 2014, 7; Deloitte 2016, 32–34.
11. Deloitte 2016, 20.
12. EMIS 2015, 10.
13. Deloitte 2016, 15; Deloitte 2015, 2.
14. The sector recorded its largest setback in 2014, when the number of infrastructure-related projects decreased from 22 to just 8 (Deloitte 2014, 22).
15. There is a substantial concentration of investment value in a few major projects, though, with the top ten projects accounting for nearly one-quarter of total project value in the region and Egypt's two major oil and gas developments—the Shorouk Concession and the West Nile Delta Project—among the largest construction projects in all of Africa (Deloitte 2016, 37–39).
16. Deloitte 2016, 32–34.
17. AfDB and WEF 2013, 8.
18. Deloitte 2016, 23; EMIS 2015, 22.
19. EMIS 2015, 22.
20. Even the primary inland waterways in Africa—the Nile River, Congo River, Niger River, Senegal River, lower Zambezi River, Lake Victoria, Lake Tanganyika, and Lake Malawi—are typically not maintained for navigation and transport, such that they remain economically serviceable only to the immediate, local economy (PIDA n.d., 37–40).
21. Deloitte 2015, 2.
22. See Estache and Garsous (2012), 5 and Tan et al. (2010) on the question of causality, and Hulten (1996) on the importance of efficiency of investment.

23. Robles 1998; Calderón and Servén 2004; Estache and Garsous 2012. See also Sahin et al. 2014, 2–6.

24. Estache and Garsous 2012.

25. Biswas 2002; Pereira and Andraz 2012.

26. Aschauer 1989; Agénor 2008; Dethier et al. 2008; Uhde 2010; Verma and Arora 2010; Cook 2011.

27. Estache and Garsous 2012; PwC 2016.

28. Sahoo et al. 2010.

29. Straub 2008; Calderón and Serven 2014.

30. Stretton 1981.

31. Portugal-Perez and Wilson 2012; Estache and Fay 2010; Hong et al. 2011; Estache and Garsous 2012.

32. Berechman et al. 2006; Alfredo and Andraz 2011; Yamaguchi 2011; Pereira and Andraz 2012.

33. Shepherd and Wilson 2009; Ismael and Mahydeen 2015.

34. Garsous 2012; UNIDO 2010.

35. With the notable exception of Europe and Central Asia, although this figure is misleading as nearly all low- and middle-income countries in this region are land-locked.

36. Wantchekon and Stanig 2016; Blimpo et al. 2013.

37. Leon and Miguel's (2016) study of Sierra Leone argues that transit barriers lead to lower value of mortality in sub-Saharan Africa, as travelers are more willing to engage in risky behavior in order to access the airport than they would be in other regions.

38. AECOM 2016, 35.

39. Following Deloitte (2016).

40. Algeria, Ethiopia, Mauritania, Mozambique, Namibia, Niger, Republic of Congo, Seychelles, Tanzania, and Zambia (World Development Indicators 2017).

41. See PIDA 2012, 2; AECOM 2016, 35, EMIS 2015, 4. Lee et al. (2012) argue that expansion of telecommunications networks in sub-Saharan Africa, especially access to mobile cellular phones, has a positive effect on the rate of economic growth.

42. Ianchovichina et al. 2012.

43. Burgess et al. 2015; Blimpo et al. 2013; Wantchekon and Stanig 2016.

44. Kiganda 2016.

45. NEPAD and United Nations 2015, 12–13.

46. V.e.n.t.u.r.e.s Onsite & Construct East Africa 2015, 3.

47. V.e.n.t.u.r.e.s Onsite & Construct East Africa 2015, 4.

48. PIDA n.d., 34.

49. Deloitte 2014.

50. Bughin et al. 2016, 8.

51. With the addition of Johannesburg, Nairobi, Khartoum, Luanda, Dar es Salaam, and Abidjan (PIDA n.d., 8; Deloitte 2016, 17).

52. See Deloitte 2015, 2.

53. Ernst and Young 2014.

54. AfDB 2017 in China Daily Africa Weekly 2017, 10; V.e.n.t.u.r.e.s Onsite & Construct East Africa 2015, 4.

55. Deloitte 2015, 27.

56. Kiganda 2016.

57. Koppenjan and Enserink 2009.

58. Okocha 2015.

59. PIDA n.d., 8.

60. Gross fixed capital formation of greater than 30 percent of GDP, according to Deloitte (2016).

61. The construction sector alone was estimated to represent just 3.6 percent of Nigeria's GDP in 2014, although it has shown impressive annual growth rates as high as 13 percent in recent years (EMIS 2015, 35).

62. Okocha 2015; GCP Global, Oxford Economics, ENR, and PwC 2015, 11.

63. In one noteworthy policy, implemented by Nigeria's former president in 2014, land was provided for free to property developers, and in order to reduce the price of building materials—90 percent of which are imported—negotiations with the manufacturing sector attempt to make locally produced materials available at factory prices. EMIS 2015, 38.

64. EMIS 2015, 40.

65. Deloitte 2014, 15.

66. Deloitte 2014, 15.

67. EMIS 2015, 40.

68. Deloitte 2014, 9.

69. EMIS 2015, 12–14.

70. EMIS 2015, 21.

71. Timetric 2016.

72. Timetric 2016.

73. African Business Central 2015; EMIS 2015, 14–22.

74. EMIS 2015, 26.

75. Beyond the economic pillar of the development plan, two other pillars focus on social development and political reform (see V.e.n.t.u.r.e.s Online & Construct East Africa 2015, 3).

76. EMIS 2015, 31.

77. Deloitte 2014, 20.

78. LAPSSET Corridor Development Authority 2016.

79. BBC News 2017.

80. Deloitte 2014.

81. PIDA 2016, 39.

82. Reuters 2016.

83. Deloitte 2015, 2.

84. Deloitte 2014, 13.

85. Deloitte 2015, 2.

86. V.e.n.t.u.r.e.s Online & Construct East Africa, 2015, 3.

87. Deloitte 2014, 13.

88. World Development Indicators 2017.

89. Bonface 2015.

90. EMIS 2015, 26.
91. Deloitte 2016, 17.
92. Bonface 2015.
93. PIDA n.d., 32.
94. PIDA n.d., 30.
95. Bonface 2015.
96. PIDA n.d., 30.
97. Ondiege et al. 2013, 77.
98. Deloitte 2015, 28.
99. Ondiege et al. 2015, 87–88.
100. Deloitte 2015, 28.
101. PIDA 2012, 2.
102. Ondiege et al. 2015.
103. Deloitte 2016, 16.
104. Calderón and Servén 2008.
105. See UNECA and NEPAD 2017 and OSAA 2015.
106. See Ezzat Othman 2013, 1.
107. Ondiege, Moyo and Verdier-Chouchane 2013; EMIS 2015, 4.
108. Zipporah 2017, 3.
109. PIDA 2016, 41.

Conclusion

1. The projections build as well from the recent publication by Leke and Signé (2019).

References

CHAPTER 1

Acemoglu, Daron, and James A. Robinson. 2010a. "Why Is Africa Poor?" *Economic History of Developing Regions* 25 (June 1): 21–50.

Acemoglu, Daron, and James Robinson. 2010b. "The Role of Institutions in Growth and Development." *Review of Economics and Institutions* 1 (2): 1–33. http://www.rei .unipg.it/rei/article/view/14.

Amâncio, R. 2017. "Why Africa? #2—Africa Is Outperforming the World in . . ." LinkedIn. May 26, 2017. https://www.linkedin.com/pulse/why-africa-2-outper forming-world-ricardo-am%C3%A2ncio-1.

Azam, J. P., B. R. Biais, and R. H. Bate. 2009. "Political Predation and Economic Development." *Economics and Politics* 21 (2): 255–277.

Banerjee, A. V. and Esther Duflo. 2008. "What Is Middle Class about the Middle Classes around the World?" *Journal of Economic Perspectives* 22 (2): 3.

Barberena, M., N. Schmeichel, and B. Corrales. 2006. "Latin American Profile, Demographics and Socio-economic Strata." European Society for Opinion and Marketing Research. October 20, 2006. https://ana.esomar.org/documents/latin-american-profile-demographics-and-socio-economic-strata.

Bates, Robert H. 1981. *Markets and States in Tropical Africa: The Political Basis of Agricultural Policies.* Berkeley: University of California Press.

Bates, Robert. 2006. "Institutions and Development." *Journal of African Economies* 15 (1): 10-61.

Bates, Robert H., and Steven A. Block. 2011. "Revisiting African Agriculture: Institutional Change and Productivity Growth." *Journal of Politics* 75, no. 2 (April 9): 372–384. https://www.jstor.org/stable/10.1017/s0022381613000078.

Bayen, M. 2018. "Africa: A Look at the 442 Active Tech Hubs of the Continent." GSM Association (blog), March 22, 2018. https://www.gsma.com/mobilefordevelop ment/blog-2/africa-a-look-at-the-442-active-tech-hubs-of-the-continent/.

Birdsall, N. 2012. "Oops: Economists in Confused Search for the Middle Class in the Developing World." Center for Global Development (blog). May 31, 2012. https:// www.cgdev.org/blog/oops-economists-confused-search-middle-class-developing- world.

Bloom, David E. and Jeffrey D. Sachs. 1998. "Geography, Demography, and Economic Growth in Africa." *Brookings Papers on Economic Activity* 1998 (2): 207-295.

Brun, J., P. S. Guillaumont, and J. Guillaumont. 1999. "How Instability Lowers African Growth." *Journal of African Economies* 8 (1): 87–107.

Chatterjee, S. and Mahama, H. E. J. D. 2017. "Promise or Peril? Africa's 830 Million Young People by 2050." United Nations Development Programme (blog), August 12, 2017. http://www.africa.undp.org/content/rba/en/home/blog/2017/8/12/Prom ise-Or-Peril-Africa-s-830-Million-Young-People-By-2050.html.

Chen, W., and R. Nord. 2018. "Reassessing Africa's Global Partnerships: Approaches for Engaging the New World Order." In *Foresight Africa: Top Priorities for the Continent in 2018*, chapter 6. Brookings Institution. January 11, 2018. https:// www.brookings.edu/multi-chapter-report/foresight-africa-top-priorities-for-the- continent-in-2018/.

Collier, Paul. 2000. "Ethnicity, Politics and Economic Performance." *Economics and Politics* 12 (3): 225–245.

Collier, Paul. 2006. "Africa: Geography and Growth." *Proceedings – Economic Policy Symposium – Jackson Hole:* 235-252.

Collier, Paul, and Jan Willem Gunning. 1999a. "Explaining African Economic Performance." *Journal of Economic Literature* 37, no. 1 (March): 64–111. https://www. researchgate.net/profile/Jan_Gunning/publication/4721034_Explaining_african_ economic_performance_J_Econ_Lit_XXXVII64-111/links/56600ee908ae4988 a7bf00fc.pdf.

Collier, Paul, and Jan Willem Gunning. 1999b. "Why Has Africa Grown Slowly?" *Journal of Economic Perspectives* 13 (3): 3–22.

Court, D., and L. Narasimhan. 2010. "Capturing the World's Emerging Middle Class." *McKinsey Quarterly.* July 2010. https://www.mckinsey.com/industries/ retail/our-insights/capturing-the-worlds-emerging-middle-class.

Dadush, U. B., and S. Ali. 2012. "In Search of the Global Middle Class: A New Index." Carnegie Endowment for International Peace. July 23, 2012. https://carne gieendowment.org/2012/07/23/in-search-of-global-middle-class-new-index- pub-48908.

Deloitte. 2014. "Africa: A 21st Century View." *The Deloitte Consumer Review.* https:// www2.deloitte.com/ng/en/pages/consumer-business/articles/consumer-review- africa.html.

Easterly, William. 2001a. *The Elusive Quest for Growth: Economists' Adventures and Misadventures in the Tropics*. Cambridge, MA: MIT Press.

Easterly, William. 2001b. "The Middle Class Consensus and Economic Development." *Journal of Economic Growth* 6, no. 4: 317–335.

Easterly, William, and Ross Levine. 1997. "Africa's Growth Tragedy: Policies and Ethnic Divisions." *Quarterly Journal of Economics* 112, no. 4 (November): 1203–1250. https://academic.oup.com/qje/article-abstract/112/4/1203/1911730?redirectedFrom=fulltext.

The Economist. 2000. "Hopeless Africa." *The Economist*. May 11, 2000. https://www.economist.com/leaders/2000/05/11/hopeless-africa.

The Economist. 2011. "The Hopeful Continent: Africa Rising." *The Economist*. December 3, 2011. https://www.economist.com/leaders/2011/12/03/africa-rising.

The Economist. 2013. *Emerging Africa: A Hopeful Continent*. Special Report. *The Economist*. March 2, 2013. https://www.economist.com/sites/default/files/20130203_emerging_africa.pdf.

The Economist. 2016. *Business in Africa: 1.2 Billion Opportunities*. Special Report. *The Economist*. April 14, 2016. https://www.economist.com/special-report/2016/04/14/12-billion-opportunities.

Fick, David. 2007. *Africa: Continent of Economic Opportunity*. Johannesburg: STE Publishers.

Fosu, A. K. 2001. "Political Instability and Economic Growth in Developing Economies: Some Specification Empirics." *Economics Letters* 70 (2): 289–294.

Fosu, A. K. 2010. "The Global Financial Crisis and Development: Whither Africa?" WIDER Working Paper Series 124. Helsinki, Finland: World Institute for Development Economic Research.

Gelb, A., C. J. Meyer, V. Ramachandran, and D. Wadhwa. 2017. "Can Africa Be a Manufacturing Destination? Labor Costs in Comparative Perspective." Center for Global Development Working Paper 466. October 15, 2017. https://www.cgdev.org/publication/can-africa-be-manufacturing-destination-labor-costs-comparative-perspective.

Gray, A. 2018. "Ethiopia Is Africa's Fastest-Growing Economy." World Economic Forum. May 4, 2018. https://www.weforum.org/agenda/2018/05/ethiopia-africa-fastest-growing-economy/.

Grosskurth, Jasper. 2010. *Future of Technology in Africa*. The Hague: STT Publications.

Guillaumont, Patrick, Sylviane Guillaumont Jeanneney, and Jean Brun. 1999. "How Instability Lowers African Growth." *Journal of African Economies* 8 (1): 87-107.

Herbst, Jeffrey I. 2000. *States and Power in Africa: Comparative Lessons in Authority and Control*. Princeton, New Jersey: Princeton University Press.

International Monetary Fund. 2018. World Economic Outlook. IMF DataMapper. October 2018.

Jayadev, Arjun, Rahul Lahoti, and Sanjay Reddy. 2015. "The Middle Muddle: Conceptualizing and Measuring the Global Middle Class." Courant Research Centre Discussion Paper 193. November 24, 2015.

Kamakura, W. A., and J. A. Mazzon. 2013. "Socioeconomic Status and Consumption in an Emerging Economy." *International Journal of Research in Marketing* 30 (1): 4–18.

Kaufmann, D., and A. Kraay. 2018. *Worldwide Governance Indicators*. World Bank Group. https://info.worldbank.org/governance/wgi/#home.

Kharas, Homi. 2010. "The Emerging Middle Class in Developing Countries." OECD Development Center Working Paper 285. Brookings Institution. January 31, 2010. https://www.brookings.edu/research/the-emerging-middle-class-in-developing-countries/.

Kharas, Homi. 2017. "The Unprecedented Expansion of the Global Middle Class: An Update." Brookings Institution Working Paper 100. Brookings Institution. February 28, 2017. https://www.brookings.edu/research/the-unprecedented-expansion-of-the-global-middle-class-2/.

Lopez-Calva, L. F., and E. Ortiz-Juarez. 2014. "A Vulnerability Approach to the Definition of the Middle Class." *Journal of Economic Inequality* 12 (1): 23–47.

Mahajan, Vijay, with Robert E. Gunther. 2009. *Africa Rising: How 900 Million African Consumers Offer More Than You Think*. Upper Saddle River, NJ: Pearson Education as Prentice Hall.

McCord, Gordon, Jeffrey D. Sachs, and Wing Thye Woo. 2005. "Understanding African Poverty: Beyond the Washington Consensus to the Millennium Development Goals Approach." In *Africa in the World Economy*: The National, Regional and International Challenges, edited by Jan Joost Teunissen and Age Akkerman, 23–45. The Hague: Fondad. https://www.earth.columbia.edu/sitefiles/file/about/director/documents/AfricaintheWorldEconomy2005withMcCordandWoo-UnderstandingAfricanPoverty.pdf.

Mo Ibrahim Foundation. 2018. 2018 IIAG. Ibrahim Index of African Governance. Index Report. October 2018. http://mo.ibrahim.foundation/iiag/.

Monga, Célestin, and Justin Yifu Lin. 2015a. *The Oxford Handbook of Africa and Economics: Volume 1: Context and Concepts*. Oxford: Oxford University Press.

Monga, Célestin, and Justin Yifu Lin. 2015b. *The Oxford Handbook of Africa and Economics: Volume 2: Policies and Practices*. Oxford: Oxford University Press.

Morgan, J. 2016. "What Is the Fourth Industrial Revolution?" *Forbes*. February 19, 2016. https://www.forbes.com/sites/jacobmorgan/2016/02/19/what-is-the-4th-industrial-revolution/#247e9ff6f392.

Mpala, D. 2018. "Five SA Biotech Companies to Watch in 2018." Ventureburn. May 22, 2018. https://ventureburn.com/2018/05/x-south-african-biotech-companies-watch-2018-digital-stars/.

Mwanza, K., and H. Wilkins. 2018. "African Startups Bet on Blockchain to Tackle Land Fraud." Reuters. February 16, 2018. https://www.reuters.com/article/us-africa-landrights-blockchain/african-startups-bet-on-blockchain-to-tackle-land-fraud-idUSKCN1G00YK.

Ndulu, Benno J. and Stephen A. O'Connell. 1999. "Governance and Growth in Sub-Saharan Africa." *Journal of Economic Perspectives* 13 (3): 41-66.

Ndulu, Benno J., Stephen A. O'Connell, Robert H. Bates, Paul Collier, and Chuckwuma C. Soludo. 2007a. *The Political Economy of Economic Growth in Africa: 1960–*

2000. Volume 1. Cambridge, UK: Cambridge University Press. Online January 2010. https://www.cambridge.org/core/books/political-economy-of-economic-growth-in-africa-19602000/5D032C32C0C978A55B5601CE95D23F2A.

Ndulu et al. 2007. *The Political Economy of Economic Growth in Africa: 1960-2000. Volume 1.* Cambridge : Cambridge University Press.

North, D. 1990. *Institutions, Institutional Change and Economic Performance.* Cambridge, UK: Cambridge University Press.

Nunn, Nathan. 2008. "The Long-Term Effects of Africa's Slave Trades." *Quarterly Journal of Economics* 123 (1): 139–176.

Przeworski, A. 2004. "Democracy and Economic Development." 2004. In Edward D. Mansfield and Richard Sisson, eds., *The Evolution of Political Knowledge: Democracy, Autonomy, and Conflict in Comparative and International Politics*, 300–324. Columbus: Ohio State University Press.

Quah, D. T. 1996. "Twin Peaks: Growth and Convergence in Models of Distribution Dynamics." *Economic Journal* 106, no. 437 (July 1996): 1045–1055.

Quest, Richard, and Sheena McKenzie. 2018. "President Mnangagwa: 'Zimbabwe Is Open for Business.'" CNN. Last updated January 24, 2018. https://www.cnn.com/2018/01/24/africa/zimbabwe-president-emmerson-mnangagwa-davos-intl/index.html.

Radelet, Steven C. 2010. *Emerging Africa: How 17 Countries Are Leading the Way.* Washington, DC: Center for Global Development.

Ravallion, M. 2010. "The Developing World's Bulging (But Vulnerable) Middle Class." *World Development* 38 (4): 445–454.

Roxburgh, C., Norbert Dörr, Acha Leke, Amine Tazi-Riffi, Arend van Wamelen, Susan Lund, Mutsa Chironga, Tarik Alatovik, Charles Atkins, Nadia Terfous, and Till Zeino-Mahmalat. 2010. *Lions on the Move: The Progress and Potential of African Economies.* McKinsey Global Institute Report. June 2010. https://www.mckinsey.com/featured-insights/middle-east-and-africa/lions-on-the-move.

Sachs, J., and A. W. Warner. 1997. "Sources of Poor Growth in African Economies." *Journal of African Economies* 6 (3): 335–376.

Schlogal, Lukas, and Andy Sumner. 2018. "Robots, Robots Everywhere. What Does It Mean for Developing Countries?" *LSE Business Review* (blog). July 10, 2018. https://blogs.lse.ac.uk/businessreview/2018/07/10/robots-robots-everywhere-what-does-it-mean-for-developing-countries/.

Schwab, K. 2018. *The Global Competitiveness Report 2018.* World Economic Forum. October 16, 2018. https://www.weforum.org/reports/the-global-competitveness-report-2018.

Signé, L. 2011. Is Africa Emerging? Economic Growth, Business Opportunities and Challenges in the 21st Century. The Global Network for Africa's Prosperity.

Signé, Landry. 2017. *Innovating Development Strategies in Africa: The Role of International, Regional, and National Actors.* Cambridge, UK: Cambridge University Press.

Signé, Landry. 2018. *African Development, African Transformation: How Institutions Shape Development Strategy.* Cambridge, UK: Cambridge University Press.

Signé, L., and C. Munyati. 2018. "What Is Next for Zimbabwe's Economy after Its

Historic Election? The Brookings Institution. *Africa in Focus* (blog). August 24, 2018. https://www.brookings.edu/blog/africa-in-focus/2018/08/24/what-is-next-for-zimbabwes-economy-after-its-historic-election/.

Sturm, N. 2013. "Two Years after Civil War's End, Côte d'Ivoire Is Still Unstable." *The Atlantic*. July 30, 2013. https://www.theatlantic.com/international/archive/2013/07/two-years-after-civil-wars-end-c-te-divoire-is-still-unstable/278210/.

Van de Walle, Nicolas. 2001. *African Economies and the Politics of Permanent Crisis, 1979–1999*. Cambridge, UK: Cambridge University Press.

Woetzel, J., A. Madgavkar, J. Seong, J. Manyika, K. Sneader, O. Tonby, A. Cadena, R. Gupta, A. Leke, H. Kim, and S. Gupta. 2018. *Outperformers: High-Growth Emerging Economies and the Companies That Propel Them*. McKinsey Global Institute Report. September 2018. https://www.mckinsey.com/featured-insights/innovation-and-growth/outperformers-high-growth-emerging-economies-and-the-companies-that-propel-them.

World Bank. 2018. *Doing Business 2019: Training for Reform*. Washington, DC: World Bank Group. https://www.doingbusiness.org/content/dam/doingBusiness/media/Annual-Reports/English/DB2019-report_web-version.pdf.

World Economic Forum. 2018. *Regional Risks for Doing Business*. Insight Report. November 12, 2018. https://www.weforum.org/reports/regional-risks-for-doing-business.

CHAPTER 2

Allen, Robert C. 2000. "Economic Structure and Agricultural Productivity in Europe, 1300–1800." *European Review of Economic History* 4 (1): 1–25.

Baldwin, Richard E., Philippe Martin, and Gianmarco I. P. Ottaviano. 2001. "Global Income Divergence, Trade, and Industrialization: The Geography of Growth Take-offs." *Journal of Economic Growth* 6 (1): 5–37.

Bates, Robert H. 1980. "States and Market Intervention: A Case Study from Africa." Working Paper.

Bughin, Jacques, Mutsa Chironga, Georges Desvaux, Tenbite Ermias, Paul Jacobson, Omid Kassiri, Acha Leke, Susan Lund, Arend van Wamelen, and Yassir Zouaoui. 2016. *Lions on the Move II: Realizing the Potential of Africa's Economies*. McKinsey Global Institute Report, September 2016. https://www.mckinsey.com/featured-insights/middle-east-and-africa/lions-on-the-move-realizing-the-potential-of-africas-economies.

Business Sweden. 2016. *Emerging Consumer Market in Maghreb and West Africa*. The Swedish Trade and Invest Council. September 2016. https://www.business-sweden.se/contentassets/d2e184b90baa489895106f886f3ab6d8/emerging-consumer-markets-in-west-africa.pdf.

Chenery, Hollis B., Sherman Robinson, and Moshe Syrquin. 1986. *Industrialization and Growth*. Washington, DC: World Bank.

Deloitte. 2013. *Africa: Tapping into Growth, Opportunities, Challenges and Strategies for Consumer Products*. Deloitte. https://www2.deloitte.com/content/dam/Deloitte/nl/Documents/consumer-business/deloitte-nl-africa-tapping-into-growth.pdf.

Deng, X., J. Huang, S. Rozelle, and E. Uchida. 2008. "Growth, Population and Industrialization, and Urban Land Expansion of China." *Journal of Urban Economics* 63 (1): 96–115.

Dihel, Nora. 2011. "Beyond the Nakumatt Generation: Distribution Services in Africa." Africa Trade Policy Note 26. World Bank. September 2011. http://site resources.worldbank.org/INTAFRREGTOPTRADE/Resources/Distribution_ services_sep_11.pdf.

Dubai Exports Agency. 2016. *The FMCG/Prepared Food Sector in Africa: An Overview and Trade Analysis.* Sector Report. January 4, 2016. http://www.dedc.gov.ae/StudiesAndResearchDocument/STR001042016-FoodAfricaFINAL.pdf.

Fay, Marianne, and Charlotte Opal. 1999. "Urbanization without Growth: A Not-So-Uncommon Phenomenon." Policy Research Working Papers. World Bank Group. November 1999. https://elibrary.worldbank.org/doi/abs/10.1596/1813-9450-2412.

Foster, Jacqueline, Takeshi Oikawa, James Spanjaard, Emmanuel Huet, Mia Kimani, and Stefano Niavas. 2016. *African Consumer Sentiment 2016: The Promise of New Markets.* Boston Consulting Group. June 21, 2016. https://www.bcgperspectives. com/content/articles/globalization-center-customer-insight-african-consumer-sentiment-2016/.

Hatch, Grant, Pieter Becker, and Michelle van Zyl. 2011. *The Dynamic African Consumer Market: Exploring Growth Opportunities in Sub-Saharan Africa.* Accenture. http://www.nubukeinvestments.com/downloads/Accenture%20The%20Dy namic%20African%20Consumer%20Market%202011.pdf.

Hattingh, Damian et al. 2012. "The Rise of African Consumer." An article from McKinsey's Africa Consumer Insights Center. McKinsey & Company. November 2012. https://www.mckinsey.com/industries/retail/our-insights/the-rise-of-the-african -consumer.

How Consumer Products & Retail Companies Are Structuring Their Operations in Sub-Saharan Africa. 2016. Ernst and Young Global Limited. https://www.weinholdlegal. com/Publication/vwLUAssets/ey-how-consumer-products-retail-companies-are-structuring-their-operations-in-sub-saharan-africa/$FILE/ey-how-consumer-products-retail-companies-are-structuring-their-operations-in-sub-saharan-africa.pdf.

Invest in Morocco. 2017. "Opportunities for Investment." http://www.invest.gov.ma/? Id=34519&lang=fr&RefCat=8&Ref=153.

Karuri, Ken; with AFP and Boston Consulting Group. 2016. "Africa's Consumer Market Promising: BCG Report." *Africanews.* June 21, 2016. http://www.africa news.com/2016/06/21/africa-s-consumer-market-promising-bcg-report/.

KPMG. 2015. *Manufacturing in Africa: Sector Report.* KPMG Africa.

KPMG. 2016. *Fast Moving Consumer Goods: Sector Report.* KPMG Africa. September 2016. https://assets.kpmg/content/dam/kpmg/br/pdf/2016/09/fast-moving-con sumer-goods.pdf.

Kpodar, Kangni R., and Mihasonirina Andrianaivo. 2011. "ICT, financial inclusion, and growth evidence from African countries." IMF Working Papers. April 1, 2011. https://www.imf.org/en/Publications/WP/Issues/2016/12/31/ICT-Finan cial-Inclusion-and-Growth-Evidence-from-African-Countries-24771.

Kuranga, David O. 2012. "Africa Rising: The Last Consumer Frontier." *Nova Capital/ Africa Analytics*. https://www.europeanbusinessreview.eu/articlefiles/nova_africa_ consumer_report.pdf.

Leke, Acha, and Dominic Barton. 2016. "3 Reasons Things Are Looking Up for African Economies." World Economic Forum on Africa. May 5, 2016. https://www.we forum.org/agenda/2016/05/what-s-the-future-of-economic-growth-in-africa/.

Martins, Johan. 2007. "The South African Consumer Market." *Global Journal of Business Research* 1 (1): 168–183. February 17, 2010. https://papers.ssrn.com/sol3/ papers.cfm?abstract_id=1542835.

Matsuyama, Kiminori. 1992. "Agricultural Productivity, Comparative Advantage, and Economic Growth." *Journal of Economic Theory* 58 (2): 317–334.

Matsuyama, Kiminori. 2002. "The Rise of Mass Consumption Societies." *Journal of Political Economy* 10 (5): 1035–1070.

Meacham, Matthew, Andrew Tymms, Tiaan Moolman, and Joelle de Montgolfier. 2012. "Growing with Africa's Consumers." *Bain & Company*. February 2. https:// www.bain.com/insights/growing-with-africas-consumers.

Mugai, Christine. 2015. "Africa's Retail Maze: Consumer Demand Rising Sharply, But You Need to Be a Wizard to Win." *Mail & Guardian Africa*. February 26, 2015. http://mgafrica.com/article/2015-02-26-incomes-are-rising-and-consumer- demand-growing-but-where-do-they-shop. On 1/19/2017.

Nielsen. 2015. *Africa: How to Navigate the Retail Distribution Labyrinth*. February 2015. https://www.nielsen.com/wp-content/uploads/sites/3/2019/04/africa-report -navigating-the-retail-dist-labyrinth-feb-2015.pdf.

Nielsen. 2016. *Consumer Confidence: Concerns and Spending Intentions around the World*. 2016 Consumer Confidence Series, 3rd ed. https://www.nielsen.com/us/en/ insights/report/2016/q3-2016-consumer-confidence-report.

O'Brien, P. K. 1996. "Path Dependency, or Why Britain Became an Industrialized and Urbanized Economy Long before France." *Economic History Review* 49 (2): 213– 249.

PwC. 2012. *South African Retail and Consumer Products Outlook 2012–2016*. South African Edition. PricewaterhouseCoopers (PwC). October 2012. https://www. pwc.co.za/en/assets/pdf/retail-and-consumer-products-outlook-2012-2016.pdf.

Quelques éléments sur la Grande Distribution au Maroc. 2006. USAID|Morocco. Ministère de l'Agriculture, du Développement Rural et des Pêches Maritimes. https://www.academia.edu/31636128/La_grand_distribution_au_maroc.

Quest, Richard, and Sheena Mackenzie. 2018. "President Mnangagwa: 'Zimbabwe Is Open for Business.'" CNN. Last updated January 24, 2018. https://www.cnn. com/2018/01/24/africa/zimbabwe-president-emmerson-mnangagwa-davos-intl/ index.html.

Rostow, Walt Whitman. 1959. "The Stages of Economic Growth." *Economic History Review* 12 (1): 1–16.

Sassi, Seifallah, and Mohamed Goaied. 2013. "Financial Development, ICT Diffu- sion and Economic Growth: Lessons from MENA Region." *Telecommunications Policy* 37 (4): 252–261.

Spence, M., P. C. Annez, and R. M. Buckley. 2009. *Urbanization and growth: commission on growth and development.* World Bank. https://openknowledge.worldbank.org/handle/10986/2582.

Spivey, Lori, Patrick Dupoux, Stefano Niavas, Tenbite Ermias, and Stéphane Heuzé. 2013. *Ten Things to Know about African Consumers: Capturing the Emerging Consumer Class.* BCG. January 25. https://www.bcg.com/en-us/publications/2013/globalization-retail-ten-things-to-know-about-african-consumers.aspx.

Steinmueller, W.E. 2001. "ICTs and Possibilities for Leapfrogging by Developing Countries." *International Labor Review* 140 (2): 1-18.

Tiffen, Mary. 2003. "Transition in Sub-Saharan Africa: Agriculture, Urbanization and Income Growth." *World Development* 31 (8): 1343–1366.

Tisdale, Hope. 1942. "The Process of Urbanization." *Social Forces* 20, no. 3 (March): 311–316.

Tyler, William G. 1981. "Growth and Export expansion in Developing Countries: Some Empirical Evidence." *Journal of Development Economics* 9 (1): 121–130.

World Bank. 2012. "The World Bank in Ethiopia." World Bank Group. Last updated April 12, 2019. http://www.worldbank.org/en/country/ethiopia/overview.

World Development Indicators. 2017. "Household Final Consumption Expenditure, etc. (% of GDP)." World Bank. https://datacatalog.worldbank.org/household-final-consumption-expenditure-etc-gdp-0.

XCOM Africa. 2009. *Consumer Market Nigeria: How to Enter One of the Largest African Markets.* https://www.africon.de/wp-content/uploads/2015/12/FMCG-in-Nigeria-XCOM-Africa.pdf.

CHAPTER 3

Africa Agriculture Status Report 2016: Progress towards Agricultural Transformation in Africa. 2016. https://reliefweb.int/sites/reliefweb.int/files/resources/assr.pdf.

African Development Bank. 2016. *Feed Africa: Strategy for Agricultural Transformation in Africa 2016–2025.* May 2016. https://www.afdb.org/fileadmin/uploads/afdb/Documents/Generic-Documents/Feed_Africa-_Strategy_for_Agricultural_Transformation_in_Africa_2016-2025.pdf.

African Development Bank, World Economic Forum, The World Bank, OECD. 2015. *The Africa Competitiveness Report 2015.* Insight Report. http://www3.weforum.org/docs/WEF_ACR_2015/Africa_Competitiveness_Report_2015.pdf.

Agricultural Input Business Development in Africa: Opportunities, Issues and Challenges. n.d. United Nations Economic Commission for Africa. Southern Africa Office. Accessed September 11, 2019. https://www.uneca.org/sites/default/files/PublicationFiles/sro-sa-agri-iputs-business-opportunities.pdf.

Alemayehu, Konde Koira. 2014. "Agribusiness in Sub-Saharan Africa: Pathways for Developing Innovative Programs for Youth and the Rural Poor." Working paper, The Master Card Foundation. August 2014. https://mastercardfdn.org/wp-content/uploads/2018/06/Agribusiness-in-Sub-Saharan-Africa-2014-accessible.pdf.

Alexandratos, Nikos, and Jelle Bruinsma. 2012. "World Agriculture Towards 2030/2050: The 2012 Revision." ESA Working Paper No. 12-03, Food and Agriculture Organization of the United Nations, Agricultural Development Economics Division. June 2012. http://www.fao.org/global-perspectives-studies/resources/detail/en/c/411108/.

Bah, El-hadj M. et al. 2015. "Assessing Africa's Competitiveness: Opportunities and Challenges to Transforming Africa's Economies." In *The Africa Competitiveness Report 2015*. Geneva: World Economic Forum. http://www3.weforum.org/docs/WEF_ACR_2015/Africa_Competitiveness_Report_2015.pdf.

Bates, Robert H. 1981. *Markets and States in Tropical Africa: The Political Basis of Agricultural Policies*. Berkeley: University of California Press.

Binswanger-Mkhize, Hans P., and Sara Savastano. 2017. "Agricultural Intensification: The Status in Six African Countries." *Food Policy* 67: 26-40.

Borger, Julian. 2008. "Rich Countries Launch Great Land Grab to Safeguard Food Supply." *The Guardian*. https://www.theguardian.com/environment/2008/nov/22/food-biofuels-land-grab.

Bremner, Jason. 2012. "Population and Food Security: Africa's Challenge." Policy Brief. Population Reference Bureau. February 2012. https://assets.aspeninstitute.org/content/uploads/files/content/docs/ee/Population_Reference_Bureau_Population_and_Food_Security_Africa_Bremner.pdf.

Bughin, Jacques, Mutsa Chironga, Georges Desvaux, Tenbite Ermias, Paul Jacobson, Omid Kassiri, Acha Leke, Susan Lund, Arend van Wamelen, and Yassir Zouaoui. 2016. *Lions on the Move II: Realizing the Potential of Africa's Economies*. McKinsey & Company Report. September 2016. https://www.mckinsey.com/featured-insights/middle-east-and-africa/lions-on-the-move-realizing-the-potential-of-africas-economies.

Byerlee, Derek, Andres F. Garcia, Asa Giertz, and Vincent Palmade. 2013. *Growing Africa: Unlocking the Potential of Agribusiness: Main Report*. World Bank. March 11. http://documents.worldbank.org/curated/en/327811467990084951/Main-report.

Chamberlin, J., and Jacob Ricker-Gilbert. 2016. "Participation in Rural Land Rental Markets in Sub-Saharan Africa: Who Benefits and By How Much? Evidence from Malawi and Zambia." *American Journal of Agricultural Economics* 98 (5): 1507-1528.

Christiaensen, Luc, Lionel Demery, and Jesper Kuhl. 2011. "The (Evolving) Role of Agriculture in Poverty Reduction – An Empirical Perspective." *Journal of Development Economics* 96 (2): 239-254.

Cotula, Lorenzo, Sonja Vermeulen, Rebeca Leonard, and James Keeley. 2009. *Land Grab or Development Opportunity? Agricultural Investment and International Land Deals in Africa*. London/Rome: IIED/FAO/IFAD.

Deininger, Klaus, Fang Xia, and Sara Savastano. 2015. "Smallholders? Land Ownership and Access in Sub-Saharan Africa: A New Landscape?" World Bank Policy Research Working Paper 7285. Washington, D.C.: World Bank.

Dorosh, Paul, Hyoung-Gun Wang, Liang You, and Emily Schmidt. 2010. "Crop Production and Road Connectivity in Sub-Saharan Africa: A Spatial Analysis." World Bank Policy Research Working Paper 5385. Washington, D.C.: World Bank.

Drechsel, Pay, Lucy Gyiele, Dagmar Kunze, and Olufunke Cofie. 2001. "Population Density, Soil Nutrient Depletion, and Economic Growth in Sub-Saharan Africa." *Ecological Economics* 38 (2): 251-258.

Hubert, Bernard, Mark Rosegrant, Martinus A. J. S. van Boekel, and Rodomiro Ortiz. 2010. "The Future of Food: Scenarios for 2050." *Crop Science* 50 (March–April): S-33–S-50. https://dl.sciencesocieties.org/publications/cs/pdfs/50/Supplement_1/S-33.

Hughes, Justin. 2009. "Coffee and Chocolate – Can We Help Developing Country Farmers Through Geographical Indications?" Report for the International Intellectual Property Institute, Washington, D.C.

International Fund for Agricultural Development (IFAD). 2016. *Fostering Inclusive Rural Transformation.* 2016. Rural Development Report 2016. IFAD. September 2016. https://www.ifad.org/en/web/knowledge/publication/asset/39240288.

Jayne, Thomas, David Mather, and Elliot Mghenyi. 2010. "Principal Challenges Confronting Smallholder Agriculture in Sub-Saharan Africa." *World Development* 38 (10): 1384-1398.

Jayne, Thomas, J. Govereh, M. Wanzala, and M. Demeke. 2003. "Fertilizer Market Development: A Comparative Analysis of Ethiopia, Kenya, and Zambia." *Food Policy* 28: 293-316.

Jin, Songqing, and Thomas Jayne. 2013. "Land Rental Markets in Kenya: Implications for Efficiency, Equity, Household Income, and Poverty." *Land Economics* 89 (2): 246-271.

Johnston, B. F. and P. Kilby. 1975. "Agriculture and Structural Transformation: Economic Strategies in Late Developing Countries." *Revue Tiers Monde* 16 (63): 699.

Kelly, Valerie A., Eric W. Crawford, and Thomas Jayne. 2003. "Agricultural Input Use and Market Development in Africa: Recent Perspectives and Insights." *Policy Synthesis for Cooperating USAID Offices and Country Missions* 70 (July).

Kowalski, Przemyslaw, Javier Lopez Gonzalez, Alexandos Ragoussis, and Cristian Ugarte. 2015. "Participation of Developing Countries in Global Value Chains: Implications for Trade and Trade-Related Policies." *OECD Trade Policy Papers.* https://www.oecd-ilibrary.org/trade/participation-of-developing-countries-in-global-value-chains_5js33lfw0xxn-en.

Lipton, Michael. 2005. *The Family Farm in a Globalizing World: The Role of Crop Science in Alleviating Poverty.* Washington, D.C.: International Food Policy Research Institute.

McCullough, Ellen B. 2017. "Labor Productivity and Employment Gaps in Sub-Saharan Africa." *Food Policy* 67: 133-152.

McCullough, Ellen B., Prabhu L. Pingali, and Kostas G. Stamoulis. 2008. "Small Farms and the Transformation of Food Systems: An Overview." In McCullough, Ellen B., Prabhu L. Pingali, and Kostas G. Stamoulis (eds.), *The Transformation of Agri-food Systems: Globalization, Supply Chains and Smallholder Farmers.* London: FAO and Earthscan.

Mellor, John W. 1976. *The New Economics of Growth.* Ithaca, NY: Cornell University Press.

Mhlanga, Nomathemba. 2010. "Private Sector Agribusiness Investment in Sub-

Saharan Africa." Agricultural Management, Marketing and Finance Working Document 27. FAO. http://www.fao.org/3/k7443e/k7443e.pdf.

Minde, Isaac, Thomas Jayne, Eric W. Crawford, Joshua Ariga, and Jones Govereh. 2008. "Promoting Fertilizer Use in Africa: Current Issues and Empirical Evidence from Malawi, Zambia, and Kenya." ReSAKSS Working Paper 13.

Mosoti, V. and S. Koroma. 2008. "Towards an African Common Market for Agricultural Products and Implications of EPAs." Paper presented at the African Workshop on EPAs, 8-10 October, Addis Ababa, Ethiopia.

Moyo, Jennifer Mbabazi, El-hadj M. Bah, and Audrey Verdier-Chouchane. 2015. "Transforming Africa's Agriculture to Improve Competitiveness." *Africa Competitiveness Report 2015*. Geneva: World Economic Forum.

Msangi, Siwa. 2012. "African Agricultural Futures: Opportunities, Challenges and Priorities." Food Security in Africa: Bridging Research and Practice. Sidney, 29–30 November. https://www.slideshare.net/ACIAR_Australia/1140-s-msangi.

Msuya, Elibariki Emmanuel. 2007. "The Impact of Foreign Direct Investment on Agricultural Productivity and Poverty Reduction in Tanzania." Munich Personal RePEc Archive Paper 3671. Munich: Munich University Library.

PricewaterhouseCoopers. 2007. "Sustainability Impact Assessment of the EU-ACP Economic Partnership Agreements, West Africa Agro-industry." Paris, Price waterhouseCoopers. May. https://ec.europa.eu/smart-regulation/evaluation/search/download.do?documentId=2447.

Rohrbach, D. D., I. J. Minde, and J. Howard. 2003. "Looking Beyond National Boundaries: Regional Harmonization of Seed Policies, Laws and Regulations." *Food Policy* 28 (4): 317-333.

Sanghvi, Sunil, Rupert Simons, and Roberto Uchoa. 2011. "Four Lessons for Transforming African Agriculture." *McKinsey*. https://www.mckinsey.com/industries/public-sector/our-insights/four-lessons-for-transforming-african-agriculture.

Sasson, Albert. 2012. "Food Security for Africa: An Urgent Global Challenge." *Agriculture and Food Security* w11, article no. 2. https://agricultureandfoodsecurity.biomedcentral.com/articles/10.1186/2048-7010-1-2.

Schaffnit-Chatterjee, Claire. 2014. "Agricultural Value Chain in Sub-Saharan Africa: From a Development Challenge to a Business Opportunity." Deutsche Bank Research. April 14. http://catalogue.unccd.int/764_Agricultural_value_chains_SSA_DB.pdf.

Sheahan, Megan, and Christopher B. Barrett. 2017. "Ten Striking Facts About Agricultural Input Use in Sub-Saharan Africa." *Food Policy* 67: 12-25.

Stoorvogel, J. J., and E. M. A. Smaling. 1990. "Assessment of soil nutrient depletion in Sub–Saharan Africa: 1983–2000." Report 20. Wageningen, The Netherlands: The Winand Staring Centre for Integrated Land, Soil and Water Research.

Swinnen, Johan F. M. 2007. *Global Supply Chains, Standards and the Poor: How the Globalization of Food Systems and Standards Affects Rural Development and Poverty*. Boston: CABI.

Timmer, C. Peter. 1988. "The Agricultural Transformation." In Chenery, H. and T. N. Srinivasan (eds.), *Handbook of Development Economics* 1: 275–331. Amsterdam: North-Holland.

Tittonell, Pablo, and Ken E. Giller. 2013. "When Yield Gaps Are Poverty Traps: The Paradigm of Ecological Intensification in African Smallholder Agriculture." *Field Crops Research* 143 (March): 76-90.

UNCTAD (United Nations Conference on Trade and Development). 2008. *World Investment Directory 2008.* Volume X (Africa). New York and Geneva: United Nations. https://unctad.org/en/Docs/iteiit20075_en.pdf.

UNCTAD (United Nations Conference on Trade and Development). 2009. *World Investment Report 2009: Transnational Corporations, Agricultural Production, and Development.* New York and Geneva: United Nations. https://unctad.org/en/Docs/wir2009_en.pdf.

UNECA (United Nations Economic Commission for Africa). 2010. *Agricultural Input Business Development in Africa: Opportunities, Issues and Challenges.* Addis Ababa: UNECA. https://www.uneca.org/sites/default/files/PublicationFiles/sro-sa-agri-iputs-business-opportunities.pdf.

UNIDO (United Nations Industrial Development Organization). 2016. *Industrialization in Africa and Least Developed Countries: Boosting Growth, Creating Jobs, Promoting Inclusiveness and Sustainability.* UNIDO. September 2016. https://www.unido.org/sites/default/files/2016-09/G20_new_UNIDO_report_industrialization_in_Africa_and_LDCs_0.pdf.

UNIDO Statistics Unit. 2013. "The Structure and Growth Pattern of Agro-industry of African Countries." Development Policy, Statistics and Research Branch Working Paper 9/2012. United Nations Industrial Organization (UNIDO). https://www.unido.org/sites/default/files/files/2018-03/WP092012_Ebook.pdf.

Van Rooyen, C. J. 2014. "Towards 2050: Trends and Scenarios for African Business." *International Food and Agribusiness Management Review* 17, special issue B. https://www.ifama.org/resources/Documents/v17ib/Rooyen.pdf.

Vermeulen, S., J. Woodhill, F. Proctor, and R. Delnoye. 2008. "Chain-wide Learning for Inclusive Agrifood Market Development. A Guide to Multi-stakeholder Processes for Linking Small-scale Producers to Modern Markets." London: IIED and Wageningen University.

Vollrath, Dietrich. 2007. "Land Distribution and International Agricultural Productivity." *American Journal of Agricultural Economics* 89 (1): 202-216.

Von Braun, Joachim, and Ruth Meinzen-Dick. 2009. "'Land grabbing' by Foreign Investors in Developing Countries: Risks and Opportunities." International Food Policy Research Institute Policy Brief 13. Washington, D.C.: IFPRI.

World Bank. 2007. *World Development Report 2008: Agriculture for Development.* Washington, D.C.: World Bank. https://openknowledge.worldbank.org/handle/10986/5990.

World Economic Forum. 2009. *The Africa Competitiveness Report 2009.* Geneva: World Economic Forum. https://www.afdb.org/fileadmin/uploads/afdb/Documents/Publications/Africa%20Competitiveness%20Report%202009.pdf.

CHAPTER 4

Adeosun, O. O., T. H. Adeosun, and I. A. Adetunde. 2009. "Strategic Application of Information and Communication Technology for Effective Service Delivery in Banking Industry." *Journal of Social Sciences* 5 (1): 47–51.

Adera, Edith Ofwona, Timothy M. Waema, Julian May, Ophelia Mascarenhas, and Kathleen Diga, eds. 2014. *ICT Pathways to Poverty Reduction: Empirical Evidence from East and Southern Africa.* Practical Action Publishing, International Development Research Centre (IDRC). January 14. https://www.idrc.ca/en/book/ict-pathways-poverty-reduction-empirical-evidence-east-and-southern-africa.

Adeya, Catherine Nyaki. 2001. Information and Communication Technologies in Africa: A Review and Selective Annotated Bibliography 1990–2000. Oxford, UK: INASP.

Afari-Kumah, Eben, and Hannah Ayaba Tanye. 2009. "Tertiary Students' View on Information and Communications Technology Usage in Ghana." *Journal of Information Technology Impact* 9 (2): 81–90.

African Union, African Development Bank, NEPAD. 2015. "Programme for Infrastructure Development in Africa (PIDA)—Information and Communication Technologies (ICT) Sector ToR." https://www.afdb.org/fileadmin/uploads/afdb/Documents/Procurement/Project-related-Procurement/PIDA%20-%20Sector-specific%20Terms%20of%20Reference%20for%20Information%20and%20Communication%20Technologies%20%28ICT%29%20Sector.pdf.

Akomea-Bonsu, Charles, and Frank Sampong. 2012. "The Impact of Information and Communication Technologies (ICT) on Small and Medium Scale Enterprises (SMEs) in the Kumasi Metropolis, Ghana, West Africa." *European Journal of Business and Management* 4 (20): 152–158.

Andrianaivo, Mihasonirin, and Kangni Kpodar. 2011. "ICT, Financial Inclusion, and Growth Evidence from African Countries." IMF Working Paper WP/11/73. International Monetary Fund. April 2011. https://www.imf.org/external/pubs/ft/wp/2011/wp1173.pdf.

Apulu, Idisemi, and Ann Latham. 2010. "Benefits of Information and Communication Technology in Small and Medium Sized Enterprises: A Case Study of a Nigerian SME." *UK Academy for Information Systems Conference Proceedings 2010.* March 23, 2010. https://pdfs.semanticscholar.org/9e18/325585bab07acf0b9e5e22965c6351a86261.pdf.

Apulu Idisemi, and Ann Latham. 2011. "Drivers for Information and Communication Technology Adoption: A Case Study of Nigerian Small and Medium Sized Enterprise." *International Journal of Business and Management* 6, no. 5 (May 2011). https://www.researchgate.net/profile/Ann_Latham/publication/229020234_Drivers_for_Information_and_Communication_Technology_Adoption_A_Case_Study_of_Nigerian_Small_and_Medium_Sized_Enterprises/links/558d1a9b08ae591c19da337a.pdf.

Asare, Sampson D., Bontle Gopolang, and Opelo Mogotlhwane. 2012. "Challenges Facing SMEs in the Adoption of ICT in B2B and B2C E-commerce: A Comparative Case Study of Botswana and Ghana." *International Journal of Commerce and Management* 22, no. 4 (November 2012): 272–285.

Ashrafi, R. and M. Murtaza. 2008. "Use and Impact of ICT on SMEs in Oman." *The Electronic Journal Information Systems Evaluation* 11: 125-138.

Baller, Silja, Attilio Di Battista, Soumitra Dutta, and Bruno Lanvin. 2016. "The Networked Readiness Index 2016." In *The Global Information Technology Report: Innovating in the Digital Economy*, chapter 1.1, World Economic Forum. http://www3.weforum.org/docs/GITR2016/WEF_GITR_Chapter1.1_2016.pdf.

Bankole, Felix Olu, and Lucas Mimbi. 2015. "ICT and Health System Performance in Africa: A Multi-Method Approach." May 4, 2016. https://arxiv.org/abs/1605.01151.

Ben-Ari, Nirit. 2014. "Big Dreams for Rwanda's ICT Sector." *Africa Renewal*, April. http://www.un.org/africarenewal/magazine/april-2014/big-dreams-rwanda%E2%80%99s-ict-sector.

Bresnahan, Timothy, Erik Brynjolfsson, and Lorin M. Hitt. 2002. "Information Technology, Workplace Organization, and the Demand for Skilled Labor: Firm-Level Evidence." *Quarterly Journal of Economics* 117 (1): 339-376.

Buhalis, Dimitrios. 2003. *eTourism: Information Technology for Strategic Tourism Management*. London, UK: Pearson Education.

Bussotti, Lucas. 2015. "Short Reflections on the History of African Communication." ISCTE-IUL, International Studies Center, Lisbon. January 2015. https://www.researchgate.net/publication/283581084_Short_reflections_on_the_history_of_African_communication.

Calandro, Enrico, Allison Gillwald, Mpho Moyo, and Christoph Stork. 2010. "Comparative ICT Sector Performance Review 2009/2010." Towards Evidence-Based ICT Policy and Regulation, Vol. 2, Policy Paper 5. https://www.researchictafrica.net/publications/Policy_Paper_Series_Towards_Evidence-based_ICT_Policy_and_Regulation_-_Volume_2/Vol_2_Paper_5_-_Comparative_ICT_Sector_Performance_Review_2009_2010.pdf.

Chibelushi, Caroline. 2008. "ICT Industry Challenges in Adopting ICT: A Case Study from the West Midlands, UK." In *CONF-IRM 2008 Proceedings*, 32. International Conference on Information Resources Management (CONF-IRM). May. https://pdfs.semanticscholar.org/c7c5/396b8e896b577692680729c4aded78a40bfe.pdf.

Chowdhury, Shyamal, and Susanna Wolf. 2003. "Use of ICTs and the Economic Performance of SMEs in East Africa." UNU-WIDER Working Paper, 6/2003. United Nations University–World Institute for Development Economics Research (UNU-WIDER). https://www.wider.unu.edu/publication/use-icts-and-economic-performance-smes-east-africa.

Cisco Systems. 2017. "Cisco Visual Networking Index: Global Mobile Data Traffic Forecast Update, 2016–2021 White Paper." Cisco Systems. April 12. http://www.czechmarketplace.cz/news/cisco-visual-networking-index-global-mobile-data-traffic-forecast-update-2016-2021-white-paper.

"Current ICT Initiatives and Projects—Republic of Kenya." 2017. IST Africa. http://www.ist-africa.org/home/default.asp?page=doc-by-id&docid=5181.

Datta, A., and S. Agarwal. 2004. "Telecommunications and Economic Growth: A Panel Data Approach." *Applied Economics* 36 (15): 1649–1654.

Deen-Swarray, Mariama, Alison N. Gillwald, and Ashleigh Morrell. 2013. "Lifting the Gender Veil on ICT Indicators in Africa." Conference Paper. *CPRSouth Conference.*

Deloitte. 2014. "The Future of Telecoms in Africa: The 'Blueprint for the Brave.'" https://www2.deloitte.com/content/dam/Deloitte/fpc/Documents/secteurs/technologies-medias-et-telecommunications/deloitte_the-future-of-telecoms-in-africa_2014.pdf.

Deloitte. 2016. *Tech Trends 2016: Innovating in the Digital Era: A Public Sector Perspective.* https://www2.deloitte.com/us/en/insights/focus/tech-trends/2016.html.

Den Hengst, Marielle, and Henk G. Sol. 2001. "The Impact of Information and Communication Technology on Interorganizational Coordination: Guidelines from Theory." *Special Series on Information Exchange in Electronic Markets* 4 (3): 129–138. http://inform.nu/Articles/Vol4/v4n4p129-138.pdf.

Di Battista, Attilio, Soumitra Dutta, Thierry Geiger, and Bruno Lanvin. 2015. "The Networked Readiness Index 2015: Taking the Pulse of the ICT Revolution." In *The Global Information Technology Report 2015.* Geneva: World Economic Forum.

Diga, K. 2013. "Local Economic Opportunities and ICTs: How ICTs Affect Livelihoods (Part II)." In *Connecting ICTs to Development: The IDRC Experience*, edited by Laurent Elder, Heloise Emdon, Richard Fuchs, and Ben Petrazzini. New York: Anthem Press, with International Development Research Center (IDRC).

Duncombe Richard, and Richard Heeks. 1999. "Information, ICTs and Small Enterprise: Findings from Botswana." Development Informatics Working Paper Series 7. Institute for Development Policy and Management, University of Manchester. November. http://unpan1.un.org/intradoc/groups/public/documents/nispacee/unpan015541.pdf.

Durrani, H., S. Khoja, A. Naseem, R. E. Scott, A. Gul, and R. Jan. 2012. "Health Needs and eHealth Readiness Assessment of Health Care Organizations in Kabul and Bamyan, Afghanistan/Évaluation des besoins en matière de santé et de la préparation à la cybersanté dans des établissements de soins de santé à Kaboul et Bamyan (Afghanistan)." *Eastern Mediterranean Health Journal* 18(6): 663-70.

Dutta, Soumitra, Thierry Geiger, and Bruno Lanvin. 2015. *The Global Information Technology Report 2015: ICTs for Inclusive Growth.* Insight Report. World Economic Forum. http://www.itweb.co.za/images/PDF/WEF_Global-IT-Report-2015.pdf.

Ewing, Javier. 2015. *ICT Competitiveness in Africa.* Washington, D.C.: World Bank. http://siteresources.worldbank.org/EXTINFORMATIONANDCOMMUNICATIONANDTECHNOLOGIES/Resources/282822-1346223280837/ICTCompetitiveness.pdf.

Farrell, Glen. 2007. "ICT in Education in Rwanda." *Survey of ICD and Education in Africa: Rwanda Country Report.* April. http://www.infodev.org/infodev-files/resource/InfodevDocuments_423.pdf.

Fink, Dieter, and Georg Disterer. 2006. "International Case Studies: To What Extent Is ICT Infused into the Operations of SMEs?" *Journal of Enterprise Information Management* 19 (6): 608–624.

Fortune of Africa. n.d. "Challenges Facing ICT Sector in Rwanda." Fortune of Africa. Accessed September 12, 2019. http://fortuneofafrica.com/rwanda/challenges-facing-ict-sector-in-rwanda/.

Fulantelli, Giovanni, and Mario Allegra. 2003. "Small Company Attitude towards ICT Based Solutions: Some Key-Elements to Improve It." *Journal of Educational Technology and Society* 6 (1): 45–49. International Forum of Educational Technology and Society. January. https://www.jstor.org/stable/jeductechsoci.6.1.45?seq=1#page_scan_tab_contents.

Internet Society. 2016. "The Future of the Internet in Africa." June.

Gillwald, Allison, and Mpho Moyo. 2014. "The Cloud over Africa." Policy paper. Research ICT Africa. https://www.researchictafrica.net/publications/Evidence_for_ICT_Policy_Action/Policy_Paper_20_-_The_cloud_over_Africa.pdf.

Grace, Jeremy, Charles Kenny, Christine Zhen-Wei Qiang, Jia Liu, and Taylor Reynolds. 2003. "Information and Communication Technologies and Broad-Based Development." World Bank Working Paper Series 12. World Bank. December 1. http://documents.worldbank.org/curated/en/998881468780319383/Information-and-communication-technologies-and-broad-based-development.

GSMA Intelligence. 2016. *The Mobile Economy: Africa 2016*. London, UK: GSMA. https://www.gsmaintelligence.com/research/?file=3bc21ea879a5b217b64d62fa24c55bdf&download.

GSMA Intelligence. 2018. *The Mobile Economy: Sub-Saharan Africa 2018*. London, UK: GSMA. https://www.gsmaintelligence.com/research/?file=809c442550e5487f3b1d025fdc70e23b&download.

Harrison, Bryant. 2005. "Information and Communication Technology Policy in Rwanda." Case study 21G-034. December 13. https://ocw.mit.edu/courses/global-studies-and-languages/21g-034-media-education-and-the-marketplace-fall-2005/projects/MIT21G_034F05_ictrwanda.pdf.

Heeks, Richard. 1999. *Information and Communication Technologies, Poverty and Development*. Development Informatics Working Paper Series 5. Manchester: Institute for Development Policy and Management, University of Manchester. http://unpan1.un.org/intradoc/groups/public/documents/nispacee/unpan015539.pdf.

Heeks, Richard. 2001. *Understanding e-Governance for Development*. i-Government Working Paper Series 11. Manchester: Institute for Development Policy and Management, University of Manchester. http://unpan1.un.org/intradoc/groups/public/documents/NISPAcee/UNPAN015484.pdf.

InfoDev, Hivos, UKaid. 2010. *Transforming East African ICT Sector by Creating a Business Engine for SMEs*. http://www.infodev.org/infodev-files/resource/Infodev Documents_1040.pdf.

Irani, Z. 2002. "Information Systems Evaluation: Navigating through the Problem Domain. *Journal of Information & Management* 40 (1): 11–24.

IST-Africa. 2012. *Guide to ICT Policy in IST-Africa Partner Countries*. April 20. http://www.ist-africa.org/home/files/IST-Africa_ICTPolicy_200412.pdf.

Jennex, Murray E., Don Amoroso, and Olayele Adelakun. 2004. "E-commerce Infrastructure Success Factors for Small Companies in Developing Economies." *Electronic Commerce Research* 4 (3): 263–286.

Jumia. 2019. *Nigeria: Mobile Report 2019*. https://www.jumia.com.ng/mobile-report.

Kenya National Bureau of Statistics and Communications Authority of Kenya. 2016. *Enterprise ICT Survey 2016*. https://ca.go.ke/wp-content/uploads/2018/02/Enter prise-ICT-Survey-Report-2016.pdf.

Khuong, Vu. 2005. "Measuring the Impact of ICT Investments on Economic Growth." Cambridge, MA: Harvard Kennedy School of Government. https://www.re searchgate.net/publication/228350121_Measuring_the_Impact_of_ICT_Invest ments_on_Economic_Growth.

Kwankam, S. Yunkap. 2004. "What e-Health Can Offer." *Bulletin of the World Health Organization* 82 (10): 800–802.

Kwapong, Olivia. 2007. "Problems of Policy Formulation and Implementation: The Case of ICT Use in Rural Women's Empowerment in Ghana." *International Journal of Education and Development using ICT* 3 (2). June 13. http://ijedict.dec.uwi.edu/ printarticle.php?id=324&layout=html.

Lal, Kaushalesh. 2004. "E-business and Export Behavior: Evidence from Indian Firms." *World Development* 32 (3): 505–517.

Lancaster, Henry. 2017. "Fixed and Mobile Broadband in Africa: An Executive Sum-mary." *Africology: The Journal of Pan African Studies* 10 (10): 171-174.

Lee, Sang H., John Levendis, and Luis Gutierrez. 2009. "Telecommunications and Economic Growth: An Empirical Analysis of Sub-Saharan Africa." *Applied Eco-nomics* 44 (4): 461–469.

Lewin, David, and Susan Sweet. 2005. "The Economic Impact of Mobile Services in Latin America." *GSM Association*: 47–49. http://citeseerx.ist.psu.edu/viewdoc/dow nload?doi=10.1.1.513.8704&rep=rep1&type=pdf.

Love, Peter E. D., Zahir Irani, Ahmad Ghoneim, and Marinos Themistocleous. 2006. "An Exploratory Study of Indirect ICT Costs Using the Structured Case Method." *International Journal of Information Management* 26 (2): 167–177.

Lucas, H. 2008. "Information and Communications Technology for Future Health Systems in Developing Countries." *Social Science and Medicine* 66 (10): 2122-32.

Lwakabamba, Silas. 2005. "The Development of ICTs in Rwanda: Pioneering Experi-ences." In *At the Crossroads: ICT Policy Making in East Africa*, edited by Florence E. Etta and Laurent Elder, 213–224. Nairobi: East African Educational Publishers.

M&G Africa Writer. 2016. "20 Striking Facts about Digital, Mobile and Tech in Africa, Including the 'Dictator's Dilemma.'" *Mail & Guardian Africa*. https://web. archive.org/web/20180521221059/http://mgafrica.com/article/2016-01-22-20-facts-about-digital-in-africa.

Maldeni, H. M. C. M., and Sanath Jayasena. 2009. "Information and Communication Technology Usage and Bank Branch Performance." *International Journal on Advances in ICT for Emerging Regions (ICTer)* 2 (2). December. https://www. researchgate.net/publication/270873721_Information_and_Communication_ Technology_Usage_and_Bank_Branch_Performance.

Mars, M. and R. E. Scott. 2015. "Telehealth in the Developing World: Current Status and Future Prospects." *Social Science and Medicine* 66 (10): 2122-2132.

Matambalya, Francis, and Susanna Wolf. 2001. "The Role of ICT for the Performance of SMEs in East Africa: Empirical Evidence from Kenya and Tanzania." ZEF–Discussion Papers on Development Policy 42. http://hdl.handle.net/10419/84717.

May, Julian, Vaughan Dutton, and Louis Munyakazi. 2014. "Information and Communication Technologies as a Pathway from Poverty: Evidence from East Africa." In Adera, Edith Ofwona, Timothy M. Waema, Julian May, Ophelia Mascarenhas, and Kathleen Diga (eds.), *ICT Pathways to Poverty Reduction: Empirical Evidence from East and Southern Africa*. London and Ottawa: Practical Action Publishing and IDRC.

Mirembe, Namugenyi Loi. 2010. "ICT Initiatives in Uganda." Presentation at eChallenges e-2010 Conference, Warsaw, Poland. *IST-Africa and UNCST.* http://www.ist-africa.org/home/files/ICTResearch_Uganda_IST-Africa.pdf.

Moahi, Kgomotso H. 2009. "ICT and Health Information in Botswana: Towards the Millennium Development Goals." *Information Development* 25 (3): 198–206.

Msimang, Mandla. 2011. *Broadband in Kenya: Build It and They Will Come*. Report. Washington DC: World Bank. January 1. http://documents.worldbank.org/curated/en/617221468331457281/Kenya-Broadband-in-Kenya-build-it-and-they-will-come.

Mutula, Stephen M., and Pieter Van Brakel. 2007. "ICT Skills Readiness for the Emerging Global Digital Economy among Small Businesses in Developing Countries: Case Study of Botswana." *Library Hi Tech* 25 (2): 231–245.

Ngwenyama, Ojelanki, and Olga Morawczynski. 2009. "Factors Affecting ICT Expansion in Emerging Economies: An Analysis of ICT Infrastructure Expansion in Five Latin American Countries." *Information Technology for Development* 15 (4): 237–258.

Nkwe, Nugi. 2012. "E-government: Challenges and Opportunities in Botswana." *International Journal of Humanities and Social Science* 2 (17): 39–48.

Obijiofor, Levi, Sohail Inayatullah, and Tony Stevenson. 2000. "Impact of New Information and Communication Technologies (ICTs) on Socioeconomic and Educational Development of Africa and the Asia-Pacific: A Pilot Study." *Journal of Futures Studies* 4, no. 2 (May). https://pdfs.semanticscholar.org/63d2/101672c097706e2b8a97292f23761278c18a.pdf.

Ongori, Henry, and Stephen O. Migiro. 2010. "Information and Communication Technologies Adoption in SMEs: Literature Review." *Journal of Chinese Entrepreneurship* 2 (1): 93–104.

Owen, Wilfred Jr. and Osei Darkwa. 1999. "Role of Multi-purpose Community Telecenters in Accelerating National Development in Ghana." *First Monday* 5 (1): 1-23.

Pepper, Robert, and John Garrity. 2015. "ICTs, Income Inequality, and Ensuring Inclusive Growth." In *The Global Information Technology Report 2015*. Geneva: World Economic Forum.

PIDA. 2012. *Africa ICT Sector Outlook—2030*. https://www.nepad.org/publication/africa-ict-sector-outlook-2030-0.

PIDA. 2014. *Sector-Specific Terms of Reference for Information and Communication Technologies (ICT) Sector*. https://www.afdb.org/fileadmin/uploads/afdb/Documents/Procurement/Project-related-Procurement/PIDA%20-%20Sector-specific%20Terms%20of%20Reference%20for%20Transport%20Sector.pdf.

Quarshie, Henry Osborn, and James Ami-Narh. 2012. "The Growth and Usage of Internet in Ghana." *Journal of Emerging Trends in Computing and Information Sciences* 3 (9): 1302–1308.

Qureshi, Kashif Naseer, Abdul Hanan Abdullah, and Raja Waseem Anwar. 2014. "The Evolution in Health Care with Information and Communication Technologies." Paper in *Proceedings of 2nd International Conference on Applied Information and Communications Technology*, April 28–29, 2014, Oman. December. https://www.researchgate.net/publication/271521684_The_Evolution_in_Health_Care_with_Information_and_Communication_Technologies.

Ramsey, Elaine, Pat Ibbotson, Jim Bell, and Brendan Gray. 2003. "E-opportunities of Service Sector SMEs: An Irish Cross-Border Study." *Journal of Small Business and Enterprise Development* 10 (3): 250–264.

Rice-Oxley, Mark, and Zoe Flood. 2016. "Can the Internet Reboot Africa?" *The Guardian*, July 25. https://www.theguardian.com/world/2016/jul/25/can-the-internet-reboot-africa.

Rizzato, Francesco. 2017. "Variable Network Quality a Key Driver of Multi-SIM Ownership." *GSMA Intelligence.* https://www.gsmaintelligence.com/research/2017/01/variable-network-quality-a-key-driver-of-multi-sim-ownership/597.

Sambo, Luis Gomes and World Health Organization (WHO). 2014. *The Health of the People: What Works: The African Regional Health Report 2014.* Geneva: World Health Organization. https://apps.who.int/iris/handle/10665/137377.

Sassi, Seifallah, and Mohamed Goaied. 2013. "Financial Development, ICT Diffusion and Economic Growth: Lessons from MENA Region." *Telecommunications Policy* 37 (4): 252–261.

Sebusang, S. E. M., and S. Masupe. 2003. "ICT Development in Botswana: Connectivity for Rural Communities." *African Journal of Information and Communication* (4): 41–51.

Shaqrah, Amin A. 2010. "Adoption of Telemedicine among Health Care Services: The Strategic Adoption." *Journal of E-health Management* 19: 66–74.

Silver, Laura and Courtney Johnson. 2018. "Majorities in sub-Saharan Africa own mobile phones, but smartphone adoption is modest." *Pew Research Center.* https://www.pewresearch.org/global/2018/10/09/majorities-in-sub-saharan-africa-own-mobile-phones-but-smartphone-adoption-is-modest.

Soremekun, Olumayokun, and Charles A. Malgwi. 2013. "Exploring Patterns in ICT Growth and Development in Africa: A Kohonen Map Analysis." *Review of Regional Studies* 43 (2): 175-190.

Spanos, Yiannis E., Gregory P. Prastacos, and Angeliki Poulymenakou. 2002. "The Relationship between Information and Communication Technologies Adoption and Management." *Information and Management* 39 (8): 659–675.

Sridhar, Kala Seetharam, and Varadharajan Sridhar. 2006. "Telecommunications and Growth: Causal Model, Quantitative and Qualitative Evidence." *Economic and Political Weekly* 41, no. 25 (June 24–29): 2611–2619. https://www.jstor.org/stable/4418381?seq=1#page_scan_tab_contents.

Sridhar, Kala Seetharam, and Varadharajan Sridhar. 2008. "Telecommunications infrastructure and economic growth: Evidence from developing countries."

Stefanski, Scott. 2014. *ICTs for Financial Services in Africa*. Washington, D.C.: World Bank. https://openknowledge.worldbank.org/handle/10986/19019.

Straub, Stéphane. 2008. *Infrastructure and growth in developing countries*. Policy Research Working Papers 4460. World Bank. January. https://openknowledge.worldbank.org/handle/10986/6458.

Tarute, Asta, and Gatautis Rimantas. 2014. "ICT Impact on SMEs Performance." *Social and Behavioral Sciences* 110 (2014): 1218–1225. https://www.sciencedirect.com/science/article/pii/S1877042813056085.

Tcheng, H., J. Huet, I. Viennois, and M. Romdhane. 2007. "Telecoms and Development in Africa: The Chicken or the Egg?" *Convergence Letter* 8.

UN (United Nations). 2018. *E-Government Survey 2018: Gearing E-Government to Support Transformation Towards Sustainable and Resilient Societies*. New York: United Nations. https://publicadministration.un.org/egovkb/Portals/egovkb/Documents/un/2018-Survey/E-Government%20Survey%202018_FINAL%20for%20web.pdf.

Vu, Khuong M. 2011. "ICT as a Source of Economic Growth in the Information Age: Empirical Evidence from the 1996–2005 Period." *Telecommunications Policy* 35 (4): 357–372.

Wangwe, Samuel M. 2007. "A Review of Methodology for Assessing ICT Impact on Development and Economic Transformation." *African Economic Research Consortium (AERC)*. https://www.africaportal.org/publications/a-review-of-methodology-for-assessing-ict-impact-on-development-and-economic-transformation.

Waverman, Leonard, Meloria Meschi, and Melvyn Fuss. 2005. "The Impact of Telecoms on Economic Growth in Developing Countries." ICT Regulation Toolkit. InfoDev, ITU. https://www.researchgate.net/publication/265758950_The_Impact_of_Telecoms_on_Economic_Growth_in_Developing_Countries.

CHAPTER 5

ACET (African Center for Economic Transformation). 2014. *Growth with Depth*. 2014 African Transformation Report. http://africantransformation.org/wp-content/uploads/2014/02/2014-african-transformation-report.pdf.

African Development Bank Group. 2018. *African Economic Outlook 2018*. Abidjan, Côte d'Ivoire: African Development Bank Group. https://www.afdb.org/fileadmin/uploads/afdb/Documents/Publications/African_Economic_Outlook_2018_-_EN.pdf.

African Union. n.d. "CFTA—Continental Free Trade Area." Accessed September 18, 2019. https://au.int/en/ti/cfta/about.

African Union Commission. 2015. *Agenda 2063: The Africa We Want: First Ten-Year Implementation Plan 2014-2023*. September. https://www.un.org/en/africa/osaa/pdf/au/agenda2063-first10yearimplementation.pdf.

Ansu, Yaw, Margaret McMillan, John Page, and Dirk Willem te Velde. 2016. "African Transformation Forum 2016: Promoting Manufacturing in Africa." African Center for Economic Transformation, African Transformation Forum, Supporting Economic Transformation. March. https://set.odi.org/wp-content/uploads/2016/03/SET-ACET-ATF-Manufacturing-Paper.pdf.

Balchin, Neil, Stephen Gelb, Jane Kennan, Hope Martin, Dirk Willem te Velde, and Carolin Williams. 2016. "Developing Export-Based Manufacturing in Sub-Saharan Africa." Research Reports and Studies. April. https://www.odi.org/publications/10395-developing-export-based-manufacturing-sub-saharan-africa.

Bates, Robert. 2014. *Markets and States in Tropical Africa: The Political Basis of Agricultural Policies.* Updated and expanded, with a new preface. California Series on Social Choice and Political Economy. University of California Press.

Bentzen, Jeanet Sinding, Nicolai Kaarsen, and Asger Moll Wingender. 2013. "The Timing of Industrialization across Countries." Discussion Paper 13-17. University of Copenhagen Department of Economics Discussion. November 18. https://www.economics.ku.dk/research/publications/wp/dp_2013/1317.pdf.

Bessant, John, and Joe Tidd. 2007. *Innovation and Entrepreneurship.* Chichester, UK: Wiley.

Bhorat, Haroon, and Finn Tarp, eds. *Africa's Lions: Growth Traps and Opportunities for Six African Economies.* Washington, DC: Brookings Institution Press, 2016.

Bhorat, Haroon, and François Steenkamp. 2018. "Manufacturing Complexity in Africa." *Foresight Africa: Top Priorities for the Continent in 2018*: 72-75. Washington D.C.: Brookings Institution. January 11. https://www.brookings.edu/wp-content/uploads/2018/01/foresight-2018_full_web_final2.pdf.

Bhorat, Haroon, Christopher Rooney, and François Steenkamp. 2016. "Africa's Manufacturing Malaise." Working Paper Series, 1 (3). United Nations Development Program Regional Bureau for Africa. September 27. http://www.africa.undp.org/content/rba/en/home/library/working-papers/africa-s-manufacturing-malaise.html.

Bhorat, Haroon, Ravi Kanbur, Christopher Rooney, and François Steenkamp. 2017. "Sub-Saharan Africa's Manufacturing Sector: Building Complexity." Working Paper Series 256. Abidjan, Côte d'Ivoire: African Development Bank Group.

Bolaky, Bineswaree. 2011. "Fostering Industrial Development in Africa in the New Global Environment: Key Policy Recommendations." *Trade Negotiations Insights* 10 (9). International Centre for Trade and Sustainable Development. December 9. http://www.ictsd.org/bridges-news/trade-negotiations-insights/news/fostering-industrial-development-in-africa-in-the-new.

Brunetti, Aymo Aart Oliver, Gregory Kisunko, and Beatrice Silvia Weder. 1997. "Institutional Obstacles to Doing Business: Region-by-Region Results from a Worldwide Survey of the Private Sector." Research Working Paper WPS 1759. World Bank. April 30. http://documents.worldbank.org/curated/en/44906146813 1976033/Institutional-obstacles-to-doing-business-region-by-region-results-from-a-worldwide-survey-of-the-private-sector.

Bughin, Jacques, Mutsa Chironga, Georges Desvaux, Tenbite Ermias, Paul Jacobson, Omid Kassiri, Acha Leke, Susan Lund, Arend Van Wamelen and Yassir Zouaoui. 2016. *Lions on The Move II: Realizing the Potential of Africa's Economies.* McKinsey Global Institute Report. September. https://www.mckinsey.com/featured-insights/middle-east-and-africa/lions-on-the-move-realizing-the-potential-of-africas-economies.

Business Sweden. 2016a. "Emerging Consumer Markets in West Africa: Fact Pack." Business Sweden. September. https://www.business-sweden.se/contentassets/d2e1 84b90baa489895106f886f3ab6d8/emerging-consumer-markets-in-west-africa .pdf.

Chenery, Hollis B. 1960. "Patterns of Industrial Growth." *American Economic Review* 50 (4): 624–654.

Chenery, Hollis B., Sherman Robinson, and Moshe Syrquin. 1986. *Industrialization and Growth.* New York: Oxford University Press.

Colin, Clark. 1940. *The Conditions of Economic Progress.* London, UK: Macmillan.

Collier, Paul. 2008. *The Bottom Billion: Why the Poorest Countries Are Failing and What Can Be Done about It.* New York: Oxford University Press.

Conde, Carlos, Philipp Heinrigs, and Anthony O'Sullivan. 2015. "Tapping the Potential of Global Value Chains for Africa." In *The Africa Competitiveness Report 2015*, 71–85. World Economic Forum. http://www3.weforum.org/docs/WEF_ ACR_2015/Africa_Competitiveness_Report_2015.pdf.

Cornwall, John. 1977. *Modern Capitalism: Its Growth and Transformation.* New York: St. Martin's Press.

Deloitte. 2016. *2016 Global Manufacturing Competitiveness Index.* https://www2. deloitte.com/content/dam/Deloitte/global/Documents/Manufacturing/gx-global-mfg-competitiveness-index-2016.pdf.

De Vries, Gaaitzen, Marcel Timmer, and Klaas De Vries. 2013. "Structural Transformation in Africa: Static Gains, Dynamic Losses." *Journal of Development Studies* 51 (6): 674–688.

Dollar, David. 2018. "African Economies and Global Value Chains." In *Foresight Africa: Top Priorities for the Continent in 2018*, 76. Washington DC: Brookings Institution. https://www.brookings.edu/wp-content/uploads/2018/01/foresight-2018_full_web_final2.pdf.

The Economist. 2014. "Manufacturing in Africa: An Awakening Giant." February 8. http://www.economist.com/news/middle-east-and-africa/21595949-if-africas-economies-are-take-africans-will-have-start-making-lot.

The Economist Intelligence Unit. 2016. "Manufacturing in Africa: Still Struggling with the Basics." March 16. http://country.eiu.com/article.aspx?articleid=77403 4461#.

Ernst and Young. 2014. "Africa 2030: Realizing the Possibilities." https://www.ey. com/Publication/vwLUAssets/EY-Africa-2030-realizing-the-possibilities/$ FILE/EY-Africa-2030-realizing-the-possibilities.pdf.

Ernst, Dieter. 2002. "Global Production Networks and the Changing Geography of Innovation Systems. Implications for Developing Countries." *Economics of Innovation and New Technology* 11 (6): 497–523.

Ernst, Dieter, and Linsu Kim. 2002. "Global Production Networks, Knowledge Diffusion and Local Capability Formation." *Research Policy* 31 (8): 1417–1429.

Erzan, Refik. 1989. "Would General Trade Liberalization in Developing Countries Expand South-South Trade?" World Bank Policy Research Working Paper Series 319. Washington, D.C.: World Bank.

Evenson, Robert, and Larry Westphal. 1995. "Technological Change and Technology Strategy." *Handbook of Development Economics* 3 (1995): 2209–2299.

Farole, Thomas. 2010. "Second Best? Investment Climate and Performance in Africa's Special Economic Zones." Working Paper 3698. Washington, DC: World Bank.

Filmer, Deon and Louise Fox. 2014. *Youth Employment in Sub-Saharan Africa*. Washington, D.C.: World Bank.

Foreign Direct Investment Intelligence. 2016a. *The Africa Investment Report 2016: Foreign Investment Broadens Its Base*. https://www.camara.es/sites/default/files/pub licaciones/the-africa-investment-report-2016.pdf.

Foreign Direct Investment Intelligence. 2016b. *The Africa Investment Report 2015: An FDI Destination on the Rise*. African Business Central. January 4. https://www. africanbusinesscentral.com/2016/01/04/the-africa-investment-report-2015-an-fdi-destination-on-the-rise-fdi-intelligencethis-is-africa-report/.

Foster, Vivien, and Cecilia Briceno-Garmendia (eds.). 2010. *Africa's Infrastructure: A Time for Transformation*. Washington, D.C.: World Bank.

Gelb, Alan, Christian J. Meyer, and Vijaya Ramachandran. 2014. "Development as Diffusion—Manufacturing Productivity and Sub-Saharan Africa's Missing Middle." CGD Working Paper 357. Washington, DC: Center for Global Development.

Gelb, Alan, Christian J. Meyer, Vijaya Ramachandran, and Divyanshi Wadhwa. 2017. "Can Africa Be a Manufacturing Destination? Labor Costs in Comparative Perspective." CGD Working Paper 466. Washington, DC: Center for Global Development.

Chang, Ha-Joon, Adam B. Elhiraika, and Jostein Lohr Hauge. 2016. Seminar on Smart Industrial Policy for Africa in the 21st Century. Chaired by Antonio Andreoni. https://www.soas.ac.uk/economics/events/economics-seminars/29feb2016 -smart-industrial-policy-for-africa-in-the-21st-century.html.

Hidalgo, César A., Bailey Klinger, A-L. Barabási, and Ricardo Hausmann. 2007. "The Product Space Conditions the Development of Nations." *Science* 317 (5837): 482–487.

Imbs, J. and R. Wacziarg. 2003. "Stages of Diversification." *American Economic Review* 93 (1): 63-86.

IPRCC and UNDP. 2015. *If Africa Builds Nests, Will the Birds Come? Comparative Study on Special Economic Zones in Africa and China*. https://www.undp.org/content/ dam/china/docs/Publications/UNDP-CH-Comparative%20Study%20on%20 SEZs%20in%20Africa%20and%20China%20-%20ENG.pdf.

Irz, Xavier, Lin Lin, Colin Thirtle, and Steve Wiggins. 2001. "Agricultural Productivity Growth and Poverty Alleviation." *Development Policy Review* 19 (4): 449–466.

Jacobs, A. J. 2019. *The Automotive Industry and European Integration: The Divergent Paths of Belgium and Spain*. Cham, Switzerland: Palgrave McMillan.

Kaldor, Nicholas. 1966. *Causes of the Slow Rate of Economic Growth of the United Kingdom: An Inaugural Lecture*. London: Cambridge University Press.

Keller, Wolfgang. 1996. "Absorptive Capacity: On the Creation and Acquisition of Technology in Development." *Journal of Development Economics* 49 (1): 199--227.

Kim, Linsu. 1980. "Stages of Development of Industrial Technology in a Developing Country: A Model." *Research Policy* 9 (3): 254–277.

KPMG. 2013. *Manufacturing in Africa: Sector Report.* https://pdfs.semanticscholar.org/d027/959638f76e2f7fe42f5bbec77be30c70b1d9.pdf.

KPMG. 2015. *Manufacturing in Africa: Sector Report.*

KPMG. 2016. *Fast-Moving Consumer Goods: Sector Report.* https://assets.kpmg/content/dam/kpmg/br/pdf/2016/09/fast-moving-consumer-goods.pdf.

Kuznets, Simon, and John Thomas Murphy. 1966. *Modern Economic Growth: Rate, Structure and Spread.* Vol. 2. New Haven: Yale University Press.

Lewis, W. Arthur. 1954. "Economic Development with Unlimited Supplies of Labour." *The Manchester School* 22 (2): 139–191. https://la.utexas.edu/users/hcleaver/368/368lewistable.pdf.

Luke, David, and Babajide Sodipo. 2015. "Launch of the Continental Free Trade Area: New Prospects for African Trade?" *Bridges Africa* 4, no. 6 (June 23). International Centre for Trade and Sustainable Development. http://www.ictsd.org/bridges-news/bridges-africa/news/launch-of-the-continental-free-trade-area-new-prospects-for-african.

Mano, Yukichi, Alhassan Iddrisu, Yutaka Yoshino, and Tetsushi Sonobe. 2012. "How can Micro and Small Enterprise in Sub-Saharan Africa Become More Productive? The Impact of Experimental Basic Managerial Training." *World Development* 40 (3): 458–468.

Manyika, James, Jeff Sinclair, Richard Dobbs, Gernot Strube, Louis Rassey, Jan Mischke, Jaana Remes, Charles Roxburgh, Katy George, David O'Halloran, and Sreenivas Ramaswamy. 2012. *Manufacturing the Future: The Next Era of Global Growth and Innovation.* Report. McKinsey Global Institute. November. https://www.mckinsey.com/business-functions/operations/our-insights/the-future-of-manufacturing.

Martin, Will, and Devashish Mitra. 2001. "Productivity Growth and Convergence in Agriculture versus Manufacturing." *Economic Development and Cultural Change* 49 (2): 403–422.

McMillan, Margaret and Dani Rodrik. 2011. "Globalization, Structural Change and Productivity Growth." In Mark Bachetta and Marion Jansen (eds.), *Making Globalization Socially Sustainable.* Geneva: International Labor Organization.

McMillan, Margaret, Dani Rodrik, and Íñigo Verduzco-Gallo. 2014. "Globalization, Structural Change and Productivity Growth, with an Update on Africa." *World Development* 63 (1): 11–32.

McPherson, Michael A. 1996. "Growth of Micro and Small Enterprises in Southern Africa." *Journal of Development Economics* 48 (1996): 253-277.

Mead, Donald C. and Carl Liedholm. 1998. "The Dynamics of Micro and Small Enterprises in Developing Countries." *World Development* 26 (1): 61-74.

Narayanan, V. K. 2001. *Managing Technology and Innovation for Competitive Advantage.* Chennai, Tamil Nadu: Pearson India Education Services.

Nelson, Richard, and Edmund Phelps. 1966. "Investment in Humans, Technological Diffusion and Economic Growth." *American Economic Review* 56 (2): 69–75.

Newfarmer, Richard, John Page, and Finn Tarp. 2018. *Industries without Smokestacks: Industrialization in Africa Reconsidered.* New York: Oxford University Press.

Newman, Carol, and John Page. 2017. "Industrial Clusters: The Case for Special Economic Zones in Africa." WIDER Working Paper 15/2017. UNU-WIDER. https://www.wider.unu.edu/publication/industrial-clusters-1.

Newman, Carol, John Page, John Rand, Abebe Shimeles, Måns Söderbom, and Finn Tarp. 2016. *Made in Africa: Learning to Compete in Industry.* Washington, DC: Brookings Institution Press.

Ng, Francis and Alexander Yeats. 1996. "Open Economies Work Better! Did Africa's Protectionist Policies Cause Its Marginalization in World Trade?" World Bank Policy Research Working Paper Series 1636. Washington, D.C.: World Bank.

Ngulube, Bekithemba. 2014. "What Is the Future of Manufacturing in South Africa?" Frontier Advisory. August. https://www2.deloitte.com/content/dam/Deloitte/za/Documents/manufacturing/za_what_is_the_future_of_manufacturing_summary_20082014.pdf.

Nichter, Simeon, and Lara Goldmark. 2009. "Small Firm Growth in Developing Countries." *World Development* 37 (9): 1453–1464.

Noble, Kenneth B. 1994. "French Devaluation of African Currency Brings Wide Unrest." *New York Times*, February 23, 1994, A6.

O'Regan, Nicholas, Abby Ghobadian, and David Gallear. 2006. "In Search of the Drivers of High Growth in Manufacturing SMEs." *Technovation* 26 (1): 30–41.

Oxford Business Group. 2015. "Bearing Fruit: Policy Changes Create New Difficulties for Small Scale Cocoa Grinders." Oxford Business Group. https://oxfordbusinessgroup.com/analysis/bearing-fruit-policy-changes-create-new-difficulties-small-scale-cocoa-grinders.

Page, John. 2018. The Road Not Taken: Structural Change in Africa Reconsidered. In *Foresight Africa: Top Priorities for the Continent in 2018.* Washington DC: Brookings Institution. 66. https://www.brookings.edu/wp-content/uploads/2018/01/foresight-2018_full_web_final2.pdf.

Patel, Suresh H. 2005. "Business Age and Characteristics of SME Performance." Working paper. Kingston Business School, Kingston University. November 1. https://www.bl.uk/collection-items/business-age-and-characteristics-of-sme-performance.

Prakash, Yamini, and Gupta Meenakshi. 2008. "Exploring the Relationship between Organisation Structure and Perceived Innovation in the Manufacturing Sector of India." *Singapore Management Review* 30 (1): 55–76.

Radelet, Steven, and Jeffrey D. Sachs. 1998. "Shipping Costs, Manufactured Exports, and Economic Growth." Presented at American Economic Association Annual Meeting, Chicago, January 3-5. https://academiccommons.columbia.edu/doi/10.7916/D8J39081.

Rodrik, Dani. 2012. "Unconditional Convergence in Manufacturing." *Quarterly Journal of Economics* 128 (1): 165–204.

Rodrik, Dani. 2016. "An African Growth Miracle?" *Journal of African Economies* 27 (1): 10–27. https://academic.oup.com/jae/article-abstract/27/1/10/2660399.

Roxburgh, C., Norbert Dörr, Acha Leke, Amine Tazi-Riffi, Arend van Wamelen, Susan Lund, Mutsa Chironga, Tarik Alatovik, Charles Atkins, Nadia Terfous, and Till Zeino-Mahmalat. 2010. *Lions on the Move: The Progress and Potential of African Economies.* McKinsey Global Institute Report. June 2010. https://www.mckinsey.com/featured-insights/middle-east-and-africa/lions-on-the-move.

Schiff, M. and A. Valdez. 1992. *The Plundering of Agriculture in Developing Countries.* Washington, D.C.: World Bank.

Schwab, Klaus, and Xavier Sali-i-Martin. 2016. *The Global Competitiveness Report 2016–2017.* Insight Report. Geneva: World Economic Forum. http://www3.weforum.org/docs/GCR2016-2017/05FullReport/TheGlobalCompetitivenessReport2016-2017_FINAL.pdf.

Schwab, Klaus, and Xavier Sali-i-Martin. 2017. *The Global Competitiveness Report 2017–2018.* Insight Report. Geneva: World Economic Forum. http://www3.weforum.org/docs/GCR2017-2018/05FullReport/TheGlobalCompetitivenessReport2017%E2%80%932018.pdf.

Signé, Landry. 2017. "3 Things to Know about Africa's Industrialization and the Continental Free Trade Area." Washington, DC: Brookings Institution. *Africa in Focus* (blog), November 22. https://www.brookings.edu/blog/africa-in-focus/2017/11/22/3-things-to-know-about-africas-industrialization-and-the-continental-free-trade-area/.

Signé, Landry. 2018. "Capturing Africa's High Return." Washington, DC: Brookings Institution. Op-ed. March 14. https://www.brookings.edu/opinions/capturing-africas-high-returns/.

Songwe, Vera. 2019. "Intra-African Trade: A Path to Economic Diversification and Inclusion." *Foresight Africa 2019.* Washington, D.C.: Brookings Institution. https://www.brookings.edu/research/intra-african-trade-a-path-to-economic-diversification-and-inclusion.

Sun, Irene Yuan. 2017. "The World's Next Great Manufacturing Center." *Harvard Business Review* 95 (May–June): 122–129. https://hbr.org/2017/05/the-worlds-next-great-manufacturing-center.

Terziovski, Mile. 2010. "Innovation Practice and Its Performance Implications in Small and Medium Enterprises (SMEs) in the Manufacturing Sector: A Resource-Based View." *Strategic Management Journal* 31 (8): 892–902.

Tushman, Michael, and William Moore. 1988. *Readings in the Management of Innovation,* 2nd ed. New York: Ballinger/Harper & Row.

Tybout, James R. 2000. "Manufacturing Firms in Developing Countries: How Well Do They Do, and Why?" *Journal of Economic Literature* 38 (1): 11-44.

United Nations Economic Commission for Africa and African Union. 2014. *Dynamic Industrial Policy in Africa: Innovative Institutions, Effective Processes and Flexible Mechanisms.* United Nations Economic Commission for Africa. March. https://www.uneca.org/sites/default/files/PublicationFiles/final_era2014_march25_en.pdf.

United Nations Industrial Development Organization. 2015. *Supporting Pharmaceutical Production in Africa.* Geneva: UNIDO.

Wheelen, Thomas L., and J. D. Hunger. 1999. *Strategic Management and Business Policy*. Reading, MA: Addison-Wesley.

World Bank. 1994. *World Development Report 1994: Infrastructure for Development*. New York: Oxford University Press.

World Bank. 1997. *World Development Report 1997: The State in a Changing World*. New York: Oxford University Press.

World Bank. 2016. *Kenya Country Economic Memorandum: From Economic Growth to Jobs and Shared Prosperity*. Washington, DC: World Bank Group.

World Bank. 2017. *World Development Report 2017: Global Value Chain: Measuring and Analyzing the Impact of GVCs on Economic Development*. Washington, DC: World Bank Group.

CHAPTER 6

Ackah-Baidoo, Abigail. 2012. "Enclave Development and 'Offshore Corporate Social Responsibility': Implications for Oil-Rich Sub-Saharan Africa." *Resources Policy* 37 (2): 152–159.

African Development Bank and The African Union. 2009. *Oil and Gas in Africa*. Oxford: Oxford University Press.

African Union Commission. 2015. *Agenda 2063 Framework Document: The Africa We Want*. https://www.un.org/en/africa/osaa/pdf/au/agenda2063-framework.pdf.

Alden, Chris, and Martyn Davies. 2006. "A Profile of the Operations of Chinese Multinationals in Africa." *South African Journal of International Affairs* 13 (1): 83–96.

Anderson, D. M., and A. J. Browne. 2011. "The Politics of Oil in Eastern Africa." *Journal of Eastern African Studies* 5 (2): 369–410.

Ariweriokuma, Soala. 2008. *The Political Economy of Oil and Gas in Africa: The Case of Nigeria*. Abingdon, UK: Routledge.

Astier, Henri. 2003. "Elf Was 'Secret Arm of French Policy.'" BBCNews Online. Last updated March 19, 2003. http://news.bbc.co.uk/2/hi/europe/2862257.stm.

Augé, Benjamin. 2015. "Oil and Gas in East Africa: Current Developments and Future Perspectives." IFRI. OCP Policy Center. Policy paper. March 5. https://www.ifri.org/en/publications/enotes/notes-de-lifri/oil-and-gas-eastern-africa-current-developments-and-future.

Auty, R. M. 2001. *Resource Abundance and Economic Development*. Oxford: Oxford University Press.

Baffes, John. M. Ayhan Kose, Franziska Ohnsorge, and Marc Stocker. 2015. *The Great Plunge in Oil Prices: Causes, Consequences, and Policy Responses*. Policy Research Note. Washington, D.C.: World Bank Group.

Beck, Thorsten, Asli Demirguc-Kunt, and Ross Levine. 2007. "Finance, Inequality, and the Poor." *Journal of Economic Growth* 12 (1): 27-49.

Bekoe, Samuel Osei, Mark Evans, Emmanuel Kuyole, Rushaiya Ibrahim-Tanko, and Adams Fusheini. 2016. "Ghana's Election: Seven Extractives Governance Recommendations for the Next Government." Briefing. Natural Resource Governance Institute. December. https://resourcegovernance.org/sites/default/files/docu

ments/ghanas-election-seven-extractives-governance-recommendations-for-the-next-government-web.pdf.

BP *Statistical Review of World Energy June 2009.* http://news.bbc.co.uk/2/shared/bsp/hi/pdfs/10_06_09_bp_report.pdf.

BP *Statistical Review of World Energy June 2015.* 64th ed. https://www.bp.com/content/dam/bp-country/es_es/spain/documents/downloads/PDF/bp-statistical-review-of-world-energy-2015-full-report.pdf.

BP *Statistical Review of World Energy 2018.* 67th ed. https://www.bp.com/content/dam/bp/business-sites/en/global/corporate/pdfs/energy-economics/statistical-review/bp-stats-review-2018-full-report.pdf.

Brown, David E. 2014. *Africa's Booming Oil and Natural Gas Exploration and Production: National Security Implications for the United States and China.* Carlisle Barracks, PA: United States Army War College Press. https://publications.armywarcollege.edu/pubs/2258.pdf.

Bughin, Jacques, Mutsa Chironga, Georges Desvaux, Tenbite Ermias, Paul Jacobson, Omid Kassiri, Acha Leke, Susan Lund, Arend van Wamelen, and Yassir Zouaoui. 2016. *Lions on the Move II: Realizing the Potential of Africa's Economies.* McKinsey Global Institute Report, September 2016. https://www.mckinsey.com/featured-insights/middle-east-and-africa/lions-on-the-move-realizing-the-potential-of-africas-economies.

Cheeseman, Nic. 2015. *Democracy in Africa: Successes, Failures, and the Struggle for Political Reform.* Cambridge, UK: Cambridge University Press.

Cilliers, Jakkie, Barry B. Hughes, and Jonathan D. Moyer. 2011. *African Futures 2050: The Next Forty Years.* AFP Monograph 175. Institute for Security Studies and Pardee Center for International Futures. https://pardee.du.edu/african-futures-2050-next-forty-years.

Collier, Paul, and Anke Hoeffler. 2005. "Resource Rents, Governance, and Conflict." *The Journal of Conflict Resolution* 49 (4): 625-633.

Delivering on the Promise: Leveraging Natural Resources to Accelerate Human Development in Africa. 2015. African Development Bank and Bill and Melinda Gates Foundation. June. https://www.afdb.org/fileadmin/uploads/afdb/Documents/Publications/Delivering_on_the_promise-Leveraging_natural_resources_to_accelerate_human_development_in_Africa.pdf.

Demirguc-Kunt, Asli, and Ross Levine. 2009. "Finance and Inequality: Theory and Evidence." *Annual Review of Financial Economics* 1: 287-318.

Demirguc-Kunt, Asli, and Leora Klapper. 2012. "Financial Inclusion in Africa: An Overview." World Bank Policy Research Working Paper 6088. Washington, D.C.: World Bank.

Diamond, Larry. 2015. *In Search of Democracy.* Abingdon, UK: Routledge.

Dunning, Thad. 2008. *Crude Democracy: Natural Resource Wealth and Political Regimes.* Cambridge, UK: Cambridge University Press.

The Economist Intelligence Unit. 2016. "Into Africa: Institutional Investor Intentions to 2016." *The Economist.* June 13. https://www.slideshare.net/Management-Thinking/into-africa-institutional-investor-intentions-to-2016.

Ellis, Stephen. 2003. "Briefing: West Africa and Its Oil." *African Affairs* 102 (406): 135–138.

Gillies, Alexandra, Marc Guéniat, and Lorenz Kummer. 2014. *Big Spenders: Swiss Trading Companies, African Oil and the Risks of Opacity.* Natural Resource Governance Institute (NRGI). July 20. https://resourcegovernance.org/analysis-tools/publications/big-spenders-swiss-trading-companies-african-oil-and-risks-opacity.

Ginsburg, Norton. 1957. "Natural Resources and Economic Development." *Annals of the Association of American Geographers* 47: 197–212.

Global Witness. 2015. "Shell and Eni's Misadventures in Nigeria." November 15. Briefing. Global Witness. November 17. https://www.globalwitness.org/en/campaigns/oil-gas-and-mining/shell-and-enis-misadventures-nigeria/.

Global Witness. 2017. "Shell Knew." April 10. Briefing. https://www.globalwitness.org/en/campaigns/oil-gas-and-mining/shell-knew/.

Gupte, Eklavya. 2016. "Nigeria Slips into Recession as Q2 Oil Output Slumps." In *African Energy Outlook.* https://web.archive.org/web/20170621211422/https://www.platts.cn/news-feature/2016/oil/african-energy-outlook/index.

Gupte, Eklavya, and George Shaw. 2016. "Angola Shelves Plans for New Oil Refinery." In *African Energy Outlook.* https://www.platts.cn/news-feature/2016/oil/african-energy-outlook/angola-oil-refinery-090116.

Gylfason, Thorvaldur. 2001. "Natural Resources, Education, and Economic Development." *European Economic Review* 45 (4-6): 847-859.

Haber, Stephen, and Victor Menaldo. 2011. "Do Natural Resources Fuel Authoritarianism? A Reappraisal of the Resource Curse." *American Political Science Review* 105 (1): 1–26.

Haggard, Stephan, and Robert R. Kaufman. 2016. *Dictators and Democrats: Masses, Elites and Regime Change.* Princeton, NJ: Princeton University Press.

Henley, John. 2003. "Gigantic Sleaze Scandal Winds Up as Former Elf Oil Chiefs Are Jailed." *The Guardian*, November 13. https://www.theguardian.com/business/2003/nov/13/france.oilandpetrol.

International Energy Agency (IEA). 2014. *Africa Energy Outlook: A Focus on Energy Prospects in Sub-Saharan African.* World Energy Outlook Special Report. International Energy Agency. https://www.iea.org/publications/freepublications/publication/WEO2014_AfricaEnergyOutlook.pdf.

International Monetary Fund (IMF). 2008. *World Economic Outlook: Housing and the Business Cycle.* Washington, D.C.: International Monetary Fund.

Kimemia, Douglas. 2018. "Multinational Corporations as Supplier of Corruption in Africa." *Africa Insight* 48 (2): 25–40. September 1. https://journals.co.za/content/journal/10520/EJC-1487e29417.

KPMG. 2013. *Oil and Gas in Africa: Africa's Reserves, Potential and Prospects.* KPMG. https://www.resourcedata.org/hr/dataset/rgi-oil-and-gas-in-africa-africa-s-reserves-potential-and-prospects/resource/f9dce625-fdda-45ac-b21f-206ab1acd5c0.

KPMG. 2015. *Oil and Gas in Africa Sector Report. KPMG Africa Blog.* http://www.blog.kpmgafrica.com/2015-sector-report-on-the-oil-and-gas-sector-in-africa/.

Liou, Yu-Ming, and Paul Musgrave. 2014. "Refining the Oil Curse: Country-Level Evidence from Exogenous Variations in Resource Income." *Comparative Political Studies* 47 (11): 1584–1610. http://citeseerx.ist.psu.edu/viewdoc/download?doi=10.1.1.1022.2907&rep=rep1&type=pdf.

Maugeri, L. 2013. "The Shale Oil Boom: A U.S. Phenomenon." Discussion Paper. Belfer Center for Science and International Affairs. Harvard Kennedy School. June. https://www.belfercenter.org/publication/shale-oil-boom-us-phenomenon.

Melina, Giovanni, and Yi Xiong. 2013. "Natural Gas, Public Investment and Debt Sustainability in Mozambique." IMF Working Papers 13/261. December 23. https://www.imf.org/en/Publications/WP/Issues/2016/12/31/Natural-Gas-Public-Investment-and-Debt-Sustainability-in-Mozambique-41166.

NRGI (Natural Resource Governance Institute). "Tanzania's 2015 Extractive Sector Legislation: Recommendations for Effective Implementation." 2016. Briefing. Natural Resource Governance Institute. November. https://resourcegovernance.org/analysis-tools/publications/tanzania-2015-extractive-sector-legislation-recommendations-effective.

Odusola, Ayodele, Giovanni Andrea Cornia, Haroon Bhorat, and Pedro Conceição, eds. 2017. *Income Inequality Trends in Sub-Saharan Africa: Divergence, Determinants and Consequences*. New York: UNDP. https://www.undp.org/content/dam/rba/docs/Reports/Overview-Income%20inequality%20Trends%20SSA-EN-web.pdf.

"Passage of the Petroleum Industry Governance Bill." 2017. *The Guardian: Opinion*, Editorial June 23, Editorial Board. https://guardian.ng/opinion/passage-of-the-petroleum-industry-governance-bill/.

Perkin, Robert, and Eklavya Gupte. 2016. "Kenya Firms Up Plan to Become First East African Oil Exporter." In *African Energy Outlook*. https://www.platts.cn/news-feature/2016/oil/african-energy-outlook/kenya-oil-exports-090116.

PwC. 2016. *Choice to Change: Africa Oil and Gas Review*. 2016. PwC. https://www.pwc.com/gx/en/industries/energy-utilities-resources/publications/change-to-change.html.

"The Race for Oil and Gas in Africa: A Look at International Oil Companies Operating across the African Continent." 2016. Al Jazeera Africa. October 23. http://www.aljazeera.com/indepth/interactive/2016/10/race-oil-gas-africa-161020104953200.html.

Readhead, Alexandra. 2016. "Transfer Pricing in the Extractive Sector in Ghana." Case Study. Natural Resource Governance Institute. March. https://resourcegovernance.org/sites/default/files/documents/nrgi_ghana_transfer-pricing-study.pdf.

Ross, Michael L. 2001. "Does Oil Hinder Democracy?" *World Polit* 53 (3): 325-361.

Ross, Michael L. 2012. *The Oil Curse: How Petroleum Wealth Shapes the Development of Nations*. Princeton, NJ: Princeton University Press.

Sayne, Aaaron, and Alexandra Gillies. 2014. *Initial Evidence of Corruption Risks in Government Oil and Gas Sales*. Natural Resource Governance Institute. https://resourcegovernance.org/analysis-tools/publications/initial-evidence-corruption-risks-government-oil-and-gas-sales.

Sayne, Aaron, Alexandra Gillies, and Christina Katsouris. 2015. *Inside NNPC Oil*

Sales: A Case for Reform in Nigeria. Natural Resource Governance Institute. August 4. https://resourcegovernance.org/analysis-tools/publications/inside-nnpc-oil-sales -case-reform-nigeria.

Schwab, Klaus, and Xavier Sali-i-Martin. 2017. *The Global Competitiveness Report 2017–2018.* Insight Report. Geneva: World Economic Forum. http://www3. weforum.org/docs/GCR2017-2018/05FullReport/TheGlobalCompetitivenessRe port2017%E2%80%932018.pdf.

Senelwa, Kennedy. 2016. "Kenya to Go It Alone in Oil Pipeline Project." *The East African.* March 5. https://www.theeastafrican.co.ke/business/Kenya-to-go-it-alone -in-oil-pipeline-project/2560-3104700-6bcobfz/index.html.

Shaxson, Nicholas. 2008. *Poisoned Wells: The Dirty Politics of African Oil.* Basingstoke, UK: Palgrave Macmillan.

Shephard, Ben. 2013. "Oil in Uganda: International Lessons for Success." Chatham House. February 1. https://www.chathamhouse.org/publications/papers/view/188959.

Teorell, Jan. 2010. *Determinants of Democratization.* Cambridge, UK: Cambridge University Press.

Time for Transparency: Coming Clean on Oil, Mining and Gas Revenue. 2004. Report. Global Witness. March 25. https://www.globalwitness.org/en/reports/time-trans parency/.

U.S. Energy Information Administration. 2015. *South Africa.* Last updated October 26, 2017. http://www.eia.gov/beta/international/analysis.cfm?iso=ZAF.

U.S. Energy Information Administration. 2016. *International Energy Outlook 2016 with Projections to 2040.* U.S. Department of Energy, Washington, DC. May. https://www.eia.gov/outlooks/ieo/pdf/0484(2016).pdf.

Vines, Alex. 2010. "Resurgent Continent? Africa and the World: Thirst for African Oil." The London School of Economics IDEAS Reports. http://eprints.lse.ac. uk/43658/1/Resurgent%20Continent_thirst%20for%20African%20oil(lsero).pdf.

World Bank Group. 2016. *Global Economic Prospects: Spillovers amid Weak Growth.* Washington, D.C.: International Bank for Reconstruction and Development/ World Bank.

Zhao, Shelly. 2011. "The China-Angola Partnership: A Case Study of China's Oil Relations in Africa." China Briefing, May 25. http://urban-africa-china.angonet. org/sites/default/files/resource_files/the_china_angola_partnership_-_shelly_ zhao_-_25_may_2011.pdf.

CHAPTER 7

Adeyeye, Adefolake. 2016. "Understanding Africa's Slow Growth in Intra-Regional Air Transport." NTU-SBF Centre for African Studies. AfricaBusiness.com. June 1. http://africabusiness.com/2016/06/01/africa-intra-regional-air-transport/.

AfDB (African Development Bank). 2016a. *Africa Visa Openness Report.* https://www. afdb.org/fileadmin/uploads/afdb/Documents/Generic-Documents/Africa_Visa_ Openness_Report_2016.pdf.

AfDB (African Development Bank). 2016b. *Africa Tourism Monitor: Sustainable Tourism through Innovation, Entrepreneurship, and Technology* 4, no. 1 (December).

Annual. https://www.afdb.org/fileadmin/uploads/afdb/Documents/Publications/Africa_Tourism_Monitor_2016.pdf.

AfDB (African Development Bank). 2017. *Africa Visa Openness Report 2017.* Visa Openness Index. https://www.afdb.org/fileadmin/uploads/afdb/Documents/Publications/2017_Africa_Visa_Openness_Report_-_Final.pdf

AfDB (African Development Bank), New York University, Africa Travel Association. 2015. *Africa Tourism Monitor: Unlocking Africa's Tourism Potential*, 3, no. 1 (October). https://www.afdb.org/fileadmin/uploads/afdb/Documents/Publications/Africa_Tourism_Monitor_-_Unlocking_Africa%E2%80%99s_Tourism_Potential_%E2%80%93_Vol_3_%E2%80%93_Issue_1.pdf.

Ashley, Caroline, and Jonathan Mitchell. 2009. *Tourism and Poverty Reduction: Pathways to Prosperity.* London, UK: Taylor & Francis.

Ashley, Caroline, and Dilys Roe. 2002. "Making Tourism Work for the Poor: Strategies and Challenges in Southern Africa." *Development Southern Africa* 19 (1): 61–82.

Ayenagbo, Kossi. 2015. "Sino-Africa Economic and Chinese Foreign Direct Investment in Africa on Bilateral Trade Relations." *Journal of African Studies and Development* 7 (7): 172–182.

Balaguer, Jacint, and Manuel Cantavella-Jorda. 2002. "Tourism as a Long-Run Economic Growth Factor: The Spanish Case." *Applied Economics* 34 (7): 877–884.

Balassa, Bela. 1978. "Exports and Economic Growth: Further Evidence." *Journal of Development Economics* 5 (2): 181–189.

Bouzahzah, Mohamed, and Younesse El Menyari. 2013. "International Tourism and Economic Growth: The Case of Morocco and Tunisia." *Journal of North African Studies* 18 (4): 592–607.

Briedenhann, Jenny, and Eugenia Wickens. 2004. "Tourism Routes as a Tool for the Economic Development of Rural Areas—Vibrant Hope or Impossible Dream?" *Tourism Management* 25 (1): 71–79.

Britton, S. G. 1982. "The Political Economy of Tourism in the Third World." *Annals of Tourism Research* 9 (3): 331–358.

Butler, R. W. 1980. "The Concept of a Tourist Area Cycle of Evolution and Implications for Management of Resources." *Canadian Geographer* 24 (1): 5–12.

Carlisle, Sheena, Martin Kunc, Eleri Jones, and Scott Tiffin. 2013. "Supporting Innovation for Tourism Development through Multi-stakeholder Approaches: Experiences from Africa." *Tourism Management* 35: 59–69.

Chen, Ching-Fu, and Song Zan Chiou-Wei. 2009. "Tourism Expansion, Tourism Uncertainty and Economic Growth: New Evidence from Taiwan And Korea." *Tourism Management* 30 (6): 812–818.

Chen, L., and J. Devereux. 1999. "Tourism and Welfare in Sub-Saharan Africa: A Theoretical Analysis." *Journal of African Economies* 8 (2): 209–227.

Christie, Iain T., and Doreen E. Crompton. 2001. "Tourism in Africa." Africa Region Working Paper Series 12. World Bank Group. February. http://web.worldbank.org/archive/AFRtrade/WEB/WP12.HTM.

Christie, Iain T., Eneida Fernandes, Hannah Messerli, and Louise Twining-Ward. 2014. *Tourism in Africa: Harnessing Tourism for Growth and Improved Livelihoods.* Washington, D.C.: World Bank. http://documents.worldbank.org/curated/en/73

8471468299123752/pdf/Tourism-in-Africa-harnessing-tourism-for-growth-and-improved-livelihoods.pdf.

De Kadt, Emanuel. 1984. *Tourism: Passport to Development? Perspectives on the Social and Cultural Effects of Tourism in Developing Countries.* World Bank Group. June 30. http://documents.worldbank.org/curated/en/223271468141894689/Tourism-passport-to-development-Perspectives-on-the-social-and-cultural-effects-of-tourism-on-developing-countries.

Dieke, Peter U. C. 2003. "Tourism in Africa's Economic Development: Policy Implications." *Management Decision* 41 (3): 287–295.

Dobruszkes, Frédéric, and Véronique Mondou. 2013. "Aviation Liberalization as a Means to Promote International Tourism: The EU–Morocco Case." *Journal of Air Transport Management* 29: 23–34.

Dritsakis, Nikolaos. 2004. "Tourism as a Long-Run Economic Growth Factor: An Empirical Investigation for Greece Using Causality Analysis." *Tourism Economics* 10 (3): 305–316.

Du Plessis, Engelina and Melville Saayman. 2017. "Aspects Contributing to Tourism Price Competitiveness of South Africa." *Tourism Economics* 24 (1).

Durbarry, Ramesh. 2004. "Tourism and Economic Growth: The Case of Mauritius." *Tourism Economics* 10 (4): 389–401.

Ernoul, L. 2009. "Residents' Perception of Tourist Development and the Environment: A Study from Morocco." *International Journal of Sustainable Development & World Ecology* 16 (4): 228–233.

Eugenio-Martin, Juan Luis, Noelia Martín Morales, and Riccardo Scarpa. 2004. "Tourism and Economic Growth in Latin American Countries: A Panel Data Approach." Working Paper 26. Fondazione Eni Enrico Mattei. February. https://www.researchgate.net/publication/5023309_Tourism_and_Economic_Growth_in_Latin_American_Countries_A_Panel_Data_Approach.

Fayissa, Bichaka, Christian Nsiah, and Badassa Tadasse. 2008. "Impact of Tourism on Economic Growth and Development in Africa." *Tourism Economics* 14 (4): 807–818.

Kim, Hyun Jeong, Ming-Hsiang Chen, and SooCheong "Shawn" Jang. 2006. "Tourism Expansion and Economic Development: The Case of Taiwan." *Tourism Management* 27 (5): 925–933.

Koens, Ko, and Rhodri Thomas. 2015. "Is Small Beautiful? Understanding the Contribution of Small Businesses in Township Tourism to Economic Development." *Development Southern Africa* 32 (3): 320–332.

Industrial Development Corporation. 2016. "Africa Poised for Tourism Success." May 9. https://www.idc.co.za/2016/05/09/africa-poised-for-tourism-success.

Jones, Pete. 2012. "Western Uganda: Crop-Raiding Elephants Call for Plan Bee." *The Guardian*, June 6. https://theguardian.com/global-development/2012/jun/06/western-uganda-crop-raiding-elephants-bees.

Lee, Chien-Chiang, and Chun-Ping Chang. 2008. "Tourism Development and Economic Growth: A Closer Look at Panels." *Tourism Management* 29 (1): 180–192.

Lee, Joomi. 2008. "Riad Fever: Heritage Tourism, Urban Renewal and the Medina

Property Boom in Old Cities of Morocco." *Economic Review of Tourism Research* 6 (4): 66–78.

Leibold, Marius, and Karsten Seibert. 2015. "Developing a Strategic Model for Branding South Africa as an International Tourism Destination, with Special Consideration of Multicultural Factors." In *Proceedings of the 1998 Multicultural Marketing Conference. Developments in Marketing Science: Proceedings of the Academy of Marketing Science*, edited by Jean-Charles Chebat and A. Ben Oumlil, 45–47. Springer. https://link.springer.com/chapter/10.1007/978-3-319-17383-2_6.

Mayaki, Ibrahim Assane. 2015. "Tourism Growth and Air Access within Africa." In *Africa Tourism Monitor: Unlocking Africa's Tourism Potential*, 3, no. 1 (October): 10–11. AfDB (African Development Bank), New York University, Africa Travel Association. https://www.afdb.org/fileadmin/uploads/afdb/Documents/Publica tions/Africa_Tourism_Monitor_-_Unlocking_Africa%E2%80%99s_Tourism_ Potential_%E2%80%93_Vol_3_%E2%80%93_Issue_1.pdf.

Milne, Simon, and Irena Ateljevic. 2001. "Tourism, Economic Development and the Global-Local Nexus: Theory Embracing Complexity." *Tourism Geographies* 3 (4): 369–393.

Milne, Simon, and Corinne Pohlmann. 1998. "Continuity and Change in the Hotel Sector: Some Evidence from Montreal." In *The Economic Geography of the Tourism Industry: A Supply-side Analysis*, edited by D. Ioannides and K. Debbage, 180–196. Abingdon, UK: Routledge.

Minca, Claudio, and Rachele Borghi. 2009. "Morocco: Restaging Colonialism for the Masses." In *Cultures of Mass Tourism: Doing the Mediterranean in the Age of Banal Mobilities*, edited by P. Obrador Pons, Mike Crang, and Penny Travlou, 21–52. Farnham, UK: Ashgate.

Mowforth, Martin, and Ian Munt. 2009. *Tourism and Sustainability: Development, Globalisation and New Tourism in the Third World*. Abingdon, UK: Routledge.

Mwiti, Lee. 2014. "20 Staggering Facts about Tourism in Sub-Saharan Africa, Including Some Real Star Performers." *Mail & Guardian Africa*, August 12. https:// web.archive.org/web/20180511070705/http://mgafrica.com/article/2014-08-11-20-staggering-facts-about-tourism-in-sub-saharan-africa-including-some-innovative-things-countries-are-doing.

Ndabeni, L. L., C. M. Rogerson, and I. Booyens. 2016. "Innovation and Local Economic Development Policy in the Global South: New South African Perspectives." *Local Economy* 31 (1–2): 299–311.

Novelli, Marina. 2016. *Tourism and Development in Sub-Saharan Africa: Current Issues and Local Realities*. Abingdon, UK: Routledge.

Nowak, Jean-Jacques, Mondher Sahli, and Isabel Cortés-Jiménez. 2007. "Tourism, Capital Good Imports and Economic Growth: Theory and Evidence for Spain." *Tourism Economics* 13 (4): 515–536.

Ntonzima, Lulamile, Mzikayise Shakespeare Binza, and Ignatius Wilhelm Ferreira. 2014. "Tourism as a Catalyst for Local Economic Development in the Transkei Wild Coast, South Africa." *SHS Web of Conferences* 12: 01055.

Oh, Chi-Ok. 2005. "The Contribution of Tourism Development to Economic Growth in the Korean Economy." *Tourism Management* 26 (1): 39–44.

Okello, Moses, and Marina Novelli. 2014. "Tourism in the East African Community (EAC): Challenges, Opportunities, and Ways Forward." *Tourism and Hospitality Research* 14 (1–2): 55–56.

Pandy, Wayde R., and Christian M. Rogerson. 2013. "The Timeshare Industry of Africa: A Study in Tourism Geography." *Bulletin of Geography. Socio-economic Series* 21: 97–109.

Pillay, Manisha, and Christian M. Rogerson. 2013. "Agriculture-Tourism Linkages and Pro-poor Impacts: The Accommodation Sector of Urban Coastal KwaZulu-Natal, South Africa." *Applied Geography* 36: 49–58.

Poon, Auliana. 1989. "Competitive Strategies for a 'New Tourism.'" In *Progress in Tourism, Recreation and Hospitality Management*, edited by C. P. Cooper, 91–102. London, UK: Belhaven Press.

Poon, Auliana. 1993. *Tourism, Technology and Competitive Strategies*. Wallingford, UK: C.A.B. International. June. https://www.cabi.org/bookshop/book/97808519 89501.

Ramukumba, Takalania. 2012. "The Local Economic Development in the Eden District Municipality, Western Cape Province, South Africa: A Case Study of Emerging Entrepreneurs in Tourism Industry." *American Journal of Tourism Research* 1 (1): 9–15.

Rogerson, C. M. 2012. "Local Economic Development and Tourism Planning in Africa: Evidence from Route Tourism in South Africa." In *Tourism Strategies and Local Responses in Southern Africa*, 27–40. Wallingford, UK: C.A.B. International.

Rogerson, C. M. 2015. "Tourism and Regional Development: The Case of South Africa's Distressed Areas." *Development Southern Africa* 32 (3): 277–291.

Rogerson, C. M. 2016. "Climate Change, Tourism and Local Economic Development in South Africa." *Local Economy* 31 (1-2): 322–331.

Rogerson, C. M., and E. Nel. 2016. "Planning for Local Economic Development in Spaces of Despair: Key Trends in South Africa's 'Distressed Areas.'" *Local Economy* 31 (1-2): 124–141.

Rogerson, Jayne M. 2013. "The Economic Geography of South Africa's Hotel Industry 1990–2010." *Urban Forum* 24 (3): 425–446.

Scherle, N. 2011. "Tourism, Neoliberal Policy and Competitiveness in the Developing World. The Case of the Master Plan of Marrakech." In *Political Economy of Tourism: A Critical Perspective*, edited by Jan Mosedale, 207–224. Abingdon, UK: Routledge.

Schlumberger, Charles E. 2010. *Open Skies for Africa: Implementing the Yamoussoukro Decision*. Washington, D.C.: World Bank.

Schubert, Stefan Franz, Juan Gabriel Brida, and Wiston Adrián Risso. 2011. "The Impacts of International Tourism Demand on Economic Growth of Small Economies Dependent on Tourism." *Tourism Management* 32 (2): 377–385.

Sequeira, Tiago Neves, and Paulo Maçãs Nunes. 2008. "Does Tourism Influence Economic Growth? A Dynamic Panel Data Approach." *Applied Economics* 40 (18): 2431–2441.

Sharpley, Richard, and David J. Telfer. 2015. *Tourism and Development: Concepts and Issues*. 2nd ed. Bristol, UK: Channel View Publications.

Shea, Griffin. 2017. "10 Budget Airlines Changing Africa's Skies." CNN. June 15. https://www.cnn.com/travel/article/10-budget-airlines-africa/index.html.

Sinclair, M. Thea. 1998. "Tourism and Economic Development: A Survey." *Journal of Development Studies* 34 (5): 1–51.

Snyman, J. A., and M. Saayman. 2009. "Key Factors Influencing Foreign Direct Investment in the Tourism Industry in South Africa." *Tourism Review* 64 (3): 49–58.

"The Sun Rises on Online Travel in Africa." 2017. EyeforTravel.com. March 6. https://eyefortravel.com/revenue-and-data-management/sun-rises-online-travel-africa.

UNCTAD (United Nations Conference on Trade and Development). 2017. *Economic Development in Africa Report 2017: Tourism for Transformative and Inclusive Growth.* https://unctad.org/en/PublicationsLibrary/aldcafrica2017_en.pdf.

UNDP (United Nations Development Program). 2011. *Tourism and Poverty Reduction Strategies in the Integrated Framework for Least Developed Countries.* Discussion paper. April. http://unwto.org/sites/all/files/pdf/undp_discussion_paper_tourism_and_poverty_reduction_strategies_in_the_integrated_framework_for_least_developed_countries.pdf.

UNWTO (United Nations World Tourism Organization). 1980. *Manila Declaration on Tourism.* Manila. https://www.univeur.org/cuebc/downloads/PDF%20carte/65.%20Manila.PDF.

UNWTO (United Nations World Tourism Organization). 2002. *Tourism and Poverty Alleviation.* https://www.e-unwto.org/doi/pdf/10.18111/9789284405497.

UNWTO (United Nations World Tourism Organization). 2015. *Tourism in Africa: A Tool for Development.* http://cf.cdn.unwto.org/sites/all/files/pdf/tourism_africa_tool_development1.compressed.pdf.

UNWTO (United Nations World Tourism Organization). 2016. *Tourism Highlights 2016 Edition.* https://www.e-unwto.org/doi/pdf/10.18111/9789284418145.

UNWTO (United Nations World Tourism Organization). 2017. *Tourism Highlights 2017 Edition.* https://www.e-unwto.org/doi/pdf/10.18111/9789284419029.

UNWTO (United Nations World Tourism Organization). 2018. *World Tourism Barometer.* http://cf.cdn.unwto.org/sites/all/files/pdf/unwto_barom18_03_june_excerpt.pdf.

Urry, J. 1990. *The Tourist Gaze: Leisure and Travel in Contemporary Societies.* Newbury Park, CA: Sage.

World Bank. 2011. *Africa Region Tourism Strategy: Transformation through Tourism—Harnessing Tourism for Growth and Improved Livelihoods.* January 20. https://openknowledge.worldbank.org/bitstream/handle/10986/12841/700990ESW0P1170ing0the0Economic0Pow.pdf?sequence=1&isAllowed=y.

World Bank. 2013. "Africa's Tourism Set to Boost Economic Growth, Create New Jobs, and Now Outpace Other Regions for New Tourism Investment." Press release, October 3. https://www.worldbank.org/en/news/press-release/2013/10/03/africa-tourism-economic-growth-new-jobs-tourism-investment.

World Economic Forum. 2015. *The Travel & Tourism Competitiveness Report 2015:*

Growth through Shocks. Insight Report. http://www3.weforum.org/docs/TT15/ WEF_Global_Travel&Tourism_Report_2015.pdf.

World Economic Forum. 2017. *The Travel & Tourism Competitiveness Report 2017: Paving the Way for a More Sustainable and Inclusive Future*. Insight Report. April 5. http://www3.weforum.org/docs/WEF_TTCR_2017_web_0401.pdf.

CHAPTER 8

Arnold, Martin, and Patrick Jenkins. 2016. "Barclays Set to Exit African Business." *Financial Times*, February 26. https://www.ft.com/content/01d64502-dca4-11e5-827d-4dfbe0213e07.

Andrianaivo, Mihasonirina and Charles Amo Yartey. 2009. "Understanding the Growth of African Financial Markets." IMF Working Paper WP/09/182. Washington, D.C.: International Monetary Fund.

Athanasoglou, Panayiotis P., Matthaios D. Delis, and Christos Staikouras. 2006. "Determinants of Bank Profitability in the South Eastern European Region." Bank of Greece Working Paper 47.

Athanasoglou, Panayiotis P., Sophocles N. Brissimis, and Matthaios D. Delis. 2008. "Bank-Specific, Industry-Specific and Macroeconomic Determinants of Bank Profitability." *Journal of International Financial Markets, Institutions and Money* 18 (2): 121–136.

Banerjee, Abhijit V. and Andrew Newman. 1993. "Occupational Choice and the Process of Development." *Journal of Political Economy* 101 (2): 274-298.

Beck, Thorsten. 2013. "Renewing the Rules for an Efficient Financial System." *Private Sector & Development* 16 (May): 18-21.

Beck, Thorsten, Ross Levine, and Norman Loayza. 2000. "Finance and the Sources of Growth." *Journal of Financial Economics* 58: 261-300.

Beck, Thorsten, Samuel Munzele Maimbo, Issa Faye, and Thouraya Triki. 2011. *Financing Africa: Through the Crisis and Beyond*. World Bank Group, Federal Ministry for Economic Cooperation and Development, African Development Bank. http://documents.worldbank.org/curated/en/633671468194645126/Financ ing-Africa-through-the-crisis-and-beyond.

Berthelemy, Jean-Claude and Aristomene Varoudakis. 1996. "Economic Growth, Convergence Clubs, and the Role of Financial Development." *Oxford Economic Papers* 48 (2): 300-328.

Calderon, Cesar and Lin Liu. 2003. "The Direction of Causality Between Financial Development and Economic Growth." *Journal of Development Economics* 72 (1): 321-334.

Clarke, G., L. Xu, and H. F. Fou. 2002. "Financial and Income Inequality: Test of Alternative Theories." World Bank Policy Research Paper 2984. Washington, D.C.: World Bank.

Coleman, B. E. 1999. "The Impact of Group Lending in Northeast Thailand." *Journal of Development Economics* 60 (1): 105-141.

David-West, Olayinka. 2018. "Constraints of the Nigerian Mobile Money Ecosystem:

A Study." *The Guardian*, May 14. https://guardian.ng/features/constraints-of-the-nigerian-mobile-money-ecosystem-a-study/.

De Gregorio, Jose. 1996. "Borrowing Constraints, Human Capital Accumulation, and Growth." *Journal of Monetary Economics* 37 (1): 49–71.

De Gregorio, Jose and Pablo E. Guidotti. 1995. "Financial Development and Economic Growth." *World Development* 23 (3): 433-448.

Demetriades, P. O., and K. Hussein. 1996. "Does Financial Development Cause Economic Growth? Time-Series Evidence from 16 Countries." *Journal of Development Economics* 51: 387-411.

Demirgüç-Kunt, Ash, and Harry Huizinga. 1999. "Determinants of Commercial Bank Interest Margins and Profitability: Some International Evidence." *World Bank Economic Review* 13 (2): 379-408.

Derreumaux, P. 2013. "The Renewal of the African Banking Sector." *Private Sector & Development* 16 (May): 2-5.

DFID (Department for International Development). 2004. "The Importance of Financial Sector Development for Growth and Poverty Reduction." Policy Division Working Paper 12886. UK Department for International Development. https://ideas.repec.org/p/ags/dfidpd/12886.html.

Dieter, Heribert. 2000. "Monetary Regionalism: Regional Integration without Financial Crises." CSGR Working Paper 52/00. November 28. https://papers.ssrn.com/sol3/papers.cfm?abstract_id=229812.

Ernst and Young. 2011. *It's Time for Africa: Ernst & Young's 2011 Africa Attractiveness Survey.* https://www.ey.com/za/en/issues/business-environment/2011-africa-attractiveness-survey.

Ernst and Young. 2014. *Sub-Saharan Africa Banking Review: 2014 Calendar Year.* Ernst & Young Global Limited, 2015. https://www.ey.com/za/en/industries/financial-services/banking---capital-markets/ey-sub-saharan-africa-banking-review-2015.

Ernst and Young. 2016. *Waves of Change Revisited: Insurance Opportunities in Sub-Saharan Africa.* Ernst & Young Global Limited. https://www.ey.com/Publication/vwLUAssets/ey-insurance-opportunities-sub-saharan-africa/$FILE/ey-insurance-opportunities-sub-saharan-africa.pdf.

European Investment Bank. 2015. *Recent Trends in Banking in Sub-Saharan Africa: From Financing to Investment.* European Investment Bank. July. https://www.eib.org/attachments/efs/economic_report_banking_africa_from_financing_to_investment_en.pdf.

Fengler, Wolfgang. 2012. "How Kenya Became a World Leader for Mobile Money." *World Bank Blogs*, July 16. http://blogs.worldbank.org/africacan/how-kenya-became-a-world-leader-for-mobile-money.

Flamini, Valentina, Calvin McDonald, and Liliana Schumacher. 2009. *The Determinants of Commercial Bank Profitability in Sub-Saharan Africa.* IMF Working Paper WP/09/15. International Monetary Fund. January. https://www.imf.org/external/pubs/ft/wp/2009/wp0915.pdf.

Galor, Oded and Joseph Zeira. 1993. "Income Distribution and Macroeconomics." *Review of Economic Studies* 60 (1): 35-52.

Goddard, John A., Philip Molyneux, and John O. S. Wilson. 2004. "Dynamics of Growth and Profitability in Banking." *Journal of Money, Credit, and Banking* 36 (6): 1069–1090.

Goldsmith, Raymond W. 1959. "Financial Structure and Development." In *The Comparative Study of Economic Growth and Structure*, 114–123. Cambridge, MA: National Bureau of Economic Research. https://www.nber.org/chapters/c4417.

Greenwood, Jeremy and Boyan Jovanovic. 2009. "Financial Development, Growth, and the Distribution of Income." *Journal of Political Economy* 98 (5, Part 1): 1076–1107.

Gupta, Sanjeev, Catherine A. Pattillo, and Smita Wagh. 2009. "Effect of Remittances on Poverty and Financial Development in Sub-Saharan Africa." *World Development* 37 (1): 104–115.

Gurley, J., and E. Shaw. 1967. "Financial Structure and Economic Development." *Economic Development and Cultural Change* 34: 333–346.

Hogan Lovells. 2018. *Financing Africa's Future: Who Is Taking the Lead in Lending?* https://www.hoganlovells.com/en/publications/financing-africas-future-who-is-taking-the-lead-in-lending.

Holden, Paul and Vassili Prokopenko. 2001. "Financial Development and Poverty Alleviation: Issues and Policy Implications for Developing and Transition Countries." International Monetary Fund Working Paper WP/01/160. Washington, D.C.: International Monetary Fund.

Honohan, Patrick. 2004. "Financial Development, Growth and Poverty: How Close Are the Links?" In Goodhart, Charles (ed.), *Financial Development and Economic Growth: Explaining the Links*. London: Palgrave. 1-37.

Hulme, David, and Paul Mosley. 1996. *Finance Against Poverty Volume 1*. London: Routledge.

International Monetary Fund (IMF). 2014. *Pan-African Banks: Opportunities and Challenges for Cross-Border Oversight*. Washington, D.C.: International Monetary Fund.

Insurance 2020: Turning Change into Opportunity. 2012. PwC. January. https://www.pwc.com/gx/en/insurance/pdf/insurance-2020-turning-change-into-opportunity.pdf.

Insurance 2020 & Beyond: Necessity Is the Mother of Reinvention. 2015. PwC. https://www.pwc.com/gx/en/insurance/publications/assets/pwc-insurance-2020-and-beyond.pdf.

Jalilian, Hossein and Colin Kirkpatrick. 2005. "Does Financial Development Contribute to Poverty Reduction?" *Journal of Development Studies* 41 (4): 636-656.

Jung, W. 1986. "Financial Development and Economic Growth: International Evidence." *Economic Development and Cultural Change* 34 (2): 333–346.

Kamau, Anne W. 2011. "Intermediation Efficiency and Productivity of the Banking Sector in Kenya." *Interdisciplinary Journal of Research in Business* 1 (9): 12–26.

Kasekende, Louis. 2010. "Developing a Sound Banking System in Sub-Saharan African Countries." In Quintyn, M. and G. Verdier (eds.), *African Finance in the 21st Century*. Washington, D.C.: International Monetary Fund.

King, Robert G., and Ross Levine. 1993a. "Financial Intermediation and Economic Development." In *Financial Intermediation in the Construction of Europe*, edited by Colin Mayer and Xavier Vives, 156–189. London: Centre for Economic Policy Research. http://faculty.haas.berkeley.edu/ross_levine/Papers/1993_Book_Mayer_ Intermediation.pdf.

King, Robert G., and Ross Levine. 1993b. "Finance and Growth: Schumpeter Might Be Right." *Quarterly Journal of Economics* 108, no. 3 (August): 717–737. https:// pdfs.semanticscholar.org/e711/b61ec85cd2b09d43a6737abe94035fa0e652.pdf.

King, Robert G., and Ross Levine. 1993c. "Finance, Entrepreneurship and Growth: Theory and Evidence." *Journal of Monetary Economics* 32 (3): 513-542. http://faculty. haas.berkeley.edu/ross_levine/papers/1993_jme_entrepreneurship.pdf.

Kouassi-Olsson, Laureen and Julien Lefilleur. 2013. "Supporting the Emergence of a Sustainable Financial Sector in Africa." *Private Sector & Development* 16 (May): 12-15.

KPMG. 2016. *Financial Services: The South African Insurance Industry Survey 2016*. July. https://assets.kpmg/content/dam/kpmg/pdf/2016/07/2016-Insurance-Survey.pdf.

KPMG Africa. 2014. "What's Driving African Banking? And Stalling It?" *KPMG Africa Blog*. http://www.blog.kpmgafrica.com/whats-driving-african-banking-whats -stalling/.

La Porta, Rafael, Florencio Lopez-de-Silanes, and Andrei Shleifer. 1998. "Law and Finance." *Journal of Political Economy* 106 (6): 1113-1155.

La Porta, Rafael, Florencio Lopez-de-Silanes, Andrei Shleifer, and Robert Vishny. 2000. "Investor Protection and Corporate Governance." *Journal of Financial Economics* 58 (2000): 3-27.

Léon, Florian. 2015. "Has Competition in African Banking Sectors Improved? Evidence from West Africa." CERDI. Universite d'Auvergne. https://editorial express.com/cgi-bin/conference/download.cgi?db_name=CSAE2015&paper_ id=91.

Levine, Ross. 1997. "Financial Development and Economic Growth: Views and Agenda." *Journal of Economic Literature* 35: 688–726.

Levine, Ross, Norman Loayza, and Thorsten Beck. 2000. "Financial Intermediation and Growth: Causality and Causes." *Journal of Monetary Economics* 46: 31–77. https://siteresources.worldbank.org/DEC/Resources/FinancialDevelopment andGrowth.pdf.

Levine, Ross and Sara Zervos. 1998. "Stock Markets, Banks, and Economic Growth." *American Economic Review* 88 (3): 537-558.

Littlefield, Elizabeth, Jonathan Morduch, and Syed Hashemi. 2003. "Is Microfinance an Effective Strategy to Reach the Millennium Development Goals?" CGAP Focus Note 24. https://www.cgap.org/sites/default/files/CGAP-Focus-Note-Is-Microfinance-an-Effective-Strategy-to-Reach-the-Millennium-Development-Goals-Jan-2003.pdf.

Lukonga, Inutu and Kay Chung. 2010. "The Cross-Border Expansion of African LCFIs: Implications for Regional Financial Stability and Regulatory Reform." African Development Bank Research Paper. https://www.afdb.org/fileadmin/

uploads/afdb/Documents/Knowledge/Session%20I.1.3_2.%20The%20Cross%20
Border%20Expansion%20of%20African%20LFCIs.pdf.

Mattei, Jean-Louis. 2013. "A French Bank's Vision of the African Banking Sector's
Evolution." *Private Sector & Development* 16 (May): 25-27.

McDonald, Calvin A. and Liliana B. Schumacher. 2007. "Financial Deepening in
Sub-Saharan Africa: Empirical Evidence on the Role of Creditor Rights Protec-
tion and Information Sharing." IMF Working Paper WP/07/203. Washington,
D.C.: International Monetary Fund.

Mecagni, Mauro, Daniela Marchettini, and Rodolfo Maino. 2015. "Evolving Banking
Trends in Sub-Saharan Africa: Key Features and Challenges." Departmental Paper
15/10. International Monetary Fund. September 16. https://www.imf.org/en/
Publications/Departmental-Papers-Policy-Papers/Issues/2016/12/31/Evolving-
Banking-Trends-in-Sub-Saharan-Africa-Key-Features-and-Challenges-43276.

Mlachila, M., S. Gil Park, and M. Yabara. 2013. "Banking in Sub-Saharan Africa: The
Macroeconomic Context." African Departmental Paper 13/03. International
Monetary Fund. September 26. https://www.imf.org/en/Publications/Depart
mental-Papers-Policy-Papers/Issues/2016/12/31/Banking-in-Sub-Saharan-
Africa-the-Macroeconomic-Context-40622.

Mlachila, Montfort, Ahmat Jidoud, Monique Newiak, Bozena Radzewicz-Bak, and
Misa Takebe. 2016. "Financial Development in Sub-Saharan Africa: Promoting
Inclusive and Sustainable Growth." Departmental Paper 16/11. International
Monetary Fund. September 14. https://www.imf.org/en/Publications/Depart
mental-Papers-Policy-Papers/Issues/2016/12/31/Financial-Development-in-Sub-
Saharan-Africa-Promoting-Inclusive-and-Sustainable-Growth-44220.

Mlambo, Kupukile, Louis Kasekende, and Victor Murinde. 2012. "Comparative
Overview of Bank Regulatory Experiences and the Impact on Bank Competition
and Intermediation Efficiency in Africa." In Murinde, Victor (ed.), *Bank Regulatory
Reform in Africa*. New York: Palgrave McMillan.

Morduch, Jonathan. 1999. "The Microfinance Promise." *Journal of Economic Literature*
37 (December): 1569-1614.

Nyantakyi, Eugene Bempong, and Mouhamadou Sy. 2015. "The Banking System in
Africa: Main Facts and Challenges." *Africa Economic Brief* 6 (5). African
Development Bank Group. October 19. https://www.afdb.org/en/documents/
document/africa-economic-brief-the-banking-system-in-africa-main-facts-and-
challenges-84186.

Odedokun, M. O. 1996. "Alternative Econometric Approaches for Analysing the Role
of the Financial Sector in Economic Growth: Time Series Evidence from LDCs."
Journal of Development Economics 50, no. 1 (June): 119–146.

Oduor, Jacob, Stephen Karingi, and Stephen Mwaura. 2011. "Efficiency of Financial
Market Intermediation in Kenya: A Comparative Analysis." *Journal of Policy Mod-
eling* 33 (2): 226–240.

Olayungbo D. O., and A. E. Akinlo. 2016. "Insurance Penetration and Economic
Growth in Africa: Dynamic Effect Analysis Using Bayesian TVP-VAR Approach."
Cogent Economics & Finance 4 (1): 1150390. February 24. https://www.tandfonline.
com/doi/full/10.1080/23322039.2016.1150390.

Ondiege, Peter. 2010. "Mobile Banking in Africa: Taking the Bank to the People." *Africa Economic Brief* 1 (8). African Development Bank Group. December. https://www.afdb.org/fileadmin/uploads/afdb/Documents/Publications/John%20brief%201_John%20brief%201.pdf.

Ondiege, Peter. 2013. "Fostering Financial Inclusion with Mobile Banking." *Private Sector & Development* 16 (May): 9–11.

Patrick, Hugh T. 1966. "Financial Development and Economic Growth in Underdeveloped Countries." *Economic Development and Cultural Change* 14 no. 2 (January): 174–189. https://www.jstor.org/stable/1152568?seq=1#page_scan_tab_contents.

Pitt, Mark and Shahidur Khandker. "The Impact of Group-Based Credit Programs on Poor Households in Bangladesh: Does the Gender of Participants Matter?" *Journal of Political Economy* 106 (5): 958-996.

Rousseau, Peter and Paul Wachtel. 1998. "Financial Intermediation and Economic Performance: Historical Evidence from Five Industrialized Countries." *Journal of Money, Credit and Banking* 30 (4): 657-678.

Saunders, Anthony and Liliana Schumacher. 2000. "The Determinants of Bank Interest Rate Margins: An International Study." *Journal of International Money and Finance* 19 (6): 813-832.

Stubos, George, and Ioannis Tsikripis. 2005. "Regional Integration Challenges in South East Europe: Banking Sector Trends." Working Papers, 24. Bank of Greece. https://econpapers.repec.org/paper/bogwpaper/24.htm.

United Nations. 2007. *Trade and Development Aspects of Insurance Services and Regulatory Frameworks*. United Nations Conference on Trade and Development. https://unctad.org/en/Docs/ditctncd20074_en.pdf.

Vaithilingam, Santha, Mahendhiran Nair, and Muthi Samudram. 2006. "Key Drivers for Soundness of the Banking Sector: Lessons for Developing Countries." *Journal of Global Business and Technology* 2 (1): 1–11.

World Bank. 2017. "The Global Findex Database 2017." https://globalfindex.worldbank.org/.

Zingales, Luigi. 2003. "The Weak Links." *Federal Reserve Bank of St. Louis Review* 85: 47–52. https://files.stlouisfed.org/files/htdocs/publications/review/03/07/Zingales.pdf.

CHAPTER 9

Acemoglu, Daron, Simon Johnson, and James A. Robinson. 2000. "The Colonial Origins of Comparative Development: An Empirical Investigation." NBER Working Paper 7771. National Bureau of Economic Research. June. https://www.nber.org/papers/w7771.

AECOM. 2016. *Africa Prosperity & Construction Cost Guide 2016*. https://www.aecom.com/za/wp-content/uploads/2016/09/Africa_Property_and_Construction_Cost_Guide_2016.pdf.

AFP. 2015. "Kenya Signs Nuclear Power Deal with China, Looks to Have Power Station up by 2025." *Mail & Guardian Africa*. https://web.archive.org/web/201712

27003928/http://mgafrica.com/article/2015-09-10-kenya-signs-nuclear-power-deal-with-china-looks-to-have-power-station-by-2025.

African Business Central. 2015. "Here Are Seven of Africa's Largest Infrastructure Projects Currently under Construction (Photos)." African Business Central. March 6. http://www.africanbusinesscentral.com/2015/03/06/seven-of-africas-largest-infra structure-projects-currently-under-construction-photos/.

African Development Bank and World Economic Forum. 2013. *Strategic Infrastructure in Africa: A Business Approach to Project Acceleration.* Abidjan and Geneva: AfDB and WEF. https://www.weforum.org/reports/strategic-infrastructure-africa-busi ness-approach-project-acceleration.

African Union, NEPAD. 2015. *Programme Infrastructure Champion Initiative (PICI) Report.* https://www.nepad.org/publication/presidential-infrastructure-champion-initiative-pici-report.

Agénor, Pierre-Richard. 2008. "Health and Infrastructure in a Model of Endogenous Growth." *Journal of Macroeconomics* 30 (4): 1407–1422.

Alfredo, M. P., and J. M. Andraz. 2011. "On the Economic and Fiscal Effects of Investments in Road Infrastructures in Portugal." *International Economic Journal* 25 (3): 465–492.

Aschauer, D. A. 1989. "Is Public Expenditure Productive?" *Journal of Monetary Economics* 23 (2): 177–200.

BBC News. 2017. "Kenya Opens Nairobi-Mombasa Madaraka Express Railway." BBC News Online, May 31. https://www.bbc.com/news/world-africa-40092600.

Berechman, Joseph, Dilruba Ozmen, and Kaan Ozbay. 2006. "Empirical Analysis of Transportation Investment." *Transportation*, no. 6 (November): 537–551. https://link.springer.com/article/10.1007/s11116-006-7472-6.

Biswas, Romita. 2002. "Determinants of Foreign Direct Investment." *Review of Development Economics* 6 (3): 492–504.

Blimpo, Moussa P., Robin Harding, and Leonard Wantchekon. 2013. "Public Investment in Rural Infrastructure: Some Political Economy Considerations." *Journal of African Economies* 22 (2): ii57–ii83.

Bonface. 2015. "Top 5 Challenges Facing Africa's Construction Industry." *Construction Review Online.* July 9. https://constructionreviewonline.com/2015/07/top-5-challenges-facing-africas-construction-industry.

Bughin, Jacques, Mutsa Chironga, Georges Desvaux, Tenbite Ermias, Paul Jacobson, Omid Kassiri, Acha Leke, Susan Lund, Arend van Wamelen, and Yassir Zouaoui. 2016. *Lions on the Move II: Realizing the Potential of Africa's Economies.* McKinsey Global Institute Report, September 2016. https://www.mckinsey.com/featured-insights/middle-east-and-africa/lions-on-the-move-realizing-the-potential-of-africas-economies.

Burgess, Robin, and Edward Miguel. 2015. "The Value of Democracy: Evidence from Road Building in Kenya." *American Economic Review* 105 (6): 1817–1851. June. https://www.researchgate.net/publication/279213172_The_Value_of_Democracy _Evidence_from_Road_Building_in_Kenya.

Burgess, Robin, Remi Jedwab, Edward Miguel, Ameet Morjaria, and Gerard Padró i

Miquel. 2015. "The Value of Democracy: Evidence from Road Building in Kenya." *American Economic Review* 105 (6): 1817-1851.

Buys, Piet, Uwe Diechmann, and David Wheeler. 2006. "Road Network Upgrading and Overland Trade Expansion in Sub-Saharan Africa." World Bank Policy Research Working Paper 4097. Washington, D.C.: World Bank. https://open knowledge.worldbank.org/handle/10986/9256.

Calderón, César, and Luis Servén. 2004. "The Effects of Infrastructure Development on Growth and Income Distribution." World Bank Policy Research Working Paper 3400. Washington, DC: World Bank. https://openknowledge.worldbank.org/handle/10986/14136.

Calderón, César, and Luis Servén. 2010. "Infrastructure and Economic Development in Sub-Saharan Africa." *Journal of African Economies* 19, suppl 1 (May 1): i13–i87. https://academic.oup.com/jae/article-abstract/19/suppl_1/i13/679403?redirect edFrom=PDF.

Calderón, César, and Luis Servén. 2014. "Infrastructure, Growth, and Inequality: An Overview." World Bank Policy Research Working Paper 7034. Washington, D.C.: World Bank.

Chakraborty, Chandana, and Banani Nandi. 2011. "'Mainline' Telecommunications Infrastructure, Levels of Development and Economic Growth: Evidence from a Panel of Developing Countries." *Telecommunications Policy* 35 (5): 441–449.

"Construction Boom Brightens Future for East Africa." 2017. Africa BuildMart. http://www.buildmartafrica.com/detail-news.php?NEWS_ID=324&PAGE_ID=7.

Cook, Paul. 2011. "Infrastructure, Rural Electrification and Development." *Energy for Sustainable Development* 15 (3): 304–313.

Datta, A., and S. Agarwal. 2004. "Telecommunications and Economic Growth: A Panel Data Approach." *Applied Economics* 36 (15): 1649–1654.

Deloitte. 2014. *Deloitte on Africa: African Construction Trends Report 2014.* https://www2.deloitte.com/content/dam/Deloitte/za/Documents/manufacturing/za_africa_construction_trends_2015_10032015.pdf.

Deloitte. 2015. *A 360° View: Africa Construction Trends Report 2015.* https://www2.deloitte.com/content/dam/Deloitte/za/Documents/manufacturing/ZA-ConstructionTrendsReport-2015.pdf.

Deloitte. 2016. *Africa's Changing Infrastructure Landscape: Africa Construction Trends Report 2016.* https://www2.deloitte.com/content/dam/Deloitte/fpc/Documents/secteurs/immobilier/DeloitteAfrica_Construction_Trends_2017_Nov2016.pdf.

Dethier, Jean-Jacques, and Alexander Moore. 2012. "Infrastructure in Developing Countries: An Overview of Some Economic Issues." ZEF-Discussion Papers on Development Policy 165. Center for Development Research (ZEF), University of Bonn. April. https://www.zef.de/uploads/tx_zefportal/Publications/zef_dp_165.pdf.

Dethier, Jean-Jacques, Maximilian Hirn, and Stephane Straub. 2008. "Explaining Enterprise Performance in Developing Countries with Business Climate Survey Data." World Bank Policy Research Working Paper 4792. Washington, D.C.: World Bank.

EMIS. 2015. *Construction Sector Sub-Saharan Africa*. EMIS. April. https://www.emis. com/sites/default/files/EMIS%20Insight%20-%20Sub-Saharan%20Africa%20 Construction%20Sector%20Report.pdf.

Ernst and Young. 2014. *Africa 2030: Realizing the Possibilities*. http://www.nubukein vestments.com/downloads/Ernst%20and%20Young%20Africa%202030%20 RealizingThe%20Possibilities%20October%202014.pdf.

Estache, A., and G. Garsous. 2012. "The Impact of Infrastructure on Growth in Developing Countries." International Finance Corporation Economic Note 1.

Estache, Antonio, and Marianne Fay. 2010. "Current Debates on Infrastructure Policy." In *Globalization and Growth: Implications for a Post-Crisis World*, edited by Michael Spence and Danny Leipziger, 151–193. Washington, DC: The World Bank, on behalf of the Commission on Growth and Development. https:// openknowledge.worldbank.org/bitstream/handle/10986/2440/542530PUB0glob 101Official0Use0Only1.pdf?sequence=1.

Ezzat Othman, Ayman Ahmed. 2013. "Challenges of Mega Construction Projects in Developing Countries." *Organization, Technology, and Management in Construction* 5 (1): 730-746.

Garsous, G. 2012. "How Productive Is Infrastructure? A Quantitative Survey." European Center for Advanced Reseach Working Paper. Brussels: Universite Libre de Bruxelles.

GCP Global, Oxford Economics, ENR, and PwC. 2015. *Global Construction 2030: A Global Forecast for the Construction Industry to 2030*. London: Global Construction Perspectives and Oxford Economics. https://www.pwc.se/sv/entreprenad/assets/ global-construction-2030.pdf.

Good, Kenneth. 1976. "Settler Colonialism: Economic Development and Class Formation." *Journal of Modern African Studies* 14 (4): 597–620.

Hong, Junjie, Zhaofang Chu, and Qiang Wang. 2011. "Transport Infrastructure and Regional Economic Growth: Evidence from China." *Transportation* 38 (5): 737–752.

Hulten, R. C. 1996. "Infrastructure Capital and Economic Growth: How Well You Use It May Be More Important Than How Much You Have." NBER Working Paper 5847. National Bureau of Economic Research. December. https://www.nber. org/papers/w5847.

Ianchovichina, Elena, Antonio Estache, Renaud Foucart, Gregoire Garsous, and Tito Yepes. 2012. "Job Creation through Infrastructure Investment in the Middle East and North Africa." World Bank Policy Research Working Paper 6164. Washington, D.C.: World Bank. https://openknowledge.worldbank.org/handle/10986/11975.

Ismael N. W., and M. J. Mahydeen. 2015. "The Impact of Infrastructure on Trade and Economic Growth in Selected Economies in Asia." ADBI Working Paper Series. ADBInstitute. https://www.adb.org/sites/default/files/publication/177093/adbi-wp 553.pdf.

Jedwab, Remi, Edward Kerby, and Alexander Moradi. 2015. "History, Path Dependence and Development: Evidence from Colonial Railroads, Settlers and Cities in Kenya." *The Economic Journal* 127 (603): 1467–1494. https://onlinelibrary.wiley. com/doi/10.1111/ecoj.12347.

Kiganda, Antony. 2016. "Top 3 Key Drivers of Construction Industry in Kenya." *Construction Review Online*, July 27. https://constructionreviewonline.com/2016 /07/ttop-3-key-drivers-of-construction-industry-in-kenya/.

Kiganda, Antony. 2016. "Construction Market Opportunities in Africa." *Construction Review Online*. September 22. https://constructionreviewonline.com/2016/05/a -south-african-company-specialized-in-civil-engineering-has-this-to-say-about-construction-market-opportunities-in-africaconstruction-market-opportunities-africa/.

Kiganda, Antony. 2017. "Top 4 Factors Driving the Growth of Africa's Construction Industry." *Construction Review Online*. March 14. https://constructionreviewonline. com/2017/03/top-4-factors-driving-the-growth-of-africas-construction-industry/.

Koppenjan, Joop F. M. and Bert Enserink. 2009. "Public–Private Partnerships in Urban Infrastructures: Reconciling Private Sector Participation and Sustainability." *Public Administration Review* 69 (2): 284–296.

LAPSSET Corridor Development Authority. 2016. *Brief on LAPSSET Corridor Project*. Nairobi: Government of Kenya. http://vision2030.go.ke/inc/uploads/2018 /05/LAPSSET-Project-Report-July-2016.pdf.

Lee, Sang Hyup, John Levendis, and Luis H. Gutierrez. 2012. "Telecommunications and Economic Growth." *Applied Economics* 44 (4): 461–469.

León, Gianmarco, and Edward Miguel. 2016. "Risky Transportation Choices and the Value of a Statistical Life." July. http://emiguel.econ.berkeley.edu/assets/miguel_research/5/SL-VSL_2016-07-07-CLEAN.pdf.

M&G Africa Reporter. 2015. "What Crisis? 16 of China's Biggest Projects in Africa—It's All Billion Dollar Territory in Here." *Mail & Guardian Africa*. https://web. archive.org/web/20180523034158/http://mgafrica.com/article/2015-09-18-multi-billion-dollar-deals-chinas-27-biggest-active-projects-in-africa.

Mahasenan, Natesan, Steve Smith, and Kenneth Humphreys. 2002. "The Cement Industry and Global Climate Change: Current and Potential Future Cement Industry CO2 Emissions." *Proceedings of the 6th International Conference on Greenhouse Gas Control Technologies*, 1–4 October 2002, Kyoto, Japan. https://www. sciencedirect.com/science/article/pii/B9780080442761501574.

Milner, Helen V. 2006. "The Digital Divide: The Role of Political Institutions in Technology Diffusion." *Comparative Political Studies* 39 (2): 176–199.

Musau, Zipporah (ed.). 2017. "Partnerships Giving Africa a New Look: Private Sector Working with Governments to Fund Mega Development Projects." *Africa Renewal* 31 (2): 3, 23.

NEPAD and United Nations. 2015. *Infrastructure Development within the Context of Africa's Cooperation with New and Emerging Development Partners*. Office of the Special Adviser on Africa. http://www.un.org/en/africa/osaa/pdf/pubs/2015infra structureanddev.pdf.

Office of the Special Adviser on Africa (OSAA). "Financing Africa's Infrastructure Development." 2015. Policy Brief. https://www.un.org/en/africa/osaa/pdf/policy briefs/2015_financing_infrastructure.pdf.

Okocha, Samuel. 2015. "Construction Industry to Drive Nigeria's Economic Growth."

Construct Africa. https://web.archive.org/web/20170306123502/http://www.con structafrica.com/news/construction-industry-drive-nigerias-economic-growth.

Ondiege, Peter, Jennifer Mbabazi Moyo, and Audrey Verdier-Chouchane. 2013. "Developing Africa's Infrastructure for Enhanced Competitiveness." *Africa Competitiveness Report 2013*. Geneva: World Economic Forum.

Pereira, A. M., and J. M.Andraz. 2012. "On the Economic Effects of Investment in Railroad Infrastructures in Portugal." *Journal of Economic Development* 37 (2): 79–107.

Portugal-Perez, Alberto, and John S. Wilson. 2012. "Export Performance and Trade Facilitation Reform: Hard and Soft Infrastructure." *World Development* 40 (7): 1295–1307.

Program for Infrastructure Development in Africa (PIDA). n.d. Accessed October 1, 2019. *Africa Infrastructure—Synthesis Report*. https://www.nepad.org/publication/africa-infrastructure-synthesis-report-0.

Program for Infrastructure Development in Africa (PIDA). 2012. *Program for Infrastructure Development in Africa: Interconnecting, Integrating and Transforming a Continent*. https://www.icafrica.org/fileadmin/documents/PIDA/PIDA%20Executive%20Summary%20-%20English_re.pdf.

Program for Infrastructure Development in Africa (PIDA). 2016. *Infrastructure Outlook 2040*. https://ab-network.jp/wp-content/uploads/2014/08/140523_ONRI-Rapport_%e8%8b%b1%e8%aa%9e.pdf.

PwC. 2016. *SA Construction 4th Edition: Highlighting Trends in the South African Construction Industry*. November. https://www.pwc.co.za/en/assets/pdf/sa-construction-2016.pdf.

Reuters. 2016. "Tanzania Makes Big Onshore Natural Gas Discovery." Reuters Market News, February 25. https://www.reuters.com/article/tanzania-gas/tanzania-makes-big-onshore-natural-gas-discovery-local-newspapers-idUSL8N16427G.

Robles, B. S. 1998. "Infrastructure Investment and Growth: Some Empirical Evidence." *Contemporary Economic Policy* 16 (1): 98–108.

Röller, L. H., and L. Waverman. 2011. "Telecommunications Infrastructure and Economic Development: A Simultaneous Approach." *American Economic Review* 91 (4): 909–923.

Sahin, Osman, Nurettin Kan, and Erkan Demirbas. 2014. "The Effects of Infrastructure Determinants on Economic Growth: European Union Sample." *Eurasian Journal of Business and Economics* 7 (13): 11–27. https://www.researchgate.net/publication/328929955_The_Effects_of_Infrastructure_Determinants_on_Economic_Growth_European_Union_Sample.

Sahoo, Pravakar, Ranjan Kumar Dash, and Geethanjali Nataraj. 2010. "Infrastructure Development and Economic Growth in China." IDE Discussion Papers 261. Institute of Developing Economics. October. https://www.ide.go.jp/English/Publish/Download/Dp/261.html.

Shepherd, Ben and John S. Wilson. 2009. "Trade Facilitation in ASEAN Member Countries: Measuring Progress and Assessing Priorities." *Journal of Asian Economics* 20 (4): 367-383.

Straub, Stéphane. 2008. *Infrastructure and growth in developing countries.* Policy Research Working Papers 4460. World Bank. January. https://openknowledge. worldbank.org/handle/10986/6458.

Stretton, Allan W. 1981. "The Building Industry and Urbanization in Third World Countries: A Philippine Case Study." *Economic Development and Cultural Change* 29 (2): 325–339.

Tan, B., K. M. Mert, and Z. A. Ozdemir. 2010. "Kamu yatırımları ve ekonomik buyume ilikisine bir bakı: Turkiye, 1969–2003." *Dokuz Eylul Universitesi ktisadi ve dari Bilimler Fakultesi Dergisi* 25 (1): 25–39.

Timetric. 2016. "Construction in South Africa: Key Trends and Opportunities to 2020." *ReportBuyer.* https://www.globaldata.com/store/report/gdcn0465mr--con struction-in-south-africa-key-trends-and-opportunities-to-2023/.

Turner & Townsend. 2016. International Construction Market Survey 2016, Over-stretched and Over-Reliant: A Polarised Market. http://www.turnerandtownsend. com/media/1518/international-construction-market-survey-2016.pdf.

Uhde, N. 2010. "Output Effects of Infrastructures in East and West German States." *Intereconomics* 45 (5):322-328. September. https://link.springer.com/article/10 .1007/s10272-010-0352-5.

United Nations Economic Commission for Africa (UNECA) and New Partnership for Africa's Development (NEPAD). 2017. *16 Infrastructure Projects for African Integration.* https://repository.uneca.org/handle/10855/23964.

United Nations Industrial Development Organization (UNIDO). 2010. *Annual Report 2009.* Vienna: UNIDO. https://www.unido.org/sites/default/files/2010-03/10-50277_Ebookb_0.pdf.

V.e.n.t.u.r.e.s Onsite & Construct East Africa. 2015. *The Emerging East Africa Construction Market 2015: Focus on Uganda, Ethiopia, Tanzania, Mozambique and Kenya.* https://www.civimec.co.in/the-emerging-east-africa.pdf.

Verma, S., and R. Arora. 2010. "Does the Indian Economy Support Wagner's Law? An Econometric Analysis." *Eurasian Journal of Business and Economics* 3 (5): 77–91.

Wantchekon, Leonard, and Piero Stanig. 2016. "The Curse of Good Soil? Land Fertility, Roads and Rural Poverty in Africa." September 20. https://ostrom workshop.indiana.edu/pdf/seriespapers/2016F_Colloq/wantchekon-paper.pdf.

Wilson, John S., Catherine L. Mann, and Tsunehiro Otsuki. 2003. "Trade Facilitation and Economic Development: Measuring the Impact." World Bank Policy Research Working Paper 2988. Washington, D.C.: World Bank.

World Development Indicators. 2017. "Gross fixed capital formation (current US$)." *World Bank.* https://data.worldbank.org/indicator/NE.GDI.FTOT.CD.

Worrell, Ernst, Lynn Price, Nathan Martin, Chris Hendriks, and Leticia Ozawa Meida. 2001. "Carbon Dioxide Emissions from the Global Cement Industry." *Annual Review of Energy and the Environment* 26: 303–329.

Yamaguchi, K. 2011. "Inter-regional Air Transport accessibility and Macro-economic Performance in Japan." *Transportation Research Part E: Logistics and Transportation Review* 43 (3): 247–258.

Zhen-Wei Qiang, Christine, Alexander Pitt, and Seth Ayers. 2003. "Contribution of Information and Communication Technologies to Growth." World Bank Working Paper 24. Washington, D.C.: World Bank. http://documents.worldbank.org/curated /en/483071468326372732/Contribution-of-information-and-communication-technologies-to-growth.

CONCLUSION

Chironga, Mutsa, Acha Leke, Arend van Wamelen, and Susan Lund. 2011. "The Globe: Cracking the Next Growth Market: Africa." *Harvard Business Review.* May. https://hbr.org/archive-toc/BR1105.

Leke, Acha, and Landry Signé. 2019. *Spotlighting Opportunities for Business in Africa and Strategies to Succeed in the World's Next Big Growth Market.* Foresight Africa 2019. Washington DC: Brookings Institution. January 11. https://www.brookings. edu/research/spotlighting-opportunities-for-business-in-africa-and-strategies-to-succeed-in-the-worlds-next-big-growth-market/.

Index